The Power of Populism and People

This collection is essential reading for our turbulent times. Profoundly relevant, this volume contributes greatly to our understanding of the relationship among modern populism, collective action, and the contemporary crises of democracy.

                        Marla Stone, Professor of History, Occidental College, USA

This masterful volume reminds us that mass mobilization does not always lead to democracy, nor are the outcomes of pro-democratic mobilization always assured. An important contribution.

                        Erica Chenoweth, Frank Stanton Professor of the First Amendment, Harvard University, USA

These far-ranging, intelligent essays in scholarly vigilance will help elevate the conversation about the prospects for viable self-government as dictatorial movements threaten to poison the future.

                        Todd Gitlin, Professor of Journalism and Sociology, and Chair, Ph. D. Program in Communications, Columbia University, USA

The Power of Populism and People

Resistance and Protest in the Modern World

Edited by
Nathan Stoltzfus and
Christopher Osmar

BLOOMSBURY ACADEMIC
LONDON • NEW YORK • OXFORD • NEW DELHI • SYDNEY

BLOOMSBURY ACADEMIC
Bloomsbury Publishing Plc
50 Bedford Square, London, WC1B 3DP, UK
1385 Broadway, New York, NY 10018, USA
29 Earlsfort Terrace, Dublin 2, Ireland

BLOOMSBURY, BLOOMSBURY ACADEMIC and the Diana logo are trademarks of Bloomsbury Publishing Plc

First published in Great Britain 2022

Copyright © Nathan Stoltzfus and Christopher Osmar, 2022

Nathan Stoltzfus and Christopher Osmar have asserted their right under the Copyright, Designs and Patents Act, 1988, to be identified as Author of this work.

Cover design: Terry Woodley
Cover image: A 'Yellow Vest' demonstration near the Arc de Triomphe on December 1, 2018 in Paris, France. (Photo by Veronique de Viguerie/Getty Images)

All rights reserved. No part of this publication may be reproduced or transmitted in any form or by any means, electronic or mechanical, including photocopying, recording, or any information storage or retrieval system, without prior permission in writing from the publishers.

Bloomsbury Publishing Plc does not have any control over, or responsibility for, any third-party websites referred to or in this book. All internet addresses given in this book were correct at the time of going to press. The author and publisher regret any inconvenience caused if addresses have changed or sites have ceased to exist, but can accept no responsibility for any such changes.

Every effort has been made to trace copyright holders and to obtain their permissions for the use of copyright material. The publisher apologizes for any errors or omissions and would be grateful if notified of any corrections that should be incorporated in future reprints or editions of this book.

A catalogue record for this book is available from the British Library.
A catalog record for this book is available from the Library of Congress.

Library of Congress Cataloging-in-Publication Data

Names: Stoltzfus, Nathan, editor. | Osmar, Christopher, editor.
Title: The power of populism and people : resistance and protest in the modern world / edited by Nathan Stoltzfus and Christopher Osmar.
Description: London ; New York, NY : Bloomsbury Academic, 2021. | Includes bibliographical references. |
Identifiers: LCCN 2020055556 (print) | LCCN 2020055557 (ebook) | ISBN 9781350202009 (paperback) | ISBN 9781350201996 (hardback) | ISBN 9781350202016 (ebook) | ISBN 9781350202023 (epub)
Subjects: LCSH: Populism—History—Cross-cultural studies. | Power (Social sciences)—Cross-cultural studies. | Protest movements—Cross-cultural studies. | Political participation—Cross-cultural studies. | Fascism—Cross-cultural studies.
Classification: LCC JC423 .P658 2021 (print) | LCC JC423 (ebook) | DDC 320.56/62—dc23
LC record available at https://lccn.loc.gov/2020055556
LC ebook record available at https://lccn.loc.gov/2020055557

ISBN: HB: 978-1-3502-0199-6
PB: 978-1-3502-0200-9
ePDF: 978-1-3502-0201-6
eBook: 978-1-3502-0202-3

Typeset by Deanta Global Publishing Services, Chennai, India

To find out more about our authors and books visit www.bloomsbury.com and sign up for our newsletters.

CONTENTS

Acknowledgements vii
Notes on contributors and editors viii

Introduction: Authoritarianism like liberal democracy is the work of the people *Nathan Stoltzfus and Christopher Osmar* 1

1 Civil resistance versus authoritarian rule: The Arab Spring and beyond *Adam Roberts* 21

2 Civil society as a threat to democracy *Grzegorz Ekiert* 53

3 The Arab uprisings and people's power: Romantic views and hard realities *Marina Ottaway* 73

4 'Maidans' and movements: Legacies, innovations and contention in independent Ukraine *Olga Onuch* 89

5 Paradoxes of reform: Protest, progress and polarization in Malaysia *Meredith L. Weiss* 115

6 People power in Putin's Russia: Social versus political protests *Laura A. Henry* 137

7 How the party-state harnessed people power in China *Diana Fu* 163

8 Caught between Kemalist and Islamist authoritarianisms: The masses as auxiliary power in Turkey, 1923 to present *Azat Zana Gündoğan* 181

9 1989 inverted: Transformative authoritarian memory and the rise of populism in Poland and Hungary *Michael Bernhard* 205

10 Protesting democracy in Africa: Popular movements and political transformation *Zachariah Mampilly* 227

11 Populism in Latin America as global history *Federico Finchelstein* 243

12 Why Trump is not the problem *Andrew J. Bacevich* 255

Index 265

ACKNOWLEDGEMENTS

Special thanks are due first of all to the Florida State University's Center for the Advancement of Human Rights (CAHR) and the Dorothy and Jonathan Rintels Professorship for Holocaust Studies, the co-sponsors of our conference in February 2019 that engendered the papers for this book. The Rintels Professorship was delighted to be a cosponsor of a CAHR conference, not least because of Executive Director Terry Coonan's extraordinary capacity together with Assistant CAHR Director Vania Llovera, to conceive and carry out ideas. With Vania's skills in conference logistics and the generous assistance of interns and volunteers, we orchestrated a fine example of multidisciplinary work across organizations that is characteristic of a fine university. The conference with its intersecting exchanges shaped the concept for this cross-disciplinary, around-the-globe perspective on the role of people in shaping the rule of recent national democracies and autocrats. Thanks especially to the Florida State Law School for providing meeting space in its charming Rotunda as well as continuous IT assistance that kept us flowing smoothly.

Thanks are also due to those who attended the conference and followed up with chapters in this book, beginning with our keynote speaker Sir Adam Roberts: Andrew J. Bacevich, Michael Bernhard, Grzegorz Ekiert, Federico Finchelstein, Diana Fu, Azat Gundogan, Laura A. Henry, Zachariah Mampilly, Olga Onuch, Marina Ottaway, Meredith L. Weiss. We express heartfelt thanks to Danielle Wirsansky, who working for the Rintels Professorship applied her boundless energy and skills to various aspects of the book's production. At Bloomsbury Publishing, thanks especially to Rhodri Mogford, Maddie Holder and Joseph Gautham for working with us so well in the book's production.

CONTRIBUTORS AND EDITORS

Andrew J. Bacevich grew up in Indiana, graduated from West Point and Princeton, served in the army, became an academic and is now a writer.

Michael Bernhard is the Ehrlich Eminent Scholar Chair in Political Science at the University of Florida and the editor of *Perspectives on Politics*. His work centres on questions of democratization and development, both globally and in the context of Europe.

Grzegorz Ekiert is Laurence A. Tisch Professor of Government at Harvard University, Director of the Minda de Gunzburg Center for European Studies and Senior Scholar at the Harvard Academy for International and Area Studies. His research and teaching interests focus on comparative politics, regime change and democratization, civil society and social movements, and East European politics and societies.

Federico Finchelstein is Professor of History at the New School for Social Research. Professor Finchelstein is the author of seven books on fascism, populism, Dirty Wars, the Holocaust and Jewish history in Latin America and Europe.

Diana Fu is Associate Professor of political science at the University of Toronto. Her research examines popular contention, state control, civil society and authoritarian citizenship in contemporary China. She is the author of *Mobilizing without the Masses: Control and Contention in China*.

Azat Gundogan, of the teaching faculty of the Florida State University Honors Program, has published on the Kurdish political movement in Turkey and on anti-urban renewal mobilization in the peripheries of Istanbul. He is at work on a book on urbanization and politics in Istanbul.

Laura A. Henry is Professor of Government at Bowdoin College who studies Russia's post-Soviet politics, civil society and social movements. Henry is the author of *Red to Green: Environmental Activism in Post-Soviet Russia* and the co-editor of *Russian Civil Society: A Critical Assessment* as well as articles in *Environmental Politics, Global Environmental Politics, Post-Soviet Affairs* and *Europe-Asia Studies*.

Zachariah Mampilly is Marxe Chair of International Affairs at the Marxe School of Public and International Affairs, CUNY. He is the author of *Rebel Rulers: Insurgent Governance and Civilian Life during War*. 2011; co-author of *Africa Uprising: Popular Protest and Political Change*; and co-editor of *Rebel Governance in Civil Wars and Rebel Rulers: Insurgent Governance and Civilian Life during War*.

Ola Onuch is Senior Lecturer in Politics at the University of Manchester and a leading scholar of protest in Eastern Europe and Latin America. Her book *Mapping Mass Mobilizations* explores the processes leading up to mass protest engagement in Ukraine and Argentina.

Christopher Osmar is Independent Scholar who received his PhD in 2018 from Florida State University, USA. His thesis, "Now I Am in Distant Germany, It Could Be That I Will Die: Colonial Precedent, Wartime Contingency, and Crisis Mentality in the Transition from Subjugation to Decimation of Foreign Workers," won the Martin-Vegue Dissertation Fellowship Award (2017).

Marina Ottaway is a Middle East Fellow at the Woodrow Wilson Center and a long-time analyst of political transformations in Africa, the Balkans and the Middle East. She is working on a project at the Wilson Center about the countries of the Arab Spring and Iraq.

Sir Adam Roberts, KCMG FBA, is Emeritus Professor of International Relations at the University of Oxford, a senior research fellow in Oxford University's Department of Politics and International Relations and an emeritus fellow of Balliol College, Oxford. He is the author and editor of numerous articles and books, including *Civil Resistance and Power Politics: The Experience of Non-violent Action from Gandhi to the Present* (2009).

Nathan Stoltzfus, Rintels Professor of Holocaust studies and of history at Florida State University, USA, has published numerous books, essays and articles including *Hitler's Compromises* (2016) and *Resistance of the Heart* (1996), co-recipient of the Institute of Contemporary History's Fraenkel Prize.

Meredith L. Weiss is Professor of Political Science at SUNY Albany. She has published widely on social mobilization and civil society and electoral politics and parties, including the books *Student Activism in Malaysia: Crucible, Mirror, Sideshow* and *Protest and Possibilities: Civil Society and Coalitions for Political Change in Malaysia*, along with numerous articles.

Introduction

Authoritarianism like liberal democracy is the work of the people

Nathan Stoltzfus and Christopher Osmar

Today, around the globe, crowds of millions join in news-making demonstrations on a daily basis. Many assert their democratic freedoms, even while millions more collect in support of autocrats who repress individual rights. Autocrats today put down unfavourable popular demonstrations as urgently as they suppress the fourth estate, another stream of independent thought. Unlike the press, with its clear organizational structure, the fifth estate of popular demonstrations often offers less clear targets for repression. Beijing has recently moved to punish protesters from intentionally leaderless demonstrations, even arresting towering figures of protest like seventy-two-year-old Jimmy Lai, who said he could choose prison over silence because that would be 'the only way to end'. Prison would cost him everything, the self-made billionaire said, but he was confident that such measures would be 'very expensive for Beijing' and thus his single life in exchange would be 'a very good bargain'.[1] Crowds and icons like Lai are stronger when they can draw on outside allies, like the tens of thousands of Lithuanians who in August of 2020 formed a human chain across their country in solidarity with the demonstrators in neighbouring Belarus, where President Alexander Lukashenko crushed a plan to build a similar chain of protest.[2] But just as crowds demonstrating in protest can challenge an authoritarian regime, crowds can also rally to the support of dictators, in common cause. Savvy autocrats know the basic principles of crowd psychology.

Popular autocracy, as a strategy for acquiring and exercising power, is not new. Last century's fascism was careful to accrue mass support and sustain it even as it used terrorizing force against 'outsiders' and 'enemies of the people'.³ This introduction will trace parallels between the development and practice of 'classic' twentieth-century dictatorships and their present-day autocratic iterations. It concludes by synthesizing the findings of cases globally, outlining how the structures of popular resistance movements have affected the efficacy of autocrats and how authoritarians employ repression while maintaining support. What is the role of the masses in strengthening or undermining democratic institutions?

Whatever their objective, disciplined crowds with a united message have an impact far beyond their number. The 'people power' protesters celebrated for prompting the fall of communism in the late twentieth century were just a fraction of their respective national populations. After the dismantling of the Soviet Bloc, Western experts encouraged rule of law institutions that promoted civil societies, building on the civilian crowds who had found the capacity to push back against communist forms of oppression. More recently, some characterized the living chain of Lebanese stretching from one side of their country to the other in 2019 as promoting a pluralism that might expand civil society and a sense of commonweal.⁴

History shows that crowds do not automatically reboot to open societies with benign government for all. In 1985 Gustav Le Bon published his classic characterization of crowds as soul-crushing, lost-to-conscience dissolvers of liberalism that destroyed civilized humanity with the siren call of irrational behaviour. But even in his time, German workers and churchgoers collectivized by Marxist parties and the Catholic Church were demonstrating that crowds could act rationally, conveying a united message to achieve a specific political goal. While Rosa Luxembourg believed that strikes could bring about a communist revolution, socialist leaders prized collective action in the form of street demonstrations as their key weapon. In 1904, socialist leader of gradualism Eduard Bernstein stated that demonstrations 'had become the main weapon for reform', while 'mob activity was counterproductive'.⁵

As a pioneering fascist Adolf Hitler was among the first to illustrate how the autocrat manages crowds to maintain support, an appearance of legitimacy outside of the law. For Elias Canetti, the post-war theorist of crowds, the ideal type had unlimited power, although it must move in a single direction to bind everyone together, and to survive the crowd will 'accept any goal'.⁶ Hitler's successful efforts to build his movement between the wars should warn us against today's rabble-rousing leaders who inflame emotions that compel crowds towards action, particularly in the context of growing rival militias and allegiance to faction over the common enlightenment language of facts and reason.

As our authors point out, powerful regimes co-opt the crowds for themselves and brutally block and punish protests. Beijing's communist leaders, long concerned with monopolizing collective action and backed by the power of popular nationalism, have shown a growing savvy in sustaining support while repressing street protests. The authoritarian state and many indebted to it also have nearly unlimited resources compared to protesters, who must maintain body and mind while mustering time and strength to stand up to injustice, all while risking being thrown into prison. Street protests can lose their appearance of discipline and legitimacy once invaded by *agents provocateur* who do not share protester tactics. Populist leaders mobilize crowds of supporters to display and build legitimacy, just as open protests create opportunities for civil solidarity and expand its political place.

Each year Freedom House draws upon a variety of indicators of political rights and civil liberties to place countries on a seven-step spectrum between 'Free', 'Partly Free' and 'Not Free'. By this metric, the freedom of countries around the globe has fallen for the past fifteen years, succumbing to leaders who maintain support even as they attack the norms and institutions of democracy, disregarding the voices and rights of dissidents and critics.[7] This trend corresponds with the decline of constitutional democracies since the early years of this century, and the corollary rise of 'defective democracies', governments not so much overthrown by coup d'état as surrendered to challenges that reduced freedoms while operating within existing constitutional systems.[8] Contributors to this volume, applying viewpoints of several disciplines, examine recent case studies of national experiences to expose the contours of phenomena that transcend our national and historical moment, and illuminate the global slide towards authoritarianism.

The same disaffection that helped to fill out the ranks of cults of personality around the world has also produced significant mass action against authoritarian rule, beginning with the emergence of popular movements in North Africa in opposition to authoritarian leaders. But even as the Arab Spring radiated out from Tunisia, displacing dictators, it failed to produce new stable democracies in any case with the exception, perhaps, of Tunisia itself. Movements in Libya and Syria that began with peaceful demonstrations developed into civil war, and the subsequent conflicts contributed to the expansion of the ongoing refugee crisis. Yet, as Roberts writes, "the hopes it raised of an essentially peaceful and cooperative form of politics have not disappeared. Popular movements showed determination and skill in asserting basic rights, both within and beyond the Arab world". Examples include the massive protests for political and economic liberalizations challenging Algerian President Abdelaziz Bouteflika that erupted in early 2019, and the 'anti-government protests in 2016-2017, against corruption, unemployment, police brutality, and neglect of the Berber population'.

The crisis of pluralist liberal democracy and the re-emergence of populism

The ideological footrace of the twentieth century appeared to have been decided with the fall of the Berlin Wall. Empowered by Mikhail Gorbachev's drive for reform and unshackled by his decision that the Soviet Union would not intervene to repress opposition to its client states, popular movements provided the catalyst for dissolving the communist regimes in Poland, Czechoslovakia and East Germany.[9] Each of these governments could have smashed the street demonstrations without Moscow, and it is important to consider why they chose not to. Since 1989 popular mobilization has often been rendered as a consistently democratizing force. Here we examine its role in supporting – or even demanding – authoritarian rule. Bearing in mind Adam Roberts's caution in his chapter against 'an often unspoken assumption that history's arrow flies in a single direction – from dictatorship to democracy', the book considers how populist and authoritarian regimes have worked to influence the behaviour and beliefs of their peoples in order to manufacture support for their rule, and how populations have independently encouraged a turn towards autocracy. Why do some civic mobilizations back dictators, and some back democracy? We investigate the emergence of populist strongmen who wish to appear to operate within a democratic context, raising the question of whether popular mobilizations are a crucial fifth estate of democracy and the extent to which the dangers which liberal democracy faces stem from a popular sense of crisis that only a strongman with the will to crack down might solve.

In the wake of the collapse of the Soviet Bloc some observers suggested that humanity was approaching its final condition, not in the utopian collective imagined by the followers of Marx, but in the triumph of pluralistic liberal democracy wielding global capitalism for the betterment of all. The democratic world revolution appeared unstoppable. All that remained was to push over a few strongmen and the people would fill the vacuum with the only system capable of representing their interests and meeting their needs: Western-style democracy. Western governments have 'often been wedded to the idea, deeply embedded in much Western political thought, that if you get rid of a bad ruler, all will be well' without a further plan, writes Roberts. American President George W. Bush's 'freedom agenda' expressed this raw, wishful notion in July 2005: 'As freedom takes root in Iraq, it will inspire millions across the Middle East to claim their liberty as well!'[10]

The failure of militarized democratization projects in Afghanistan and Iraq in the context of the 'war on terror' early in the century demonstrated the bankruptcy of the notion that peoples will choose liberal democracy when unrestrained, leading to continued interventions some now see as unending wars. The consequences of globalization in the post–Cold War period also called into question the viability of capitalist liberal democracy as a vehicle for promoting people's welfare. Open markets have certainly improved the material standard of living for many, while also greatly exacerbating inequality – itself a condition favouring autocracy – and creating a space for economic alternatives such as China's state capitalism to thrive. Outside militaries cannot build nations. Instead, each free generation which prizes civil liberties and political freedoms must secure and guard those rights to prevent the return of authoritarianism.

The opening years of our new millennium have made it dramatically clear that there will be no inexorable advance of democracy once repression is lifted. The twentieth-first century is known for crises occurring simultaneously, some exacerbated or caused by incompetent leaders themselves.[11] The 2008 global financial crisis, culture wars sharpened by a concerted new advance of terrorism, a massive exodus of refugees yearning to become citizens of stable societies and the twin shocks of global pandemic and economic recession in 2020 have perhaps encouraged some civilians to line up behind demagogues who promise security, material goods and a rightful standing for their country in the world, in exchange for a surrender of liberal individual rights. There are other compelling explanations for the weakening of the democracies established after 1989. Ivan Krastev and Stephen Holmes argue that having just found freedom from communism, countries felt expected to put on the attitudes and institutions of Western Europe and the United States. Pressure for 'copycat Westernization' caused a political backlash against liberalism.[12]

While the full consequences of the Covid-19 pandemic have yet to play out, governments have assumed responsibility for handling similar health crises since the early modern period. Science and international organizations are necessary as authorities to inform individual actions and coordinate responses across national borders, while deceptions and repression of information from the top-down are dangerous, whether in autocracies or democracies. It is easy for autocrats to demand a change in everyday practices but more difficult for them to enforce their order.

Reflecting on the 2020 pandemic in an overview of 'Pandemics and Politics', Adam Roberts concluded that 'epidemics, and action to control them, do sometimes play a part in increased authoritarianism, but they can also give rise to more positive initiatives of various kinds'. Pandemics in particular frequently spur fundamental changes and social unrest, illustrated by latest iteration of the Black Lives Matter protests that began in the United States in May 2020 and spread across the globe. The following month, representing the repressions of liberal rights that accompanied the Covid-19 crisis, Beijing imposed a 'National Security Law' on Hong Kong, arresting protesters and disqualifying oppositional contenders for elected office. With its poor response to the coronavirus, the reputation of the United States 'as a serious international actor has undergone a major decline', which in fact may have increased Beijing's prerogative to crack down without facing concerted international reprisals.[13] While some leaders have likened fighting the social calamity of a pandemic with war, the cooperative, bottom-up force of collective civil action might make for better analogies. On the one hand, individual conscientious practices, taken on behalf of others in order to stymie the invading virus (masks, social distancing), are essential, recalling Václav Havel's model for resisting tyranny by attempting 'to live in the truth', according to conscience.[14] At the same time, collective and aggregate civil noncompliance has been richly illustrated by pandemic-deniers and mask-protesters representing culture wars and vehement individualism or stubbornness.

Still, the pandemic is only one of several crises that have jeopardized the stability of democracies in the West. In Europe and the United States the popular political right, in coalitions encouraged by political leaders, has weaponized the threat of terror and the flood of refugees, incorporating them into anti-global and xenophobic narratives as dangerous outsiders who threaten democratic traditions and sovereignty. This has fuelled popular movements that promote nationalisms centred on the notion that the 'real' people are under threat from enemies, enemies which are increasingly cast as radical leftists coming from within the country rather than from without, while rejecting open borders and free trade. This sentiment has been strong enough to produce electoral majorities in support of people and policies that upend precedent and threaten existing democratic institutions in the name of resolving the crisis. One autocracy encourages and demonstrates the tactics to others.

Similar movements towards autocracy have emerged across the globe, however, in opposition to the spectre of foreign threats to the lives and livelihoods of the people who compose the idealized nation, but feel 'insufficiently regarded to count for something among the cultures of the world'.[15] The populist shift, a response to a sense of crisis commonly manufactured by the demagogues who name scapegoats and claim to have fixes, was manifest in Brexit, in Trump's wall and travel ban, in the turn to protectionism, and in the abandonment of truth in favour of a narrative of grievance and fear. The PiS Party in Poland and Fidesz in Hungary have embraced Euroscepticism and erected barriers to the immigration of refugees while degrading institutional checks on their power. More entrenched authoritarians have also appealed to a sense of patriotic nationalism to discredit their opposition. An embattled Nicholás Maduro attempted to cast his struggle with the last intact democratic institution in Venezuela, the National Assembly, as an effort to upset a foreign plot, while the Chinese and Russian governments have deployed a similar rationalization for suppressing internal dissent with greater success.[16]

The popular appeal of fascism and populist nationalism in history

Just as the end of the Cold War invited hopes that democracies would naturally take root in dismantled single-party states, the creation of new states in the wake of the First World War on the basis of national self-determination also promised to allow democracies to flourish. During the interwar years, however, these new states had to contend with the advance of communism as the Soviet Union swallowed up some and attempted to export revolution to the rest. As communist opposition formed political parties operating within the national electoral systems that they had vowed to destroy, a fear of the revolutionary threat and widespread support for suppressing communism escalated. The onset of the Great Depression deepened this fear and further discredited constitutional capitalist democracy and its inability to cope with the economic crisis. In this environment, proponents of a third-way alternate to liberalism and communism built a following. Rejecting both liberalism and class conflict, fascism promised to unite the people behind notions of nation or race by furnishing a leader that was capable of acting boldly in their interest, unfettered by norms, institutions or constitutional constraints.[17]

In Germany, Adolf Hitler embodied this third-way alternative. In place of democracy he imagined a system predicated on a leadership principle: a genius leader, if ordained by the people and faithful to Germany's true interests, might overcome the obstructions and compromises presented by democratic institutions in order to ensure the nation's survival. Dismissive of representative democracy, he nonetheless grounded his authority and legitimacy in the support of the people. He won this following by promising to improve economic conditions and to restore order and security to the streets of Germany while confronting the communist threat directly, but made no secret of his intentions to dismantle the new German democracy. Underlining the political significance of mass mobilizations for the Nazis, Prussian Interior Minister Hermann Goering banned communist demonstrations on 2 February 1933, and in May the regime banned all demonstrations without prior police approval, followed by a ban on all public gatherings other than traditional processions and pilgrimages.[18]

Even after he obtained dictatorial power, legally, Hitler was careful to shore up his power by appropriating, rather than jettisoning, the pillars of traditional leadership. He remained concerned, for example, with preserving the appearance that everything was proceeding according to legal precedents and procedures which had been developed and honoured in Germany over the course of generations. He would suppress opposition parties, and the Communists in particular, within months of becoming Chancellor, but even these repressive measures – which included the creation and population of concentration camps – were legitimized in a decree that President Hindenburg issued on the basis of constitutional emergency powers. With the German Communist Party dismantled, only the Social Democrats and the Catholic Centre Party remained within the Reichstag parliament to voice opposition to a measure that allotted dictatorial powers to Hitler for four years. This Enabling Act passed when only the German socialist delegates voted against it, and in the coming years Hitler expanded his popular acclaim to levels that obviated any need for a further extension of the measure.

Although the National Socialist regime left the structures created by the Weimar constitution in place, it nonetheless proceeded to challenge the norms that had been built up around that system of government. Hitler's apparent deference to traditional German values, along with headlines acclaiming the victories of the German nation, soothed the German people and distracted them from the radical changes that he was making. He hoped that his people would soon agree that exchanging the old Christian and democratic way of life for his dictatorial leadership was the best path towards what had really been important to them all along: growing prosperity and national pride, a sense of belonging in the 'national community' and a purpose in world history.

Hitler would turn to the people to legitimize specific policies in plebiscites, and the Reichstag went on meeting, albeit as little more than an applause chamber. Hitler's effort to reshape society and build a national community, working within the confines of strict legality while suppressing political opposition in order to fortify the image of a receptive German people, won him spectacular adulation as an unparalleled leader. As long as he seemed to solve the problems that German leaders before him had failed to conquer, the romance between Hitler and his followers continued, allowing him to think, as he said in March 1939 with characteristic subtlety, 'I will go down as the greatest German in history.'[19]

The crises that led the Weimar Republic to dissolve were certainly more severe than those that confront the present day, and the Third Reich's violent repression of its opponents was often more extreme than the methods of modern populist regimes. Nonetheless, the parallels between twentieth-century fascism and twenty-first-century authoritarian populism point towards a similar understanding of how autocrats secure and exercise power.[20] Both establish their base in a grievance community, which swells in times of crisis, and both call on this community to identify with the nation, and often in opposition to those seen as dangerous to that nation. Like Hitler, the populist claims to understand the will of the people and justifies circumventing traditional or institutional barriers in the name of directly carrying out that will, sometimes by manufacturing a crisis and then claiming to offer the only solution.

As a state of mind, crisis remains subjective and relative – it is not absolute privation that prompts this anxiety but a sense that a turning point has been reached which threatens a particular way of life. The improvement in the standard of living in the United States and Europe over the course of the past century, itself a product of the global dominance of democracy, decreased the threshold for the development of a crisis mentality. The unprecedented disruption of the Covid-19 pandemic and the sudden curtailment of economic activity in 2020, however, have surpassed this threshold for many. This new crisis may open the way for perceived existential threats that could facilitate the demise of fundamental democratic institutions. Still, the system of the *ancien régime* is never entirely upset. Once in power, modern populism, like its fascist forbearers, prefers the appearance of continuity to revolutionary restructuring, whether justified as expanded rule during emergencies, lifting constitutional checks on the executive or engineering electoral victories.

Fascism does depart from contemporary autocracies in its approach to organized opposition. Hitler's dictatorship operated within a single-party state created by the criminalization of organized political opposition. Today's populists, on the other hand, require an opposition in order to preserve the premise that the leader is accountable to the people and could be replaced through a popular and legal process. In the case of both fascism and today's populists the opposition must be, in reality, politically weak. The ruler must maintain popular support for repression of political opposition or despite it, regardless of infringements on civil liberties. And a leader who has built sufficient popularity to eclipse all opposition can begin leveraging the power of the state to ensure that the opposition will never be a threat.

The persistence of multiple political parties and the staging of regular elections, however, are not alone sufficient markers of democracy. Erdogan's Turkey, for example, has more than a dozen political parties with four represented in the legislature as of 2015, although like Putin and others bent on centralizing their rule over a nation, Erdogan has found it essential to intimidate and destroy popular protests as well as independently minded journalists. Mass collective actions that seek to circumvent institutional government have proven to be politically significant both during the last century and today. While Hitler did not allow opposition parties, like popular autocrats today he sought to erase every sign of popular dissent expressed in protests and demonstrations, throttling popular demonstrations as strenuously as the press. For pretenders to the role of consensus leader, free assembly and speech can be just as challenging as opposition parties and more difficult to discredit, particularly in cases where independent journalism or public mass mobilizations might be more effective in communicating a political alternative than opposition parties. Mass demonstrations against strongmen are as potent as they are perilous because they evoke emotion and images, broad brushstrokes upon which strongmen depend, and because they avoid the specificity of clear-cut words and policies, particularly on controversial matters that divide popular loyalties.

The efficacy of popular mobilization in opposing authoritarianism

Liberal democracies and populist strongmen alike stake their claims to legitimacy on the premise that they represent the will of the people, either enshrined in a set of institutions or embodied in an individual. Mass public mobilizations offer an alternative informal channel of popular representation, using or creating public spaces where the people themselves express their needs, desires and discontents directly. While these mobilization cannot encompass the entire population, a minority that is willing and able to be collectively seen and heard has more influence than its numerical strength might suggest. Societies that embrace popular direct action are capable of incorporating demonstrations and protests into the system of rule as something of a fifth estate. By regulating rather than suppressing voices of opposition and providing mechanisms to respond to calls from the street, open societies blunt challenges to their legitimacy that such movements might otherwise produce. Authoritarian regimes do engage in efforts to co-opt popular mass movements towards their own ends, shaping the content of those movements while repressing opposition that cannot be channelled to their purposes.

Civil resistance may be roughly divided into two categories: spontaneous and organized.[21] Spontaneous resistance arises because regime policies have so offended a segment of the population that individuals take initiative alone, without a leader, find solidarity in a shared grievance and begin to act collectively. While they are usually specific about what they oppose, the absence of recognized leadership and policy prescriptions hinders the development of viable alternatives, demonstrated in France by the 'Gilets jaunes'. The decentralized nature of such a mobilization conveys a kind of authenticity, a sense that the voice in the street reflects the genuine will of the people unmediated by other political interests. Consequently, spontaneous mobilizations can represent a direct, and even fatal, challenge to the regime's claim to legitimacy on the basis of representing the popular will. Efforts to counteract this de-legitimization have succeeded in China and Russia, where protesters are vilified as the puppets of a foreign plot – 'enemies of the people'.

Even where they have been successful in unseating strongmen, these spontaneous movements struggle to exercise power beyond a regime-change event. In her contribution to this volume, Marina Ottaway considers the failure of spontaneous opposition movements within the Arab Spring to construct successor democracies after catalysing revolution. Further, Ottaway does not find convincing evidence that women have had leadership positions in the Arab Spring uprisings, or that these popular protests have benefitted the status of women in relationship to men. She suggests that bottom-up movements may upset the status quo, but that they are unable to sustain themselves long term, or produce significant social change. Unless these popular demonstrations succeed in unsettling the established organizations that wield power – by dividing their leadership for example – these organizations will determine the institutions of political power after the demonstrations subside. The primary actors in the remaking of North Africa, Ottaway points out, have been organizations structurally modelled after Leninism, such as the Muslim Brotherhood, as well as old institutions like the military and bureaucracy. Adam Roberts, who also writes on the Arab Spring, agrees here that 'to call for the fall of a regime without a clear view of what is to replace it is hugely problematic', adding that this is also a failure of Western governments who think toppling bad rulers is sufficient, a 'central delusion both of the US-led invasion of Iraq in 2003, and of the Arab Spring movements that began in 2011'.

Of course, not all instances of popular collective action result from this kind of spontaneous upwelling of unrest. Organized opposition, whether legal or underground, can direct activism strategically in pursuit of a specific agenda. They also possess a more enduring character than their spontaneous counterpart, as organizational structure and hierarchy allow these movements to reproduce themselves across multiple demonstration events, while established leadership can learn from previous mistakes and adapt to contingency. More importantly, organizations can maintain momentum beyond a flashpoint mass mobilization that produces a regime change and thereafter pursue a programmatic change in society. Olga Onuch traces organized popular opposition in the Ukraine through a series of upheavals from 1990 to 2014, demonstrating how efforts by dissident groups and opposition parties to coordinate and cooperate while controlling the flow of information and communicating a master frame brought success in the Revolution on the Granite and enabled these networks to reproduce themselves in the Orange Revolution. She argues that the turn to violence during the EuroMaidan demonstrations in 2014, which deepened divides between east and west, was a consequence of the fracturing of coordinated control of demonstrators and their message. Meredith Weiss observes a similar pattern in her exploration of the Pakatan Harapan coalition's electoral victory in Malaysia over the Barisan Nasional coalition, which had controlled the country since its independence. Despite Malaysia's entrenched electoral authoritarianism, opposition parties and civil society had been permitted to develop, and when former Prime Minister Mahathir Mohamad threw in his lot with the opposition they were able to unify behind him to unseat Barisan Nasional.

Spontaneous and organized popular movements differ in their structure and in their strengths, but both are capable of acting either against or within the existing political system. An authoritarian regime might respond to an organized challenge to its rule through repression, or it may discredit a spontaneous movement for regime change as working for foreign interests, but activism that challenges specific policies rather than the legitimacy of the regime itself is not as vulnerable. In her examination of protests in Russia, Laura Henry differentiates between political protests aimed at changing the government and social protests which centre around single-issue quality of life matters. While Vladimir Putin's government has managed to defang popular opposition to its rule through indiscriminate repression of protesters and by presenting them as unpatriotic, the weapons that it deploys against political protests are not as effective when directed at social protests. Social protests do not challenge the regime itself, instead working to make the government more responsive without displacing it. The power of this approach stems from its recognition of the legitimacy of the powers that be, she finds, even as it calls upon them to demonstrate that legitimacy by meeting the needs of the people. Social protest does not itself threaten the regime, though state repression of such a movement or even failure to deliver adequate concessions could endanger its claim to represent the people and open it to a more existential danger. Successful compromise between the social protest and the authoritarian state, on the other hand, might strengthen the latter's claim to legitimacy.

The rise of social media has, of late, complicated the way that people mobilize politically as well as the avenues available to powerful state and corporate actors to shape their behaviour. In decentralizing control of media content creation, and providing a platform for instantaneous mass peer-to-peer communication, the internet promised to be a democratizing influence. Whereas the radio, film and the loudspeaker had offered cutting-edge tools for homogenizing peoples under fascism and communism, social media was to advance pluralism. Indeed, new media has been effective in mobilizing people in the face of abuses of state power, much as the fax machine as the newest medium was useful for mobilizing the protests on Tiananmen Square. Viral videos of police brutality, the kinds of images rarely captured or circulated before the smart phone became ubiquitous, show the American city on a hill shining in blue and red light. Likewise, in Tunisia and Egypt social media aided in the development of a narrative of police repression, transforming people like Mohamed Bouazizi and Khaled Saeed into figureheads for what would become Arab Spring, a movement bolstered by interventions such as Asmaa Mahfouz's appeal on YouTube for protest in Tahrir Square.

Despite its power to disseminate dissent, social media has not entirely delivered on its promise of facilitating democratization. The kind of movements that benefit most from the new technology are spontaneous and decentralized, just as these are the most likely means for visibly challenging autocratic regimes. While martyrs might mobilize they cannot lead, and maintaining momentum or avoiding co-optation once the object of popular ire has been removed proves difficult. Social media has had a centrifugal influence on other popular mass movements, allowing more extreme or violent factions to gain traction, as happened during the EuroMaidan demonstrations in Ukraine. The same tool is also capable of promoting inaction or counteraction in the face of unrest. The digitization of the protest space allows it to reach more people, but might also create the impression of participation through the superficial activity that is the 'like' button and the retweet. More nefariously, because virtual civil society exists outside of the walled garden that is traditional media it does not have the protection of recognized and accountable gatekeepers. This opens it to infiltration by state actors seeking to sow disinformation abroad or to shape the popular discourse at home. Even absent state intervention, new media has the potential to create conditions conducive to a populist consolidation of power. Internet echo chambers, producing sensationalist and often competing truths, have created an atomized sense of reality that might only find its resolution in the strongman, who through strategic use of new media can generate increased atomization.

The people and authoritarian advance

While authoritarian states often do resort to force and coercion to control public dissent, outright repression is not always the most efficient tool for this purpose. Particularly in populist authoritarian regimes, where the claim to leadership is grounded in the appearance of a supportive people, violent suppressions of popular demonstrations risks alienating this popular foundation and possibly losing legitimacy. On the other hand, if the regime can generally portray the targets of its repression as the 'enemy of the people', it is free to proceed against them without endangering the appearance of popular backing. If an opposition movement cannot be checked through counter-demonstration, broken up through repression of individual leaders or discredited as illegitimate – for example by presenting them as under the influence of a foreign power – then the recourse left to the regime is either to make concessions or to counter mass mobilization with force. Electing to use force in the face of a mass movement demonstrating in public carries a level of risk. The populist authoritarian that appears to be acting against the people might not be able to command the loyalty of the state's instruments of violence, and if the military or police refuse the order to disperse a crowd by force and instead join the protesters, then the entire regime is liable to collapse.

Violent repression of popular movements can be risky for a popular authoritarian regime once the movement reaches the streets, particularly in the case of the spontaneous movement that cannot be delegitimized or decapitated by doing away with organizers. Repression geared towards preventing the development of open demonstrations in the first place has seen wider use and success. While Hitler and his National Socialists had long recognized the potentials and hazards posed by public mobilizations that were not initiated by the Nazi Party, Russia, Turkey and others today have resorted to imprisoning or murdering journalists in an effort to control the public narrative and forestall public unrest this century.

Because forceful repression of dissent can be both counterproductive and expensive, entrenched authoritarian regimes have developed techniques to shape public conversation proactively. While the People's Republic of China has a long history of suppressing dissent in a heavy-handed manner, it has begun to retool this approach under Xi Jinping. Diana Fu chronicles changes in the Chinese repertoire for controlling the masses from Mao to Xi. Traditional mechanism geared towards influencing the people included appeals to culture, exploitation of class conflict and party propaganda. The current regime has developed these techniques further, while reorienting its image towards fostering support rather than forcing compliance. Televised confessions connected with the anti-corruption campaign, during which citizens are invited to vote on the most sincere confession online, have replaced the "struggle sessions" of the Cultural Revolution. The old approach of silencing opposition by stoking class conflict has been abandoned in favour of dismissing dissent as the work of foreign powers, a tactic used extensively in response to the protests in Hong Kong. This has become a common technique of authoritarian governments that must explain opposition while preaching the unity of the people; a system of propaganda that once centred around official messages broadcast on loudspeakers has become less overt and more disguised. Censorship of communication on WeChat, the country's prominent internet communication platform, as well as the seeding of pro-regime sentiment has enabled the state to steer, if not fully control, public discourse.

Where Fu identifies changes in the way that the Chinese state exercises control over its people, Azat Gundogan sees longer-term continuities in Turkish efforts to construct and control an idea of a people. Though the country has passed through periods of Kemalist and Islamist rule, both have suppressed the left, preached historical revisionism and persecuted non-Muslim and non-Turkish peoples. Mass mobilizations in Turkey have consistently been co-opted by the state and redeployed as auxiliary power, with their energies channelled against out-groups, sometimes violently, rather than against the state itself.

In less repressive states, mobilization of support for illiberal rule has also fuelled democratic backsliding. Michael Bernhard argues that structural properties shared by Hungary and Poland, resulting from what he calls their path of extrication from communism, facilitated the development of memory politics hostile to liberal democracy. This trend has gained greater traction with the public following the financial crisis of 2008 and the influx of refugees following Arab Spring. He contends that the process by which *both* Poland and Hungary sloughed off single-party rule included elements of contention and negotiation, allowing for the development of post-communist parties that remained competitive with the fractured remains of the former opposition. The persistence of post-communist parties promoted a counter-narrative that cast the revolutions as incomplete and beneficial only to the elites, while divisions within the former opposition prompted smaller parties on the right to radicalize to fortify their following. FiDeSz in Hungary and the Law and Justice Party in Poland played on memory politics, pushing revisionist histories that rehabilitated pre-communist anti-democratic traditions while denigrating the revolutions of 1989. While both parties had been in power as of the early 2000s, they moved to the right during a subsequent period in opposition – a period that also saw the global financial crisis. In the case of FiDeSz this radicalization came in response to growing popular support for the far-right party Jobbik. Once they had recaptured the majority, both moved to solidify their new grip on power by modifying electoral structures, democratic institutions and constitutions. Grzegorz Ekiert explores the Polish case further in his contribution. Contentious reformism in Poland, he says, bolstered the development of civil society, but also fuelled culture wars and facilitated the development of a nationalist civil society. Recently Polish civil society has become increasingly pillarized, dividing the country between a nationalist anti-liberal wing on the right and a pro-European liberal wing on the left, each of which has lent their sizable popular support to competing political parties.

The people, democratic structures and power

Well-functioning pluralist liberal democracies are capable of responding to the needs of a diverse population, facilitating gradual change in a climate of competing interests, identities and ideas. They give people a public voice and influence over governance, while protecting the system itself from co-optation by individuals or domination by a majority. The core components for successful and responsive democracies have been legal protections for the expression of ideas, formal mechanisms that allow the people to select leaders and policies, and institutions that check one another. Tolerance of peaceful opposition to the government in the form of a free press, as well as freedom of association and assembly, is a necessary prerequisite for the development and propagation of ideas. Elections and referendums provide an avenue for the people to exercise choice, transforming the popular will developed within a free civil society into action. Finally, institutions protect rights and the rule of law while checking the accumulation of power in the hands of a single group and applying drag to efforts aimed at radical change. The absence of any one of these components can lead to the degradation of democracy and its replacement by dictatorship or populist authoritarianism.

As Zachariah Mampilly shows in this volume, healthy democracies require more than just electoral participation. He traces the development of ostensibly democratic governments in Africa following waves of protests in the late 1980s and early 1990s, in which the ruling elite across the continent were able to capture opposition and channel it into demands for competitive elections. He suggests that while these movements precipitated widespread adoption of democratic forms, lauded in the West, elections have not provided a vehicle for real social or economic change. These elections do offer a choice between candidates and can result in the removal of long-standing leaders, as was the case in Joseph Kabila's ouster from the helm of the Democratic Republic of Congo in 2018, but they rarely present a challenge to the prevailing neoliberal order. Despite the failure of elections to deliver change, the international community and organizations like Freedom House continue to privilege electoral form in evaluating the relative success of African democracies. What these metrics miss, writes Mampilly, is the importance of freedom of assembly and speech, and the popular protest movements that they facilitate. Popular movements provide a more inclusive environment than party politics, while allowing for more organic and dynamic expression of ideas geared towards change, although an independent judiciary is important as well.

Just as favouring democratic form in the absence of venues for popular expression can produce choiceless democracies, an emphasis on realizing popular will by circumventing institutional constraints can result in populist authoritarianism. Federico Finchelstein historicizes populism and presents it as a transnational phenomenon that develops in response to a crisis of representation, that is, to a popular sense that liberal democracy is not responding to the needs of the people. Finchelstein traces the genealogy of modern populism back to late-nineteenth-century movements that pitted 'the people', singularly conceived, against elites. Fascism welded anti-liberalism and anti-communism onto this frame in the interwar period while dismantling democracy, presenting this approach as a third-way alternative that empowered the people through their leader. Following the defeat of fascism, populism re-emerged in Latin America, preserving the notion that the people are best represented by a strong leader who is in touch with their interests while operating within a democratic context and eschewing the discredited racism and violence of fascism. Juan Perón, who had toured both Mussolini's Italy and the Third Reich, championed this transition in Argentina. He styled his rule as a new third way, a universalizable solution to the crisis of representation that might liberate people after communism and capitalism, both built on exploitation, strangled each other to death. Today, Finchelstein suggests, the world is experiencing the third way's third wave, a new transnational embrace of nationalism and anti-politics in which the racism that characterized fascism has returned once again as global xenophobia.

In the United States the norms of forbearance in the application of power and toleration of opposing political views have eroded significantly.[22] Still, protections for free expression remain and the institutional foundations of the republic, though eroded, have not collapsed. Andrew Bacevich confronts America under the Trump administration in this book's coda, contending that Donald Trump's election reflected a deeper crisis in American politics, including an outsized obsession with the power of the presidency and a mirroring disregard for other institutions and loci of power at the national, regional and local levels. After the conclusion of the Cold War both of the major political parties embraced the proliferation of corporate capitalism around the world, the displacement of traditional social norms in favour of individual autonomy and American interventionism abroad. While this post–Cold War consensus benefitted some, the experience for many Americans has been one of inequality, alienation and perpetual war. In 2016 disillusionment with this outmoded consensus, and the failure of the establishment wings of either party to offer a vision for something new, delivered frustrated voters to Donald Trump. The policies that he has introduced since then, Bacevich points out, can be undone, and Congress is still perfectly capable of applying institutional brakes to a runaway presidency so long as the conductors can be persuaded to act. Still, neither of these tacks will alleviate the underlying problem. Instead, he says, what is needed are new ideas, a replacement of the shattered post–Cold War consensus with a new consensus predicated upon the pursuit of the common good, although the temptation is to tack towards the comforting myth of the national glory of 1945, the country as the back-to-back winner of world wars.

Liberal democracy, in any case, is not the inevitable end of history. It is not necessarily fragile, but it is mortal. A system of government predicated on empowering the people will always be vulnerable to the possibility that those same people might choose to abandon it. Times of crisis, inevitable regardless of advancements in the standard of living, will fortify this desire to defend an old way of life with a new system of government, to trade the role of hungry citizen for that of the well-fed subject. Democracy will hold where institutions are resilient and where leaders respect the norms of democracy. It can prevail where elections offer real choice, and where the people demand it. Populist nationalism will grow where these values and norms are compromised. But the dictator and the populist strongman fear crisis too. When they fail to meet the people's needs or stretch their norms too far, they will face unrest. They may repress opposition, but they can only wield force so long as they retain the loyalty of the majority and the military. The people spontaneously taking to the streets can shatter the authoritarian mindset and disarm the state so that it is no longer able to resist the resistance. Populists who lean on the façade of elections to legitimize themselves can be defeated, while organized opposition can coordinate diverse interests for a sustained campaign to mobilize the public to both remove and replace a repressive regime. Authoritarianism, like liberal democracy, is driven by the people.

Notes

1 *The Daily Podcast*, 3 September 2020, https://www.nytimes.com/2020/09/03/podcasts/the-daily/hong-kong-china-jimmy-lai.html.

2 'What Is Happening in Minsk', *BBC News*, 23 August 2020, https://www.bbc.com/news/world-europe-53882062.

3 Wendy Z. Goldman, *Inventing the Enemy: Denunciation and Terror in Stalin's Russia* (Cambridge: Cambridge University Press, 2011); Ryan Stackhouse, *Enemies of the People: Hitler's Critics and the Gestapo* (Cambridge: Cambridge University Press, forthcoming 2021).

4 Deutsche Welle News, Lebanon Protesters Form Human Chain across the Country, 27 October 2019, https://www.dw.com/en/lebanon-protesters-form-human-chain-across-the-country/a-51009905.

5 Eric D. Weitz, *Creating German Communism, 1890-1990: From Popular Protests to Socialist State* (Princeton: Princeton University Press, 1997), 43–5, 79; *Als die Deutschen demonstrieren lernten: Das Kulturmuster „friedliche Strassendemonstration" im preußischen Wahlrechtskampf 1908 – 1910*, ed. Bernd Jürgen Warneken (Tübingen: Ludwig-Uhland-Institut für Empirische Kulturwissenschaft, 1986), 7–8.

6 Elias Canetti, *Crowds and Power* (New York: Continuum, 1981), 29.

7   Freedom House report on 'Freedom in the World 2020', https://freedomhouse.org/sites/default/files/2020-02/FIW_2020_REPORT_BOOKLET_Final.pdf.
8   Wolfgang Merkel, 'The Consolidation of Post-Autocratic Democracies: A Multi-Level Model', *Democratization*, 5, no. 3 (Autumn 1998): 33–67, here 57.
9   Charles S. Maier, *Dissolution: The Crisis of Communism and the End of East Germany* (Princeton: Princeton University Press, 1999).
10 *Evolution of U.S. Counterterrorism Policy*, vol. 1, Yonah Alexander and Michael B. Kraft, eds. (Praeger, 2007), 301.
11 See the increasing attention to crises conglomeration beginning with Christopher Bones, *The Cult of the Leader* (Chichester: John Wiley & Sons, 2012), 1ff.
12 Ivan Krastev and Stephen Holmes, *The Light that Failed: Why the West Is Losing the Fight for Democracy* (New York: Pegasus Books, 2020).
13 Adam Roberts, 'Pandemics and Politics', The Survival Editors' Blog, https://www.iiss.org/blogs/survival-blog/2020/09/pandemics-and-politics. Roberts, 'Pandemics', 8, 30, 41. Pandemics have previously been associated with the rise of religion and popular surrender to a strongman who promises a path out of the crisis. Italian leaders who successfully mobilized massive resources to manage the plague of 1575–8 produced a glorification of individual leaders and boosted absolutism. Samuel K. Cohn, *Cultures of Plague: Medical Thinking at the End of the Renaissance* (Oxford: Oxford university Press, 2010), 8.
14 Václav Havel, 'The Power of the Powerless', in *The Power of the Powerless: Citizens Against the State in Central-Eastern Europe* (New York and London: Routledge 2009 [1985]), 23–96; Roberts, 'Pandemics', 26.
15 Isaiah Berlin, *The Crooked Timbers of Humanity* (Princeton: Princeton University Press, 2013 [1947]), 278.
16 Adam Przeworski, *Crisis of Democracy* (Cambridge: Cambridge University Press, 2019), 172ff.
17 See, for example, William Sheridan Allen, *The Nazi Seizure of Power: The Experience of a Single German Town 1930-1935* (New York: New Viewpoints, 1973).
18 Marie-Luise Ehls, *Protest und Propaganda: Demonstrationen in Berlin zur Zeit der Weimarer Republik* (Berlin: de Gruyter, 1997), 208.
19 Ian Kershaw, *Hitler, 1936-45: Nemesis* (New York: Norton, 2001), 171.
20 Among the proliferation of recent books on populism and its history are Barry Eichengreen, *Populist Temptation: Economic Grievance and Political Reaction in the Modern Era* (Oxford: Oxford University Press, 2020) and Federico Finchelstein, *From Fascism to Populism in History* (Oakland: University of California Press, 2019).
21 *Civil Resistance and Power Politics: The Experience of Nonviolent Action from Gandhi to the Present*, eds Adam Roberts and Timothy Garton Ash (Oxford: Oxford University Press, 2011).
22 See Steven Levitsky and Daniel Ziblatt, *How Democracies Die* (New York: Crown, 2018).

References

Albrecht, Joachim and Bernd Jürgen Warneken, eds. *Als die Deutschen demonstrieren lernten: Das Kulturmuster „friedliche Strassendemonstration" im preußischen Wahlrechtskampf 1908–1910*. Tübingen: Ludwig-Uhland-Institut für Empirische Kulturwissenschaft, 1986.

Allen, William Sheridan. *The Nazi Seizure of Power: The Experience of a Single German Town 1930–1935*. New York: New Viewpoints, 1973.

Berlin, Isaiah. *The Crooked Timbers of Humanity*. Princeton: Princeton University Press 2013 [1947].

Bones, Christopher. *The Cult of the Leader*. Chichester: John Wiley & Sons, 2012.

Canetti, Elias. *Crowds and Power*. New York: Continuum, 1981.

Cohn, Samuel K. *Cultures of Plague: Medical Thinking at the End of the Renaissance*. Oxford: Oxford University Press, 2010.

Ehls, Marie-Luise. *Protest und Propaganda: Demonstrationen in Berlin zur Zeit der Weimarer Republik*. Berlin: de Gruyter, 1997.

Eichengreen, Barry. *Populist Temptation: Economic Grievance and Political Reaction in the Modern Era*. Oxford: Oxford University Press, 2020.

Finchelstein, Federico. *From Fascism to Populism in History*. Oakland: University of California Press, 2019.

Goldman, Wendy Z. *Inventing the Enemy: Denunciation and Terror in Stalin's Russia*. Cambridge: Cambridge University Press, 2011.

Havel, Václav. 'The Power of the Powerless'. In *The Power of the Powerless: Citizens Against the State in Central-Eastern Europe*. New York and London: Routledge 2009 [1985].

Kershaw, Ian. *Hitler, 1936–45: Nemesis*. New York: Norton, 2001.

Krastev, Ivan and Stephen Holmes. *The Light that Failed: Why the West Is Losing the Fight for Democracy*. New York: Pegasus Books, 2020.

Levitsky, Steven and Daniel Ziblatt. *How Democracies Die*. New York: Crown, 2018.

Maier, Charles S. *Dissolution: The Crisis of Communism and the End of East Germany*. Princeton: Princeton University Press, 1999.

Merkel, Wolfgang. 'The Consolidation of Post-Autocratic Democracies: A Multi-Level Model'. *Democratization* 5, no. 3 (Autumn 1998): 33–67.

Przeworski, Adam. *Crisis of Democracy*. Cambridge: Cambridge University Press, 2019.

Roberts, Adam and Timothy Garton Ash, eds. *Civil Resistance and Power Politics: The Experience of Nonviolent Action from Gandhi to the Present*. Oxford: Oxford University Press, 2011.

Stackhouse, Ryan. *Enemies of the People: Hitler's Critics and the Gestapo*. Cambridge: Cambridge University Press, forthcoming 2021.

Weitz, Eric D. *Creating German Communism, 1890–1990: From Popular Protests to Socialist State*. Princeton: Princeton University Press, 1997.

1

Civil resistance versus authoritarian rule

The Arab Spring and beyond

Adam Roberts

The authors of this book have been offered some propositions, and have been set some questions, that are politically sensitive and also intellectually difficult.

> This century is seeing a new proclivity toward populist dictatorships that few would have predicted two or three decades ago. At the same time, the world is witnessing an increased use of mass collective actions, a surge in 'people power' protests and grassroots initiatives together with human rights activism, that resist advances in tyranny. Individual autocrats are often blamed for autocracy. But how have peoples facilitated dictatorships or democracies in recent national histories? What (perceived) circumstances of opportunity or grievance explain the success of strongmen and their repression of democracy?[1]

The first question in this statement, *our* question, is worth repeating. How have peoples facilitated dictatorships or democracies in recent national histories? It is the master question under which a host of other matters can and will be up for exploration. Among these is the puzzle: Why, two decades into the twenty-first century, have autocratic regimes of various kinds been on the increase?

Here I will explore, in necessarily abbreviated form, eight topics that bear on the opportunities and problems of civil resistance against dictatorship.

1. Overview of 'civil resistance', and its connections with struggles against dictatorship. The notion of 'political jiu-jitsu' that informs the line taken by nonviolent movements when faced with violence by adversaries. Recent examination of the question why civil resistance works. Civil resistance not presented here as a panacea.
2. The theory of voluntary servitude, which is more than 450 years old, yet resonates today. It sees tyranny as a consequence of the acquiescence of citizens in oppressive rule by an individual, and it suggests a simple (perhaps over-simple) solution.
3. The view of the world that sees history, and especially the history of our own era, as a long series of struggles between dictatorship and democracy, in which history's arrow points in a democratic direction.
4. The changing nature of threats to democracy today, including populism and 'illiberal democracy'.
5. The use of civil resistance in the movements in the Middle East and North Africa in the early 2010s, known as the Arab Spring, which in many cases were followed by war or dictatorship, or both; and the tough lessons that can be learned from these catastrophic setbacks.
6. The continued extensive (but by no means always successful) use of civil resistance in anti-dictatorial movements in numerous countries and territories, including Hong Kong, Morocco, Sudan, Armenia and Belarus.
7. The role of women, including in frontline and leadership roles, in many of these movements.
8. Conclusion on whether, in recent national histories, peoples facilitated dictatorships or democracies; and on ways in which civil resistance has become an issue in the international politics of our time, but with mixed results.

Overview of civil resistance

Since at least the early twentieth century, civil resistance has had a significant role in world politics. This role has been especially evident since the late 1980s. Through the revolutions in Eastern Europe and the Soviet Union in 1989–91, civil resistance played some part in the downfall of Soviet-style rule. Then in Serbia in 2000, Georgia in 2003 and Ukraine in 2004, it proved a powerful mechanism for undermining brittle authoritarian systems and in particular challenging regimes that had falsified the results of elections. These and many other cases in many parts of the world strongly suggest that there is a link between civil resistance and the idea of democratic constitutional government.

To capture the character and modes of action of some or all of the movements involved, a rich variety of terms has been employed: 'mass collective actions', 'people power', 'passive resistance', 'nonviolent action' and 'colour revolution'. Here I mainly use the term 'civil resistance'. This abbreviated definition indicates one way of using it:

> CIVIL RESISTANCE is a type of political action that relies on the use of nonviolent methods. It involves a range of widespread and sustained activities that challenge a particular power, force, policy or regime– hence the term 'resistance'. The adjective 'civil' in this context denotes that which pertains to a citizen or society, implying that a movement's goals are 'civil' in the sense of being widely shared in a society; and it generally denotes that the action concerned is non-military or nonviolent in character.
>
> Civil resistance, precursors of which can be found throughout history, has been used in many types of struggle in modern times: for example, against colonialism, foreign occupations, military *coups d'état*, dictatorial regimes, electoral malpractice, corruption, environmental despoliation and racial, religious and gender discrimination. It has been used not only against tyrannical rule, but also against democratically elected governments, over such issues as maintenance of key elements of the constitutional order, preservation of regional autonomy within a country, defence of minority rights, environmental protection and opposition to involvement in certain military interventions and wars.
>
> Civil resistance operates through several mechanisms of change. These are not limited to forms of protest, nor to attempts to appeal to the adversary. They can involve pressure and coercion – by increasing the costs to the adversary of pursuing particular policies, weakening the adversary's capacity to pursue a particular policy or even undermining completely the adversary's sources of legitimacy and power, whether domestic or international. Campaigns of civil resistance involve strategy – i.e. projecting and directing the movements and elements of a campaign.
>
> There is no assumption that the adversary power against which civil resistance is aimed necessarily avoids resort to violence. Nor is there an assumption that there cannot be various forms of understanding or cooperation between civil resisters and certain governments or other entities with a capacity to use force. Often the reasons for a movement's avoidance of violence are related to the context, pragmatic calculation and ethical preference, rather than to any absolute ethical principle.[2]

A critical and multifaceted question, often posed by events, is how a civil resistance movement in a given country relates to institutions and groups wielding force – whether they are adversaries of the movement or potential allies. One long-standing attempt at an answer is that, if the regime being opposed resorts to violence and repression, nonviolent resisters use the asymmetry of the methods used by the two sides to throw the opposition off balance politically: this has been called 'political ju-jitsu'. Gene Sharp

(1928–2018), the leading theorist of civil resistance, explained it thus: 'The opponents' repression, when confronted with the discipline, solidarity, and persistence of the nonviolent actionists, brings attention to the opponents in the worst possible light. This produces shifts in opinion and power relationships favorable to the nonviolent group.' It may even lead to defections by members of the armed forces.[3] Sometimes political ju-jitsu has worked, and has been crucial to the success of particular struggles. Efforts to suppress or instil fear into a nonviolent movement can indeed have the effect of reinforcing that movement's resolve and momentum, not least by increasing its public and international support. Yet, as we will see, it does not always work: there are several pathways by which a contest between popular nonviolent action and state repression can end in tears.

Many observers of civil resistance have concentrated on the choice of method of struggle as a key factor in determining outcomes. The clearest expression of this approach was in Erica Chenoweth and Maria Stephan's important and influential study of *Why Civil Resistance Works*, published as a book in 2011. This work greatly advanced both academic and public understanding of the role of civil resistance. On the basis of their data set (global in scope) on 'Nonviolent and Violent Campaigns and Outcomes', the two authors reached this succinct and important conclusion:

> The most striking finding is that between 1900 and 2006, nonviolent resistance campaigns were nearly twice as likely to achieve full or partial success as their violent counterparts. . . . the effects of resistance type on the probability of campaign success are robust even when we take into account potential confounding factors, such as target regime type, repression, and target regime capabilities.[4]

This conclusion depends, of course, on how cases are selected, compared and evaluated. Three obvious difficulties arise. The first is the question of how to select campaigns for inclusion in a list of cases where the purpose is to compare the effects of violent and nonviolent resistance. For example, in a list of 'Twenty-five largest resistance campaigns, 1900–2006', the Czechoslovak resistance to the Soviet-led occupation in 1968 (a very extensive civil resistance campaign which was by conventional criteria a failure, as is recognized elsewhere in the book) is omitted, while the more successful resistance movement in the 1989 'Velvet Revolution' is included. Second is the difficulty of deciding whether a campaign is to be classified as violent or nonviolent, when on the ground, at least in some cases, both strategies may co-exist in several ways – or indeed follow each other, or compete. Third, forming judgements about whether a campaign is a success or failure involves elements of uncertainty: the answer may depend on the timeframe used, and on necessarily subjective judgements about what constitutes success. Even taking full account of their commendably explicit criteria, some of Chenoweth's and Stephan's decisions on particular campaigns, reported in *Why Civil Resistance Works*, offer an over-optimistic view of their effects. For example, the German 'passive resistance' in 1923 against the Franco-Belgian occupation of the Ruhr area is designated, implausibly, as a success; and the Druze resistance in the Israeli-occupied Golan Heights in 1981–2 as a partial success. In the epilogue, written sometime after the fall of President Mubarak in Egypt on 11 February 2011, the authors uphold Egypt as 'a particularly stunning example of why civil resistance works'.[5]

Although the study of civil resistance has advanced significantly in recent years, there is still (as Chenoweth and Stephan acknowledge) scope for more work on cases of failure, and on the reasons for it.[6] The grim fate of many of the countries involved in the Arab Spring confirms the need for rigorous consideration of such cases. A focus on failures as well as successes may identify some common problems which need to be addressed if the risk of further failures is to be reduced. It may also provide some parts of an answer to the question: how have peoples facilitated dictatorships or democracies in recent national histories?

Civil resistance is not a panacea: it does not offer anything like a complete replacement for all threats and uses of force within and between human societies. Moreover, its effects can be ambiguous: sometimes it has helped to ensure the emergence, survival and effectiveness of democratic systems, but at other times, indirectly and unintentionally, it may have facilitated the survival and even growth of autocracy. It has also become a bone of contention in international politics. I will return to these problems.[7]

Theory of voluntary servitude

The idea that autocracy is far from being inevitable and immutable, but depends for its continued existence on the cooperation of citizens, has a long and instructive history, and offers a clear – indeed, suspiciously clear – answer to our question. Famously, in his manuscript essay 'Discourse on Voluntary Servitude', unpublished in his lifetime, Étienne de la Boétie (1530–63), at the remarkably young age of 17 or 18, explored the social and psychological roots of obedience. His starting point was simple and elegantly stated:

> I should like merely to understand how it happens that so many men, so many villages, so many cities, so many nations, sometimes suffer under a single tyrant who has no other power than the power they give him.[8]

In the same passage he grieves at 'the spectacle of a million men serving in wretchedness, their necks under the yoke', and all of them constrained by 'one man alone'. He repeatedly conjures up this image of one tyrant, alone, oppressing vast numbers of people. Then the connection between this central theme and nonviolent forms of resistance is evident:

> I do not ask that you place hands upon the tyrant to topple him over, but simply that you support him no longer; then you will behold him, like a great Colossus whose pedestal has been pulled away, fall of his own weight and break in pieces.[9]

Or, as his American translator put it even more optimistically:

> His method of redress against dictators is much more subtle and effective than violence, and might be substantially described as 'passive resistance'. He sought political reform not by overt deeds involving bloodshed, but by a refusal of obedience to the orders of tyrants.[10]

This observation appears to neglect another side of La Boétie's work – his enthusiasm for past wars against tyranny. He writes of 'battles fought in Greece for the welfare of the Greeks and as an example to the world'. He asks what gave the ancient Greeks the power and courage to resist much larger Persian forces: 'What was it but the fact that in those glorious days this struggle represented not so much a fight of Greeks against Persians as a victory of liberty over domination, of freedom over greed?'[11] Today, in the twenty-first-century public debates, we are still as confused as La Boétie was about whether freedom should be extended by peaceful struggle or the sword.

The fact that this essay was not published in the lifetime of La Boétie, who was a distinguished lawyer and writer, is evidence of the extreme sensitivity of the question he was addressing. When in due course it was published – after his death, and only in anonymous pirated editions – it was largely as an instrument in the hands of Protestants to foment rebellions. Bearing all this in mind, his close friend and literary executor Michel de Montaigne (1533–92) explained his refusal to publish this essay in a collection of La Boétie's works thus:

> Because I have discovered that this work has since been published, and with an evil purpose, by those who seek to disturb and change the form of our government without caring whether they better it, and who mixed it in with other grist from their own mills, I have decided not to print it here.[12]

We may regret Montaigne's decision not to publish it then. However, he was right to be sceptical about the theory of voluntary servitude. It would be extremely controversial to accept La Boétie's theory uncritically. It has two interlinked faults. The first is that it is implicitly universalist: it presents one form of action as a means of undermining all dictatorships, irrespective of local conditions. The second is that the theory easily morphs into blaming the citizens for the system that oppresses them. As La Boétie himself put it: 'It is therefore the inhabitants themselves who permit, or rather bring about, their own subjection, since by ceasing to submit they would put an end to their own servitude.' And then, in another passage: 'Poor, wretched, and stupid peoples, nations determined on your own misfortune and blind to your own good!'[13]

La Boétie presents too simple a view of domination as one dictator versus a million citizens. His theory takes too little account of the regional, tribal, class and religious divisions within a society of which autocrats can take advantage in order to prop up their rule, and which mean that at least some parts of the population have a strong material stake in the regime. There is profundity in Montaigne's implicit recognition that events can be much more tangled than theories, and that simply opposing dictatorial rule may not open up a road to its replacement. The story of the Arab Spring will illustrate these points.

La Boétie's essay can itself be seen as part of a tradition, which has continued to the present, of viewing international history as a story of struggle between democracy and dictatorship. Hence the dedication to the 1942 American translation of his work on voluntary servitude:

> This call to freedom ringing down the corridors of four centuries is sounded again here for the sake of peoples in all totalitarian countries today who dare not freely declare their thought.
>
> It will also ring dear and beautiful in the ears of those who still live freely and who by faith and power will contribute to the liberation of the rest of mankind from the horrors of political serfdom.[14]

La Boétie's work established an early connection between the analysis of tyranny and proposals for popular non-cooperation. Yet despite its many merits, it is not the only theoretical basis for civil resistance even in those cases where what is being opposed is plainly tyranny. The element of universalism in its approach can easily amount to obliviousness to different situations, different political spaces and different times. Such universalism still has echoes in contemporary debates, especially in those about democracy and dictatorship.

History as struggle between democracy and dictatorship

The view of history as a struggle between democracy and dictatorship has a long, important and intellectually interesting history of its own. At various times in both the nineteenth and twentieth centuries it played a significant role in the formulation of both British and US foreign policies. From the abolition of the slave trade to the end of communist rule in the former Soviet empire, many great and important victories have been won on the basis of this view.

Yet there are some obvious weaknesses in a view of world history as one long series of struggles between democracy and dictatorship. In particular, the political system of democracy (in its modern meaning of universal suffrage and multiparty systems) is not on its own the most relevant answer to each and every abuse of power and failure of government. One criticism is that elections are widely seen as the be-all and end-all of democracy, yet they are inherently unsatisfactory as means of giving the citizenry any real participation in decision-making.[15] A second comes from Frank Fukuyama, who has argued at length that building up an efficient administrative system, respecting the rule of law and supporting independent and fact-based news media may be equally important, and may themselves be preconditions for successful democracy.[16]

Moreover, the single-minded view of democracy as historical destiny tends to neglect, or play down, the difficult issue of whether all societies are structurally suited to making the transition from autocracy to democracy. John Stuart Mill was an advocate of self-determination but, unusually for liberal political philosophers of his time, he did recognize – if only in the most general terms – that the very existence of different nationalities within the same country may be a factor preventing the implementation of the ideal of self-determination:

> Where the sentiment of nationality exists in any force, there is a *prima facie* case for uniting all the members of the nationality under the same government, and a government to themselves apart. This is merely saying that the question of government ought to be decided by the governed. One hardly knows what any division of the human race should be free to do, if not to determine, with which of the various collective bodies of human beings they choose to associate themselves. But, when a people are ripe for free institutions, there is a still more vital consideration. Free institutions are next to impossible in a country made up of different nationalities.[17]

Mill was right to point out that it is hard to establish free democratic institutions in deeply divided countries. Yet he was aware of exceptions to this generalization. Just before the earlier-quoted passage, he had alluded briefly to the interesting case of Switzerland, which, despite differences of race, language and religion, had survived as a federal state with a democratic constitutional framework.[18]

Certain autocratic systems have been viewed widely (whether at home or abroad) with a degree of tolerance because of awareness that the state concerned encompassed bitter historical rivalries between different nationalities or religious groupings, making the introduction of multiparty democracy potentially divisive. One such case was Yugoslavia, ruled by the League of Communists of Yugoslavia under Jozip Broz Tito from 1945 until his death in 1980. When I was doing research in Yugoslavia in 1972, I was impressed by the depth of concern about the prospects for the country after Tito's death: not only that it might break up into its six component republics, but that within several of them – including Croatia, Bosnia and Serbia – there was potential for civil war. These fears were fully borne out by the way in which wars erupted in the former Yugoslavia in the 1990s. These wars were preceded in 1990 by free elections in all the republics of Yugoslavia. In every one of these republics, parties based on ethnic/communal loyalties prevailed, leading ultimately to demands for independent statehood and to three major and long-running wars, over Croatia, Bosnia and Kosovo.

A related problem with the democracy v. dictatorship view of world history is that the record of fighting wars that have been defined in these terms is at best patchy. For example, US wars since 1945 that have been defined largely in terms of opposing autocracy and supporting democracy have included those in Vietnam, Afghanistan, the second US intervention in Iraq (2003–) and the NATO-led intervention in Libya (2011). There is room for doubt about the proposition of spreading democracy by the sword, about whether these countries were ready for democracy and about the extent to which democracy has taken root in them.

A worrying aspect of the democracy v. dictatorship world view is that it tends to rest on an often-unspoken assumption that history's arrow flies in a single direction – from dictatorship to democracy. Then, when the arrow starts flying in a completely different direction, as it has been doing lately (and has of course done before), disillusion and panic quickly set in. Indeed, we now see the gloomy assumption being made – not universally, but quite widely – that all of history's arrows are flying in the reverse direction.

Writers on civil resistance have warned that merely getting rid of a dictatorial government is not enough. Gene Sharp's 1993 essay *From Dictatorship to Democracy* contained the warning: 'Nor should this analysis be interpreted to mean that when a specific dictatorship is ended, all other problems will also disappear. The fall of one regime does not bring in a utopia.'[19]

It is for good reasons that civil resistance, which has been used in many pro-democratic campaigns, tends to be associated with struggles for democracy. Yet it is not synonymous with the single cause of democracy promotion. Thinking of civil resistance as tied exclusively to the struggle for democracy can give rise to two main hazards. Firstly, it narrows the range of causes. Civil resistance has often been to advance other social, economic, legal and national goals, which may or may not in specific cases be connected to, and supportive of, existing democratic institutions. For example, it has sometimes been used in defence of the rights of a minority that feels threatened by decisions or laws even when they have been approved by a democratic legislature. Some of the most significant civil resistance campaigns have been against racism, sexism or class discrimination, not against authoritarian political regimes as such. The second hazard of equating civil resistance with democracy is that it can lead to an undifferentiated approach, as if all dictatorships are more or less the same and can be opposed by a standard range of methods and tactics. Indeed, if it is assumed that history's arrow is following the democratic direction, there may be a tendency to underestimate the adversary, and thereby increase the risks of failure.

Changing threats: Populism and 'illiberal democracy'

Today, in many parts of the world, multiparty democratic political systems face a huge range of fundamental challenges. Take the case of the convulsions in two countries, the United States and the United Kingdom, that have traditionally seen themselves as torchbearers for constitutional democracy. Both the June 2016 UK referendum on membership of the European Union and the November 2016 US presidential election reflected widespread public dissatisfaction with existing systems of government and international roles. In both cases there was, and still is, a public perception that, in an era of austerity, whole industries, whole cities, indeed whole areas of the country, have suffered disproportionately. In both cases the electorate made decisions that broke with convention and challenged key liberal assumptions – not least about the benefits of globalization, and about the useful role played by certain international institutions, including the EU. In both the United States and the United Kingdom, immigration, and fears that it risked getting out of control, played a part in a lurch to the Right.

In both the United States and the United Kingdom, populism had reared its ugly head. Populism is a form of politics in which 'the people' are upheld and are presented as victims of corrupt and self-serving elites. Populist political leaders (who may be of the political Left or Right) often present wilfully distorted pictures of the world and grotesquely simplified policy proposals. It is easy to accuse key political players in both the United States and the United Kingdom in recent years of a variety of political sins which are typical of populism: lack of attention to policy detail, making absurd promises, flattering audiences, using insulting language about ethnic or religious minorities, whipping up fears of foreigners, falsifying election results and resorting to outright lies. Such conduct seems to flourish with renewed vigour in and age of electronic media. In both countries there were concerns that the populist revolt was aided and abetted by foreign, and most particularly Russian, involvement in electoral processes, mainly through the financing of parties and electoral campaigns, and using electronic media under cover of anonymity. Yet populist appeals have always been a feature of democratic politics and cannot be entirely eliminated. A crucial task for democracies is to introduce tough measures addressing some of the worst abuses such as foreign interference in political processes, hate speech, anonymous political messaging and secret political funding. More work is needed to ensure that factual corrections are given as much prominence as the original error.

Since populism has often played a part in the emergence of authoritarian regimes, it represents one worrying answer to the question: how have peoples facilitated dictatorships? A simple answer is: people have facilitated dictatorship by being so gullible to populist appeals. A more considered answer would have to take into account the existence of strong and genuine grievances.

Democracy can be further undermined if governments fail in their basic task of protecting their citizens. In 2020 neither the United States nor the United Kingdom managed the initial phases of the Covid-19 pandemic effectively. Their populist leaders – US President Trump and UK Prime Minister Johnson – initially failed to take the crisis seriously. The figures for deaths due to Covid-19 per million of population in both countries were extraordinarily high. In the United States the number (up to 25 September 2020) was 612, and in the UK 617.[20] Both of these leading constitutional democracies were thus, for a time at least, in the inglorious position of being among the twelve worst-performing countries in the world so far as Covid-19 death rates are concerned.

In recent decades, departures from democracy and the rule of law have affected not only, and not even mainly, the Anglosphere centred on the United States and the United Kingdom, but a large number of other countries. For example, in Brazil, Hungary, the Philippines, Russia, Turkey and Venezuela, new authoritarian forms of rule have emerged, and some old forms have re-emerged.

In Putin's Russia there have been some straightforward examples of anti-liberal stances being seen as a good way of strengthening nationalism and raising suspicions about foreign influences. One example is the founding in 2005 of the *Nashi* (Russian for "Ours"), a Kremlin-supported youth movement whose stated mission is to protect Russia from liberals, communists and fascists. This is a classic GONGO – a government-organized NGO.

The forms of the new authoritarian rule have been very varied. They have included the phenomenon of 'illiberal democracy' – of elected regimes that preside over systems in which the information available to the public is limited, parties do not compete on equal terms, constitutional restrictions on governmental power are whittled away and the rule of law is undermined. As Fareed Zakaria wrote in 1997, in a pioneering article on this phenomenon: 'Today the two strands of liberal democracy, interwoven in the Western political fabric, are coming apart in the rest of the world. Democracy is flourishing; constitutional liberalism is not.'[21]

In a few cases, the cause of 'illiberal democracy' has even been advanced by politicians who had come to prominence earlier through movements of national civil resistance against authoritarian rule. One such case is Viktor Orbán in Hungary. In 1989 he had been a prominent figure in the pro-democracy movement that helped to end over four decades of communist rule in the country, replacing it with multiparty democracy. Yet he gradually became more authoritarian. In the years after 2011, as the flow of migrants from Middle Eastern countries intensified and many were heading for Europe, he increasingly styled himself and his country as defenders of Europe against the 'poison' of immigration. He attacked not only specific policies, but also some of the fundamentals of liberal democracy. In 2014, serving in his second term as Hungarian prime minister, he said this in a long speech delivered at a predominantly Hungarian summer school held annually in Romania:

> The liberal democracy was incapable of openly stating and committing the prevailing government, including through the use of its constitutional powers, to serving the interests of the nation with their work. And it in fact challenged the very idea of the existence of national interests. . . .
>
> The new state that we are constructing in Hungary is an illiberal state, a non-liberal state. It does not reject the fundamental principles of liberalism such as freedom, and I could list a few more, but it does not make this ideology the central element of state organization, but instead includes a different, special, national approach.[22]

In early 2020, as the crisis over the Covid-19 pandemic intensified, Orbán took a significant step in an authoritarian direction. At his instigation, on 30 March the Hungarian parliament passed a law ('Act on Protection against the Coronavirus') enabling the government to rule by decree, to the extent that is necessary to address the pandemic's consequences. The special legal order that he thus established was widely criticized. On 17 April it was condemned by the European Parliament as 'totally incompatible with European values'. The Hungarian emergency formally ended on 20 June. Orbán pronounced it a great success, but the legal provisions for its future renewal were such as to leave suspicions that the end of the emergency was an illusion. Moreover, by November 2020 Hungary's cumulative Covid-19 mortality rate had increased more than sixfold from where it had been at the beginning of June, so the overall record was far from impressive.

Although the official figures on coronavirus deaths were much lower, in certain other respects (although certainly not in all) the role of Rodrigo Duterte in the Philippines is comparable. It prompts the question: how could the peaceful and successful struggle in 1983–6 against the corrupt and election-fiddling rule of President Marcos have resulted, thirty years later, in Duterte's notably populist and violent form of politics? That struggle, triggered by the assassination of the opposition politician Benigno Aquino in 1983, had led to the election to the presidency of his widow Corazon Aquino in February 1986. It was in that same year, in the immediate aftermath of the 'people power' revolution in his country, that Duterte became deputy-mayor of Davao City, the third largest in the Philippines. In that post, and later in the post of mayor, he encouraged and supported extrajudicial killings of drug dealers and other criminals. When he became President of the Philippines in June 2016, he continued to encourage exceptionally violent approaches to law and order. Then, after UN human-rights experts had criticized the numerous extrajudicial killings, President Duterte threatened to withdraw the Philippines from the UN, and impulsively suggested forming a new organization with China and African states.[23] In 2017 he issued orders removing police from operations in the war on drugs, placing the Philippine Drug Enforcement Agency in charge.[24]

Various explanations have been offered for the pattern of violent politics in the Philippines. Underlying all of them is a widespread awareness that the revolution of 1986 still left many of the same old elite in charge of the country, which it saddled with a centralizing constitution. As one observer wrote at the time of the 2016 presidential election, Duterte was seen as the only one of the six candidates who had 'no substantive political link to the national political elite'.[25] Another observer, concerned about the Duterte phenomenon, noted a regular pattern whereby, since 1998, the presidency had alternately been occupied by 'reformist' and 'populist' personalities; and noted that, while Duterte is far to the left of Trump, there are similarities in the two presidents' use of political theatricality and new communications technologies.[26] The Philippines under President Duterte is clearly very different from Hungary under Prime Minister Orbán but does belong in the same category of 'illiberal democracy'. This case confirms that the experience of a national civil resistance struggle does not in any way guarantee immunity from future illiberalism.

Among the new authoritarian regimes there are huge differences in attitudes to capitalism, to welfare and to the use of violence, particularly torture. Yet some aspects of the new authoritarianism are common across several different cases, and some of them distinguish the new authoritarianism from some earlier (and still surviving) forms of dictatorial or totalitarian rule. Here is one list of features commonly, but not invariably, encountered in authoritarian regimes today. They are all consistent with the idea of 'illiberal democracy':

- Strong emphasis on nationalism, and on pursuit of the national interest.
- Heavy reliance on populist slogans and rhetoric.
- The absence, in most cases, of a fully developed ideology.
- The holding of periodic elections, but with varying practices about the possibility of different parties competing, fairness of media coverage and acceptance of international election observers.
- Freedom of citizens to travel, work and study abroad.

- A mixture of attempts to control domestic and international information flows on the one hand, and acceptance of their continued independent existence on the other.
- Hostility towards acceptance of large numbers of migrants and refugees in the country.
- Suspicion of many political and social activities that are foreign-funded or foreign-supported.
- Continued membership of most international organizations, combined with high-profile criticism of some of them.
- Entertaining the idea of establishing a common front of authoritarian regimes against what they see as dangerous liberal influence.

The Arab Spring: Ten propositions

Many questions about the long-term consequences of campaigns of civil resistance were raised by the Arab Spring of 2011. Starting with the self-immolation of Mohammed Bouazizi on 17 December 2010, the Arab Spring was a significant, but also tragic, series of cases of civil resistance. The outcomes were varied, for reasons lucidly outlined in Marina Ottaway's excellent chapter in this book.[27] They included, on the positive side, a still-ongoing process of constitutional change in Tunisia, and some modest incremental changes in Morocco, Jordan, Algeria and other countries. However, the list of negative outcomes is much longer: a Saudi Arabian military intervention in Bahrain to maintain the existing system of government there, the revival of an old system of authoritarian rule in Egypt, internationalized civil wars in Yemen and Syria, a lack of central authority and ensuing civil war in Libya. This is a grim record of failure: it needs to be taken fully into account in any evaluation of the potential of popular action against authoritarian rulers.

There were some striking similarities between the various movements that comprised the Arab Spring. Their early demands included calls for greater democracy: these were problematic because introducing a democratic system in a previously authoritarian state is inherently difficult, as some friendly critics of the Arab Spring pointed out.[28] There were also striking differences in the situations faced by the movements. Some took place in republics, others in monarchies. Some demanded the fall of the regime; others called for reform. Some had active participation of existing bodies such as trade unions; others did not. There were huge differences in the size of the countries concerned, and in their unemployment rates and in their economic levels.

What follows is an extremely brief survey of certain issues raised by the highly variegated phenomenon of the Arab Spring.[29] I first mention five misleading generalizations, and then explore at slightly greater length ten more credible propositions.

What lessons will the citizens of these countries, and indeed the world generally, learn from the Arab Spring? There is already a danger that simple, fundamentally misleading, conclusions might gain traction, including, for example, these five notably broad generalizations:

- Arab countries are unsuited to democracy and cannot make it work.
- Countries with Muslim populations are unsuited to democracy.
- Civil resistance was the result of foreign influence, pressure or even conspiracy.
- Civil resistance was a failure, and is likely to be so in the future.
- The pursuit of power politics is a normal state of affairs that civil resistance cannot stop or even modify.

The first two involve racist caricatures and imply the inferiority of the Arab world. The third lacks serious evidence, and ignores the long record of civil resistance in the Arab world. The last two ignore the degree of (modest) success in Tunisia, and also in Lebanon in the 'Cedar Revolution' of 2005. Yet such broad generalizations have the merit that they recognize the seriousness of the failures of the Arab Spring. Rather than criticizing these generalizations one by one, I will suggest some more fine-grained propositions that might be drawn from the Arab Spring. Granted the disasters encountered in the Arab Spring, and the evident failure of civil resistance to lead to peaceful change in many of the countries concerned, it is urgent to consider what propositions follow, both in the region and more generally? Ten are proposed here.

1. Conditions, both within a country and internationally, are important in determining outcomes. In 2011–12 there was a tendency to generalize wildly about the prospects of the Arab Spring, as if all the countries involved could be expected to have a similar outcome. In reality, each country and situation is different. Many types of conditions can make it harder, or easier, for a movement to achieve success. They include the degree of self-belief, or the lack of it, of the ruling party or clique; the ethnic, religious and socio-economic composition of a society, attitudes to political violence, traditions of thought whether authoritarian or otherwise, the past performance of political parties and the presence or absence of a functioning legal framework and administrative system. 'Conditions' also encompasses international factors, such as the readiness of neighbouring states, major powers and international institutions to support or oppose change.

2. Civil resistance campaigns face multiple forms of repression. Sometimes civil resistance movements can be strengthened by acts of state repression against them. It was precisely police insensitivity and repression that sparked the revolutions in Tunisia and Egypt in the first place. In both countries, early attempts to repress the civil movement failed to slow the momentum of demonstrations. Thus the concept of political ju-jitsu was at least partially vindicated.

Yet the Arab Spring confirmed that there are many forms of interaction between civil resistance and uses of force. In a challenging article published in 2014 that directly addressed the claims made about political ju-jitsu, Dr. Thomas Davies considered the extent of failure of civil resistance campaigns in four countries involved in the Arab Spring, and suggested that 'adherence to principles of strategic nonviolent action may be insufficient in contributing towards success, and how, in contrast to the assumptions of the 'political ju-jitsu' model, nonviolent strategy itself may contribute towards failure'. He argued, thoughtfully and persuasively, that there are four pathways by which nonviolent action may be counterproductive (and, at least by implication, lead to uses of force). These four pathways can be summarized as follows.[30]

(i) *Suppression.* Nonviolent action may provide a highly vulnerable target for a regime with the will and the means to repress it, especially if neighbouring states assist the repression. Bahrain in 2011 is an example.

(ii) *Cosmetic reforms.* The regime makes certain changes, generally intended to have the effect of deflecting both internal and external criticism of the regime, but key problems remain unaddressed and repression continues. Egypt in 2011–12 provides examples, showing in particular how civil–military relations can remain difficult. The slogan of the demonstrators, 'the army and people are one', may have contributed in the short term to divisions between the military command and Mubarak, all of which helped the civil resistance, but in the long term it helped to legitimize the pre-eminence of the military.

(iii) *Partial military defections leading to the militarization of a conflict.* Sections of the armed forces defect, but remain armed, gain some external financial support and continue their military roles, albeit now on the rebel side. This is one pathway to the outbreak of civil war. Syria in 2011–12 provides an example of such a process.

(iv) *Military intervention by outside armed forces to stop the regime's repression of resisters.* This may depose an old regime but create uncertainty and chaos about who is governing the country. The NATO-led campaign in Libya in 2011 is an example.

These four pathways, relating to four countries involved in the Arab Spring, do not exhaust the types of pathways that were experienced in the Arab Spring, or indeed in countless other past and present cases of civil resistance. If the dynamics facilitating the failure of nonviolent action are to be avoided, it is important for the strategists of nonviolent action to address the national and international circumstances that can lead to the use of violence and/or the failure of a civil resistance campaign.

To put the same issue more crudely, the Arab Spring shows how, even after campaigns of civil resistance, fear remains an important factor in many, and perhaps even most, political systems, and can impact on civil resistance movements. In Egypt, after the *coup d'état* of 3 July 2013, the use of harsh measures against any and all demonstrations did instil fear. And in Bahrain in the early months of the Arab Spring, the Saudi-led military intervention on 14 March 2011, followed by the regime's demolition of the Pearl Roundabout (a famous focus for demonstrations), did limit the actions of the protest movement.

3. Even in the absence of external military intervention, the problems of creating a successor government in the wake of a fallen regime can lead to social disorder and even to war. If civil resistance can bring down a regime but lacks convincing arrangements for its replacement, it has a major weakness for which a high price may be paid. One form of succession problem is the power of the 'deep state' to continue within the administration and security services despite the decapitation of the regime. A second problem is the emergence of power vacuums and ungoverned spaces: these are situations in which, in the absence of state power and effective policing, areas of a state may be exploited by private security companies, non-state entities, drug dealers, pirates, religious fanatics, human traffickers, regional states and more. Egypt in 2011–13 provides examples of both of these types of problems.

In countries, such as Syria and Yemen, where from 2011–12 onwards demonstrations were gradually eclipsed by armed struggle and internationalized civil war, there was another serious consequence. Many citizens made the desperate decision to emigrate, thus creating pressures on both neighbouring and more distant states to accept large numbers of migrants. These pressures contributed to the rise of authoritarian politics in many countries.

4. Constitutional democracy remains one principal means by which political conflicts are played out with minimal violence. The movements of the Arab Spring generally called for an enhancement of democracy and the rule of law: they particularly emphasized accountability in public life and better treatment of citizens. Their focus was *not* on such issues as changing the frontiers of Middle Eastern or North African states. (These issues hardly arose at all within the Arab Spring movements themselves.) The Arab Spring focus on constitutional democracy seems heroic now, since in the past few years there has been a trend in many parts of the world towards right-wing authoritarian regimes. Yet maybe some civil resistance movements need to be more explicit that their aim is to support constitutional systems of government, including of course the right of government to use force against certain types of threat; and they need to be more involved in parliamentary processes to create and implement constitutional systems.

5. The characterization of existing rulers as 'dictators' can be problematic. In the Arab Spring, there was a tendency to describe as 'dictators' all the leaders who were being opposed. While such an attribution may be justified in many cases, there are two potential problems associated with it. Firstly, it risks oversimplifying the roles of authoritarian leaders. Even in the absence of formal democratic constitutional constraints, some such leaders may not rule on the basis of personal interest or whim. They may even be continuously engaged in reacting to a range of regional, confessional or other pressures within the state, as well as from outside, and may be aware that their rule depends on the consent of their subjects. Secondly, when political leaders characterize certain rulers as dictators there is sometimes an implicit assumption that, if the people can only break free from their chains, if the ruler who is the source of oppression can be removed, all will be well. This has plainly not been the case in many countries affected by the Arab Spring. During that period, a mistake commonly made in some Western countries was to assume that once people power had seen off an old regime, progress to a new democratic order would be smooth. This was a nonviolent equivalent of the Rumsfeld doctrine as applied in Iraq from 2003 onwards – that the deposition of a dictator by light ground forces backed up by air power will quickly be followed by an advance to democracy.

6. **The movements' initial successes in overthrowing rulers in Tunisia and Egypt were misleading.** These extraordinary successes were deceptive for two solid reasons. Firstly, because, in those countries where a regime was overthrown, building a constitutional political order proved to be a longer and harder task; and secondly, because in some other countries, and most notably Syria, the existing regimes had a greater degree of legitimacy or capacity for survival – so could not be overthrown as easily as those in Tunis and Cairo in the early months of 2011.

7. **The decentralized and ad hoc quality of the leadership of some of the movements in the Arab Spring hindered their performance.** While the movements' leaders showed great qualities, many of them had problems regarding three key tasks: preparation for post-revolutionary governance of the country, making necessary compromises with other political forces and producing a convincing plan for economic development. These problems were especially evident in Egypt. In Yemen, the leadership of the street movement was a miscellaneous group whose only common objective was to get rid of President Saleh: essentially there were many leaders, or none. In many Middle Eastern and North African countries, it was not realistic to respond to such difficulties by urging young activists to form or join a political party: such parties were, and are, commonly seen as ineffectual bit-players in a political pantomime.

Yet, as the story of Tunisia shows, organization and leadership are crucial. In 2010–11 the trade unions played a central role in the events; and thereafter, as indicated by the role of the En Nahda Party, it was political parties' careful preparation for transition, and their explicit willingness to leave office if they lose an election, that made ultimate success in Tunisia thinkable. In January 2019 I spent a week in Tunisia with colleagues who (unlike myself) are specialists on North Africa. Our interviews with officials, politicians, lawyers and activists persuaded us that, despite problems of a sluggish economy, low voter participation, coming to terms with the past, and disorder in neighbouring countries, Tunisians are managing the democratization process seriously and effectively.

8. **Citizens can become weary of prolonged or repeated civil resistance campaigns.** This problem can be especially severe if continued activism is seen as damaging the economy of a country. Leadership of a movement requires skill in ending campaigns, or pursuing them in imaginative ways that do not antagonize the public. It calls for skilful use of the many different methods of nonviolent action. There are particular dangers in focusing exclusively on the strategy of prolonged occupation of symbolically important places. Such a strategy may expose the participants or the places to high risk of repression or destruction.

9. **There is sometimes a tendency in civil resistance movements to regard the crowd as itself a fount of legitimacy.** This is one of the many worrying aspects of populism. In Egypt, in June 2013 the Tahrir Square demonstrators conveyed a message implying that the elected government (of the Muslim Brotherhood) should step down, or be forcibly replaced, on their say-so. Such a view of the legitimacy of crowds becomes a problem if it assumes superiority over constitutional arrangements, demonstrates overconfidence about the capacity of crowds to remove regimes or becomes a justification for a *coup d'état* by the armed forces. Moreover, as evidenced in Cairo, Damascus and Manama, ruling regimes can often assemble large crowds as a means of demonstrating that they too have crowd-based legitimacy.

10. **International factors of various kinds influence outcomes.** In many fields, including medicine, business and politics, transnational influences have for centuries been facts of life. The most powerful international influences on autocratic systems may consist, not of any specific action or plan, but of the mere existence of better societies. The power of example is impressive.

Civil resistance is often assisted by the power of example (including in other countries); by the international spread of ideas through books, pamphlets and media; and by the fact that a few key people have had training in its basics. If it is to be effective, civil resistance often needs *both* strong local roots *and* some forms of external influence and support. Its application in any given country, and the outcome there, depend first and foremost on the interests, beliefs and political culture of that country's citizens. Outside support may also be important, especially if that helps to level the playing field against a powerful government apparatus. Civil resistance campaigns against authoritarian rulers have sometimes succeeded in inducing foreign democratic countries (especially the United States) to reorient their policies away from cosy relations with the authoritarian rulers, and in favour of demanding their resignation.

Foreign assistance to civil resistance movements can often be controversial, even to the point of being seen as part of a foreign conspiracy. This is not a new phenomenon. Long before the Arab Spring there were cases of authoritarian states viewing civil resistance as an externally inspired threat. Indeed, over fifty years ago, shortly after the Soviet-led invasion of Czechoslovakia, the East German communist leader Walter Ulbricht sought to justify the invasion as a response to 'the various forms and methods of the imperialist policy of expansion', claiming repeatedly that there had been a Western plot for a 'nonviolent uprising'.[31] Similarly, in a speech in 2011, President Assad of Syria suggested that civil resistance in Arab countries was largely the result of 'sedition'.[32] In the same spirit, in speeches in 2014 President Putin of Russia said that "color revolutions" in the post-Soviet world are the products of an externally controlled seizure of power.[33] These speeches of Assad and Putin repay careful study. This is not because they contain any serious evidence of external control: they do not, and indeed the evidence for this appears to be flimsy. The significance of these speeches lies in the way in which they manage to present civil resistance as part of a grand external conspiracy. They provide a useful buttress for xenophobia and authoritarianism. Even if they are unconvincing to most international audiences, they may be believed by many citizens of the authoritarian state, and especially by members of its security forces.

At the same time, another international development may be making life harder for nascent opposition movements. The period when such movements had the lead in using new electronic media seems to be coming to an end. Now the worry is that powerful corporations and states, including not just Russia and China but also many established constitutional democracies, can use the new electronic forms of communication both at home and abroad. They use them not only for surveillance, but also for spreading misleading information from anonymous sources, which is a pernicious form of 'fake news'. This can divide societies and even undermine trust in political action of all kinds. The root of this problem is not (as is sometimes suggested) the mere existence of social media: rather, it is the systematic use of information gained from a variety of sources (including social media and much else besides) to provide a basis for crude populist and commercial campaigns. Democracies in particular need to grasp this problem and to create a legal framework preventing its worst excesses.

Overall, the story of the Arab Spring needs to be understood for what it is: the story of a tragedy, but with some sparks of hope. I have suggested that the answer to the first question is this: yes, in many cases the peoples, by their actions or failures to act, have indeed played some part, however unintentional, in facilitating the return of dictatorship. Even at the risk of repetition, the extent of the tragedy needs to be spelt out. A largely familiar system of military autocratic rule is now firmly re-established in the region's most populous country, Egypt. There has been a return to foreign-assisted authoritarian rule in Bahrain. In at least three countries – Syria, Yemen and Libya – the initially more hopeful events of the Arab Spring have been followed by civil wars with extensive external military involvements. Against this pattern of disaster, more positive signs are relatively few. In the country where it started, Tunisia, the Arab Spring facilitated the emergence of a democratic constitutional system. As a result, there is a tendency to view Tunisia as a model. This is a label that many of Tunisia's leaders view with some concern. It does not help their cause to present them as offering a model for the whole region, especially as for good practical reasons they need to collaborate closely with all their neighbours.

Movements after the Arab Spring

However sobering the ten propositions about the Arab Spring may be, they did not, and do not, exclude the possibility of comparable movements emerging in the future, whether in the Arab world or elsewhere. And while these propositions may be thought to apply to all the countries in the region, they contain many indications that every country is different. Both within the region, and in the global coverage of events there, there was a tendency to view the regimes in Arab states as mere dominoes. This was a mistake. Equally, to assert that all the setbacks faced by the Arab Spring movements were due to one single cause is a mistake. There is no substitute for understanding each country as having its own unique history and its own political traditions, divisions – and possibilities.

The story of the Arab Spring is not over. The experience of it, and its suppression, has shaped, and continues to shape, the politics of many states in the region and beyond. The hopes it raised of an essentially peaceful and cooperative form of politics have not disappeared. Popular movements showed determination and skill in asserting basic rights, both within and beyond the Arab world. There were also setbacks, A few examples follow.

In Morocco there were anti-government protests in 2016–17, against corruption, unemployment, police brutality and neglect of the Berber population, leading to a government crackdown in June 2017. In Jordan in 2018 there were extensive demonstrations, and a general strike, against tax increases and rises in fuel prices, leading to government concessions. In Algeria, huge peaceful protests in January–March 2019 led in April to the resignation of Abdelaziz Bouteflika, who had been president for twenty years; demonstrations have continued, calling for fundamental changes of the political system.

In Sudan, a period of nonviolent protests began in January 2018 and spread rapidly from December 2018 onwards. Two consistent themes were opposition to the continued rule of Omar al-Bashir, who had been the country's president (with a number of different titles) since 1989; and popular concern over the economy, especially high inflation and increases in the price of bread. The demonstrations occurred in many parts of the country, and had the support of a large coalition, eventually named Forces of Freedom and Change (FFC). Slogans used have included 'Just fall–That is all', and the classic Arab Spring statement: 'The people demand the fall of the regime.' The regime and its security apparatus responded to the demonstrations with a mixture of repression and occasional tolerance; and received strong statements of support from Bahrain, Egypt, Saudi Arabia and other predictable authoritarian sources. On 11 April 2019, in what appeared to be a *coup d'état*, the Sudanese armed forces removed al-Bashir from power, arrested him, suspended the constitution and set up a new body to run the country, the Transitional Military Council (TMC). This by no means ended the crisis: demonstrators continued to demand that the military hand over power to a civilian government, and that members of the former regime be tried for crimes against humanity. For obvious reasons, some neighbouring and regional states opposed such moves. On 3 June sixty or more demonstrators were shot dead in Khartoum. The opposition responded with a three-day general strike. Both Ethiopia and the African Union made efforts to mediate. On 17 July, after long negotiations, an outline agreement was signed by representatives of the TMC and FFC, providing for a 39-month process of transition back to democracy. One of many concerns about the agreement was that Mohamed Hamdan Dagalo, former commander of the notorious Janjaweed militias, remained in a position of power. Some groups opposed the agreement, and discussions continued on key issues. The process of major reform continued. One striking development was the agreement of 3 September 2020 to separate religion and state, and an outlawing of religious discrimination. This complex and unfinished story is a reminder of four things: that civil resistance remains a powerful weapon; that authoritarians, especially but not only in the Arab world, look after their own; that the demand for civilian constitutional government, and for an end to official criminality and corruption, remains strong; and that civil resistance movements need to be prepared for a phase of detailed constitutional and legal negotiation.

Beyond the Arab world, events in Armenia in April 2018 also confirmed that civil resistance still had potency. Nikol Pashinyan, a member of the Armenian parliament, a campaigner against corruption and a candidate for the prime ministership, led a series of marches, demonstrations and strikes to prevent his rival Serzh Sargsyan from a constitutionally improper continuation of his ten-year tenure (2008–18) of the highest offices in the country – the prime ministership and the presidency. Sargsyan's plan to continue as prime minister ultimately failed because of massive and peaceful public opposition. On 8 May 2018, in a vote in parliament, Pashinyan was elected as prime minister; and in parliamentary elections held on 9 December, he won. On 14 January 2019 he was sworn in as prime minister. This was a victory that confirmed how crucial a constitutional framework can be for the success of civil resistance.[34]

However, the events in Armenia also provide the basis for a more disturbing lesson. The experience of civil resistance in an internal struggle is no guarantee that the same methods will be used in external crises. On 27 September 2020, within two years of the democratic success in Armenia, the country was plunged into hostilities with its neighbour Azerbaijan over the long-standing issue of Nagorno-Karabakh, the Armenian enclave within

Azerbaijan. Nikol Pashinyan, still the Armenian prime minister, made an impassioned address in the Armenian parliament: 'We all should be prepared to devote ourselves to a single mission that we call final victory. Each of us must be ready to be on the forefront of that victory. We will win! We are sure to win! Rest assured that victory will be on our side!'[35] Armenia lost much territory in this short war, and on 9 November Pashinyan had to agree to the Russian-brokered terms of an armistice agreement in which it ceded large swathes of territory to Armenia. There appeared to be no escape from the harsh realities of power politics.

In Hong Kong, the problems that provoked demonstrations and, in 2020, a major crisis were of long standing. The 1984 Sino-British Joint Declaration, the international treaty guaranteeing Hong Kong's autonomy except in foreign affairs and defence, was supposed to chart the status of the Hong Kong Special Administrative Region for fifty years from the restoration of the territory to China on 1 July 1997. Among the inhabitants, there were fears that the existing degree of autonomy would be eroded. From 2005 onwards, in the absence of a strong system of parliamentary representation, there were many large and mainly nonviolent demonstrations. The 2014 student-led 'Umbrella Movement', demanding reforms of Hong Kong's election laws, was strikingly well organized. Then, from June 2019, huge demonstrations, mainly student-led, were triggered by fears about a proposed new Hong Kong law that would have provided for extradition to Mainland China of fugitive offenders. Carrie Lam, chief executive of Hong Kong, withdrew the bill on 4 September, but would not concede the demonstrators' other demands, which included, for example, her own resignation, retraction of the designation of certain demonstrations as 'riots' and an independent investigation of police brutality. Protests continued, being countered, as before, by extensive police use of tear gas. There was also increasing violence from a small but significant minority of the demonstrators. Parties supporting the demonstrators' aims won a landslide victory in the Hong Kong District Council elections on 24 November 2019. In early 2020, the Covid-19 pandemic appeared to increase the determination of the authorities in Hong Kong and Beijing to end the embarrassing displays of public hostility. In March 2020, on the pretext of disease control, the Hong Kong authorities passed a regulation prohibiting gatherings of more than four people. It failed to stop the demonstrations. Then, bypassing the Hong Kong authorities completely, the Standing Committee of the National People's Congress in Beijing passed a sweeping new 'National Security Law' for Hong Kong on 30 June. The new law pays lip service to 'ensuring the resolute, full and faithful implementation of the policy of One Country, Two Systems under which the people of Hong Kong administer Hong Kong with a high degree of autonomy'. It includes an article on human rights, stipulating that the provisions of both the International Covenant on Civil and Political Rights, and the one on Economic, Social and Cultural Rights, are to be protected. But its main thrust is its enunciation of new rights and powers for the Chinese authorities in Hong Kong, and its listing of a range of loosely defined offences. In a long list of 'terrorist activities', Article 24 includes 'dangerous activities which seriously jeopardize public health, safety or security'. Article 20, on secession, prohibits many acts 'whether or not by force or threat of force', effectively criminalizing even nonviolent forms of political action. Following the law's passage, the Hong Kong government became harsher. On 30 July, 12 pro-democracy politicians were disqualified from standing in elections to the Legislative Council scheduled for 6 September 2020. A day later, these elections were postponed for a year under the Emergency Regulations Ordinance – according to Lam, 'purely on the basis of protecting the health and safety of the Hong Kong people'.

The civil resistance in Hong Kong can easily be seen as a failure. This could be attributed to any of several possible causes. Perhaps there was an underestimation of the power and determination of the People's Republic of China. There may also have been an overestimation of the willingness of the UK to take action when China in effect tore up the One Country, Two Systems arrangement. Perhaps there was a naïve belief that President Donald Trump could be relied on to take tough action against China – which could be seen as a dangerous alliance between civil resisters and an autocratically minded foreign leader.[36] Perhaps the extent of the resistance, and its worrying turns towards violence, actually made a difficult situation worse, by provoking China into extreme measures. Although it now looks like One Country, One System, the story of Hong Kong is far from being over. The underlying disparity between the interests of China and those of the inhabitants of Hong Kong continues, and is likely to manifest itself in new political developments in the future.

As we enter the 2020s, countless other movements and networks are using the methods of civil resistance to advance the cause of democratic and constitutional rule, and to oppose racism. These have already included:

- In Thailand, from February 2020 onwards, a series of large demonstrations, mainly by students, called for extensive constitutional change, including reform of the monarchy.
- Black Lives Matter, founded in 2013, gained exceptional international prominence when George Floyd, an African-American man, was killed in Minneapolis on 25 May 2020 by a policeman kneeling on his neck for over eight minutes.
- A wave of demonstrations in Belarus denounced the faked results of the presidential election of 9 August 2020, which had been improbably claimed as a victory for the incumbent president, Alexander Lukashenko.

The emergence and growth of so many movements around the world in the past eight or nine years is remarkable. It shows that the failures of some of the Arab Spring movements have not led to any general abandonment of civil resistance. It suggests that despite being no magic recipe, civil resistance meets a need of the times: for a mode of action that exposes the hollowness of autocratic rule, and enables better ways of ordering public life to be placed centre stage.

The role of women in civil resistance movements

A striking feature of many civil resistance movement is the role of women. This is not a new phenomenon. Throughout history, and especially from the early twentieth century onwards, women have played extraordinary roles in civil resistance movements. In the first half of the nineteenth century, women played an important and notably active role in the campaigns against the slave trade and against slavery itself.[37] In the struggles for women's suffrage in many countries in the decades before 1914, women showed extraordinary determination and initiative, which opened the way to their involvement in many subsequent campaigns on a huge range of issues. Indeed, it strengthened the idea that women could be leaders and frontline campaigners as well as followers. Although movements against European colonial rule were almost invariably led by men, women had growing influence. Remarkably, in 1917–18, at a time when it was moving in the direction of national independence, the president of the Indian National Congress was a woman, Annie Besant.

In the years since 1945, women have led many campaigns. Sometimes they have been cast into such roles almost involuntarily: in Argentina, it was parents of people who had disappeared, such as the Mothers of the Plaza del Mayo from 1977 onwards; in the Philippines; it was Corazon Aquino, whose husband Benigno Aquino had been assassinated at Manila airport in 1983, leading to her leadership of the movement against President Marcos in 1983–6; and in Belarus it was Svetlana Tikhanovskaya, whose husband Sergei Tikhanovsky had been jailed in May 2020, who took his place as candidate for the presidency in elections in August in which the incumbent, Alexander Lukashenko, was widely seen as having engaged in massive electoral fraud. Tikhanovskaya was ably supported by two women colleagues who had been similarly forced into the limelight by circumstances: Veronika Tsepkalo and Maria Kolesnikova. All of these women showed skills, energy and flair.

Increasingly it became completely normal, from Tunis to Tomsk, for women to play leading parts in civil resistance movements. The three main founders of Black Lives Matter Network – Patrice Cullors, Alicia Garza and Opal Tometi – aimed from the start in 2013 to set down shared principles and goals for what has become increasingly an international movement: there are hazards in their form of leadership, operating without a central structure or hierarchy, but there has also been a remarkable re-ignition of the civil rights movement, and not only in the United States.

The remarkable roles of women in civil resistance from ancient times up to the present century have been usefully surveyed by Anne-Marie Codur and Mary King, who wisely circumvent the question of whether women are drawn to nonviolent resistance because of biological reasons, or because a range of historical and social circumstances that result in 'a perceptible pattern of women's preference for nonviolent action being more frequent and systematic than that of men'.[38]

Erica Chenoweth has authored a characteristically clear and lucid study of the effect of women's participation on the outcomes of a wide variety of campaigns. For this study she made a revised data set identifying both violent and nonviolent campaigns throughout the world from 1945 to 2014, and placing major emphasis on the role of women as participants, and also as leaders. She limited this data set to campaigns making major demands (such as the fall of a regime or territorial self-determination). In all, she catalogued a total of 338 such campaigns, of which 168 were classified as violent, and 170 as nonviolent. Of these nonviolent campaigns, 52 had what she usefully calls "nonviolent flanks" – meaning that at some point during the overwhelmingly nonviolent campaign, some individuals used violence. The main conclusions of her study can be briefly summarized thus:

- Especially in nonviolent movements, there has been an increase over time in women's participation and leadership. Remarkably, 99 per cent of nonviolent campaigns featured frontline women's participation compared with 76 per cent of violent campaigns.
- Nonviolent campaigns with high degrees of frontline women's participation are also likelier to elicit loyalty shifts from security forces.
- Frontline women's participation is highly correlated with successful resistance campaigns, even when accounting for other factors such as campaign size. A similar effect holds for campaigns that feature gender-inclusive ideologies, which are more likely to succeed than campaigns without such ideologies.[39]

Conclusions: People power and dictatorships

This chapter has focused on some of the issues that arise when dictatorship and people power confront each other. While recognizing many successes, it also notes the twin tragedies that civil resistance can sometimes lead to defeat and/or be followed by war. It further notes the paradox that in this age which has seen a considerable rise of civil resistance, there has also been a rise in various forms of populist authoritarianism. It has presented some evidence that, in particular cases, not only have peoples sometimes facilitated and voted for non-democratic systems of rule, but also some campaigns of civil resistance may have contributed, unintentionally, to authoritarian outcomes. Eight themes emerge from this short survey.

1. Civil resistance has achieved many important results in struggles against authoritarian rule. It has repeatedly challenged and

undermined dictatorships. It has played a part in democratization processes in many previously authoritarian countries, from Portugal to Poland, from Chile to Czechoslovakia, and from South Africa to Sudan. It continues to be at the centre of struggles for decent government under properly functioning constitutions – in Algeria, Belarus, Thailand, Myanmar and more.

2. Leaders of civil resistance campaigns may choose to rely on nonviolent methods for a variety of ethical, legal and practical reasons. They may view a particular regime of government as vulnerable to a sustained nonviolent campaign, especially in cases where the regime's ideology is weak or a government has clung on to power through fraudulent elections. Leaders are not necessarily committed to a rejection of the use of violence in all circumstances. Many, after the movement has achieved power, may accept the value of police forces for internal security and military forces for national defence and international security roles.

3. Women have increasingly played a leading part in civil resistance movements, and have contributed to their success.

4. Yet there are distinct concerns about the limits of civil resistance in confronting authoritarian rulers. Seldom, if ever, does it work in the attractively simple fashion envisaged by La Boétie. Sometimes – as in China in 1989, in Syria in 2011 and in Hong Kong in 2020 – it fails. There has been too little analysis of failed campaigns, and the many reasons for their defeat.

5. There are several distinct pathways that can lead from civil resistance to violence. These are more numerous and complex than is recognized in much of the literature. They can include, but are not limited to, suppression by regime forces; cosmetic reforms that fail to satisfy the resisters, who may then resort to more violent methods; partial military defections leading to militarized conflict; military intervention by outside armed forces to stop repression of resisters and, finally, use of *agents provocateurs* by the regime to discredit the demonstrators as rioters or worse – a little-studied, but important aspect, of the subject. Cases in which some of these pathways can be found include the civil rights movement in Northern Ireland in 1967–72, the Kosovo struggle against Serb rule in 1990–8 and the turn in Syria in 2011 from nonviolent struggle to civil war.

6. Even after a significant success in removing the previous system of rule, an apparent victory for people power may be followed, after a number of years, by a reversion to a form of populist authoritarianism. In the 2010s, Egypt, Hungary and the Philippines were examples. In such cases, could it be the hopes raised by the earlier revolutions that led to disillusion and disappointment, constituting a possible causal link between civil resistance and autocracy?

7. To call for the fall of a regime without a clear view of what is to replace it is hugely problematic. Transition to democracy is an inherently difficult and hazard-strewn process. A movement challenging an autocratic regime needs to have a clear idea of the kind of constitutional state that it aspires to establish. Any failures on this front are not failures of peoples alone. They are also failures of Western governments which have themselves often been wedded to the idea, deeply embedded in much Western political thought, that if you get rid of a bad ruler, all will be well. This was the central delusion both of the US-led invasion of Iraq in 2003, and of the Arab Spring movements that began in 2011. Regimes do not collapse in the simple manner envisaged by La Boétie. A lesson of many nonviolent campaigns is that, within any society, some trusted intermediary bodies are needed to facilitate negotiation between civil resisters and governments: in some difficult situations, such as Syria or Belarus, such bodies are in very limited supply.

8. A core question remains. How helpful is it, either analytically or as a policy framework, to view global events as part of a great overall struggle between democracy and dictatorship? We cannot escape completely from that framework, nor can democrats ignore long-held convictions of the importance of human rights. However, both the difficulty of creating new democracies, and the practical need to collaborate with other states on a huge range of issues, not least the urgent problem of preventing environmental despoliation and life-threatening pandemics, suggest the need for democratic enthusiasm to be tempered by both prudence and patience.

Notes

1 Extract from overview document for conference on 'The Power of Populism and People: Resistance and Protest in the Modern World', Florida State University, Tallahassee, 20–22 February 2019, 1.

2 Adapted from the longer definition in Adam Roberts, 'Introduction', in Roberts and Timothy Garton Ash (eds), *Civil Resistance and Power Politics: The Experience of Non-violent Action from Gandhi to the Present* (Oxford: Oxford University Press, 2009), 2–3.

3 Gene Sharp, *Sharp's Dictionary of Power and Struggle: Language of Civil Resistance in Conflicts* (New York: Oxford University Press, 2012), 223. He had also emphasized the idea of 'political jiu-jitsu' in many of his earlier writings, including in his magnum opus, Sharp, *The Politics of Nonviolent Action* (Boston: Porter Sargent, 1973), especially 110 and 657–703.

4 Erica Chenoweth and Maria J. Stephan, *Why Civil Resistance Works: The Strategic Logic of Nonviolent Conflict* (New York: Columbia University Press, 2011), 7.

5 Chenoweth and Stephan, *Why Civil Resistance Works*, 33, 234, 235 and 229. The three designations cited here of success or partial success follow those in the authors' Nonviolent and Violent Campaigns and Outcomes (NAVCO) data set. These designations are unaltered in the latest version, NAVCO 1.3, 17 March 2020, available at dataverse.harvard.edu.

6 Chenoweth and Stephan, *Why Civil Resistance Works*, 5.

7 On Syrian, Russian and other criticisms of civil resistance, see the last portions of the section 'The Arab Spring: Ten propositions' of this chapter (p. 39–41).

8 Étienne de La Boétie, *Discours de la servitude volontaire, ou le Contr'un*, written c. 1548 and first published (anonymously) five times between 1574 and 1578. I have cited the translation by Harry Kurz in *Anti-dictator, the Discours sur la servitude volontaire of Étienne de La Boétie* (New York: Columbia University Press, 1942), 4.

9 La Boétie, *Anti-dictator*, 12–13.

10 La Boétie, *Anti-dictator*, Introduction, xxi.

11 La Boétie, *Anti-dictator*, 8.

12 La Boétie, *Anti-dictator*, Introduction, xvi. The information about the five unofficial editions between 1574 and 1578 is at xvii.

13 La Boétie, *Anti-dictator*, 9 and 11.

14 La Boétie, *Anti-dictator*, Dedication. Presumably this was written by the translator, Dr Harry Kurz (1889–1973), who was a professor at Queens College, New York.

15 A classic exposition of this highly critical view of elections is David Van Reybrouck, *Against Elections: The Case for Democracy*, trans. Liz Waters (London: Bodley Head, 2016).

16 Francis Fukuyama, *Political Order and Political Decay: From the Industrial Revolution to the Globalization of Democracy* (London: Profile Books, 2014).

17 J. S. Mill, *Considerations on Representative Government* (London: Parker, Son, & Bourn, 1861), chap. xvi, 289. *Collected Works of J.S. Mill*, vol. XIX, 547.

18 Mill, *Considerations on Representative Government*, chap. xvi, 287. *Collected Works*, vol. XIX, 546.

19 Gene Sharp, *From Dictatorship to Democracy: A Conceptual Framework for Liberation* (Boston: Albert Einstein Institution, 1993), vii.

20 Data on cumulative confirmed Covid-19 fatalities, and rates per million people, from Oxford Martin School 'Our World in Data' (which includes virtually all countries). https://ourworldindata.org/coronavirus, accessed 25 September 2020. This source, which is based on data from the European Centre for Disease Prevention and Control, contains explanations of the numerous inherent limitations of Covid-19 death statistics.

21 Fareed Zakaria, 'The Rise of Illiberal Democracy', *Foreign Affairs*, New York, 76, no. 6 (November–December 1997): 22.

22 Viktor Orbán, speech 25th Bálványos Summer Free University and Student Camp, 26 July 2014.

https://www.kormany.hu/en/the-prime-minister/the-prime-minister-s-speeches/prime-minister-viktor-orban-s-speech-at-the-25th-balvanyos-summer-free-university-and-student-camp.

23 'Philippines' Duterte Threatens to Quit UN after Drugs War Censure', Reuters report from Manila, 21 August 2016. Nothing more has been heard of this plan.

24 'Duterte Pulls Police from War on Drugs and Berates the West', Reuters report from Manila, *The Guardian*, London, 13 October 2017.

25 Ramon C. Casiple, 'The Duterte Presidency as a Phenomenon', *Contemporary Southeast Asia* 38, no. 2 (August 2016): 180–1.

26 Nicole Curato, 'Flirting with Authoritarian Fantasies? Rodrigo Duterte and the New Terms of Philippine Populism', *Journal of Contemporary Asia* 47, no. 1 (2017): 141 and 145–6.

27 See chapter 3 of this book.

28 Sheri Berman, 'The Promise of the Arab Spring: In Political Development, No Gain Without Pain', *Foreign Affairs*, New York, 92, no. 1 (January–February 2013): 64–74.

29 This part draws on some material in chapter 11 of Adam Roberts, Michael J. Willis, Rory McCarthy and Timothy Garton Ash (eds), *Civil Resistance in the Arab Spring: Triumphs and Disasters* (Oxford: Oxford University Press, 2016). This book contains accounts of the Arab Spring's effects in the different countries of the region. An Arabic translation was published by All Prints, Beirut, in 2017.

30 Thomas Richard Davies, 'The Failure of Strategic Nonviolent Action in Bahrain, Egypt, Libya and Syria: "political ju-jitsu" in Reverse', *Global Change, Peace & Security* 26, no. 3 (2014): 299 and 310–13.

31 Walter Ulbricht, speech on 12 October 1968, published in pamphlet form in English as *The Role of the Socialist State in the Shaping of the Developed Social System of Socialism* (Dresden: Verlag Zeit im Bild, 1968), 8 and 13–14.

32 Bashar al-Assad, speech to the Syrian parliament, 30 March 2011, http://www.al-bab.com/arab/docs/syria/bashar_assad_speech_110330.htm.

33 Vladimir Putin, Address by President of the Russian Federation to State Duma deputies, Federation Council members and others, Kremlin, Moscow, 18 March 2014, http://eng.kremlin.ru/news/6889; and Vladimir Putin, speech at Valdai International Discussion Club, XI session, Sochi, 24 October 2014, http://eng.kremlin.ru/transcripts/23137.

34 Laurence Broers and Anna Ohanyan (eds), *Armenia's Velvet Revolution: Authoritarian Decline and Civil Resistance in a Multipolar World* (London: I.B. Tauris, 2020).

35 Nikol Pashinyan, address to the nation, Yerevan, 3 October 2020, https://www.primeminister.am/en/statements-and-messages/item/2020/10/03/Nikol-Pashinyan-message/.

36 Helen Davidson, 'Unlikely Hero: Fans of Trump in Hong Kong Democracy Movement', report datelined Taiwan in *The Guardian*, London, 14 November 2020.

37 On the role of women in the UK, see Mary Midgley, *Women Against Slavery: The British Campaigns, 1780–1870* (London: Routledge, 1992).

38 Anne-Marie Codur and Mary Elizabeth King, 'Women in Civil Resistance', in Mariam M. Kurtz and Lester R. Kurtz (eds), *Women, War and Violence: Topography, Resistance and Hope* (New York: Praeger, 2 vols., 2015), vol. 2: 403–4.

39 Erica Chenoweth, *Women's Participation and the Fate of Nonviolent Campaigns: A Report on the Women in Resistance (WiRe) Data Set* (Broomfield: One Earth Future Foundation, 2019), 1–2 and 6–8.

References

Berman, Sheri. 'The Promise of the Arab Spring: In Political Development, No Gain Without Pain'. *Foreign Affairs* 92, no. 1 (2013): 64–74.

Broers, Laurence and Anna Ohanyan, eds. *Armenia's Velvet Revolution: Authoritarian Decline and Civil Resistance in a Multipolar World*. London: I.B. Tauris, 2020.

Casiple, Ramon C. 'The Duterte Presidency as a Phenomenon'. *Contemporary Southeast Asia* 38, no. 2 (2016): 179–84.

Chenoweth, Erica. *Women's Participation and the Fate of Nonviolent Campaigns: A Report on the Women in Resistance (WiRe) Data Set*. Broomfield: One Earth Future Foundation, 2019.

Chenoweth, Erica and Maria J. Stephan. *Why Civil Resistance Works: The Strategic Logic of Nonviolent Conflict*. New York: Columbia University Press, 2011.

Codur, Anne-Marie and Mary Elizabeth King. 'Women in Civil Resistance'. In Mariam M. Kurtz and Lester R. Kurtz (eds), *Women, War and Violence: Topography, Resistance and Hope*, 2 vols. New York: Praeger, 2015.

Curato, Nicole. 'Flirting with Authoritarian Fantasies? Rodrigo Duterte and the New Terms of Philippine Populism'. *Journal of Contemporary Asia* 47, no. 1 (2017): 142–53.

Davies, Thomas Richard. 'The Failure of Strategic Nonviolent Action in Bahrain, Egypt, Libya and Syria: "political ju-jitsu" in Reverse'. *Global Change, Peace & Security* 26, no. 3 (2014): 299–313.

Fukuyama, Francis. *Political Order and Political Decay: From the Industrial Revolution to the Globalization of Democracy*. London: Profile Books, 2014.

Kurz, Harry, trans. *Anti-dictator, the Discours sur la servitude volontaire of Étienne de La Boétie*. New York: Columbia University Press, 1942.

Midgley, Mary. *Women against Slavery: The British Campaigns, 1780–1870*. London: Routledge, 1992.

Mill, J. S. *Considerations on Representative Government*. London: Parker, Son, & Bourn, 1861.

Roberts, Adam and Timothy Garton Ash, eds. *Civil Resistance and Power Politics: The Experience of Non-violent Action from Gandhi to the Present*. Oxford: Oxford University Press, 2009.

Roberts, Adam, Michael J. Willis, Rory McCarthy and Timothy Garton Ash, eds. *Civil Resistance in the Arab Spring: Triumphs and Disasters*. Oxford: Oxford University Press, 2016.

Robson, John M. eds. *Collected Works of John Stuart Mill*, 33 vols. Toronto: University of Toronto Press, 1963–91.

Sharp, Gene. *From Dictatorship to Democracy: A Conceptual Framework for Liberation*. Boston: Albert Einstein Institution, 1993.

Sharp, Gene. *The Politics of Nonviolent Action*. Boston: Porter Sargent, 1973.

Sharp, Gene. *Sharp's Dictionary of Power and Struggle: Language of Civil Resistance in Conflicts*. New York: Oxford University Press, 2012.

Van Reybrouck, David. *Against Elections: The Case for Democracy*, trans. Liz Waters. London: Bodley Head, 2016.

Zakaria, Fareed. 'The Rise of Illiberal Democracy'. *Foreign Affairs* 76, no. 6 (1997): 22–43.

AR, 25 November 2020.

2

Civil society as a threat to democracy

Grzegorz Ekiert

In this chapter, I explore a distinctive trajectory of civil society transformation that has provided organizational foundations for cultural and political polarization and the current turn to authoritarianism in Poland.[1] Regime transitions both towards democracy and authoritarianism are not exclusively elite-level affairs or coercive impositions. They always involve a significant level of popular support and collective action by ordinary people, social movements and civil society organizations. In this process, a particular organizational structure of civil society, its sectoral composition and prevailing cleavages can facilitate and shape both the transition and consolidation of a new regime. From this perspective, the well-established assumptions of mutually beneficial relations between civil society and democracy and the inherent virtuousness and prevailing liberal orientation of civil society actors need to be reassessed. Consequently, real civil societies, depending on their organizational characteristics and general normative orientation of their actors, in some cases strengthen and in other undermine liberal democracy. One of the discernible organizational forms of civil society that may endanger democracy is a 'pillarized – that is a vertically divided – civil society'. While historically it was considered to be a phenomenon particular to the Low Countries in the nineteenth century, this form of civil society has become increasingly common in contemporary societies.

In my view, a pillarized civil society has emerged in Poland since the country's transition to democracy in 1989, and its pillars are deeply divided along cultural, ideological and political cleavages. This vertically divided civil society has enabled extreme cultural and political polarization of Polish society; facilitated mobilization of far-right, nationalist and conservative religious movements; and recently provided support for the anti-liberal and anti-European policies of the current Polish government dominated by the Law and Justice party (PiS). While my analysis points to the crucial role of the associational sphere and its specific organizational characteristics in the U-turn towards authoritarianism unfolding in Poland, I also suggest that this is a more general phenomenon in many contemporary societies both democratic and authoritarian. Today, in many countries around the world, including the United States, Turkey, Lebanon, Israel and India, civil society or rather a significant part of civil society supports political extremism, populist leaders and their anti-liberal policies and increasingly becomes an obstacle to political liberalization or a threat to democracy. Pillarized civil societies tend to emerge in countries characterized by societies deeply divided along ethnic, religious, ideological, cultural or economic cleavages. In turn, pillarization of civil society reinforces dominant cleavages and transforms politics into a zero-sum game.

* * *

The idea of civil society was reintroduced into both political and academic discourse in the late 1970s to describe two parallel political developments.[2] First, there was the emergence of new opposition movements that challenged communist rule in East-Central Europe. Their leaders rejected Marxist revisionism and advocated reviving a pluralist associational sphere and building autonomous social networks (a parallel *polis*) as a strategy by which to defy the totalitarian state. Organizations such as the Workers' Defence Committee (KOR) in Poland and the Czechoslovak Charter 77 demanded respect for human-rights and fundamental freedoms. They also developed a new discourse centred on the notion of inalienable rights, societal self-organization and unequivocal support for liberal democracy and the rule of law. In their activities they espoused transparency, public debate, non-violence and reforms based on negotiations and compromise. They defined their mission as non-political, rejected utopianism and political maximalism, and endorsed the simple ethical postulate of 'living in truth' proposed by Vaclav Havel. In Poland, they also urged broad, inclusive alliances across traditional class and political divisions, including those between the church and the left, and between the workers and intellectuals. The Solidarity movement in Poland embodied all these principles in its challenge to the Polish party-state in 1980–1.[3]

Second, political ferment in East-Central Europe was preceded by a period of intense social and political activism within Western democracies. New social movements emerging at the end of the 1960s and 1970s challenged paternalistic welfare states and criticized the encroachment of bureaucracies and markets into the public domain and private lives. They protested the shallow nature of Western democracies, environmental degradation and the arms race, and championed rights of women and excluded groups and minorities. They also sought to reconstitute a pluralist public realm where citizens would be free to debate critical issues, pursue their passions and interests, and reassert their individual and collective identities.[4]

Despite their different intellectual origins, political concerns and ideological optics, these two political currents converged around the idea that the independent public sphere, with its associational domain and individual autonomy, needed to be defended from rampant commodification and bureaucratization in the West and from the totalitarian ambitions of the communist state in the East. The concept of civil society provided a good framework for understanding these concerns, goals and political practices, since it was articulated by thinkers who were concerned by threats to liberty and were searching for the optimal model of relations between states, markets and societies. These theorists range from the philosophers of the Scottish Enlightenment to Tocqueville, Gramsci, Habermas and Gellner. They shared a set of normative concerns emphasizing liberty, freedom, justice, equality, tolerance, individualism and pluralism.[5]

In the early 1980s, the idea of civil society acquired a rarely challenged positive connotation. Social scientists and policy makers assigned civil society a key role in driving progressive social, political and economic transformation. Robust civil society was considered a panacea for a wide variety of social and political ills. Its quality, density and strength became a major yardstick for assessing the condition of a democratic system. It was widely believed that without a system of associations mediating between kinship groups, markets and the state, individuals would be less effective in articulating their common interests and identities, and society would remain politically stagnant and vulnerable to rising inequalities, corruption and authoritarianism.

Vibrant civil society was seen not only as a guarantor and defender of freedom, equality and justice but also as a mechanism for improving the institutional performance of democracy. As Robert Putnam put it, 'Tocqueville was right: democratic government is strengthened, not weakened, when it faces a vigorous civil society.'[6] As a result, Tocqueville's apotheosis of American associational life as a shield against tyranny replaced Karl Marx's critique of capitalism as the self-evident truth guiding change-oriented political activism. Paradoxically, this belief in the inherent virtue of a robust associational life based on voluntary participation and solidarity came to be shared by the political right and left, by liberals as well as the foes of liberal politics, and also by politicians and intellectuals. President George H. W. Bush, in his speech to the Republican Convention in 1988, compared America's voluntary associations to 'a brilliant diversity spread like stars, like a thousand points of light on a broad and peaceful sky'. In the social science literature that followed, civil society emerged as the main driver of democratic transformation, a source of high-quality democratic performance and an indispensable actor in disaster relief, poverty reduction, welfare provision and the fight against political corruption.

Reflecting this consensus on the beneficial role of civil society organizations in political and social life, Larry Diamond listed a number of specific functions that make them essential in strengthening and protecting democracy: they limit state power and make politicians accountable; provide alternative channels for political participation; increase citizens' political skills and efficacy; promote a better understanding of the rights and obligations that constitute democratic life; foster the development and communication of democratic norms; provide channels for articulation, aggregation and representation of different interests and identities; mitigate political conflicts; provide training and experience for future political leaders; facilitate unbiased monitoring of political activities and government policies; advance the development and provision of information; and help build political coalitions and improve the functioning of the state.[7] Given all these assumed beneficial effects, no wonder that civil society has become a focus of scholarly attention, and its strengthening around the world an urgent priority for policymakers and international organizations.

Consequently, in recent decades foundations, states and international organizations have spent billions of dollars on building civil society and supporting its projects. The promotion of civil society has become a crucial aspect of development aid for countries recovering from economic crises, civil wars and decades of authoritarian rule. And it has been considered the best hope for introducing and consolidating liberal political institutions, fighting poverty and protecting human rights. Since the 1990s, Western governments have significantly increased their support for domestic and international NGOs, promoting the expansion of their role and institutionalizing a formal partnership between civil society organizations and the state in the provision of social services. An increasing amount of official development aid has been dispensed through NGOs. Private foundations supporting liberal causes have strengthened the capacity of watchdog organizations monitoring governments. Transnational NGOs have become formally recognized consultative partners to all international and multilateral organizations, in the process emerging as influential political actors in their own right that support progressive causes around the world.[8]

In turn, authoritarian rulers of various stripes have become increasingly concerned about the growing influence of Western-backed NGOs and have reacted by imposing an array of new regulations and constraints designed to limit their role and access to resources, or else banned them altogether. They have also actively promoted the top-down process of building alternative civil society organizations and movements supportive of government policies.[9] Thus, the civil society arena has become a domain of intensifying political conflicts, competition and struggle. Paradoxically, the authoritarian rulers' fear of civil society organizations, coupled with efforts to restrict their activities, has reinforced the general belief in their unquestioned role in promoting and protecting democracy.

Yet the neo-Tocquevillian, overly affirmative views of civil society's role and impact have not been universally shared nor its potentially harmful impact on democracy entirely ignored. Nancy Bermeo rightly noted that the previous generation of political scientists viewed active civil society as a source of political instability and as posing a threat to democracy rather than as a support for it, especially in countries with weak political institutions.[10] In his influential book *Political Order in Changing Societies*, Samuel Huntington noted that 'societies which have high levels of middle-class participation have strong tendencies towards instability'.[11] From this perspective, robust civil society and its actions may not always be beneficial or supportive of democratic outcomes, but may also destabilize and endanger democracy, aiding the rise of populist leaders and precipitating an authoritarian takeover. In fact, a number of important historical cases exemplify such an outcome.

Sheri Berman, for example, argues that an organizationally robust and politically divided civil society exerting pressure on the deficient political structures of the Weimar Republic after the First World War might have been one of the important preconditions for the Nazi takeover.[12] Similarly, Dylan Riley shows that development of robust civil societies in Italy, Spain and Romania in the early twentieth century not only did not produce stable democracy but instead undermined their nascent liberal regimes and facilitated the rise of fascism. Arguing against Robert Putnam's conclusions about the benefits of dense social capital and a strong civil society, Riley demonstrates that some regions of Northern Italy that had dense social capital became hotbeds of Italian fascism.[13] Finally, examining European experiences, Bermeo and Nord point out that 'burgeoning civil society translated into a democratization of public life in certain instances but by no means always'. Moreover, 'civic activism may well be the bedrock of democratic life, but not all civil societies, however dense and vibrant, give birth to democratic polities'.[14]

All these arguments belong to what can be called a neo-Huntingtonian perspective, whose basic premise is that in places where political institutions are not able to accommodate a proliferation of voluntary associations, nor to translate popular demands via democratic channels of interest articulation, nor find remedies for civil society's politicization and polarization, the development of a strong and mobilized civil society may give rise to authoritarianism or fascism. Thus, there is a dark side to the strength of civil society and its activity. In specific political contexts, civil society actors may even facilitate the demise of democracy and contribute to an authoritarian takeover. In fact, authoritarian leaders often ride on the back of a robust and mobilized civil society and maintain their power with its support.

Neo-Huntingtonian arguments emphasize the structural/institutional deficiencies of political institutions and party systems that make the actions of civil society actors potentially destructive to democracy. Yet, there is another set of arguments focusing on the specific features of particular civil societies that may have a potentially toxic impact on democracy. Such arguments emphasize the organizational characteristics of civil society and the normative orientations of its actors. The prevalence of certain types of organizations within civil society (representing plutocratic elites, large corporate actors, fundamentalist religious organizations, extremist political movements) may increase the risk of an authoritarian takeover as well as providing stability to authoritarian rule.

Similarly, illiberal and exclusionary ideologies may provide fuel to civil society activities that not only accelerate political polarization but also endanger the stability and the very existence of democracy. As Stanley Hoffmann once quipped when commenting on Robert Putnam's ideas of social capital, 'it is not important how many choral societies a country has but what kind of songs they sing.' In fact, in the past many civil society organizations supported anti-liberal and anti-democratic agendas, advocated exclusionary national and religious identities, and endorsed violent tactics to accomplish extremist political goals. In turn, normative orientations have their organizational consequences. According to Philip Nord, in the context of the nineteenth-century European democratization, 'Catholics riposted to the secularizing policies of a dominant liberalism entrenching themselves in a formidable associational bulwark.'[15] Chambers and Kopstein label such organizations in the contemporary United States as 'bad civil society'.[16] Kopecky and Mudde call them 'uncivil society',[17] and Richard Youngs and his co-authors define them as 'conservative civil society'. As they argue, 'the rise of conservative civil society poses serious challenges to liberal democracy', since 'conservative activism is the search for protection – protection from change, from outside economic pressures, from new kinds of identities and moral norms. Curiously, these groups generally want a stronger state and more robust government intervention to provide this protection'.[18]

Such groups and organizations are a part of the civil society landscape in all contemporary societies. In specific places and periods, especially with the support of governments having authoritarian ambitions, uncivil or illiberal parts of civil society may grow and expand from the margins of associational life to colonize the domains of public space surrendered by other actors. Protected and supported by the government or other powerful social actors, they monopolize civil society activities. In extreme cases, this leads to profound cultural and subsequently political polarization and to the emergence of 'pillarized' civil societies that Phillipe Schmitter[19] diagnosed as a potential threat to democracy. Pillarization is the vertical segregation of civil society into distinct compartments with limited interaction across a dividing boundary (be it religious, ethnic or political). This creates the potential for social conflicts, contentious mobilization and political instability. In fact, the recent rise of populism can be traced to the emergence of pillarized civil societies across the world. In the 1980s and 1990s the so-called culture wars became common in many countries. Cultural polarization should be considered a precursor, if not a necessary condition, to the populist political movements and parties we see today. As Youngs observed,

> in many countries in the developing and post-communist worlds, as well as in long-established Western democracies, conservative forms of civic

activism have been multiplying and gaining traction. In some cases, new conservative civic movements and groups are closely associated with illiberal political actors and appear to be an integral part of the well-chronicled global pushback against Western liberal democratic norms.[20]

Moreover, the collapse of traditional democratic media regimes[21] and the technological and digital revolution play an important part in this growing polarization and in facilitating the emergence of the illiberal pillar of civil society. A fragmented and ideologically divided media landscape and the expanding social media scene facilitate the pillarization process by enabling smaller groups and movements to mobilize and communicate by building separate cultural silos with their own narratives, symbols and 'alternative facts'. The combination of grassroots illiberal organizations and radical social media platforms provides increasing mobilizational capacity overcoming the traditional collective action problems. Bennet and Segerberg describe this new capacity as 'connective-collective' action network model.[22] Thus, social media can be as much a tool of liberalization[23] as a facilitator of cultural wars and of the pillarization of civil society.[24]

The emergence of pillarized civil societies has crucial political consequences. Their actors, driven by a zero-sum vision of politics, fuel cultural and political polarization, support populist leaders and undermine centrist political parties. They are the source of radicalization, political instability and electoral backlash against liberal values and the affiliated political forces. They provide foot soldiers for protests against liberal elites and in support for emerging populist parties. In turn, illiberal and conservative pillars benefit from the electoral successes of such radical populist parties. Where populist parties take over the government, liberal pillars are constrained and starved of resources, while public funds are allocated exclusively to the organizations belonging to conservative and illiberal pillar of civil society. Moreover, the legal framework regulating civil society activities is purposefully altered to restrict the liberal pillar and to expand opportunities for illiberal movements and organizations.[25]

The playbook for governments with authoritarian ambitions attempting to control civil society includes: licensing NGOs by tightening registration procedures and reporting requirements; starving them of resources by prohibiting foreign funding; centralizing resources for civil society activities under state control and changing funding priorities; stigmatizing liberal NGOs through, for example, introducing so-called foreign agent laws; aggressively favouring organizations that are ideologically aligned with the government by providing additional funding and friendly regulations; escalating repression and intimidation of civil society activists from the liberal pillar and shielding activists from the illiberal pillar from prosecution for illegal and violent acts; restricting the rights of assembly and protest by imposing cumbersome regulations; introducing censorship and controls on media and the internet; bringing civil society organizations under state control and expanding the domain of *Ersatz* social movements and government-organized NGOs (GONGOs). All these actions can be described as *re-étatization* of the illiberal pillar of civil society and were tested and perfected in places like Russia, Turkey or Hungary. Such *re-étatization* results in the hardening of boundaries between the pillars of civil society and deepens its ideological polarization, fuelling political conflicts and divisions in the short run. In the long run, it may provide the organizational and cultural foundations for an authoritarian takeover.

* * *

Nowhere is the Schmitterian dilemma of pillarized and polarized civil society more apparent than in contemporary Poland. After 1989, Polish civil society was reconstituted with considerable speed and determination as the result of four distinct and overlapping processes.[26] First, the initial years of transition witnessed the process of *reconstitution* and *recombination* in which the dense network of social organizations inherited from the old regimes adapted itself to new democratic conditions[27] and a large number of new organizations and social initiatives sprang up across the country. In a parallel development, a process of *de-étatization* was underway, with the state relinquishing or losing control over professional and social organizations that were previously tightly controlled by the communist party-state. Polish civil society also experienced *de-corporatization*, a process in which large professional organizations and trade unions lost their privileged role in civil society and in politics, along with their influence on policy making. Thus, during the first two decades of post-communist transformation, Polish civil society grew rapidly. Its centre of gravity shifted from large, formal membership-based organizations, such as trade unions and professional associations (mostly inherited from the old regime), to a highly varied sector of small, professionalized NGOs that rely on voluntary involvement as well as diversified and decentralized funding that is both public and private. Their activities spanned the entire range of services, objectives, goals and styles of action similar to those present in developed democratic societies. And these organizations had a decidedly liberal and pro-European orientation. Finally, during the first two decades of the twenty-first century, civil society has become increasingly professionalized, resulting in the emergence of tens of thousands of highly specialized NGOs and foundations. These mostly small organizations are run by professional staff and rely on public funding, fundraising and volunteers. They focus on a wide range of local and national issues and initiatives and operate in a well-structured and (until 2016) friendly legal environment on both national and local levels.[28]

Poland's accession to the European Union in 2004 led to the growing internationalization of its civil society. This process had both symbolic significance and tangible economic consequences. It signalled to civil society organizations the possibility of transcending national boundaries, forming links with like-minded partners in other EU countries and supporting transnational causes. The process of Europeanization changed both the structure and institutional culture of numerous organizations. It also opened significant funding opportunities (from both official EU sources and Western civil society partners) for different initiatives and projects.[29]

Based on the sheer number of newly registered organizations, the growth of Polish civil society since 1989 has been remarkable. Until 2000, the rate of new registrations was exceptional. Since then it has stabilized at a relatively high level of around 5,000 organizations and 800 foundations per year with no major declines. By 2018, the Klon/Jawor Association, an infrastructural NGO conducting research on civil society, had nearly 140,000 new organizations in its database. New NGOs have emerged in all sectors of civil society and in all types of localities. At the same time, the survival rate of associations from the old regime has also been very high. These two trends together produce a relatively dense and consistently growing civil society. Moreover, the number of Poles who have participated in voluntary and charitable activities has expanded considerably. In recent years, over 20 per cent of Poles declare they have volunteered and over 50 per cent have donated money to charitable causes. This is on par with levels registered in many established Western democracies.

Yet, since the early 2000s, Polish civil society has experienced increasing organizational and ideological pillarization as a result of the emergence and institutionalization of far-right, conservative, nationalistic, anti-liberal and faith-based networks of organizations. They have their own national and local media, social networks, symbolic frames of reference, political narratives and resources provided by the Catholic Church, right-wing political parties, conservative foundations and individuals, and increasingly by the Polish state following PiS win in the 2015 elections. The PiS government considers the civil society domain to be an important battleground in the domination of the country's politics. Consequently, it tries to alter the composition of Poland's civil society by throwing its weight behind its allied organizations within civil society.

The illiberal, nationalistic pillar of civil society was a late arrival in the development of civil society in Poland. Although nationalist and extreme right-wing organizations and movements were always a part of the associational landscape, they were marginal and weak during the first decade of the post-communist transition.[30] At the same time, the clerical sector of the illiberal pillar was gradually gaining strength and resources since the early 1990s. The single most important organization of this segment of civil society – Radio Maryja – was founded as a local radio station in 1991 and quickly spawned a dense network of organizations across the country. By the end of 1990s it had a weekly audience of 5.5 million and a large network of organizations called the Family of Radio Maryja. The Lux Veritas Foundation, founded in 1996, was the first significant supporter of extremist religious and nationalist organizations and initiatives. The debate and referendum on the new Polish constitution in 1997 became a pivotal moment that galvanized anti-liberal and anti-European forces and movements in support of traditional values, Polish Catholic traditions and rabid nationalism.

Churches and religious institutions have become a significant factor in sustaining the faith-based pillar of civil society. Both the Catholic Church and other denominations have created networks of organizations tied to churches.[31] They have formed a diverse system of national, regional and local organizations that are controlled to a varying degree by the church hierarchy. These grassroots organizations usually have small, informal memberships. The most popular types are prayer and charitable groups, as well as groups organizing sport and leisure activities. They are usually created jointly by parish priests and lay people. The Catholic Church Statistical Institute reported that in 1998, there were already some 40,000 such organizations with over 2 million members in total. By 2008, their number had increased to over 60,000 and membership reached nearly 2.7 million. The Polish Main Statistical Office (2017: 148–46) estimated that 9 per cent of Poles are active in religious organizations, which is almost as many as in all other (non-religious) civil society organizations.

These organizations not only focused on local activities but have been increasingly present in the country's politics. They were able to initiate and coordinate spectacular nationwide campaigns, such as collecting some 7 million signatures for a petition in support of Radio Maryja in the late 1990s, organizing a get-together of Radio Maryja families in Częstochowa in 2005 with some half a million participants or the Rosary to the Borders event in 2017. The latter brought together 1 million Polish Catholics who took part in a massive collective prayer to fend off immigrants that took place in 4,000 prayer zones along the full length of the Polish border, including the beaches of the Baltic Sea and at international airports.[32]

The institutionalization of the clerical sector belonging to the illiberal pillar of Polish civil society was followed by the emergence of a whole plethora of movements (skinheads, soccer hooligans, far-right extremists), right-wing organizations and media outlets representing nationalist, xenophobic and homophobic ideas. They declare support for traditional family values and fundamentalist Catholicism and represent themselves as heirs of the traditional Polish extreme right from the interwar period. Since the early 2000s, this set of loosely connected newspapers, clubs and associations institutionalized a dense network of relations, enhanced their media presence and developed political alliances with right-wing political parties and moderated its activities.[33] In the last presidential elections in 2020, the candidate representing these organizations received almost 7 per cent of votes.

The growth of this extreme right-wing sector of Polish civil society has been fuelled by the migration crisis in Europe, which has not affected Poland directly but has engendered anxiety further exacerbated by anti-migrant rhetoric often utilizing traditional anti-Semitic tropes. The intensification of nationalist and anti-liberal sentiments has been facilitated also by the prolonged legitimacy crisis of the EU and its institutions. As a result, illiberal and nationalistic forces have become visible in protest politics, and their quest for 'xenophobic normality'[34] has been increasingly successful, especially during the first PiS government in 2005–7 and after return of PiS to power in 2015. This is most vividly illustrated by the Independence Marches organized by extremist organizations to mark the anniversary of Poland's independence. Dubbed by European media as the largest 'neo-fascist' events in Europe (some 200,000 participants in 2018), these marches' symbols and slogans revolve around the theme of 'Poland for the Poles, Poles for Poland' and its symbolic décor (the sea of national flags, flaming torches, aggressive chanting and glorification of violence) is reminiscent of the Nazis. The decision by the Polish government to join forces with extreme right organizations in the Independence March in 2018 sends a clear signal of government's support for the most radical segment of the illiberal pillar of civil society.[35]

The institutionalization of the illiberal/nationalist pillar of Poland's civil society took yet another crucial turn in 2015 with the presidential and parliamentary elections, in which the right-wing, populist Law and Justice party (PiS) won the country's presidency and the parliamentary majority. The new nationalistic government fomented a constitutional crisis by failing to observe the decisions of the Constitutional Tribunal and by engaging in a controversial partisan takeover of the public media, other public institutions and boards of state-owned companies. It also launched a crusade against liberal values and organizations and institutions that supported such values. As PiS leader Jaroslaw Kaczynski recently stated, liberal ideas 'threaten Polish identity as well as the survival of the Polish nation and of the Polish state'. Since in his view these ideas have nothing to do with Polish national identity (Polishness) and are imported from the West, Polish society must be grounded in the teachings of the Catholic Church, and 'questioning the church's fundamental role in Poland is unpatriotic'.[36] Thus, the 2015 presidential and parliamentary elections exacerbated existing cultural-ideological divisions between the two pillars of Polish civil society. On the one hand, elections legitimized and reinforced the nationalist-religious-populist camp now associated with the new government, and on the other, they galvanized the liberal, pro-European opposition, which resulted in spectacular protests against government policies. In turn, these protests spawned a large number of counter-protests in support of the PiS government. Both pillars have deep and wide roots in society and their media networks, which is reflected, for instance, in their ability to mobilize large groups of people for protests, demonstrations and participation in elections. They also actively support self-organization of citizens and their involvement in politics.

After its 2015 election victory, the PiS government took over the public media and lent its full political and economic support to the illiberal pillar of civil society. In December 2016 Poland's vice-premier Piotr Gliński, speaking to *Gazeta Polska* clubs (organizations associated with one of the most militant nationalist newspapers),[37] declared: 'You are the true Polish civil society. Thanks to your efforts Poland is changing and the Polish government is able to preside over the country's responsible and stable development.' Government-controlled resources have started to flow to such organizations as well.[38] State-owned companies have been directed to place their advertising only in the illiberal/nationalist media. At the same time, foundations run by these companies started limiting their support almost exclusively to organizations and initiatives belonging to the illiberal pillar of civil society. As recent data on advertising in the print media by state-owned companies shows, their support for the right-wing media has increased substantially since PiS came to power. For example, *Gazeta Polska* had received 91,000 zlotys from such advertising in 2015. This increased to 8.8 million in 2018. Similarly, while advertising from state-owned companies provides only 0.37 per cent of the liberal weekly *Polityka* revenues, it provides 44.85 per cent for *Gazeta Polska* and 39.77 per cent for the weekly *Sieci Prawdy* – the two most important publications of the illiberal camp. Thus, the pillarization of Polish civil society was followed and reinforced by the *re-étatization* of its illiberal pillar through the active involvement of the government in supporting illiberal organizations and initiatives. This in turn reinvigorated liberal advocacy groups and media and gave rise to new NGOs, such as the Committee for the Defence of Democracy (KOD). Since 2015, Poland's liberal organizations and movements have successfully mobilized thousands of people to show their opposition to PiS policies and to defend the rule of law in Poland. Yet, their ability to defend the liberal order has been weakened by the solidifying alliance of the state, church and illiberal civil society. This is the alliance whose interests are well protected in a system in which democratic checks and balances have already been seriously undermined.

The process of *re-étatization,* which was designed to benefit and strengthen the illiberal pillar of civil society, has political, legal and economic dimensions. First, the various sources of funding for civil society organizations and initiatives have been centralized under the newly established National Institute of Freedom, which has been formally charged with supporting nationalist causes and 'patriotic' civil society organizations. As a result, long-standing public support for various liberal organizations, cultural institutions, campaigns and artistic events has been significantly reduced. Many civil society organizations have been forced to replace state funding with private donations to continue their work. The government also created the Polish National Foundation funded by the seventeen biggest state-owned companies to the tune of 100 million zloty per year to support educational, academic and cultural activities aimed at the preservation and nurturing of the Polish national tradition, dissemination of the knowledge of the modern Polish history and popularization of 'martyrology and heroism' of the Polish nation. Organizations with long record and expertise in social policy are losing public funding that is redirected to newly registered organizations led by right-wing activists without any expertise and experiences in providing social services. The government also attempts (so far without much success) to take control of EU funds that are distributed directly to civil society organizations.

The legal framework regulating civil society activities has also been altered. For example, the new law on public gatherings favours organizations associated with the government and the church over citizen movements associated with the political opposition. Increasingly, activists of liberal movements and organizations, as well as journalists from the liberal media, have been intimidated and harassed by the security forces and by public prosecutors to deter them from pursuing investigations and expressing critical views of the government and its policies. Meanwhile, members of xenophobic and neo-fascist organizations involved in illegal activities and violent acts are shielded by state-appointed prosecutors, who delay investigations or refuse to press charges.

Thus, after three decades of democratic transformation, Polish civil society has evolved into a deeply divided and polarized entity, with two distinct organizational pillars representing antithetical value systems, visions of politics and scenarios for Poland's future development. Moreover, the unholy alliance between the state with its authoritarian ambitions and the illiberal/nationalist pillar of civil society has created new opportunities for far-right extremism to flourish, intensified Poland's culture wars and changed the underlying structure of Polish politics. As a result, Poland is drifting towards right-wing political extremism, authoritarianism and Catholic fundamentalism and away from European democratic values. The escalating conflict over the rule of law in Poland threatens the decision-making process within the EU and has become a major challenge to the EU.

Jaroslaw Kurski, editor of *Gazeta Wyborcza* and a leading critic of the Polish government, stated during the hearing in the European Parliament in 2018 that 'in today's Poland a full-fledged nationalist revolution is under way. Its casualties include the legal foundations of the state, democratic procedures and open society'. I suggested in this chapter that the illiberal civil society that emerged in Poland after 1989 provides the organizational foundation and shock troops for this revolution. The alliance of this part of civil society with right-wing political parties threatens the future of liberal democracy in Poland and the country's membership in the European Union. Poland is not alone in this predicament. Cultural and political pillarization of civil society has become a distinct feature of the contemporary political landscape across the world. Pillarized civil societies fuel cultural and political polarization, radicalization, xenophobia and nationalism. Poland may well be a crucial testing ground for the political consequences of deeply divided civil societies and may offer ideas of how such divisions can be overcome.

Notes

1. This chapter has benefitted from the ongoing research project on the development of civil society in Poland, co-directed by Grzegorz Ekiert and Jan Kubik. Some of the early results of our work have been published in Grzegorz Ekiert and Jan Kubik, *Rebellious Civil Society: Popular Protest and Democratic Consolidation in Poland* (Ann Arbor: University of Michigan Press, 1999); Grzegorz Ekiert and Jan Kubik, 'Myths and Realities of Civil Society', *Journal of Democracy* 25 (2014): 46–58; and Grzegorz Ekiert, Jan Kubik and Michal Wenzel, 'Civil Society and Three Dimensions of Inequality in Post-1989 Poland', *Comparative Politics* 49, no. 3 (2017): 331–50. Ekiert and Kubik 1999, Ekiert and Kubik 2014 and Ekiert, Kubik and Wenzel 2017. It is a revised and expanded version of the essay that was published in Polish in Jacek Żakowski, ed., *Almanach Concilium Civitas 2019/2020* (Warszawa: Fundacja Collegium Civitas, 2019) – a publication prepared for the first meeting of Concilium Civitas in Warsaw in July 2019. I would also like to thank Bart Bonikowski, Emmanuel Gerard, Peter Hall, Bart Pattyn and fellows from the Metaforum project on Democracy at the University of Leuven as well as editors of this volume for their comments on the early drafts of this chapter.
2. See John Keane, *Civil Society and the State: New European Perspectives* (London: Verso, 1988).
3. See, for example, Timothy Garton Ash, *The Polish Revolution: Solidarity*, 3rd edn (New Haven: Yale University Press, 2002); Ekiert and Kubik, *Rebellious Civil Society*; Jan Kubik, *The Power of Symbols against Symbols of Power* (University Park: Penn State University Press, 1994); Alain Touraine, *Solidarity* (Cambridge: Cambridge University Press, 1983).
4. See, for example, Claus Offe, 'Challenging the Boundaries of Institutional Politics: Social Movements since the 1960s', in Charles Maier (ed.), *Changing Boundaries of Political* (Cambridge: Cambridge University Press, 1987), 63–105; Enrique Larana, Hank Johnston and Joseph Gusfield, eds, *New Social Movements. From Ideology to Identity* (Philadelphia: Temple University Press, 1994); Hanspeter Kriesi et al., *New Social Movements in Western Europe* (Minneapolis: University of Minnesota Press, 1995).
5. For the review of various traditions and theories of civil society see, for example, John A. Hall, ed., *Civil Society: Theory, History, Comparison* (Cambridge: Polity Press, 1995); Adam B. Seligman, *The Idea of Civil Society* (Princeton: Princeton University Press, 1992); Sudipta Kaviraj and Sunil Khilnani, *Civil Society: History and Possibilities* (Cambridge: Cambridge University Press, 2001); Jeffrey C. Alexander, *The Civil Sphere* (Oxford: Oxford University Press, 2006); Victor Perez-Diaz, *Civil Society: A Multi-layered Concept* (Sociopedia.isa, 2011), www.isa-sociology.org/publ/sociopedia-isa; Grzegorz Ekiert, 'Civil Society Approach', in Wolfgang Merkel, Raj Kollmorgen and Hans-Jurgen Wagener (eds), *Handbook of Political, Social and Economic Transformations* (Oxford: Oxford University Press, 2019).
6. Robert D. Putnam, Robert Leonardi and Raffaella Y. Nanetti, *Making Democracy Work: Civic Traditions in Modern Italy* (Princeton: Princeton University Press, 1993).

7   Larry Diamond, *Developing Democracy: Toward Consolidation* (Baltimore: The Johns Hopkins University Press, 1999).

8   Margaret Keck and Kathryn Sikkink, *Activists beyond Borders* (Ithaca: Cornell University Press, 1998).

9   See, for example, Grzegorz Ekiert, Elizabeth Perry and Xiaojun Yan, eds., *Ruling by Other Means: State Mobilized Movements* (Cambridge: Cambridge University Press, 2020).

10 Nancy Bermeo, *Ordinary People in Extraordinary Times: The Citizenry and the Breakdown of Democracy* (Princeton: Princeton University Press, 2003).

11 Samuel Huntington, *Political Order in Changing Societies* (New Haven: Yale University Press, 1968).

12 Sheri Berman, 'Civil Society and the Collapse of the Weimar Republic', *World Politics* 49, no. 3 (1997): 401–29.

13 Dylan Riley, *The Civic Foundations of Fascism in Europe* (London: Verso, 2019).

14 Nancy Bermeo and Philip Nord, eds, *Civil Society before Democracy: Lessons from Nineteenth-Century Europe* (Lanham: Rowman & Littlefield, 2000).

15 Bermeo and Nord, *Civil Society before Democracy*, XXV.

16 Simone Chambers and Jeffery Kopstein, 'Bad Civil Society', *Political Theory* 29, no. 3 (2001): 837–65.

17 Petr Kopecky and Cas Mudde, eds, *Uncivil Society? Contentious Politics in Post-Communist Europe* (London: Routledge, 2003).

18 Richard Youngs et al., *The Mobilization of Conservative Civil Society* (Washington: Carnegie Endowment for International Peace, 2018).

19 Philippe C. Schmitter, 'Civil Society: East and West', in Larry Diamond, Marc F. Plattner, Yunhan Chu and Hung-mao Tien (eds), *Consolidating the Third Wave Democracies: Themes and Perspectives* (Baltimore: The Johns Hopkins University Press, 1997), 239–62. The concept of 'pillarized civil society' has its roots in the nineteenth-century political experiences of Belgium and the Netherlands, where religious and ethnic divisions led to emergence of divided civil societies in the context of expanding mass political participation. See, for example, Thomas Ertman, 'Liberalization, Democratization, and the Origins pf "Pillarized" Civil Society in Nineteenth-Century Belgium and Netherlands', in Nancy Bermeo and Philip Nord (eds), *Civil Society before Democracy: Lessons from Nineteenth-Century Europe* (Lanham: Rowman & Littlefield, 2000) and Remieg Aerts, 'Civil Society or Democracy? A Dutch Paradox', *Low Countries Historical Review* 125, nos. 2–3 (2010): 209–36.

20 Youngs, *The Mobilization of Conservative Civil Society*, 7.

21 Bruce William and Michael Delli Carpini, *After Broadcast News: Media Regimes and the New Information Environment* (Cambridge: Cambridge University Press, 2011).

22 W. Lance Bennett and Alexandra Segerberg, 'The Logic of Connective Action: Digital Media and the Personalization of Contentious Politics', *Information, Communication & Society* 15, no. 5 (2012): 739–62.

23 Larry Diamond, 'Liberation Technology', *Journal of Democracy* 21, no. 3 (2010): 69–83.
24 Joshua Tucker et al., 'From Liberation to Turmoil: Social Media and Democracy', *Journal of Democracy* 28, no. 4 (2017): 46–59; Larry Diamond, 'The Threat of Postmodern Totalitarianism', *Journal of Democracy* 30, no. 1 (2019): 20–4.
25 See, for example, Bela Greskovits, 'Rebuilding the Hungarian Right through Conquering Civil Society: The Civic Circles Movement', *East European Politics* 36, no. 2 (2020): 248–9.
26 Ekiert and Kubik, 'Myths and Realities of Civil Society', 46–58.
27 Michael Magner, 'Civil Society in Poland after 1989: A Legacy of Socialism?', *Canadian Slavonic Papers* 47, nos. 1–2 (2015): 49–69.
28 Ekiert and Kubik, 'Myths and Realities of Civil Society'.
29 Grzegorz Ekiert, Jan Kubik and Michal Wenzel, *Civil Society in Central and Eastern Europe: Challenges and Opportunities*, eds Peter Vandor, Nicole Traxler, Reinhard Miller and Michael Meyer (Vienna ERSTE Foundation, 2017), 76–91.
30 See Daniel Platek and Piotr Pluciennciczak, 'Mobilizing on the Extreme Right in Poland: Marginalization, Institutionalization and Radicalization', in Kerstin Jacobsson and Elzbieta Korolczuk (eds), *Civil Society Revisited. Lessons from Poland* (Oxford: Berghahn Books, 2017).
31 Magner, 'Civil Society in Poland after 1989', 63–7.
32 See Marta Kotwas and Jan Kubik, 'Symbolic Thickening of Public Culture and the Rise of Right-Wing Populism in Poland', *East European Politics and Societies, and Cultures* 33, no. 2 (2019): 435–71.
33 Platek and Pluciennciczak, 'Mobilizing on the Extreme Right in Poland'.
34 Agnieszka Graff, 'Gender, Sexuality, and Nation – Here and Now: Reflections on the Gendered and Sexualized Aspects of Contemporary Polish Nationalism', in E. H. Oleksy (ed.), *Intimate Citizenship: Gender, Sexualities, Politics* (London: Routledge, 2009), 133–47.
35 See Frances Cayton, 'Poland's March of Independence as a Tool in Building Illiberal Civil Society', unpublished paper, 2020; Kotwas and Kubik, 'Symbolic Thickening of Public Culture and the Rise of Right-Wing Populism in Poland', 435–71.
36 Marek Beylin, 'PiS: dumni nosiciele nacjonalistycznej choroby', *Gazeta Wyborcza* 25 (April 2019).
37 The idea of creating clubs emerged in 2005, and by 2016 there were some 400 clubs (including 70 abroad) with some 10,000 members and thousands more sympathizers and participants in meetings. These have played an active role in organizing monthly demonstrations in Warsaw to commemorate the crash of the presidential plane in Smolensk in 2010, which was blamed on Russia and the liberal Polish government of the day.
38 Paweł Marczewski, 'Freedom to Exclude: Conservative CSOs in Law and Justice Poland – The Mobilization of Conservative Civil Society' (Carnegie Europe, 2018). https://carnegieeurope.eu/2018/10/04/freedom-to-exclude-conservative-csos-in-law-and-justice-poland-pub-77377.

References

Aerts, Remieg. 'Civil Society or Democracy? A Dutch Paradox'. *Low Countries Historical Review* 125, nos. 2–3 (2010): 209–236.
Alexander, Jeffrey C. *The Civil Sphere*. Oxford: Oxford University Press, 2006.
Ash, Timothy Garton. *The Polish Revolution: Solidarity*, third edition. New Haven: Yale University Press, 2002.
Bennett, W. Lance and Alexandra Segerberg. 'The Logic of Connective Action: Digital Media and the Personalization of Contentious Politics'. *Information, Communication & Society* 15, no. 5 (2012): 739–62.
Berman, Sheri. 'Civil Society and the Collapse of the Weimar Republic'. *World Politics* 49, no. 3 (1997): 401–29.
Bermeo, Nancy. *Ordinary People in Extraordinary Times: The Citizenry and the Breakdown of Democracy*. Princeton: Princeton University Press, 2003.
Bermeo, Nancy and Philip Nord, eds. *Civil Society before Democracy: Lessons from Nineteenth-Century Europe*. Lanham: Rowman & Littlefield, 2000.
Beylin, Marek. 'PiS: dumni nosiciele nacjonalistycznej choroby'. *Gazeta Wyborcza* 25 (April 2019), accessed online.
Cayton, Frances. 'Poland's March of Independence as a Tool in Building Illiberal Civil Society' (unpublished paper. 2020).
Chambers, Simone and Jeffery Kopstein. 'Bad Civil Society'. *Political Theory* 29, no. 3 (2001): 837–65.
Diamond, Larry. *Developing Democracy: Toward Consolidation*. Baltimore: The Johns Hopkins University Press, 1999.
Diamond, Larry. 'Liberation Technology'. *Journal of Democracy* 21, no. 3 (2010): 69–83.
Diamond, Larry. 'The Threat of Postmodern Totalitarianism'. *Journal of Democracy* 30, no. 1 (2019): 20–4.
Ekiert, Grzegorz. 'Civil Society Approach'. In Wolfgang Merkel, Raj Kollmorgen and Hans-Jurgen Wagener (eds), *Handbook of Political, Social and Economic Transformations*. Oxford: Oxford University Press, 2019, pp. 151–160.
Ekiert, Grzegorz, Elizabeth Perry and Xiaojun Yan, eds. *Ruling by Other Means: State Mobilized Movements*. Cambridge: Cambridge University Press, 2020.
Ekiert, Grzegorz and Jan Kubik. 'Myths and Realities of Civil Society'. *Journal of Democracy* 25 (2014): 46–58.
Ekiert, Grzegorz and Jan Kubik. *Rebellious Civil Society: Popular Protest and Democratic Consolidation in Poland*. Ann Arbor: University of Michigan Press, 1999.
Ekiert, Grzegorz, Jan Kubik and Michal Wenzel. *Civil Society in Central and Eastern Europe: Challenges and Opportunities*, eds Peter Vandor, Nicole Traxler, Reinhard Miller and Michael Meyer, 76–91. Vienna ERSTE Foundation, 2017.
Ekiert, Grzegorz, Jan Kubik and Michal Wenzel. 'Civil Society and Three Dimensions of Inequality in Post-1989 Poland'. *Comparative Politics* 49, no. 3 (2017): 331–50.
Ertman, Thomas. 'Liberalization, Democratization, and the Origins pf "Pillarized" Civil Society in Nineteenth-Century Belgium and Netherlands'. In Nancy Bermeo and Philip Nord (eds), *Civil Society before Democracy: Lessons from Nineteenth-Century Europe*. Lanham: Rowman & Littlefield, 2000, pp. 155–178.

Główny Urząd Statystyczny. *Jakość życia w Polsce w 2015 r. Wyniki badań spójności społecznej*. Warszawa, 2017.

Graff, Agnieszka. 'Gender, Sexuality, and Nation – Here and Now: Reflections on the Gendered and Sexualized Aspects of Contemporary Polish Nationalism'. In E. H. Oleksy (eds), *Intimate Citizenship: Gender, Sexualities, Politics*, 133–47. London: Routledge, 2009.

Greskovits, Bela. 'Rebuilding the Hungarian Right through Conquering Civil Society: The Civic Circles Movement'. *East European Politics* 36, no. 2 (2020): 248–9.

Hall, John A., ed. *Civil Society: Theory, History, Comparison*. Cambridge: Polity Press, 1995.

Huntington, Samuel. *Political Order in Changing Societies*, New Haven: Yale University Press, 1968.

Kaviraj, Sudipta and Sunil Khilnani. *Civil Society: History and Possibilities*. Cambridge: Cambridge University Press, 2001.

Keane, John. *Civil Society and the State: New European Perspectives*. London: Verso, 1988.

Keck, Margaret and Kathryn Sikkink. *Activists beyond Borders*. Ithaca: Cornell University Press, 1998.

Kopecky, Petr and Cas Mudde, eds. *Uncivil Society? Contentious Politics in Post-Communist Europe*. London: Routledge, 2003.

Kotwas, Marta and Jan Kubik. 'Symbolic Thickening of Public Culture and the Rise of Right-Wing Populism in Poland'. *East European Politics and Societies, and Cultures* 33, no. 2 (2019): 435–71.

Kriesi, Hanspeter, Ruud Koopmans, Jan Willem Duyvendak and Marco Giugni. *New Social Movements in Western Europe*. Minneapolis: University of Minnesota Press, 1995.

Kubik, Jan. *The Power of Symbols against Symbols of Power*. University Park: Penn State University Press, 1994.

Larana, Enrique, Hank Johnston and Joseph Gusfield, eds. *New Social Movements. From Ideology to Identity*. Philadelphia: Temple University Press, 1994.

Magner, Michael. 'Civil Society in Poland after 1989: A Legacy of Socialism?'. *Canadian Slavonic Papers* 47, nos. 1–2 (2015): 49–69.

Marczewski, Paweł. 'Freedom to Exclude: Conservative CSOs in Law and Justice Poland – The Mobilization of Conservative Civil Society'. Carnegie Europe, 2018. https://carnegieeurope.eu/2018/10/04/freedom-to-exclude-conservative-csos-in-law-and-justice-poland-pub-77377.

Nord, Philip. 'Introduction'. In Nancy Bermeo and Philip Nord (eds), *Civil Society before Democracy: Lessons from Nineteenth-Century Europe*. Lanham: Rowman & Littlefield, 2002.

Offe, Claus. 'Challenging the Boundaries of Institutional Politics: Social Movements since the 1960s'. In Charles Maier (ed.), *Changing Boundaries of Political*, 63–105. Cambridge: Cambridge University Press, 1987.

Perez-Diaz, Victor. *Civil Society: A Multi-layered Concept*. Sociopedia.isa, 2011. www.isa-sociology.org/publ/sociopedia-isa.

Platek, Daniel and Piotr Plucienniczak. 'Mobilizing on the Extreme Right in Poland: Marginalization, Institutionalization and Radicalization'. In Kerstin Jacobsson and Elzbieta Korolczuk (eds), *Civil Society Revisited: Lessons from Poland*. Oxford: Berghahn Books, 2017, pp. 286–313.

Putnam, Robert D., Robert Leonardi and Raffaella Y. Nanetti. *Making Democracy Work: Civic Traditions in Modern Italy*. Princeton: Princeton University Press, 1993.
Riley, Dylan. *The Civic Foundations of Fascism in Europe*, London: Verso, 2019.
Schmitter, Philippe C. 'Civil Society: East and West'. In Larry Diamond, Marc F. Plattner, Yunhan Chu and Hung-mao Tien (eds), *Consolidating the Third Wave Democracies: Themes and Perspectives*, 239–62. Baltimore: The Johns Hopkins University Press, 1997.
Seligman, Adam B. *The Idea of Civil Society*. Princeton: Princeton University Press, 1992.
Touraine, Alain. *Solidarity*. Cambridge: Cambridge University Press, 1983.
Tucker, Joshua, Yannis Theodurakis, Margaret Roberts and Pablo Barbera. 'From Liberation to Turmoil: Social Media and Democracy'. *Journal of Democracy* 28, no. 4 (2017): 46–59.
William, Bruce and Michael Delli Carpini. *After Broadcast News: Media Regimes and the New Information Environment*. Cambridge: Cambridge University Press, 2011.
Youngs, Richard, Gareth Fowler, Arthur Larok, Paweł Marczewski, Vijayan Mj, Ghia Nodia, Natalia Shapovalova, Janjira Sombatpoonsiri, Marisa Von Bülow, Özge Zihnioğlu. *The Mobilization of Conservative Civil Society*. Washington: Carnegie Endowment for International Peace, 2018.
Żakowski, Jacek, ed. *Almanach Concilium Civitas 2019/2020*, Warszawa: Fundacja Collegium Civitas, 2019.

3

The Arab uprisings and people's power

Romantic views and hard realities

Marina Ottaway

Popular uprisings rattled the Arab world beginning in December 2010, with a second wave starting in Algeria and Sudan in 2019. At the outset, many saw the uprisings as proof that even the most authoritarian regimes cannot resist the force of popular mobilization and that the people, youth in particular, had changed the Middle East forever. As challenged regimes increasingly succeeded in maintaining or quickly re-establishing their authority, the romantic view of people's power gave way to a deep pessimism about the resilience of authoritarianism, and the powerlessness of grassroots movements.

In reality, the uprisings brought about considerable change in the seven countries where they took place: Tunisia, Egypt, Yemen, Bahrain, Libya, Morocco and Syria. (The countries are listed here in the order in which popular movement erupted between December 2010 and late March 2011. Jordan, Saudi Arabia, Oman and Iraq are omitted from the list because protests there never gained real traction.) The extent and nature of the changes vary considerably among the seven countries: in Syria, Yemen and Libya, the uprisings led to the collapse of the states. In Bahrain, the outcome was the de facto takeover of the country by Saudi Arabia, which intervened to save the monarchy but stayed on to establish a virtual and seemingly permanent protectorate. In Egypt, the popular uprising eventually led to the emergence of a military regime more repressive than any the country had seen since the days of Gamal Abdel Nasser in the 1950s and 1960s. In Tunisia and Morocco, protest led to new regimes that incorporated Islamist parties in the body politic, a major and often overlooked phenomenon.[1]

These are not trifling changes and there is no doubt that in all seven countries it was popular movements and mass demonstration that served as catalysts. Past the initial moment, however, the movement passed from the protesters in the streets to organized forces – domestic and foreign armed ones in Libya, Yemen, Syria and Bahrain, and political ones in the remaining three countries. The popular uprisings themselves proved powerful but ephemeral.

This analysis will concentrate on Tunisia, Morocco and Egypt, the three countries where change took place largely through a political process – even in Egypt, the military gained power through politics and political repression, not through military means. These three countries most clearly show both the short-term considerable impact of spontaneous, bottom-up movements and their longer-term vulnerability. I do not believe that the limited effectiveness of popular movements is exclusive to the Arab world and other chapters in this collection tend to confirm this idea.

The limited effectiveness of bottom-up movements is the result of several factors. First, such movements are difficult to sustain over time. People can stay out on the streets only for a limited time before the pressures of daily life – the necessity of making a living, looking after families and more broadly taking care of life – impose themselves. Students and youth with fewer responsibilities usually continue their protest the longest, but even they eventually have to give up. Organized political forces can remain active much longer, continuing to bear pressure on the authorities without causing untenable hardship for individuals. Workers, for example, cannot stay out on strike indefinitely, but well-organized labour unions can keep up pressure on the government and the private sector indefinitely, as we see in Tunisia, where the major labour federation remains a major pressure group eight years after the uprising.

The second, most important and definitely non-romantic reason for the limited effectiveness of bottom-up protest is that lasting change can come only from the top, i.e. from the government itself. Crowds can demand change, they can even tear apart a government, perhaps even set up for a time popular committees that try to rule from the bottom-up. But eventually, the old government comes back and possibly implements some reforms, or a new government and political system are set up, and they will make changes, although not necessarily the ones the protesters wanted.

Protesters might occasionally seize control of an area, declare it liberated and enforce their own rules. For example during the 'Black Lives Matter' protests in the United States in June 2020, citizens seized a six-block area of Seattle and declared it a liberated zone from which the police were excluded. The authorities tolerated the situation for three weeks, until an outbreak of violence caused them to end the autonomy of those few blocks. Lasting police reform will need the intervention of the authorities.

Crowds cannot govern. The process by which protesters overthrow a government or force it to reconsider its policies is quite different from the process of adopting and implementing new laws and regulation, which must come from the top, hopefully in consultation with civil society.

The uprisings

In Tunisia, Egypt and Morocco the mass mobilization phase of the uprisings was quickly over. It lasted the longest in Tunisia, where the protest started in a remote area and had to make its way gradually to the capital before the pressure on the government became overwhelming. Although few noticed it at the time, the protest would not have spread over a period of weeks without the intervention of the Tunisian federation of labour unions (Union Generale Tunisienne du Travail, or UGTT) that provided organizational skills and resources the protesters themselves did not have.[2] Shortly after the protest reached the capital, President Ben Ali took the route of exile with his family. At that point, the crowds largely lost their role, except for occasional burst of activity at sensitive points in the transition. When it came to designing a transition process and setting up a new government, the youthful protesters had nothing to offer. In fact, for a process of change triggered by an act of desperation by an unemployed fruit seller, the transition in Tunisia was a very top-down process, led by older people many of whom were part of the country's well-entrenched political establishment not only under President Ben Ali but also under his predecessor, Habib Bourguiba.

The semi-spontaneous phase of the Arab uprisings ran its course quickly everywhere. The mass movements captured international attention and headlines, with pictures of squares teeming with youthful participants holding placards and demanding their rulers get out. All movements exploded between December 2010 and March 2011 and then started petering out. The process of change continued, but the initiative passed to organized political forces (or to armed groups leading to the disintegration of the countries where it happened) and that is when real change started taking place. It would not have happened without the mass protest, to be sure, but the crowds were only the catalyst. In Egypt, the initiative was seized by the military and the Muslim Brotherhood, while the poorly organized secular parties were largely sidelined and protesters relegated to an even lesser role. Protesters in Tunisia started fading from the streets shortly after President Ben Ali left the country, although they returned sporadically. In Morocco, the initiative passed from the streets to the palace in a matter of days. In Yemen, Libya and Syria military action quickly superseded political action.

The quick fading of mass protests provided the answer to the question dissident movements had been debating for some time: how best to organize? In the new IT environment of the twenty-first century, did the bureaucratic and hierarchical traditional forms of organizing – what we will call the Leninist model – still make sense? Or was it an archaic approach to be replaced by new, more nimble, decentralized networks coordinating through the use of social media, infinitely flexible and thus less susceptible to dismantling by the security forces? In other words, should Lenin be scuttled in favour of Wael Ghonim, the young Egyptian computer engineer who preached a new age revolution?[3]

The issue was the subject of a lively and, at times, surprisingly acrimonious debate at a meeting of representatives of protest groups from half a dozen Arab countries organized by the Carnegie Endowment for International Peace, where I worked at the time, in Beirut, Lebanon, in late 2009. Signs of unrest were becoming increasingly evident around the region, from the Maghreb to the Gulf. During the conference, participants never agreed on an answer.[4]

The events of 2011 showed the greater staying power, thus effectiveness, of organizations embracing the Leninist model: the youth networks, which relied on call to action through social media, were effective in summoning the crowds, but were quickly sidelined after setting the process of change in motion. The real battles were fought by organizations that were definitively hierarchical and bureaucratic even when they stood for change. The Muslim Brotherhood in Egypt and the UGTT in Tunisia were structurally Leninist organizations par excellence. The Leninist influence in the UGTT was direct and explicit; there is a tantalizing piece of research to be carried out whether the Muslim Brotherhood's patterns of organization and recruiting just bore an accidental resemblance to the Leninist model or were inspired by it and, if so, through which channels. These hierarchical organizations proved capable of participating and winning not just the battles to challenge the old system but also those to create new systems. The young protesters later accused the old established organizations – the Muslim Brotherhood and the military in Egypt, the UGTT and the Islamist Ennahda party in Tunisia, the Islamist Party for Justice and Development and the palace in Morocco – of having "hijacked" their uprisings. To put it in more dispassionate terms, strong organizations took over because they had the capacity to carry on what the more spontaneous, less-hierarchical groups could only set into motion. But of course strong organizations also had their own agendas that differed from those of the youth groups.

I will elaborate these points by examining in greater detail three issues: the interplay of spontaneous upheavals and the intervention of strong organizations in Tunisia, Egypt and Morocco; the sad experience of women, who participated in substantial numbers in the uprising, but saw no lasting change in their status; and the takeover of the process by strongly organized forces.

Bottom-up participation and its limits

Bottom-up participation was important to the outcome of the uprising, but only in conjunction with the actions of organized political forces, political institutions or the military. The three case studies show that popular upheavals were extremely successful in shaking up the old system, but not in building something new and different. It is an old story: Lenin believed in revolution, but he developed a strong, bureaucratic vanguard party to carry it out.

Tunisia, Egypt and Morocco all illustrate this point vividly. The David and Goliath image of uprisings as a heroic struggle waged by young idealists rising against the forces of repressive states first emerged in Tunisia. It was an appealing narrative, but not an accurate one. The young Tunisian fruit vendor that set in motion the chain reaction leading to the overthrow of President Ben Ali was a frustrated young man who immolated himself in a fit of rage, not an idealist giving his life for a higher cause. Second, what turned an individual act of desperation into an uprising were the deliberate efforts of the UGTT to spread unrest from the small, obscure town of Sidi Bouzid to larger towns on the coast and eventually to Tunis. The UGTT involvement in turn was the result of an internal revolt by mid-level cadres against the national leadership of the UGTT in Tunis, which was closely associated with the Ben Ali regime and a few years earlier had refused to support a major strike in the country's gritty "mining basin" not far from Sidi Bouzid.[5]

This does not mean that there was no grassroots uprising against the Ben Ali regime. The crowds were large and enthusiastic and participants wanted the president to leave. But when he did so, opting for exile in Saudi Arabia, the initiative reverted to government officials, members of the established elite and political parties. Over the following years, the crowds returned to the streets at crucial times when the political process appeared to be grinding to a halt. However, the major protagonists of the process that led to real change were not the crowds, but organized forces. They included the Islamist party Ennahda; the representatives of the left including parties and the UGTT; the employers' federation the Tunisian Confederation of Industry, Trade and Handicrafts (UTICA) ; the Tunisian Human Rights League; the Tunisian Order of Lawyers; and eventually a new centrist political party called Nida Tounes, led by Beji Caid Essebsi, an octogenarian veteran of the Bourguiba regime. These were the political forces that made Tunisia what it is today, much to the frustration of the youthful rebels who feel betrayed and appear to have withdrawn from politics.

With the exception of Nida Tounes, a new centrist party only held together by hostility towards Ennahda, all the influential actors controlled strong organizations. In fact, Nida Tounes has demonstrated the need for strong structures: it fell prey to internal rivalries and by 2018 it was a spent political force, although it was not officially disbanded.

Egypt tells a similar story. With its huge crowds camped out in Tahrir Square and keeping it into a state of permanent occupation until President Hosni Mubarak left, Egypt became the symbol of what people's power could achieve. Crowds reappeared periodically in times of crisis, culminating in massive countrywide demonstrations on 30 June 2013, the first anniversary of President Mohammed Morsi's inauguration. The latter demonstrations, however, were far from spontaneous or the result of a bottom-up effort. Rather, they were organized by the security services. They provided the military with the excuse it sought to seize power and claim that it was not carrying out a coup d'état, but simply responding to a popular demand so overwhelming that it had no choice but to comply. This was the last time the "people" played any role in Egyptian politics. The military quickly consolidated its power, repressing any form of protest or popular participation.

As in the case of Tunisia, what prevented the protesters in Egypt from becoming players in the effort to develop a new political system was the absence of structure and leadership. The instrument the youth movements had chosen to mobilize people – social media – was indeed quick, nimble and difficult for the security forces to silence. However, it did not generate power. It was not a tool for sustaining concerted action, organizing for elections or designing a plan for the future. It took strong organizations to do that. Thus, it was the military that forced Mubarak from power, while he insisted on hanging on despite the protests. It was the Muslim Brotherhood that won the parliamentary elections, sidelining the dozens of weakly organized secular parties vying for seats. It was the judiciary that disbanded the parliament on a flimsy juridical pretext. Finally, it was the security forces that collected signatures on a petition against Morsi and organized the June 2013 demonstrations. Not surprisingly, the process culminated with the strongest organization of them all, the military, openly in full control.

In Morocco, grassroots movements played an even smaller role, because as soon as protest broke out the king and the palace moved very fast to assert their leadership and impose their own process of limited change. When the February 20 Movement, which took its name from the date of the first demonstrations, erupted, the king responded in days by announcing that a new constitution would be drafted by experts in consultation with a broader committee also named by the king, and that elections would be held as soon as feasible following the approval of the constitution. It all happened smoothly as promised and by October 2011, Morocco had a new constitution, had held elections and formed a new government headed by the general-secretary of the Party for Justice and Development, the Islamist organization that had received the plurality of the vote. But despite some changes in the constitution that appeared to increase the power of the prime minister, the king and the palace were still in control. Demand for change from the bottom became change from the top, cautiously doled out so as not to rock the boat, with the full agreement of an Islamist party that had deliberately chosen cooperation over confrontation.

In conclusion, both sides in the pre-uprisings debates about the pros and cons of hierarchy and strong organization versus flexible networks were partially correct. It was the nimble networks that were able to start off the blocks fast, dramatizing the widespread discontent. It was the old-fashioned, hierarchical and bureaucratic organizations, headed by the same old leaders, that demonstrated the staying power needed to have a long-lasting impact.

The problem of informal networks, as far as their long-term effectiveness, is that they are too egalitarian and democratic to accomplish much in practice. There are a few exceptions; for example an international loose network of NGOs waged a campaign in the mid-1990s that led to the signing of most world governments of the Antipersonnel Mine Convention in 1997. But such successes are rare. Insistence on complete egalitarianism is appealing in theory, but it is also a recipe for disaster. Non-hierarchical organizations have trouble speaking with one voice, because many feel equally entitled to speak for the organization. After its success in mobilizing people to take to the streets, the April 6 movements in Egypt started splintering into factions while demonstrators were still in Tahrir Square. Of course, even hierarchical bureaucratic organizations experience factionalism and power struggles, but this tendency is kept in check by the rules that govern the organization. There were factions within the Egyptian Muslim Brotherhood, but there was also an official hierarchy and fights were filtered through the rules of the organization and the requirement that decisions should follow certain paths to become binding. But in networks that rejected on principle formal leadership structures there were no rules and the door to participation was open to all – a model of participatory democracy but an invitation to chaos.

Another problem manifested by informal networks is that they can be taken over easily by stronger organizations. During 2013 in Egypt, a youth organization called Tamarrod attracted a lot of attention when it announced its intention to collect a million signatures on a petition demanding Morsi's resignation as president of Egypt. To some, the rise of Tamarrod suggested that the glory days of the uprising were coming back. Other activists originally dismissed Tamarrod as being at best a "rolodex" of names of people that might be mobilized for more street activity to bring pressure on the government. Soon, however, Tamarrod turned into a formidable machine for collecting signatures, well organized and efficient. This unexpected success was eventually shown to be the result of the organization's takeover by state security agents, who provided it with structure, leadership and money. We will probably never know how many Tamarrod members realized they were being manipulated by the state security agency. Statements later issued by Tamarrod leaders were highly ambiguous.[6] As for the followers, we really do not know what their position was.

Women and the uprisings

In all countries that experienced uprisings, women were well represented among the demonstrators. Although there are no reliable estimates of the percentage of women among protesters in any country, there is a lot of circumstantial evidence from pictures and press reports that they were well represented. A few women , such as Tawakkol Karman in Yemen, rose to prominence because of their role – Tawakkol became known as the 'mother of the revolution' and won the 2011 Nobel Peace Prize. In general, however, few women emerged as leaders in the protest movements – the names that came to the fore during the often chaotic events were overwhelmingly those of men.

Despite the importance of their participation, women have so far not benefitted from the uprisings. This is the almost unanimous, albeit reluctant, conclusion reached by scholars and commentators writing on the issue in the years after the uprisings.[7] It is mostly those writing during the early days who drew optimistic conclusions about the likely impact of women's participation.[8] By now, it is clear that in no country did the uprising lead to a significant change in the status of women, no matter how active they were in the street. The noticeable increase in the number of Tunisian women in political positions stemmed less from their activism than from deliberate decisions by political organizations, particularly Ennahda, to show that they held progressive social views and thus to put more women on their election lists.

It is not surprising that the uprisings did not prove to be a turning point for women. First, real social revolutions are exceedingly rare even in the face of violent uprisings. Even revolutions that manage to create a new political elite, as was the case in France, Russia or China, put power in the hands not of the weakest members of the society, but of an alternative elite that has the resources and the know-how to take advantage of the opportunities. The downtrodden masses of Sans Culottes, proletarians or peasants in whose names revolutions are fought never gain power. Indeed, many studies point to the fact that in situations where new leadership positions open up, not just during a revolution, but also during other period of rapid change – for example when Tanzania launched Ujamaa villages in the 1960s and villagers elected their local leaders – people at the bottom of the social ladder rarely rise the top. Women, it should be remembered, are at the bottom of the hierarchy in Arab societies.

There is another reason why the Arab uprisings did little to enhance the position of women. In many countries the movements weakened the very women's organizations that had been most successful in promoting women's rights. Much to the resentment of committed independent feminists, it was the official, government-recognized women's organizations, usually enjoying the patronage of the first lady, which managed to get some laws changed in a way that benefitted women. Similarly, Morocco made substantial, pro-women changes to its personal status code when the king embraced the ideas set forth by well-connected upper-class women's organizations.

As I pointed out earlier, reforms in Arab societies, as elsewhere, ultimately come from the top, and that is as true concerning the position of women as in other areas. Egypt is a case in point. Women suffered a setback when

Mubarak was deposed and his wife Suzanne ceased to be the link through which pressure was brought to bear on the government concerning women issues. Furthermore, the election law of 2012 eliminated quotas for women, and the result was that only fifteen women were elected to the parliament's two chambers, with an additional two appointed. Most women were Islamists. We will never know whether their presence was purely cosmetic or whether it would have led to a push for reform of policies affecting women. The courts dissolved the parliament in June 2012, on the pretext that the election law was unconstitutional, but in reality to annul the victory of the Muslim Brotherhood. By the time a new parliament was elected in 2015, the election law had been changed once again and quotas for women were reinstated. As a result, the new parliament included the largest number of women ever. Unfortunately, the parliament essentially limited itself to rubber-stamping government decisions, so the presence of more women had no discernible impact on policy.

In Tunisia, the 2014 elections resulted in one third of deputies being women – a high proportion for any country outside Scandinavia, let alone an Arab one. This was the result of several factors: the 2014 constitution embraced, after much debate, not only the principle of women equality but also that of parity of representation in leadership position for men and women, pushing political parties to increase the number of women on their candidate lists. Ennahda was particularly anxious to put women at the top in order to counter the image of a retrograde, fundamentalist party stuck in medieval thinking secularists were trying to foist on it; and in general, the entire political class was under pressure to project an image of progressivism.

The change was welcomed by women, but the fact that it came not from the bottom-up, through women's own efforts and their participation in the uprising, but from the top-down, as a result of a new found 'state feminism' outraged some. The relation between women activism and their political impact was mediated through decisions taken by governments and political parties. One question still unanswered is whether the presence of more women in the legislature and in ministerial positions, no matter what determined the increase, will lead to more changes favourable to women.

It is not only the recent examples of Tunisia, Morocco and Egypt that suggest that women's direct participation in revolutionary movements does not inevitably ameliorate their position in society. The Algerian war of independence provides a similar sad lesson. During the war, Franz Fanon, an early advocate of Third World revolutions, wrote a book, translated in English as *A Dying Colonialism*, which documented the deep social changes he believed the fight against France had brought about in Algerian society.[9] He argued, among others, that the position of women was deeply and permanently altered by their participation in the war in which they had fought bravely, including in the urban warfare of the battle of Algiers. Yet, once independence was achieved, women were pushed back into their old roles. The veil, which had been a useful tool during the war by making it easier for women to transport weapons and plant bombs, turned again into a symbol of societal control and their inferior position. Few women wear the veil in Algeria today, but this is the result of a slow and still incomplete evolution, not revolutionary change.

The uprising that started in Sudan in early 2019, leading to the overthrow of the old regime and the setting up of a joint civilian–military transitional arrangement in September of the same year, has seen the participation of many women and thus has rekindled the hope that their role in a political upheaval will empower Sudanese women in an unprecedented way.[10] It is of course too early to tell, but I am deeply sceptical that this will turn out to be a real turning point. It takes more than a few months, or even years, and the lacing of a few, highly qualified women in high positions to change deeply ingrained social attitudes. New laws are crucial, but it usually takes a long time before legal rights and social attitudes start realigning.

It is worthwhile recalling what happened in the United States as a result of women's participation in the upheavals of the late 1960s to early 1970s on university campuses, when students took over building demanding reforms. Literally and figuratively, women were manning the barricades alongside their male colleagues, but discovered that the latter still expected them to keep the occupied buildings tidy and make coffee. The resentment created by these experiences was still palpable among women on university campuses in the following years. It contributed, together with many other factors, to the revival of a feminist movement in the United States, and eventually contributed to the still slow progress towards gender equality. It is possible that future historians will be able to establish a link between women participation in the uprisings and a new Arab feminism, but right now no such link is visible.

The most likely outcome, judging from previous experience, is that the return to a more normal political situation will be a setback for women, whether or not there is a change of regime. But it is possible that the experience of challenging the regime alongside the men will lead women to remain politically active and willing to defy society in fighting for their rights. Right now, this is a hope rather than a reality.

Why strong organizations prevail

I have argued that organized political forces had a much greater impact on the outcome of the uprising than the masses of demonstrators that captured the attention and the imaginations of domestic and foreign observers. However, organizations capable of playing an independent political role outside the control of the government have always been severely and deliberately restricted in most Arab countries. As a result, the organizational scene has been seriously distorted, with only groups closely connected to the government thriving, while truly independent voluntary associations are weak, with the exception of Islamic ones, which appear to have devised ways to survive repression. Official organizations that influenced the aftermath of Arab uprisings include the military, the bureaucracy and the judiciary, although their weight differs from country to country. Influential independent organizations were overwhelmingly Islamist ones.

The military was central to the outcome of the uprising in Egypt, but not in Tunisia and Morocco. In Morocco, where the power of the monarchy was never really threatened, the military remained in the position it always occupied, as protector of the status quo at the service of the king. In Tunisia, the fact that the military remained aloof from politics is more remarkable, because after the departure of President Ben Ali there was a vacuum of power in the country and the military could easily have tried to step in. Instead, the tradition dating back to the beginning of Tunisian independence, that the military should remain apolitical, prevailed and soldiers stayed in the barracks, leaving civilians to build a new political system.

The case of Egypt is quite different. The military quickly became the centre of post-Mubarak politics, maintaining the continuity of the regime even while removing the president. The military has been a central political actor in the country since the 1952 Free Officers coup and the rise to power of Gamal Abdel Nasser. It rarely used military force in imposing its control – the most notable episode recently was the removal of an encampment of Morsi supporters in August 2013.[11] The key to the military's political power has been the presence of former officers at all levels of government and the control of important parts of the economy – exactly how much is a hotly disputed issue.[12]

By the end of the presidency of Hosni Mubarak, himself a former military man, the role of the military had become more discreet, to the point that there was growing speculation among analysts that the political importance of the military might be declining. But as soon as the uprising started, the military and security apparatus were back on centre stage. They deposed President Hosni Mubarak in 2011 and have been running the country since that time, openly from the overthrow of Mubarak to the election of Morsi in June 2012, covertly during the Morsi presidency and then overtly again after the coup d'état of 3 July 2013. In theory, President Abdel Fattah al-Sisi has resigned from the military and is now a civilian, but there is no doubt that he remains part of the military and above all that he owes his power to the military. Key to the military's success in exercising power was not the force of weapons but organization. It placed retired high-ranking officers in important government positions, not only in the central government and administration, but also in all governorates. Of course, the threat of force always remained in the background, but on the surface the Egyptian military state was a law-abiding bureaucracy

Political parties, except for the Islamist ones, were not sufficiently strong to have much say during the post-uprising period, the consequence of decades of authoritarian government and but also of a deeply undemocratic political culture that kept secular parties from building strong organizations and reaching out to constituencies. Islamist parties, on the other hand, developed a tradition of organizing early on, not in order to win elections, but in order to reform their societies. The ultimate goal of Hassan al-Banna, who founded the Egyptian Muslim Brotherhood in 1928, was to build a true Islamic state, where people would live and be governed by the precepts of Islam.[13] But he also believed that such state could not be built in Egypt or elsewhere until the society itself was reformed. The immediate goal for the Muslim Brotherhood was thus that of reforming the society. *Dawa*, preaching and proselytizing, rather than political activity, was the immediate task to which the Muslim Brotherhood should devote itself, and this required organizing. When the leaders of the Muslim Brotherhood reached the conclusions in the 1990s that the organization should participate in the legal politics of Egypt, it benefitted from the strong organization it had developed over decades of preaching and proselytizing.

The same happened in other countries. Islamists entered politics wherever they could and made a strong showing because they were well organized. In Morocco, where the government accepted a degree of Islamist presence, the Party for Justice and Development (PJD) and its predecessors steadily increased their presence in parliament. In Egypt and Tunisia, frightened governments curbed Islamist participation, arresting thousands and, in the case of Tunisia, sending many into exile. But even in these countries, the strength of the organizations helped Islamists to survive as a political force. When the political process was freed up in the aftermath of the uprisings, Islamist showed their strength. In Egypt, the Muslim Brotherhood in alliance with a Salafi party won 70 per cent of the vote, while Ennahda won a plurality in Tunisia and the PJD in Morocco.

Secular parties did not suffer the same degree of repression in any of the free countries, but they never developed strong organizations. An American observer to the 2012 parliamentary elections, who was deployed in Upper Egypt, for example, told me he had not seen an office of any party except for the Islamist ones during his mission. In fact, Egyptian secular politicians sometimes showed great reluctance to get involved with constituents, looking down on campaigning as an activity beneath their dignity. The same was true in Tunisia: secular parties were mostly centred on promoting a specific leader and remain so to this day. Nida Tounes, the party launched by the Bourguiba-era politician Beji Caid Essebsi in order to defeat Ennahda, received the plurality of votes in the 2014 elections based on its leader's reputation and political acumen. But it never consolidated the party organization or even held a party congress. As a result, it splintered into many factions and it is a spent political force.

Morocco is a partial exception, in that some of its secular parties have survived for decades and show some resilience. Key to their survival, however, are the ties to the monarchy they developed, rather than the ties to their constituents.[14]

Another organization that has been surprisingly influential in determining the outcome of the uprisings, particularly in Egypt, is the bureaucracy. Arab bureaucracies are not Weberian constructs, politically neutral and ready to serve whichever government is in power. Rather, they are part of a particular regime and of the elite associated with it and work to perpetuate it and limit change – not surprising in countries when leaders stay in power for decades and have the time to populate the top echelon of the bureaucratic apparatus with their people. Egypt again offers the best example. The bureaucracy was a centre of resistance to Morsi, sabotaging the implementation of decisions and deliberately mismanaging tasks in order to create discontent – electricity cuts and shortage of cooking gas became chronic problems under Morsi but ended suspiciously fast, at least for a time, as soon as he was deposed.

Much of the political elite in various countries is in fact rooted in the top level of the bureaucracy, including state-controlled entities such as newspapers and public agencies, rather than in the parties and the political institutions. This has proven to be the greatest obstacle to political renewal, even in the countries with new governments, new constitutions and new political parties in government. Bottom-up uprisings have proven ineffective against the inertia of these organizations

In the end

The Arab uprisings of 2011 confirm what students of revolutions have long pointed out: the impact of grassroots participation and spontaneous action is limited. Mass participation is important and can be transformative for a short period, but it quickly wanes, giving way to the deliberate actions of organized political forces and institutions old and new. It is a pessimistic conclusion, but it is rooted in an analysis of the differences in the power of large organization and of ephemeral networks, confirmed by the failure so far of most Arab opposition movements, other than Islamist ones. It does not mean that grassroots movements capable of remaining effective in the long run could never arise. But it is not likely, because to be effective, particularly in the struggle with an authoritarian government, opposition forces need to generate power and that requires leadership and organization. In other words, to be successful opposition forces need to become less grassroots.

Mass street movements led by idealistic young protesters are infinitely more appealing than bureaucratic, hierarchical organizations, no matter which ideology they embrace. They get better coverage in the media, but they do not have a good track record of getting things done. And in the end, what really matters to those who rise up is concrete change.

Notes

1   For more on the consequence of the Arab uprisings, see Marina Ottaway and David Ottaway, *A Tale of Four Worlds: The Arab Region after the Uprisings* (London: Hurst Publishers, 2019).

2 Kasper Ly Netterstrøm, 'The Tunisian General Labor Union and the Advent of Democracy', *The Middle East Journal* 70, no. 3 (2016): 383–98. https://muse.jhu.edu/ (accessed 24 June 2019).

3 See Mike Giglio, 'How Wael Ghonim Sparked Egypt's Uprising', *Newsweek*, 13 February 2011, https://www.newsweek.com/how-wael-ghonim-sparked-egypts-uprising-68727 (accessed 18 June 2019); and Jose Antonio Vargas, 'Spring Awakening: How an Egyptian Revolution Began on Facebook', *New York Times*, 17 February 2012, https://www.nytimes.com/2012/02/19/books/review/how-an-egyptian-revolution-began-on-facebook.html (accessed 18 June 2019).

4 The mounting discontent that preceded the uprising is discussed in Marina Ottaway and Amr Hamzawy, 'Protest Movements and Political Change in the Arab World', Carnegie Endowment for International Peace, 28 January 2011, http://casdcenter.com/wp-content/uploads/2016/09/Protest_Movements_and_Political_Change_in_the_Arab_World.pdf (accessed 26 June 2020).

5 See Netterstrøm. Much information also comes from interviews conducted by the author with UGTT cadres carried out over a period of several years after 2011.

6 See Asma Alsharif and Yasmine Saleh, 'The Real Force behind Egypt's "revolution of the state"', Reuters Special Report, 10 December 2013, https://uk.reuters.com/article/us-egypt-interior-specialreport-idUSBRE99908D20131010 (accessed 7 July 2018); and Hamza Hendawi, 'Dispute between Morsi, Military Led to Coup', Associated Press, 18 July 2013, https://www.yahoo.com/news/disputes-between-morsi-military-led-egypt-coup-205809544.html (accessed 25 June 2019).

7 See, for example, Tawakkol Karman, 'Women and the Arab Spring', *Un Chronicle,* December 2016, https://unchronicle.un.org/artile/women-and-the-Arab-Spring (accessed 14 July 2020); Abdallhadi Alijla, 'Women and the Arab Spring: A Dream Turned Nightmare', *Open Democracy*, 20 March 2015, https://www.opendemocracy.net/en/north-africa-weat-asia/women-and-arab-spring-dream-turned-nightmare (accessed 14 July 2020); Shazia Arshad, 'The Arab Spring, What Did It Do for Women', *Middle East Monitor,* 24 January 2014, https://middleeastmonitor.com/20140124-the-arab-spring-what-did-it-do-for-women (accessed 14 July 2020); Haleh Easfandiari and Kendra Heideman, 'The Role and Status of Women after the Uprisings', IEMed, Mediterranean Yearbook 2015, 303–8. In a collection of short essays *Five Years after the Arab Spring: What's Next for Women in the Arab World*, published by the Woodrow Wilson International Centers for Scholars in 2016, contributors generally saw little progress, although a few remained optimistic about the future.

8 See, for example, 'Women have Emerged as Key Players in the Arab Spring', *The Guardian,* 22 April 2011, https://www.theguardian.com/world/2011/april/22/women-arab-spring (accessed 15 July 2020).

9 Franz Fanon, *A Dying Colonialism* (London: Writers and Readers, 1965).

10 Max Bearak, 'Women of Sudan—"Suppressed by Any Means"—Are Protesting for Equal Rights in Post-Bashir Era', *The Washington Post*, 26 April 2019, https://www.washingtonpost.com/world/africa/women-of-sudan--suppressed

-by-any-means--are-protesting-for-equal-rights-in-the-post-bashir-era/2019/04/26/917a1f0a-6133-11e9-bf24-db4b9fb62aa2_story.html?utm_term=.f460bf858418 (accessed 27 June 2019).

11 Shadi Hamid, 'The Massacre That Ended the Arab Spring', *The Atlantic*, 14 August 2017, https://www.theatlantic.com/international/archive/2017/08/arab-spring-rabaa-massacre/536847/ (accessed 26 June 2019).

12 For good analyses of the military's role in the economy, Yezid Sayegh, *Owners of the Republic: Anatomy of Egypt's Political Economy* (Washington, DC: Carnegie Endowment for International Peace); Zeinab Abdul-Magd, *Militarizing the Nation: The Army, Business, and Revolution in Egypt* (New York: Columbia University Press, 2016); Yazid Sayigh, 'Above the State: The Officers' Republic in Egypt', Carnegie Middle East Center, 1 August 2012, http://carnegie-mec.org/2012/08/01/above-state-officers-republic-in-egypt-pub-48972 (accessed 20 June 2019); Robert Springborg, *Egypt* (Cambridge: Polity Press, 2018); and Marina Ottaway, 'Al-Sisi's Egypt: The Military Moves on the Economy', Wilson Center Middle East Program, Summer 2015, https://www.wilsoncenter.org/publication/al-sisis-egypt-the-military-moves-the-economy (accessed 20 June 2019).

13 Carrie Rosefsky Wickham, *The Moslem Brotherhood: The Evolution of an Islamist Movement* (Princeton: Princeton University Press, 2013).

14 The problem of the organizational weakness of political parties is explored in Marina Ottaway and Amr Hamzawy, eds, *Getting to Pluralism: Political Actors in the Arab World* (Carnegie Endowment for International Peace, 2012).

References

Abdul-Magd, Zeinab. *Militarizing the Nation: The Army, Business, and Revolution in Egypt*. New York: Columbia University Press, 2016.
Alijla, Abdallhadi. 'Women and the Arab Spring: A Dream Turned Nightmare'. *Open Democracy*, 20 March 2015.
Alsharif, Asma and Yasmine Saleh. 'The Real Force behind Egypt's "revolution of the state"'. *Reuters Special Report*, 10 December 2013.
Arshad, Shazia. 'The Arab Spring, What Did It Do for Women'. *Middle East Monitor*, 24 January 2014.
Bearak, Max. 'Women of Sudan—"Suppressed by Any Means"—Are Protesting for Equal Rights in Post-Bashir Era'. *The Washington Post*, 26 April 2019.
Easfandiari, Haleh and Kendra Heideman, 'The Role and Status of Women after the Uprisings'. IEMed, Mediterranean Yearbook 2015.
Fanon, Franz. *A Dying Colonialism*. London: Writers and Readers, 1965.
Giglio, Mike. 'How Wael Ghonim Sparked Egypt's Uprising'. *Newsweek*, 13 February 2011.
Hamid, Shadi. 'The Massacre That Ended the Arab Spring'. *The Atlantic*, 14 August 2017.
Hendawi, Hamza. 'Dispute between Morsi, Military Led to Coup'. *Associated Press*, 18 July 2013.

Karman, Tawakkol. 'Women and the Arab Spring'. *Un Chronicle*, December 2016.
Netterstrøm, Kasper Ly. 'The Tunisian General Labor Union and the Advent of Democracy'. *The Middle East Journal* 70, no. 3 (2016): 383–98.
Ottaway, Marina. 'Al-Sisi's Egypt: The Military Moves on the Economy'. Wilson Center Middle East Program, Summer 2015.
Ottaway, Marina and Amr Hamzawy, eds. *Getting to Pluralism: Political Actors in the Arab World*. Carnegie Endowment for International Peace, 2012.
Ottaway, Marina and David Ottaway. *A Tale of Four Worlds: The Arab Region after the Uprisings*. London: Hurst Publishers, 2019.
Sayigh, Yazid. 'Above the State: The Officers' Republic in Egypt'. Carnegie Middle East Center, 1 August 2012.
Sayigh, Yazid. *Owners of the Republic: Anatomy of Egypt's Political Economy*. Washington, DC: Carnegie Endowment for International Peace.
Springborg, Robert. *Egypt*. Cambridge: Polity Press, 2018.
Vargas, Jose Antonio. 'Spring Awakening: How an Egyptian Revolution Began on Facebook'. *New York Times*, 17 February 2012.

4

'Maidans' and movements

Legacies, innovations and contention in independent Ukraine

Olga Onuch

Introduction

What happens when long-established rituals of contention are altered or replaced? Scholars agree that particularly significant past mobilizations are not only a source of inspiration for contemporary episodes but also provide the foundations and boundaries for future action.[1] This can include the mimicking, adaptation and routinization of the: repertoires (marches or occupations), grievances and claims (civic rights based or materialist, nationalist, or socialist) and sites of the protests. But what happens when activists are unable or unwilling to follow a tried-and-tested protest playbook? How does this affect their ability to control the crowd, the protests and their outcome?

Contemporary Ukraine, once thought to be a country where activism struggled to flourish,[2] is now a poster child for studying contentious politics. Ukrainians' impressive capacity to repeatedly stage mass protests, called *Maidans*,[3] that stop rulers from sliding the country back into authoritarianism has garnered a great deal of attention.[4] But few studies have focused on the internal dynamics of activism, and even fewer have managed to connect past protest to more recent waves. This omission has hampered our ability to understand why in 2013/2014, during the EuroMaidan mass mobilization, for first time in contemporary history, the protest playbook included violent repertoires. This unexpected 'turn to violence' took seasoned observers of Ukrainian contention by surprise, not least because, from the 1960s onwards, most Ukrainian activists ritualistically employed innovative cultural repertoires and relied solely on nonviolent protest tactics. Employing peaceful protest tactics was not only part of the ethos of Ukrainian activism, past research[5] also shows that leaders understood that violent repertoires were correlated with protest failure, societal polarization,[6] and would likely lead to higher rates of repression and state violence.[7] Unexpectedly, in 2013/2014, experienced activist leaders began to 'lose control of the crowd,' and for the first time violent direct action was a feature (albeit not the main feature[8]) of mass mobilization in democratic Ukraine. What can help us understand this shift?

Informal, yet commonly accepted, explanations rely on the logic that President Viktor Yanukovych's (2010–14) repressive tactics coupled with the presence and participation of Radical Right Wing (RRW) social movement organizations (SMOs) and an uneven gender balance that favoured male protesters resulted in the unprecedented turn to violent repertoires. But while these may be important factors, these alone are unsatisfactory explanations – for two reasons. First, during several past waves of mass mobilization, activists also faced extreme repression and state violence. Second, not only did RRW parties and organizations represent only a tiny minority of the participants in 2014,[9] they also represented small minorities of participants in past mobilizations, and the gender balance among the protesters or gendered tactics (like young women holding flowers in front of militia) was no different from past events. And thus, if regime repression, the participation of RRW SMOs and higher rate of male participants in the protests were not *alone* enough to push protesters to use violence in the past, why would it be enough in 2013/2014?

To explore this 'turn to violence' this chapter compares three historical mass mobilizations (or 'Maidans') in Ukraine to the case of the EuroMaidan. The following analysis helps us understand how internal (inter-movement) practices can alter not only the mobilization process but also the outcome. First, I present a theoretical framework. In three sections that follow I unpack patterns in the mobilizational processes of three historical 'Maidans': The Revolution on the Granite (1990), The Ukraine without Kuchma protests (2000–01) and The 'Orange Revolution' (2004). To this end, I identify patterns of a Ukrainian protest playbook, comparing how these were reproduced in the past and yet differed significantly during the EuroMaidan.[10] In a fourth section, and in comparative perspective with these three events, I demonstrate how EuroMaidan mobilization represents a significant break with past patterns of mobilization in Ukraine. I propose that the ability of activists to form cross-sectoral coalitions and develop coordination strategies (including pooling of resources and intergenerational learning) gives activist leaders control over the spread of information, which in turn increases their ability to manage 'the crowd', It is argued that during the EuroMaidan not only were the first two variables missing, the informational context also changed significantly and leaders struggled to adapt. For a divided opposition, social media, initially seen as a *panacea* for mobilization, became their *Achilles* heel.

Patterns of Past Contention in Ukraine

Ukraine has had a long history of contention, and protest waves have repeatedly followed a particular pattern of five rituals of mobilization.

1) As *per* Tilly's (1993a) expectation about the reproduction of protest repertoires over time, Ukraine can be considered a poster child (until 2014). Post–Second World War mobilization retained a calculated, cultivated and even ritualistic use of *cultural and nonviolent repertoires*. From Soviet dissidents (1970s–1980s), to independence (1990s), and pro-democracy activists (2000s), the hard core of protest leaders was drawn from the *cultural sphere* (artists, writers, journalists and musicians).[11] The use of creative nonviolent tactics was another calculated choice. Hunger strikes, peaceful demos at sites of commemoration (e.g.: at Shevchenko[12] monuments), poetry readings, quiet processions, work stoppages and even self-emulations were the repertoires of choice in the face of mass repression by the Soviet regime. For observers, these 'cultural choices' were key to the success of Ukrainian activism, where there were more dissidents per capita than elsewhere in the Soviet Union. But this required *discipline, coordination* and a *united master frame* and was made possible through the next four protest practices.

2) In line with research on the role of social networks[13] and specifically the importance of combining weak and strong ties[14] in successful mobilization, leaders of various protest waves in Ukraine were particularly apt at making and maintaining *cross-sector and cross-cleavage coalitions*. For instance, in the 1960s and 1970s the *Shistdesyatnyky* (Sixtiers, a cultural dissident group) were able to draw members of different ethnic, linguistic and religious backgrounds across Ukraine – and unite them using universalist human-rights claims and grievances. Their engagement, built on cross-cutting networks, facilitated cooperation between 'critical' communist party members, shipyard workers in Odessa and Mykolaiv, miners in the industrial east of the country and union bosses.[15] Reproducing and maintaining these network ties and coalitions over time did not only strengthen the movements, it fostered structural opportunities for cooperation and coordination as the leaders knew, and had high levels of trust in, each other.

3) During each protest wave network ties were reactivated and *formal and informal agreements were struck by different SMO leaders*, ensuring clear lines of *cooperation and coordination* of activists across sectors, ideological positions and even regions in Ukraine. When necessary, this coordination also involved 'falling in line' – behind one political leader or one 'brand' in order to present a united front.

4) In line with resource mobilization theory,[16] coalition building and coordination made it possible for activist leaders to *pool resources*, be it financial, material, technical/informational or generational 'knowhow'. *Intergenerational* training was specifically important in strengthening younger activists' capacity to mobilize, avoid repression and maintain order among novice protesters.

5) Finally, corresponding to the expectations of,[17] the earlier four factors facilitated *control over the dissemination of information and the channels through which it travelled*. Formalized coordination and the pooling of resources enabled swift *communication of a unified master frame* throughout vast diverse networks simultaneously. In turn, a clear and consistent chain of communication increased activists' *capacity to control the message, the repertoires and the 'crowd'*. Ordinary citizens who joined the protests knew (or could easily find out) who its leaders were, where to turn for trusted information, and were reassured by a united stance.

By tracing these factors historically and in comparative perspective, I am able to elucidate how and which rituals of contention were reproduced over time (1990–2004) yet broke down in 2013/2014.

Revolution on the Granite: Developing the Ukrainian protest playbook

The 'Revolution on the Granite' (RotG) was the first *Maidan* and was immensely significant in creating a legacy of contention in independent Ukraine. The protest wave, also referred to as the 'Students Hunger Strike', took place between 2 and 17 October 1990, and it set a precedent that the creation of *cross-cleavage/cross-sector coalitions* and their unwavering public unity, coupled with the *use of cultural nonviolent repertoires*, were a recipe for success.

In the midst of a wave of mobilizations across the Eastern Bloc (1986–1991) Ukrainian activists – many recovering from imprisonment – were coordinating various pro-democracy activities. Although a new Ukrainian SSR Parliament was elected in March 1990 – the opposition was unsatisfied with the outcome, whereby 331 seats in the Parliament went to the Communist Party. In the context of the velvet revolutions, this result was surprising, and foul play was suspected. To quell opposition, on 16 July 1990 the Parliament made a pre-emptive declaration of State Sovereignty of Ukraine.[18] This did not satisfy opposition groups and the protest events that followed brought together a broad coalition of actors.

Rukh, the most active SMO of the period, launched a fresh wave of protests on 16 September 1990. By 30 September an estimated 100,000 ordinary citizens joined the dissident led marches in Kyiv and Lviv.[19] As students returned to their universities and reconnected with their networks, they launched local strikes. Simultaneously, labour union leaders – who staged a series of strikes earlier in the year – coordinated with the cross-partisan opposition in parliament and organized a national strike, during which they made public statements supporting *Rukh* and student protest actions. On 2 October, *Rukh* again led a 100,000-strong rally in Kyiv.[20] Students from Lviv, Kyiv and Kharkiv travelled to the capital to join the rallies; 150–200 students set up a camp on the then-called 'October Revolution Square' (*Ploshcha Zhovtnevoyi revolyutsii*, now called Independence Square *or Maidan Nezalezhnosty*), that evening. With this action the students declared the launch of the all-Ukrainian 'Student Hunger Strike'.

Cooperation, coordination and coalition

The occupation of the square was highly symbolic as it reclaimed a space associated with the violent overthrow of a regime employing nonviolent tactics. The students, dissident and opposition-party supporters took turns making speeches, reciting poetry and singing songs from a small stage. While the core of the protest was small – 150 to 200 students on hunger strike and an estimated 2000 rank-and-file participants[21] – it was periodically joined by larger groups of ordinary citizens during Sunday afternoon gatherings called *viches*[22] and after work during the week.[23] The students, referencing a list of demands made by striking miners earlier that year, composed a list of their own demands. On 17 October the Parliament, facing internal pressures and the threat of a national strike, published a response to the students agreeing to most of their demands.[24]

The 'Revolution on the Granite' reflected the coming together of vastly different networks, including: established dissidents, opposition-party MPs entrenched in the Communist System, miners in the east and south of the country, Kyiv based workers, students and ordinary citizens. These groups' coordinated cooperation, although not bound by a written agreement, facilitated diverse actors to pool their resources. Unexpected by the regime, their unity was their greatest strength – as the repression of one element was seen as an attack on all.

Intergenerational pooling of resources

The intergenerational pooling of resources was particularly important for the RotG. While the students could offer to mobilize university youth, dissident leaders offered access to an all-Ukrainian network that would help channel information throughout the country. Over years of struggle and imprisonment (1970s and 1980s) dissidents developed strong network ties with leaders of workers' unions.[25] These pre-existing ties made it easier for workers to join and support the actions. Through public statements of their solidarity with the student hunger strike, workers – like those of the Arsenal Plant in Kyiv[26] – helped legitimize the protest in the Soviet system. These acts of solidarity made it difficult for Soviet leaders to discount student protests especially, when workers – the central heroes of communism – were siding with them.[27]

These were coordinated acts and presented a multidimensional threat to the regime. Highly visible public occupations by sympathetic, attractive and peaceful students (singing songs and reciting poetry), mass work stoppages and strikes by workers at a time of economic unease, a coordinated political opposition in parliament, coupled with Moscow's own disintegration, quickly resulted in political defections at the top, making governing the Ukrainian SSR nearly impossible.[28] This coming together of diverse cross-sectoral networks placed pressure on the Soviet regime in Ukraine from all angles. Nonetheless, it was the ability of these diverse actors to fall in line around a united master narrative that enabled them to control the trajectory of contention.

Control over informational channel and capacity to control the 'crowd'

Older experienced activists (with personal experience of repression/imprisonment) as well as eager youth (many disappointed with older generations' lack of success) understood the need to remain humble in their interactions.[29] Older generation leaders not only advised how demands should be composed but also amplified the students' claims. Established dissidents took on student and worker claims as their own, presenting a united front when making public speeches.[30] Similarly, in 1991 the students were keen to take on-board the recommendations of older cultural leaders who they respected immensely. Together they employed personal ties to lobby opposition-party MPs sympathetic to their cause.[31] Once on-board, opposition MPs used their position to amplify the protest master narrative at formal political proceedings. Repetition and amplification of claims throughout diverse cross-sectoral networks built momentum around the movement and allowed organizers to control the spread of information about the protests and their aims

This cross-cleavage coalition was at times an uneasy one. While united by a common enemy the leaders found themselves at the crossroads of three different ideological strands. The ideological differences existed not only between the different networks but also within them.[32] But their ability to fall in line (following negotiations and deliberation) was impressive. Even the most extreme disagreements within their groups never resulted in public disparaging of each other or the abandonment of cooperation and came to light only in the movement's aftermath.[33] The activists never lost control of the master narrative – presenting a united front in the public sphere.[34]

And while these protests saw a higher proportion of male participants, the involvement of right-wing organizations, and faced serious repression, the leaders of RotG developed a playbook of peaceful Ukrainian contention detailing what to do (coordinated and sustained nonviolent protest actions) and how to do it (through formation of broad coalitions of actors, pooling their resources and coordinating around one master narrative), setting a precedent for a pathway to protest success in independent Ukraine.

Ukraine without Kuchma: Failures in the application of the protest playbook

Following an initial period of democratization, the second half of the 1990s was a period of significant democratic backsliding in Ukraine. President Leonid Kuchma (1994–2004) eliminated political opponents and sought to control any activists, journalists and cultural figures who opposed him. His administration produced daily *temnyky* (dark notes) detailing 'accepted' news. Journalists who did not obey risked intimidation, imprisonment and even death.[35] Journalists and cultural figures – fought back against this *Kuchmism* – by reproducing rituals of past contention. Alas, few could imagine how far Kuchma would go in his repression of opposition.

Cooperation, coordination and coalition

The final trigger of mobilization came in 2000 with the disappearance (16 September), then surfacing of the beheaded corpse (3 November), of Heorhiy Gongadze. The death of Gongadze, an investigative journalist highly critical of the president and his regime, sparked Ukraine's next significant mass protest. On 28 November, Oleksandr Moroz – Socialist Party Leader, publicized tapes[36] implicating Kuchma in Gongadze's murder.[37] Former RotG leaders distributed transcripts of the recordings on the *Maidan Inform* website,[38] and, together with journalists, activists, and opposition politicians, they began to mobilize against Kuchma.[39]

Coordination was hampered by the fact that two separate *tusovky* (cliques) were organizing separately. It is not clear from activist interviews if they knew of each other's activities and purposefully organized separately, or if this was the result of their reliance on personalistic network ties.[40] In hindsight, for those who participated in the events,[41] it is clear that coordinating sooner could have increased the likelihood of success of their mobilization. Following in the footsteps of RotG leaders, the two groups attempted to expand their network as broadly as possible. Volodymyr Chemerys, a founding member of the dissident era Helsinki Human Rights Union in Ukraine, and Yuriy Lutsenko, a student leader of the RotG, were the de facto leaders.[42] But, not only were the groups divided in their membership, like in the case of their predecessors they were also divided along ideological lines. Participants[43] argue that these multilayered divisions set the protests up for failure. While government insiders reported that this made the opposition look weak, opening it up to external provocations.

This protest wave, or the second 'Maidan', was called 'Ukraine without Kuchma' (*Ukraiina Bez Kuchmy*, UBK) and took place between November 2000 and March 2001. The first wave of actions took place between 15 and 27 December and replicated the RotG playbook. Activists chose the same site for the protests – the *Maidan Nezalezhnosty* – where they erected a small tent-city and a stage.[44] Recalling the successes of RotG – Kuchma ordered the clearing of the tent city. This act of repression highlighted, to the two anti-Kuchma groups, that divisions weakened their cause and they began coordinating their actions and pooling their resources.[45]

Pooling of resources and intergenerational training

Beginning 14 January 2001, the groups commenced a *coordinated* second wave of UBK protests. Leaders attempted to pool their resources to strengthen the mobilization.[46] In interviews leaders noted that they understood that while students and youth groups had the resource of time – likely to result in larger numbers of participants in the streets – political parties had financial resources which could pay for a new tent city and stage. To raise youth turnout and re-create the atmosphere of the RotG, live concerts by pop stars were scheduled, and food distribution points were set up.[47] Former dissidents relied on their tried-and-tested protest pamphlets (e.g.: on how to spot a provocateur), and journalists systematically spread information through reliable and uncompromised channels.[48]

Control over informational channel and capacity to control the 'crowd': A collapse of the coalition

Even though the groups coalesced around an anti-Kuchma master narrative, personal disagreements divided the leadership and some even sided with the regime.⁴⁹ This made it difficult for activists to control the crowd – specifically with the involvement of numerous inexperienced youth. Leaders noted in interviews that the they did not foresee the need to coordinate their own security to better control radically minded participants.

To this end, informants also explained that they were split on the involvement of right-wing groups. When small acts of vandalism were reported, they were taken as a signal of poor protester discipline and, thus, a weakness of its leadership.⁵⁰ With this major departure from the RotG playbook, the regime – sensing weakness – ordered the first mass repressions and arrest of protesters on 1 March 2001.

With trust being compromised, the groups decided to organize two separate protest events for 8/9 March 2001: one at the Shevchenko monument and the other outside the Presidential Administration. To unsympathetic eyes both events looked small and inconsequential. Activists admitted in interviews that this division of activities (even if united on claims) presented an image of disorganized campaigns.⁵¹ It is believed that the Kuchma regime and police used this disorganization to infiltrate the movement with provocateurs who disseminated conflicting information and encouraged vandalism.⁵² On 9 March, 300 people were arrested with some activists receiving sentences of up to five years in prison, many others were beaten and seriously injured by police.⁵³ But lessons were learned.

Again, neither the willingness of the regime to use repression nor the presence of right-wing groups or gendered repertoires played a key role in the unravelling of this protest wave. Instead, activists understood that that internal conflicts, made public by the organization of competing events, exposed the weaknesses of the movement and compromised their ability to control the spread of misinformation and protest the crowd itself.⁵⁴ This weakness was not only exploited by a repressive regime but also turned away potential supporters. The organizers knew that they would have to return to the rituals of RotG playbook if they were to succeed. Even if failing in important ways, UBK still strengthened key networks and intergenerational ties – laying the groundwork for future cooperation. There was a common enemy and goal – they would seek to put an end to *Kuchmism*.

Orange Revolution: Return to broad coalitions and coordination

The so-called Orange Revolution (OR) was in many ways a repeat of previous 'Maidans' but also involved a great deal of intergenerational learning from UBK mistakes. Leaders noted in interviews that they understood the necessity to avoid provocation and employ only nonviolent repertoires, but also that they understood that in order to do so they would need to foster strong coalitions, coordinate their actions and employ one united master narrative.[55]

Cooperation and coordination

The OR's mobilization process unfolded over six overlapping stages. During the first stage, September 2003 to February 2004, activists expanded their SMO networks (both within and outside the country), frequently attending conferences where they nurtured cross-sectoral alliances.[56] During the second stage, February to April 2004, activists composed blueprints, detailing the when and how of the mobilization process. Weary of the division that plagued political opposition in 2001 and, thus, not knowing if they could rely on opposition-party resources, activists pre-emptively began organizing meetings with public figures and business elite to attract independent financial and in-kind resources in order to strengthen their position.

Pooling of resources and intergenerational training

Similar to past 'Maidans' older generation activists reached out to youth networks and actively incorporated them in the third stage (April to August) of mobilization. But this outreach was systematic, coordinated and rigorous. Activists applied for grants (from local and foreign NGOs) in order to run trainings across all of Ukraine. Although much has been assumed about the imposition of foreign actors' and knowhow, the author's own assessment of training documents was that they were taken directly from the RotG playbook; pamphlets made in 1990 and 2001 were reprinted for this purpose.[57] Experienced activists (with two 'Maidans' under their belt) were directly involved in the trainings. In interviews, leaders recalled that they understood that in order to be able to control the protest 'crowd' they needed to have a ready cohort of trained youth who could guide and manage the protesters from within.

Between September and November 2004, this training phase was followed by, an expansive information dissemination campaign focused on one master narrative targeting *Kuchmizm*. Like in 1991, when appearing publicly, printing pamphlets or making stickers, activists asked: 'what is *Kuchmizm?*'. Each time they gave the same answer: 'corruption, repression, and poor quality of life . . .', pointing out that Kuchma's chosen successor Viktor Yanukovych was the embodiment of this. This coordinated campaign was so successful that it provoked the regime to threaten, imprison and even beat up activist leaders.[58]

Yet, having learned from past mistakes, the repression did *not* divide the opposition and it provoked opposition-party leaders to formally cooperate with activists and on 15 November they signed a plan of action.[59] Together they agreed to back one politician (Viktor Yushchenko) in the elections, and to fully coordinate all protest activities and pool their resources. At the same time, the agreement gave activist enough autonomy to not compromise their legitimacy in the eyes of ordinary Ukrainians. Finally, already united around the negative master frame – against *Kuchmism* – they also agreed to publicly support the *Yushchenko Tak!* (or Yushchenko Yes!) slogan. The stage was set, the rank and file trained, coordination formalized and united message agreed upon – all the activists and opposition-party leaders had to do was wait for the expected fraud to occur.

Control over informational channels and capacity to control the 'crowd'

On 21 November, the day of the second round of the presidential election the fraud was widespread (invisible ink, armed thugs stealing ballot boxes, carrousel voting, ballot box stuffing and over 100 per cent turnout were reported across the country.[60] And while exit polls overwhelmingly predicted that Yushchenko would win, the Central Electoral Commission (CEC) announced Yanukovych the winner. The coordinated protest action that followed was impeccable. Within minutes of the announcement various opposition-party leaders flooded the airwaves with identical slogans. Down with *Kuchmizm!* and *Yushchenko Tak!* were repeated over and again by different actors representing different political and ideological cleavages. They acknowledged one leader and fell in line behind one protest brand. Simultaneously, activists led 100,000 university students from their campuses, through the streets of the Kyiv, to the *Maidan Nezalezhnosty* shouting, 'Kyiv Stavay! [Kyiv Wake-up/Stand-up!]'.[61] Youth and activists from across the country boarded pre-booked buses and trains headed for the capital.[62] By dawn the *Maidan Nezalezhnosty* was overflowing. In the 72-hour period that followed 'ordinary' Ukrainians also joined in the protests en masse.

After this point (21 November to 10 December 2004), the phenomenon was no longer one of activist and opposition mobilization, but rather a mass mobilization with an estimated 1.5–2 million ordinary citizens participating. Controlling information channels and the protest 'crowd' would prove to be particularly important. But activists and opposition politicians remained united in their management of the masses in the streets. This unity not only motivated more 'ordinary' citizens to join in, seeing that the protests were well managed and peaceful, but also put pressure on the regime.

Reproducing the RotG playbook, activists erected a large stage and a tent city on the square. Speeches from the stage repeated the same slogans and were consistent.[63] Representatives of different ideological groups, sectors and cleavages all took to the stage in a show of unity. The recitals, performances and speeches were all broadcast live on television – on oligarch Petro Proshenko's TV channel. Activists were able to convince journalists to also start broadcasting live from the protest site – losing control over channels of information was a devastating blow for the regime. They could no longer paint the activist as terrorists or ignore the protest altogether.

The youth rank and file, having gone through months of training, were prepared and militantly devoted to the cause, having signed agreements committing themselves to nonviolent repertoires and sobriety on the protest site.[64] Activists who belonged to 'right wing' organizations, previously seen as a potential weakness during the UBK, were recruited to take on the role of security of the Maidan.[65] Young women and grandmothers, on the other hand, were placed in front of the barricades 'keeping the young men in check' and making repression unthinkable.[66] These 'crowd control' mechanisms were pre-arranged with the help of former dissidents and RotG and UBK activists, and movement discipline was key.[67]

The regime was outmanoeuvred by a disciplined united front, and Kuchma was unable to use the divide-and rule-approach that served him in 2001.[68] A well-trained youth contingent knew how to avoid violence, while radically minded activists were given a valued role in the protection of the protesters. Thus, there was little room for escalation and military personnel could not stomach using violence against peaceful singing youth. What followed were a series of major public defections among key players in the state media, judiciary, CEC, police and secrete services.[69] The crowd's peaceful presence forced negotiations, resulting in an overturning of the results. Nonetheless, the activists stayed in the streets until the victory of Yushchenko was formally confirmed.

The Kuchma regime used targeted violence and imprisoned activists but by the time the protesters were in the streets there were so many of them, the regime backed off from wholesale violence while still brutalizing individual activist leaders. Right wingers, even if few in number, were incorporated into the fold of the organizing committee and were given a key role to play, and while young women were used as a shield between the 'crowd' and the militia, men still participated in the protests at higher rates. And so, yet again, it was the coordination of a broad cross-sectoral coalition, intergenerational training coupled with the ability to maintain and disseminate a unified master narrative that once again proved to be the best protest playbook.

Yet, five years later Ukraine's 'revolutionary' hero Yushchenko lost the presidency to Yanukovych in 2009/2010. This was a blow to activists, and some started to openly doubt the use of nonviolent tactics five years earlier.[70] The period that followed saw significant democratic backsliding. Within one year Ukraine was once again listed as 'partially free' – with a significant decline in both political right and civil liberties.[71] Prime Minister Mykola Azarov enacted a series of laws (on education, taxes and language) that were perceived to be anti-democratic. Simultaneously, the country saw economic decline (with GDP contracting by 6 per cent between 2010 and 2014). These events resulted in a series of protests: The Language 'Maidan', The Campaign to Stop the Degradation of Education, the Tax 'Maidan' and the Car 'Maidan',.[72] The final straw came on 21 November 2013, when it was announced that Ukraine would not sign the Free Trade and Association Agreements with the EU – and so began the European 'Maidan' or simply EuroMaidan.

The EuroMaidan: Protest playbook abandoned

In reaction to the announcement, several small groups of activists and journalists began taking steps to launch a protest action. The main issue was not that the spark came to soon – they were already organizing protests against the regime for three years – it was that the activist were not ready to cooperate. Ideological and personal differences divided them. Coalition building and coordination take not only time, but also goodwill. Specifically, opposition politicians were not forgiven for their attempts to co-opt activists in 2004 and RRW organizations did not see eye to eye with liberal SMOs and their leaders. Moreover, in the period since 2004, there was also little training of youth. And, thus, the younger generations were not connected to the old guard in the same ways as in the past. They may have known of each other but did not know each other personally. Where ties did exist, they were weaker than ever before. Youth felt very disconnected with older generations and explained in interviews that older generations did do enough to change the regime.[73] Similarly, key journalists/activists credited with starting the protests publicly stated their belief that there was no 'real' history of activism and/or civil society in Ukraine, firmly believing that they were inventing mobilization practices anew.[74] And thus, while there were multiple actors in the mix, they were all preparing separately with different visions in mind.

Finally, in 2013, the informational context had completely changed. Social media and information and communication technology (ICT) proliferation made it possible for anyone post anything on a blog, streaming or social media site and become an instant citizen journalist, meaning that thousands of new actors joined the process and there was no way to control them. And in the weeks that followed, while journalists, activists and opposition politicians also attempted to use ICTs to their advantage, they hugely underestimated how hard it would be to control these channels of information, and what effect that would have on their ability to control the protest crowd.

Divided, lacking initial coordination and faced with the double challenge of new informational context and heightened regime repression, the activist leaders lost control of the 'crowd'. The aforementioned factors, and not a different gender balance, the presence of RRW groups, made mobilization and coordination challenging and were on display from the very first night of the protests.

Lack of coordination and coalition building from the beginning

The now much popularized 'origin story' of the EuroMaidan is that it all began with one Facebook post, by one journalist, around which others quickly coordinated.[75] Thus, the first step in understanding what went wrong is to understand that this 'origin story' is not *entirely* correct. Detailed process tracing of post activity and communication by activists and journalists shows that on 21 November 2013, *'not one but hundreds*[76] of activists and journalists . . . took to their Livejournal blogs, Facebook, and VKontakte pages and Twitter feeds' calling for protest action.[77] Calls for people to take to the streets began at approximately 19:00, when Yuriy Andreyev called for activists and journalists to head to the *Maidan* at 22:00. Other messages followed. My own analysis of these initial posts shows that although the internet allowed for the speedy travel of *reactions* to the regime's announcement these messages were uncoordinated.[78] The personalization of the 'call to action' (it is often believed journalist Mustafa Nayem was responsible) also highlights the lack of initial coordination at the SMO level. It represents a departure from past practices whereby activists previously used a collective 'we' to mobilize. Much of these initial patterns can be linked to the way that social media work. Connectivity on the internet is assumed, but yet, much of our activity online is individual (if not even lonely).

And even though the internet saw hundreds of posts calling people to action, few people actually showed up to the square on that first night. Those who *did* come to the *Maidan* that first night were *already* known activists, journalists and university professors[79] and many lament that – unlike in 1991, 2001 or 2004 when activists and journalist first met in small groups to set up coordination strategies and identify possible allies and coalition partners – this time, they skipped this initial step and went straight to the Maidan without a strategy, without knowing who would show up and without any clear leaders to turn to.

Low levels of pooling resources and intergenerational interaction

While the EuroMaidan has been described as a swift coming together, this is not what a detailed process tracing of the initial hours, days and weeks of the protests shows. Experienced activists recalled in interviews that coordination was difficult and there was a great deal of distrust between different opposition groups.[80] They also explained that it did not help that 'new' faces (who had little experience of protest organization), at least initially, avoided leaders of past protest events and 'did it on their own'.[81] The same, they argue, could be said for younger NGO workers and university students (who were teens and children in 2004) – they too did not a reach out to the 'older' generations of activists like Doniy, Chemerys, Vyatrovych, Kaskiv and Svystovych for advice.[82] Because these 'new' actors planned actions independently they hampered the attempts of more experienced activists to coordinate the protests. One long-time activist even dubbed this initial period as one of trying to 'reinvent the wheel'.[83]

On 24 November a diverse set of SMOs and opposition parties organized concurrent, but uncoordinated, marches across Ukraine with the largest, estimated at 200,000, taking place in Kyiv. Although they were able to share information with the speed of the internet, there was confusion among participants and observers. In Kyiv, competing march organizers set up different meeting points, two different marching routes and two different 'end points'. Students and activists went to the *Maidan Nezalezhnosty* and opposition politicians ended up on the *Yevropeyska Ploshcha* (European Square) some 900 meters away from the *Maidan*.[84] Replicating past protest playbook practices, a professional stage was erected by the politicians and two blocks down activists and students used the base of a large monument on the *Maidan* to host popular indie bands, poetry readings and dance parties. Older generation activists (like Viatrovych) came to help organize the protest and began running the stage. The different organizers kept these two separate protest sites going for one week – leaving the activists and students exposed to attack. Their initial inability to present a united front signalled to an increasingly authoritarian regime that the opposition was weak and divided.

Over the next seven days, even though students regularly joined the protests and ordinary Kyivites attended the meetings in the two squares after work, the protests were losing momentum. By all accounts the lack of coordination was likely to result in the dying-off of the protests in the week that followed. Yet, in a surprise move, on the eve of 30 November the regime sent in special-ops *Berkut* forces to clear the Maidan and an unprecedented beating of students and journalists took place. This was the event that *finally* forced a coordinated response from the opposition. By 1 December the protest swelled to approximately 800,000 in Kyiv with an estimated 2 million across the entire country. In this second phase, protesters also demanded the resignation of Yanukovych. But because of the initial lack of coordination the leaders of different opposition networks were *already* unable to control the crowd.

Low capacity to control the 'crowd' and no control over informational channels

Thanks to social media, information of the brutal beatings travelled quickly – but so did calls by RRW groups to take back the streets by force. Activists had no control over what was being shared online and by whom. More radically minded groups (although very small in number) held marches in Kyiv, came armed with batons and chains, and set up a barricade outside the Presidential Administration on 1 December. There was no system in place to control them, unlike in 2004; they had no key role to play in securing the Maidan. The regime revelled in this lack of coordination. There was no urgency to negotiate with the opposition, because it was clear that they were not in control. Moreover, they had photographic evidence of 'radical and violent protesters' which could be shared online to delegitimize the protests. And, thus, competing versions of the protesters, their aims and tactics were being disseminated to millions across Ukraine and beyond. To some, these were peaceful protesters demanding basic rights and unjustly beaten up. To others, these were violent radicals who deserved a strong police response. It did not matter that the second version was far from representative of the general protests.

Former leaders of key SMOs from 2004, other key activists and high-profile NGO workers saw their inability to control the crowed as a direct result of their lack of coordination.[85] They also saw that while small and insignificant, according to on-site survey data representing about 5 per cent of all protest participants,[86] the RRW willingness to use violence would only further weaken the movement leaving it exposed more repressions. Older generation activists reached out within their personal networks and set up an important new SMO *Hromadskyi sector* (Civic Sector). They also attempted to coordinate actions following the Ukrainian protest playbook – coordinating a new stage and bringing together politicians and activists and using creative tactics.[87]

The Civic Sector *(Hromadskyi Sektor)* SMO also embarked on the task of tracking and correcting disinformation and fake news posted in Ukraine and abroad.[88] They began writing daily news bulletins and making e-posters and e-pamphlets on what to bring to protest, how to spot a provocateur at a protest and why it is important to stick to peaceful nonviolent actions. These instruction guides relied on the information they had on hand from past protest events but had to be redesigned for online context – information was not enough; it had to be designed to go 'viral'.[89] They also tried gendered tactic of protest, to 'put the women upfront' with flowers and mirrors to pacify the militia.[90] Yet, as activists reported, no matter what steps they took next, to useful peaceful tactics and coordinate with opposition politicians (like by setting-up the *Rada Maidanu* [The Maidan Council]) – once immortalized in a tweet, the option to use violent repertoires remained from 1 December onwards.[91] As one experienced activist explained in private correspondence, 'what could we do? The Pandora's box was opened.'[92] They were keenly aware that they had already lost control of certain channels of communication and of some parts of the 'crowd.'

Not coordination but coexistence

Opposition politicians were also unable to fall behind one leader. They decided to always appear as a group of three: centrist *UDAR!* Party leader and former boxer Vitaliy Klitchko, liberal *Front for Change* party leader and former presidential candidate Arseniy Yatseniuk, and right-wing *Svoboda* Party leader Oleh Tyahnybok. Although this strategy was an attempt to demonstrate a united-front, it backfired – signalling to the regime that the opposition was more divided they would like to let on.[93] Regime insiders, who were more sympathetic to finding a negotiated resolution, made clear that it was difficult to know who was in charge and who they should negotiate with.[94] And although activists and politicians came together in the *Rada Maidanu* meetings, it was evident that this was not where the shots were called.[95] Some participants of these proceedings reported that they realized that the *Rada* was a way to appease youth and the more difficult to control activists.[96] These attempts to show a collective front did not result in coordination but only in a negotiated coexistence of diverse opposition actors. This practice made it difficult not only to control the crowd but also negotiate with and convincingly threaten the Regime.

A vicious and uncontrollable cycle of repression and violence

As the protests unfolded, it was also evident that the 'crowd', or at least a portion of it, was not listening to the *Rada*'s instructions. In the tent city encampment on the Maidan, militia-style *Sotnyi* groups were formed with the help of former Afghan war soldiers. They tasked themselves with the protection of the Maidan and held their own meetings of *Sotnya* leaders.[97] While some of these *Sotni* 'fell in line' with the *Rada*'s decisions, many groups took matters into their own hands – and coordinated their own activities especially when faced with further repression. These groups were not only uncontrollable, they were also easily confused with being RRW organizations – they wore balaclavas, military fatigue and helmets, and would soon perfect the production of Molotov cocktails. This is central to the framing of EuroMaidan story. Those left-wing, liberal and centre-right activists that were willing to use violent tactics were often mislabelled as RRW. The *en mass* use of violent repertoires, even if in retaliation to the regime, gave the impression that there were more RRW-ers in the square than there were and gave the regime an excuse to escalate.

On 16 January 2014, the parliament enacted the 'dictatorship' laws[98] and the regime escalated the violence and used live bullets for the first time against the protesters. In response the protesters threw rocks and devised improvised Molotov cocktails. Whist Civic Sector and other activist SMOs tried to maintain nonviolent and cultural repertoires they could not control the actions of a few individuals that were willing to engage in direct violent retaliation against the regime.⁹⁹ Photos and videos of small acts of violence went viral. Disinformation tactics often relied on half-truths, using some original footage of protesters throwing Molotov cocktails but branding all of them as RRW nationalists, and even manipulating and altering the images (like adding a Hitler poster behind the crowd).¹⁰⁰ It would have been difficult for a coordinated opposition to counter this disinformation – but for a competing and only co-existing one, it became impossible.

With an excuse that it needed to rid the capital of extremists, the regime continued to escalate its violent repression. In the week of 18–20 February, 100 civilians died at the hands of government snipers and militia.¹⁰¹ The *finale* of the EuroMaidan perfectly summed the lack of coordination and control over the crowd. One protester, Volodymyr Parasiuk, stormed the stage uninvited, grabbed the microphone and declared that there was no room for negotiation and that if necessary, he and his comrades would storm the Presidential Administration, no matter what the leaders told them.¹⁰² The politicians and activist leaders had to leave the stage as the crowd booed them. Unlike in 1991, 2001 and 2004, in 2014, no party, movement or leader had any real legitimacy.

Their initial inability to coordinate, form a cross-cleavage, cross-generational coalition, employ united message and control information channels left activists exposed to an extremely repressive regime. The internet, initially seen as a source that would facilitate their own speedy dissemination of information, became the movement's *Achilles* heel. With multiple actors, voices and versions of the truth shared simultaneously, activists could not control the image of the protests. Internal ideological disagreements and 'new generation's' hubris made it only possible for these diverse actors to co-exist in the Maidan and not control it or the crowd that stood upon in.

Conclusion

As the analysis we have discussed demonstrates, the five practices of the Ukrainian protest playbook were altered in 2013/2014. Unlike those who preceded them, EuroMaidan activists were unable to form cross-sectoral coalitions in order to coordinate protest activities. This was exponentially made worse by their inability, to at least initially, effectively employ intergenerational learning and pool their resources. Two of the main practices of old guard – to rely on creative and cultural repertoires while centralizing informational channels – were certainly more difficult to achieve in the context of 2013/2014. Unlike past generations of activists EuroMaidan generation were unable to fall in line behind one leader. Attempts at horizontal leadership were seen by some observers as inauthentic and a weakness by regime insiders. And it was a lack of initial coordination, coupled with inexperience, that led activists to rely on the internet. They, almost immediately, loss of control over informational channels. By the time opposition leaders did manage to cooperate, by forming the *Rada Maidanu* and Civic Sector, and appearing together during press conferences, the Pandora's box of viral images of RRW-ers and violent repertoires was already opened.

Finally, although social media was seen as a panacea for activist information and coordination, it was also used to spread disinformation. Leaders quickly lost the war when it came to branding their own protest. All of these factors put together meant that activists also lost the control of the 'crowd' both on the Maidan and in the country.

While observers fail to understand that the violence observed in Kyiv in 2013/2014 was not an example of 'a move to the right' nor that it can simply be explained by the regime's repression alone, they also failed to learn key lessons about the role of activist disunity, delay in coordination and loss of control over the dissemination of information. And, thus, these mistakes were repeated in other sectors of Ukrainian politics since.

Leading up to the 2019 presidential elections, then-President Petro Poroshenko also failed to understand that the uniting ethos of the opposition in 2014 was not based in right-wing or national rhetoric. His campaign's focus on 'Army, Language, and Faith' misunderstood what shaped the cross-class cross-cleavage coalition in 2013/2014. With the post-EuroMaidan leadership once again internally embattled and divided, the ill-conceived campaign only further pushed away the median voter, opening up space for a new populist leader that connected to Ukrainians on their level to emerge. And so 2019 saw the election of movie star, comedian and entertainment mogul Volodymyr Zelensky to the presidency and a complete collapse of Petro Poroshenko's vote who received less than a quarter of votes cast.

Notes

1 Doug McAdam, Sidney Tarrow and Charles Tilly, *Dynamics of Contention* (New York and London: Cambridge University Press, 2001); Charles Tilly, 'Social Movements as Historically Specific Clusters of Political Performances', *Berkeley Journal of Sociology* 38 (1993): 1–30.
2 See: Marc Morjé Howard, *The Weakness of Civil Society in Post-Communist Europe* (Cambridge: Cambridge University Press, 2003).
3 Because all of the major protests in Ukraine since 1991 have tended to take place on the 'Maidan Nezalezhnosty' or Independence Square in Kyiv, scholars, journalists and activists alike frequently refer to the protests as 'maidans' or 'squares'.
4 Mark Beissinger, 'The Semblance of Democratic Revolution: Coalitions in Ukraine's Orange Revolution', *American Political Science Review*, FirstView (2013): 1–19; Adam Meirowitz and Joshua A. Tucker, 'People Power or a

One-Shot Deal? A Dynamic Model of Protest', *American Journal of Political Science* 57, no. 2 (2013): 478–90; Olga Onuch, *Mapping Mass Mobilizations: Understanding Revolutionary Moments in Ukraine and Argentina* (London: Palgrave MacMillan, 2014a).

5   See: Onuch, *Mapping Mass Mobilizations*.

6   Erica Chenoweth and Maria J. Stephan, *Why Civil Resistance Works: The Strategic Logic of Nonviolent Conflict* (New York: Columbia University Press, 2011).

7   See: Sabine C. Carey, 'The Dynamic Relationship between Protest and Repression', *Political Research Quarterly* 59, no. 1 (2006): 1–11.

8   See Olga Onuch and Gwendolyn Sasse, 'Maidan in Movement: Protest Cycles, Diversity of Actors, and Violence', *Europe-Asia Studies* 68, no. 4 (2016): 556–87 for overview of the phases and cycles of contention and the estimated number of Radical Right Wing party and organization supporting protesters.

9   See Onuch and Sasse, 'Maidan in Movement'.

10 The empirical findings discussed here are based on the analysis of data collected during three periods of field research in Ukraine. The first (2005–10) includes the collection of interviews (98) and focus group (15) data covering the 2004 protests, past mobilizations and activism in Ukraine. The second, conducted on-site during the EuroMaidan, includes a protest survey, rapid on-site interviews and digital photos of slogans and posters. Finally, 68 interviews (with activists, journalists and politicians) and nine focus groups (with activists and 'ordinary' citizens) were collected throughout 2014/2015. Interviewees, where requested, have been anonymized to protect their identities. Process tracing methodology (Andrew Bennett, 'Process Tracing and Causal Inference', 2010. http://philsci-archive.pitt.edu/8872/; David Collier, 'Process Tracing: Introduction and Exercises', *Beta Version*, 22 September 2010) was employed by the author to comparatively analyse the data.

11 Onuch, *Mapping Mass Mobilizations*.

12 Taras Shevchenko (9 March 1814–10 March 1861) is considered the Bard of Ukraine.

13 McAdam, Tarrow and Tilly, *Dynamics of Contention*.

14 Roger V. Gould, 'Collective Action and Network Structure', *American Sociological Review* 58, no. 2 (1993): 182–96.

15 Onuch, *Mapping Mass Mobilizations*.

16 J. Craig Jenkins, 'Resource Mobilization Theory and the Study of Social Movements'. *Annual Review of Sociology* 9 (1983): 527–53.

17 Susanne Lohmann, 'The Dynamics of Informational Cascades', *World Politics* 47, no. 1 (1994): 42–101.

18 David R. Marples, *Ukraine under Perestroika: Ecology, Economics and the Workers' Revolt* (New York: Springer, 1991).

19 The Ukrainian Weekly, '100,000 in Kiev March to Protest Union Treaty', *The Ukrainian Weekly*, 7 October 1990, 40 edition.

20 Mary Mycio, 'Ukrainian SSR Government Bows to Students' Demands Maso Macr Agrees to Resign', *The Ukrainian Weekly*, 21 October 1990, 42 edition.
21 Mycio, 'Ukrainian SSR Government Bows to Students' Demands Maso Macr Agrees to Resign'.
22 *Viche* means a mass gathering of the population or mass rally. In Ukrainian Rus it is referred to as a 'People's Assembly' – the highest authority in some cities.
23 Interview, OD, student leader of Revolution on the Granite, 06 July 2008, Kyiv.
24 Verkhovna Rada Ukrayiny, 'Postanova Verkhovnoyi Rady Ukrayinskoyi RSR Pro Rozhlyad Vymoh Studentiv, Yaki Provodyat Holoduvannya V M. Kyyevi Z 2 Zhovtnya 1990 Roku № 402-XII'. 402-XII, 1990. Online Archive of Verkhovna Rada Ukrayiny.
25 Onuch, *Mapping Mass Mobilizations*.
26 See: Taras Kuzio and Andrew Wilson, *Ukraine: Perestroika to Independence* (Edmonton: CIUS Press, 1994).
27 Interview, Unnamed Former MP, 20 July 2009, Kyiv.
28 Interview, MS, activist, journalist and founder of Maidan Inform website, 30 July 2007, Kyiv.
29 Interview, VC, coordinator of Ukraine Without Kuchma Campaign, activist, National Deputy, 10 July 2008, Kyiv.
30 Interview, OD, National Deputy (unaffiliated) and student leader of Revolution on the Granite and the Last Barricade Movement, 6 July 2008. Kyiv.
31 Interview, Unnamed Former MP, 6 August 2008, Kyiv.
32 Author's private communication with Doniy, Kyrylenko, and Ivashchyshyn, at 3R Symposium in Natolin at College D'Europe, 28 February 2017.
33 Author's private communication with Doniy, Kyrylenko, and Ivashchyshyn, at 3R Symposium in Natolin at College D'Europe, 28 February 2017.
34 Author's private communication with Doniy, Kyrylenko, and Ivashchyshyn, at 3R Symposium in Natolin at College D'Europe, 28 February 2017.
35 Interview, Unnamed Channel 5 anchor, 8 August 2009, Kyiv.
36 Secretly recorded by Mykola Melnychenko, Kuchma's bodyguard.
37 'Ukrainian Transcripts of the Melnychenko Tapes', 2001. http://www.perehid.org.ua/look/25_11_2000.phtml.
38 MS, 30 July 2007.
39 MS, 30 July 2007.
40 VC, 10 July 2008.
41 VC, 10 July 2008; MS, 30 July 2007.
42 VC, 10 July 2008; MS, 30 July 2007.
43 VC, 10 July 2008; MS, 30 July 2007.

44 VC, 10 July 2008; MS, 30 July 2007; OD, 06 July 2008.
45 VC, 10 July 2008.
46 MS, 30 July 2007; VC, 10 July 2008; VV, 10 July 2007.
47 VC, 10 July 2008.
48 MS, 30 July 2007; VV, 10 July 2007.
49 VC, 10 July 2008.
50 Interview, Unnamed Kuchma Presidential Administration insider 3, 7 July 2008, Kyiv.
51 MS, 30 July 2007; OD, 06 July 2008.
52 VV, 10 July 2007.
53 "Maidan Website." 2002. *Maidan Website*. http://maidanua.org/static/news/1032796245.html; "Ukraine Without Kuchma." 2001. *Ukraine Without Kuchma*. http://www.bezkuchmi.narod.ru/.
54 VK, 19 April 2008.
55 VK, 19 April 2008.
56 Interview, YY, black *Pora* Activist, 16 April 2008, Kyiv.
57 Interview, OK, yellow Pora activist and journalist, 18 July 2007, Kyiv.
58 Interview, OK, yellow Pora activist and journalist, 18 July 2007, Kyiv.
59 Interview, YZ, yellow Pora and human rights activist, 9 July 2008, Kyiv.
60 2005. *Ukrain Presidential Election. 31 October, 21 November and 26 December 2004, OSCE/ODIHR Election Observation Mission Final Report*. Warsaw: Office for Democratic Institutions and Human Rights, OSCE.
61 Interview, YP, yellow Pora Kyiv activist, 3 August 2008, Kyiv.
62 Interview, TM, former student activist and sociologist, 18 August 2007, Kyiv.
63 Interview, Unnamed Yushchenko Presidential Campaign assistant-manager, 22 April 2007, Kyiv.
64 YY, 16 April 2008.
65 Interview, RR, Sprotyv activist and leader, security at Maidan, 28 April 2008, Lviv.
66 Tamara Martsynyuk, 16 April 2008.
67 Unnamed Yushchenko Presidential Campaign assistant-manager, 22 April 2007.
68 Unnamed Kuchma Presidential Administration insider 3, 7 July 2008.
69 Unnamed Channel 5 anchor, 8 August 2009.
70 Interview, Unnamed Activist Leader, 09 July 2010.
71 Freedom House, 'Ukraine in 2011: Freedom House Report', 2011. https://freedomhouse.org/report/freedom-world/2011/ukraine.
72 See: Anastasiya Zanuda, '"Podatkovyy" maydan: rik potomu Anastasiya Zanuda BBC Ukrayina 23 lystopada 2011', *BBC News Ukraine*, 23 November 2011. https://www.bbc.com/ukrainian/business/2011/11/111122_tax_maidan_one_year_az.shtml; Oleksandr Suprunyuk, 'Avtomaydan, Abo Rozvidka Boyem', 24 March 2011. http://maidan.org.ua/arch/arch2011/1300969540

.html; Avtomaydan, 'Avtomaydan 2012', 19 March 2012. http://chp.com.ua/all-news/item/16442-avtomaydan-2012; Maidan.org, 'Perelik Tem Forumu Osvita 2010/01', 2010. https://maidan.org.ua/arch/osvita/2010_01.html.

73 Olga Onuch, 'Social Networks and Social Media in Ukrainian "Euromaidan" Protests', *Washington Post* (blog), 2014b, 2 January 2014. http://www.washingtonpost.com/blogs/monkey-cage/wp/2014/01/02/social-networks-and-social-media-in-ukrainian-euromaidan-protests-2/.

74 Interview, Unnamed Journalist, Activist, Politician, 30 March 2017, NYC.

75 "Maidan Website." 2002. *Maidan Website.* http://maidanua.org/static/news/1032796245.html; "Ukraine Without Kuchma." 2001. *Ukraine Without Kuchma.* http://www.bezkuchmi.narod.ru/.

76 For examples, see Yak Facebook Vidreahuvav Na Vidmovu Vid Yevrointehratsiyi, (YouTube 2013).

77 Olga Onuch, '"Facebook Helped Me Do It": Understanding the EuroMaidan Protester "Tool-Kit"', *Studies in Ethnicity and Nationalism* 15, no. 1 (2015): 170–84.

78 Onuch, '"Facebook Helped Me Do It"'.

79 Interview, Unnamed journalist/politician, 17 December 2013.

80 Interview, Unnamed Civic Sector Activist 2, 20 July 2014, Kyiv.

81 Interview, Unnamed Civic Sector Activist 5, 30 November 2013.

82 Interview, Unnamed Civic Sector Activist 5, 30 November 2013.

83 Unnamed journalist/politician, 17 December 2013.

84 Interview, Unnamed Civic Sector Activist 3, 26 August 2014, Kyiv.

85 Unnamed Civic Sector Activist 4, 26 August 2014, Kyiv.

86 See: Onuch and Sasse, 'Maidan in Movement'.

87 Interview, Unnamed Member of the *Rada Maidanu,* Negotiator during Roundtables, 14 May 2015, Kyiv.

88 Unnamed Civic Sector Activist 5, 30 November 2013.

89 Unnamed Civic Sector Activist 5, 30 November 2013.

90 Unnamed Civic Sector Activist 5, 30 November 2013.

91 Unnamed Civic Sector Activist 4, 26 August 2014, Kyiv.

92 Unnamed Civic Sector Activist 4, 26 August 2014, Kyiv.

93 Unnamed Member of the *Rada Maidanu,* 14 May 2015.

94 Telephone interview, Unnamed former Yanukovych administration insider, 26 June 2014.

95 Unnamed Member of the *Rada Maidanu,* 14 May 2015.

96 Unnamed Member of the *Rada Maidanu,* 14 May 2015.

97 Interview, Unnamed SamoOboran Sotnya Leader 1, 13 May 2015, Kyiv.

98 Civic Solidarity, 'Ukraine: Brief Legal Analysis of "Dictatorship Law"', 20 January 2014. http://civicsolidarity.org/article/880/ukraine-brief-legal-analysis-dictatorship-law.

99 Unnamed Civic Sector Activist 2, 20 July 2014, Kyiv.
100 StopFake.org. 'Stop Fake EuroMaidan', 1 March 2014. https://www.stopfake.org/en/tag/euromaidan/.
101 Onuch and Sasse, 'Maidan in Movement'.
102 For full video of the speech see: https://www.youtube.com/watch?v=Ude6JX3YxVI.

References

Avtomaydan. 'Avtomaydan 2012', 19 March 2012. http://chp.com.ua/all-news/item/16442-avtomaydan-2012.

Beissinger, Mark. 'The Semblance of Democratic Revolution: Coalitions in Ukraine's Orange Revolution'. *American Political Science Review*, FirstView (2013): 1–19.

Bennett, Andrew. 'Process Tracing and Causal Inference', 2010. http://philsci-archive.pitt.edu/8872/.

Carey, Sabine C. 'The Dynamic Relationship between Protest and Repression'. *Political Research Quarterly* 59, no. 1 (2006): 1–11.

Chenoweth, Erica and Maria J. Stephan. *Why Civil Resistance Works: The Strategic Logic of Nonviolent Conflict*. New York: Columbia University Press, 2011.

Civic Solidarity. 'Ukraine: Brief Legal Analysis of "Dictatorship Law"', 20 January 2014. http://civicsolidarity.org/article/880/ukraine-brief-legal-analysis-dictatorship-law.

Collier, David. 'Process Tracing: Introduction and Exercises'. *Beta Version*, 22 September 2010.

Diani, Mario and Doug McAdam. *Social Movements and Networks: Relational Approaches to Collective Action: Relational Approaches to Collective Action*. New York: Oxford University Press, 2003.

Freedom House. 'Ukraine in 2011: Freedom House Report', 2011. https://freedomhouse.org/report/freedom-world/2011/ukraine.

Gould, Roger V. 'Collective Action and Network Structure'. *American Sociological Review* 58, no. 2 (1993): 182–96. https://doi.org/10.2307/2095965.

Howard, Marc Morjé. *The Weakness of Civil Society in Post-Communist Europe*. Cambridge: Cambridge University Press, 2003.

Jenkins, J. Craig. 'Resource Mobilization Theory and the Study of Social Movements'. *Annual Review of Sociology* 9 (1983): 527–53.

Kuzio, Taras and Andrew Wilson. *Ukraine: Perestroika to Independence*. Edmonton: CIUS Press, 1994.

Lohmann, Susanne. 'The Dynamics of Informational Cascades'. *World Politics* 47, no. 1 (1994): 42–101.

Maidan.org. 'Perelik Tem Forumu Osvita 2010/01', 2010. https://maidan.org.ua/arch/osvita/2010_01.html.

Marples, David R. *Ukraine under Perestroika: Ecology, Economics and the Workers' Revolt*. New York: Springer, 1991.

McAdam, Doug, Sidney Tarrow and Charles Tilly. *Dynamics of Contention*. New York and London: Cambridge University Press, 2001.

Meirowitz, Adam and Joshua A. Tucker. 'People Power or a One-Shot Deal? A Dynamic Model of Protest'. *American Journal of Political Science* 57, no. 2 (2013): 478–90. https://doi.org/10.1111/ajps.12017.

Mycio, Mary. 'Ukrainian SSR Government Bows to Students' Demands Maso Macr Agrees to Resign'. *The Ukrainian Weekly*, 21 October 1990, 42 edition. http://ukrweekly.com/archive/1990/The_Ukrainian_Weekly_1990-42.pdf.

Oleksandr Doniy, National Deputy (unaffiliated) and student leader of Revolution on the Granite and the Last Barricade Movement, 06 July 2008. Kyiv. Interview.

Onuch, Olga. *Mapping Mass Mobilizations: Understanding Revolutionary Moments in Ukraine and Argentina*. London: Palgrave MacMillan, 2014a.

Onuch, Olga. 'Social Networks and Social Media in Ukrainian "Euromaidan" Protests'. *Washington Post* (blog), 2014b, 2 January 2014. http://www.washingtonpost.com/blogs/monkey-cage/wp/2014/01/02/social-networks-and-social-media-in-ukrainian-euromaidan-protests-2/.

Onuch, Olga. '"Facebook Helped Me Do It": Understanding the EuroMaidan Protester "Tool-Kit"'. *Studies in Ethnicity and Nationalism* 15, no. 1 (2015): 170–84. https://doi.org/10.1111/sena.12129.

Onuch, Olga and Gwendolyn Sasse. 'Maidan in Movement: Protest Cycles, Diversity of Actors, and Violence'. *Europe-Asia Studies* 68, no. 4 (2016): 556–87.

Pavlo Kachur, former National Depute and Minister of Construction and Architecture of Ukraine, Rukh Party, 20 July 2009. Kyiv. Interview.

StopFake.org. 'Stop Fake EuroMaidan', 1 March 2014. https://www.stopfake.org/en/tag/euromaidan/.

Suprunyuk, Oleksandr. 'Avtomaydan, Abo Rozvidka Boyem', 24 March 2011. http://maidan.org.ua/arch/arch2011/1300969540.html.

The Ukrainian Weekly. '100,000 in Kiev March to Protest Union Treaty'. *The Ukrainian Weekly*, 7 October 1990, 40 edition.

Tilly, Charles. 'Social Movements as Historically Specific Clusters of Political Performances'. *Berkeley Journal of Sociology* 38 (1993): 1–30.

'Ukrainian Transcripts of the Melnychenko Tapes', 2001. http://www.perehid.org.ua/look/25_11_2000.phtml.

Verkhovna Rada Ukrayiny. 'Postanova Verkhovnoyi Rady Ukrayinskoyi RSR Pro Rozhlyad Vymoh Studentiv, Yaki Provodyat Holoduvannya V M. Kyyevi Z 2 Zhovtnya 1990 Roku № 402-XII'. 402-XII, 1990. Online Archive of Verkhovna Rada Ukrayiny. http://zakon1.rada.gov.ua/laws/show/402-12.

Yak Facebook Vidreahuvav Na Vidmovu Vid Yevrointehratsiyi, 2013. https://www.youtube.com/watch?v=jFgLZXeW0aw&feature=youtube_gdata_player.

Zanuda, Anastasiya. '"Podatkovyy" maydan: rik potomu Anastasiya Zanuda BBC Ukrayina 23 lystopada 2011'. *BBC News Ukraine*, 23 November 2011. https://www.bbc.com/ukrainian/business/2011/11/111122_tax_maidan_one_year_az.shtml.

5

Paradoxes of reform

Protest, progress and polarization in Malaysia

Meredith L. Weiss

Amid a widespread global trend towards democratic decline – source of much anguished hair-pulling, soul-searching, op-ed-writing and protest-marching in recent years – one state seemed for a time to be bucking the trend: Malaysia. Having lived under one of the world's longest-lasting dominant-party electoral-authoritarian regimes since independence from Britain in 1957, Malaysian voters elected a new government, the Pakatan Harapan (Alliance of Hope, Pakatan) coalition, in May 2018. To do so required persistent, careful opposition-party coordination, massive missteps among incumbent Barisan Nasional (National Front, BN) coalition leaders and economic restructuring that increased inequality and anxious precarity. But the change also entailed substantial, sustained mobilization in civil society. While the emphasis among politicians, pundits and academics alike has been on '905' – the 9 May 2018 election result – a more panoptic lens situates that moment within a much wider frame. That frame captures, too, the collapse of Pakatan nearly two years later, to be replaced by the cobbled-together Perikatan Nasional (National Alliance, PN, inclusive of the BN), centred substantially on the rights of the Malay-Muslim majority.

Before Malaysians cast their ballots in 2018, ongoing mass protest played a pivotally important role in exposing causes for grievance, in pressing and helping parties to craft platforms responsive to popular needs, and in mobilizing support for those alternative ideas and parties, including for the decidedly unusual credentialing of the BN's former long-time prime minister as acceptable to head the opposition coalition. Post-transition, a broad cluster of civil society organizations (CSOs) continued to goad, monitor and assist the new government. Meanwhile, vehement ethnonationalist protests by another CSO cluster stymied Pakatan's efforts at institutional reforms and coherent messaging, laying the ground for PN's palace-backed parliamentary coup.

The first of these transitions warrants especial attention, given the longevity of the government it upended and the path it cleared for subsequent turnover. The fact that protest mattered in the peaceful ejection of a dominant party is not itself so shocking. We see such a role in many or most polities in which an illiberal regime topples. Nor is it so unusual that opposition to the new regime united the ousted, diminished remnants of the BN with their own civil-societal backers. What distinguishes this one case – apart from its against-the-current timing – are, first, the specific attributes of the array of CSOs and political-party partners, not all of which are 'liberal' or 'progressive', and second, the extent to which protesters' expectations and parties' strategic realities are at odds. That mismatch is most manifest in the fact that a key catalyst in Pakatan Harapan's win was its embrace as leader of former BN prime minister Mahathir Mohamad, long the nemesis of CSOs that came, perversely, to welcome him back. In this chapter, I explore the multifaceted place of civil society within Malaysian political developments, and consider whether this rare forward-flying arrow is likely more definitively to hit its mark (to borrow the analogy with which Chris Osmar and Nathan Stoltzfus begin this volume). I will first briefly sketch the key contributions of civil-societal mobilization in the 2018 election and its aftermath, then consider the composition of that civil society, before turning to activists' paradoxical endorsement of Mahathir, concluding with a more speculative assessment of the path since then and still ahead for Malaysian politics.

All told, the Malaysian case defies pithy summation or pigeonholing. It is testament to the extent to which efforts within civil society may counter or support elements within the state, may work in coordination or at cross-purposes with each other, and may resist or endorse the sort of strong leaders who might give democratic deconsolidation theorists pause. In Malaysia popular support and dissent *both* support *and* limit illiberal rule, and have *both* been pivotal in a transition towards formal democracy *and* key to efforts towards its reversal. Above all, Malaysian experience offers two especially relevant insights. The first is a stark reminder that 'civil society' is not simply progressive, urban, web-savvy NGOs; may be highly partisan or entangled with parties; and may be every bit as consequential in comparatively authoritarian as in truly democratic states. The second is an acknowledgement that political constraint may breed creativity: in Malaysia, less despite than *because of* curbs on elections (disproportionality between votes and seats, limits on campaigning, etc.), but still consistent effort to confirm a noncoerced electoral mandate, we find a tendency towards more consistent mobilization. That engagement is punctuated by, but not limited to, electoral cycles, in which CSOs seek to hold the parties with which they align to the promises they have pressed those parties to make. We can expect, then, simultaneous progress towards both short- and long-term objectives, not always in the same direction; broader participation and the practical need to both fit within and expand beyond the boundaries of the current system make for a messy process.

Civil society in the 2018 electoral upset . . . and in what came next

The outcome of Malaysia's 2018 general elections, the country's 14th – referred to as 'GE14' – was neither widely anticipated nor all that shocking, really. Malaysia's core opposition parties have drifted in and out of coalitions for decades, but more consistently so since the late 1990s *Reformasi* movement, at the turbulent confluence of the Asian Financial Crisis and more generic political jockeying. In 2008, a set of parties contested together, then formalized their alliance as the Pakatan Rakyat (People's Pact) after a strong performance at the polls. Apart from winning an unprecedented five of thirteen state governments that year, the parties of Pakatan Rakyat deprived the incumbent BN of its two-thirds majority in Parliament – and, hence, of the assured votes to enact constitutional amendments. The next election in 2013 saw even greater Pakatan gains. This time, the opposition coalition won only three states (they had lost control of one of the other two in the interim), but secured the majority of popular votes at the federal level. Given the disproportionality in translating votes to seats in Malaysia's single-member-district, majoritarian electoral system, the BN retained control of Parliament, but with a diminished mandate. Moreover, in 2013, Prime Minister Najib Razak was popular – more so than his coalition – and hence a vote-wooing asset. By 2018, mired in colossal corruption allegations, Najib was a decided liability, while other scandals left the BN as a whole struggling. So for the already-organized, experienced opposition to make further headway was hardly surprising, on face.

Except for three key factors. First, Pakatan Rakyat had partly collapsed, then reconstituted itself. Riven by tension particularly over a proposal to strengthen the penalties states could impose for Muslim convicted criminals under shariah law, the coalition fractured. The Pan-Malaysian Islamist Party (PAS), sponsor of the bill, left the coalition. PAS's 'progressive' wing itself splintered off, reorganizing as a new party (Parti Amanah Nasional, or National Trust Party), still allied with the two remaining parties in Pakatan Rakyat (the Democratic Action Party or DAP, and Parti Keadilan Rakyat: People's Justice Party, or PKR). Pakatan Rakyat reformed as Pakatan

Harapan in 2015. The following year, ex–prime minister Mahathir exited the United Malays National Organisation (UMNO), declaring its leadership irredeemably corrupt, and launched Parti Pribumi Bersatu Malaysia (United Malaysian Indigenous Party, Bersatu). That party, too, soon joined Pakatan Harapan. Yet Bersatu had a communal (Malay-ethnic) premise, echoing UMNO's in the pseudo-consociational BN; Pakatan, by contrast, had until then taken noncommunal politics as its ostensible premise.[1] (In early 2020, segments from PKR and Bersatu left Pakatan to join with PAS and what remained of the BN in Perikatan Nasional; by mid-year Bersatu reconsolidated without Mahathir and his circle – who disdained alliance with UMNO – following which Mahathir launched yet another Malay-communal party, Parti Pejuang Tanah Air, Fighters of the Nation Party.)

Mahathir's entry into Pakatan Harapan in advance of the 2018 elections was expected to attract Malay votes, given his long record as a champion of pro-Malay policies. But he was less natural a draw for the approximately 40 per cent non-Malay population, and had been the chief target of the Reformasi movement that gave rise to PKR and the progenitor of Pakatan, Barisan Alternatif (Alternative Front), in the first place. That all Pakatan Harapan candidates contested under the PKR logo likely helped to assuage some such doubts in the end, reinforcing the appearance of common purpose and of the coalition's *not* being just Mahathir's personal vehicle. (Still, his participation, as a charismatic and perplexingly spry nonagenarian, surely did woo voters opposed to Najib, but not keen on too-dramatic reform of the extant order otherwise.) Mahathir needed a vehicle broader than his own fledgling party; reformists needed a sharper kick to lob themselves over the electoral hurdle – the result was mutual, and mutually advantageous, co-optation.

Second, PAS was now a spoiler, informally allied, it appeared, with UMNO. (The parties later acknowledged and solidified that collaboration, formalizing the Muafakat Nasional, National Consensus, in late 2019 as precursor to PN.) Strongest along the east coast of peninsular Malaysia, PAS opted to wage a massive nationwide campaign, standing in far more than its usual selection of seats. Ubiquitous rumours suggested the BN was funding those challenges, in hopes of splitting the opposition vote. Even if Malay voters *were* prepared to defect from UMNO, then, they might not flow towards Mahathir and Pakatan Harapan. In the end, the strategy, whether truly PAS's own or indeed an UMNO plot, hurt the BN more than Pakatan Harapan: as a third-party spoiler, PAS siphoned off Malay support not only from Pakatan Harapan but at least as much from UMNO.[2]

And third, the BN had used its authority over the electoral process further to tilt an already skewed electoral playing field. An exemplar of the 'real but unfair' competition of competitive authoritarianism,[3] the BN structured its legitimacy along both performance and electoral axes, sustaining space for opponents, but twisting the system around to make it especially hard for the latter to win. Among other measures, a redistricting exercise prior to the election forged or fortified likely BN-leaning seats and further packed much larger opposition-inclined states and constituencies;[4] the government denied voter petitions against the redelineation as well as complaints about the electoral rolls; and the (partisanized) Election Commission organized the election for a Wednesday rather than the usual weekend, complicating the efforts of 'outstation' or overseas (particularly Singapore-based) voters to return to vote. Hence the general expectation, bolstered by most credible, nonpartisan polling data, at least until the cusp of polling day, indicating a result either in the BN's favour or too close to call.

But what was the role of civil society in all this? In a word: crucial. Most important and high-profile was over a decade's activism by electoral-reform coalition Bersih, the Movement for Clean and Fair Elections. Bersih (the organization or individual activists involved), offshoots thereof and allied efforts, such as among independent online media and anti-corruption watchdog groups, publicized otherwise largely suppressed information about recent corruption scandals, to persuade voters to care and vote accordingly; produced and released detailed information on specific problems with the electoral system and governance more broadly; campaigned for particular candidates and even coordinated a last-minute, transnational effort to mobilize transport for voters and absentee ballots, to help voters and votes reach their polling stations in time. At the same time, other pockets within civil society rallied to the support of UMNO as well as PAS, particularly around the theme of Malay-Muslim rights (and Pakatan Harapan's less-convincing commitment thereto). Largely bereft of urban and non-Malay support (those categories overlapping), UMNO had doubled down in its pursuit of Malay votes, whatever the consequences for its appeal among other constituencies.[5] Both encouraging and assisting in that shift have been a set of 'Malay-chauvinist' groups, rallying, for instance, in red T-shirts to counter the yellow T-shirts Bersih adopted, in angry parallel with Bersih marches. Those groups sustained the fight post-election, arguably blazing UMNO's trail back to office, this time together with PAS and much of Bersatu, to save the day for Malays.

In short, civil-societal activism was clearly not the only force behind Malaysia's seeming 'democratization by election' and the reversal thereof, nor will it be the only force that determines whether electoral turnover, if that is to be the pattern going forward, ultimately yields regime transformation – whether democracy consolidates. But it was a critically important factor, in publicizing issues, encouraging voters to see a political crisis and an electoral solution, and even just turning out the vote. At the same time, civil-societal agitation activated ethnonationalist margins more inclined towards the old order, as well, heightening polarization and leaving the stability of the regime transition in doubt from the outset. Moreover, we might expect similar camps within civil society to play cognate roles next time. These forces will not be the only ones that determine the result of GE15, but they surely will play an important role in rallying all manner of troops.

The composition of civil society

To understand this mixed role for civil society, in both enabling electoral turnover *and* bolstering illiberal incumbents, we might take a step back, to consider the makeup of Malaysia's civil society. The domain occupies a comparatively unusual place in the Malaysian polity, shaped by over six decades' competitive-authoritarian governance: elections failed to generate leadership change (until at long last, they did), but the regime was only moderately repressive, allowing challengers to form and engage, both as parties and otherwise. Formal and informal channels have never been exclusive, facilitating more sustainable, if incremental, progress than the less institutionalized, more episodic outbursts of, for instance, the Arab Spring (see Ottoway, this volume).

The organizations that comprised early civil society (before the term was widely used) and Malaysia's (initially Malaya's) inaugural political parties developed approximately in tandem in the early twentieth century, ahead of independence from Britain in 1957. UMNO, for instance, developed out of state-based Malay organizations in 1946; the DAP, formed of the remnant of Singapore's People's Action Party in the peninsula after Singapore's brief merger with Malaysia in 1963–5, gained vitality as powerful Chinese-education-movement organizations shifted increasingly from the side of the BN-component Malaysian Chinese Association to theirs in the 1980s. More broadly, the efforts of political parties have intertwined since the earliest elections with those of CSOs. Indeed, structurally disadvantaged, resource-strapped opposition parties have been especially prone not only to function rather like CSOs themselves – providing advocacy work and other services, across the electoral cycle, to nurture a base and ideological profile while seemingly intractably out of office – but also to rely on non-party allies for ideas, validation and mobilizational help.[6] Hence, we might see the innovation-encouraging constraints of electoral authoritarianism, particularly during Mahathir's first protracted stint as prime minister, from 1981 through 2003 – coinciding with much of the heydays of NGOs', mass Islamist organizations' and other CSOs' efflorescence amid an increasingly middle-class, educated, globally networked society – as, counterintuitively, enabling and empowering CSOs. Legal curbs notwithstanding, CSOs secured an unusually influential and important niche within the polity.

Given this salience, CSOs have worked alongside parties to structure the electorate: propounding the axes along which voters align and (given, perhaps, CSOs' own lack of a specific electoral imperative) fostering multipolarity rather than tidy consolidation around an ideological/policy median. Importantly, too, given different recruitment patterns and stakes, CSOs have offered women, youths and other groups more space for leadership than have parties (a point to which we return later in the chapter). At the same time, by developing social capital as well as coalitional capital – trust among not just key individuals but also organizations, accumulated through experience of working in tandem – those same party-overlapping CSOs facilitate opposition coalition building.[7] It is the legacy of CSOs able simultaneously to occupy and organize discrete niches *and* to build strategic bridges between them that we see in play today. CSOs' reinforcement substantially enabled Pakatan Harapan to cohere and to prevail, but continued also to breathe life into an enfeebled UMNO and nudge it from pluralist power-sharing towards near-exclusive communalism alongside PAS – and Islamist *dakwah* organizations are a mainstay of PAS's permeation among Malay students and other potential supporters.

We now find a Malaysian polity likely to remain multipolar. Centred on the east coast is an Islamist core: PAS, with ranks of affiliated, generally mass, grassroots-based, ideologically tuned organizations. Centred in the rest of peninsular Malaysia after the 2018 elections were at least three blocs. One was a comparatively 'progressive' and 'justice'-oriented set of parties, secular and otherwise: the rump of Pakatan Rakyat, allied with a raft especially of advocacy-oriented NGOs and coalitions. The second was a Malay-rights segment comprised of UMNO as well as what we might gloss as the Malay-chauvinist segment of civil society. Its core players were thrown into some disarray once Mahathir left UMNO, but still comprised engaged Najib or more broadly *ancien régime* loyalists, engaging from outside the party even if some were surely also UMNO members. The third was a Malay-rights-within-Pakatan piece, lacking similar civil-societal backing, but oriented around Mahathir and his party. With the regime flip of early 2020, the various Malay-rights-oriented segments, both CSOs and parties (absent Mahathir and his inner circle), joined forces, however tenuously, to oppose the 'progressive' party–CSO bloc.

In Sabah and Sarawak, the Borneo states of East Malaysia, we find a more jumbled picture. The opposition won in Sabah in 2018, spearheaded by a party allied with, but not formally part of, Pakatan Harapan: Parti Warisan Sabah (Sabah Heritage Party, or Warisan). In Sarawak, a coalition of state-specific parties formerly in the BN won both in state elections held two years prior to GE14 (only Sarawak held its state elections separately), and the majority of the state's seats in the federal parliament, but that coalition broke off from the BN soon after GE14, forming the independent Gabungan Parti Sarawak (Coalition of Sarawak Parties, GPS). Sabah's Warisan and its partners, as well as the DAP in Sarawak, benefitted from Bersih and similar efforts, albeit with a Borneoist tinge. (Sabah's state government collapsed within months of PN's rise, however, amid politicians' opportunistic party-hopping.) In Sarawak, the parties of GPS have gained arguably more salient ideological ballast from states'-rights mobilization within civil society, most notably the Sarawak for Sarawakians (S4S) movement (itself now birthing a Parti S4S). The rise of PN saw GPS align with the new government – but with S4S intent on remaining a third force.[8]

Although patterns are not absolute, roughly speaking, at least in peninsular Malaysia, parties associated with Islam and Malays tend to find support in nationwide, mass-based Islamist and/or Malay-students' groups; parties specific to the Chinese community tend to seek support in identity-based educational, occupational and cultural associations; and noncommunal parties (most of which claim an at least loosely social-democratic orientation) rely on urban-centred issue-oriented NGOs and coalitions (e.g. oriented around particular rights or societal goods). That mix of backers and the extent to which opposition parties in particular have tended to rely upon ongoing support from civil society help to shape and sustain parties' regional distribution of strength. Augmenting those leanings are feedback effects, in the sense of perceptions of which parties, in office, are most open to input and influence from CSO allies.

Given this mélange of forms and foci, even more than in many other countries, we cannot assume the politically engaged mien of civil society to be unilaterally 'progressive' or pro-democratic, nor its impacts to lean more towards advancing political liberalization than otherwise. Hence the sense in Malaysia that however important CSOs and movements such as Bersih clearly were and continue to be to the rise and consolidation of a new government, other CSOs and activists that might oppose too-aggressive pursuit of, say, reforms to communally structured preferential policies limited that government's range of action.[9] That said, Pakatan's win was at least marginally positive for those 'core components for successful and responsive democracies' Osmar and Stoltzfus identify in their introduction: 'legal protections for the expression of ideas, formal mechanisms that allow the people to select leaders and policies, and institutions that check one another', given pressure from CSO backers and component parties alike to tweak the BN's institutional model.

Importantly, leaders, both as sources of ideas and as charismatic icons, matter enormously to politics in Malaysia; that rule extends to civil society. However pivotal the impact Bersih had in mobilizing Malaysians to hold the BN accountable for its leaders' malfeasance in the 2018 election, for instance, their effort may well have fallen short if not for the simple fact of Mahathir's presence within opposition ranks. Within civil society, spokespeople (often specifically spokeswomen) such as Ambiga Sreenivasan or Maria Chin Abdullah, for example, both long-time advocates for core causes, but both also leaders of Bersih, carry moral authority – but also are readily pulled towards formal politics when they see a valid opening to pursue their goals from within. (The Pakatan Harapan government named the former to an influential Institutional Reforms Committee; the latter became a Pakatan member of Parliament.)

It is worth noting that, however problematic an overreliance on key personalities rather than enduring institutional frameworks, civil-societal activism has been a more consistently viable channel for women's political influence than parties. Women remain seriously under-represented still in formal politics (even more so in executive than legislative office), but loom large among the ranks of high-profile leaders in civil society – for some, opening a path also to election. Indeed, women's-rights activists kept pressure on Pakatan to fulfil its promises of appointing more women to top leadership positions after GE14, drawing in heretofore under-tapped expertise and projecting a message of inclusivity, albeit still without either meeting the coalition's own stated targets or fundamentally addressing the structural constraints that define and confine gender roles.[10] Nor does even the elevation, however important, of Malaysia's first-ever female deputy prime minister and chief justice under Pakatan, and female Deputy Speaker of Parliament under PN, for instance, clear a path towards 'state feminism', or policy machineries that embed pursuit of women's equal status in state agencies,[11] or towards other means of ensuring not just women's presence in government but their policy influence. Moreover, given activists-turned-legislators' prominence and contributions, their co-optation into formal politics runs the risk of enervating their segments within civil society and weakening ongoing checks.[12]

Return of a strongman, rebranded

One of the oddest quirks of this politically efficacious civil society, in an era of surging populism elsewhere, is its role in sweeping Mahathir Mohamad – Malaysia's closest thing to a populist[13] – back into office. As prime minister previously, Mahathir oversaw the consolidation of a regime marked by a highly centralized executive and concentration of power under that executive; of deep intermeshing of politics and business, particularly through UMNO and its BN partners' own holdings; and of staunch imperviousness to cries for democracy and civil liberties. Now – even after his government's collapse – Mahathir claims to have turned over a dramatic new leaf, cracking jokes during the campaign about how he used to be a dictator and lock up his now-colleagues, but insisting that in his dotage, he values good governance above all. Many of his one-time opponents chose to take Mahathir at his word, propelled by an opposition *ini kalilah!* (now is the time!) sentiment recommending due consideration of *all* tools for ousting Najib, and reassured by the notion that Mahathir would not have emerged from comfortable retirement if he were not sincere and committed to a quick clean-up of the sullied polity.

For his part, explains Khoo Boo Teik, Mahathir 'was gratified to be accepted by oppositionists and dissidents, some of whom he had previously imprisoned'. This alliance 'taught him to value the basic parameters for checking the abuse of power and protecting civil liberties and human rights: genuine separation of powers, the rule of law, nonpartisan state institutions, and freedom of the mass media'.[14] Indeed, after coming back into office, Mahathir *did* prioritize governance reforms – not just attacking corruption in its various guises but also potentially significant reforms to the electoral system, parliamentary rules, and more – although even fairly low-hanging fruit in terms of civil liberties (the promised repeal of an overreaching Sedition Act, for instance) remained unplucked when the government fell.

But the about-face is still astounding, and speaks to the balance and interplay between civil society and political parties in shaping Malaysian political outcomes. In particular, Mahathir's October 1987 Operasi Lalang saw over one hundred, mostly left-leaning, opposition-party and civil society activists detained without trial under the since-replaced Internal Security Act (ISA) and four newspapers' licenses suspended. The crackdown came in the wake of a serious rift within UMNO and CSO challenges to government policies especially related to ethnicity. It was ostensibly to quell racial tensions and prevent 'riots'. The arrests not only removed key leaders from the fray, some for well over a year, but also had a strong deterrent effect on would-be activists and organizations – especially since Mahathir's government used the incident as justification for tightening laws further on the press and assembly.[15] The crackdown also instigated the launch of human-rights group Suaram, through which several now-Pakatan leaders cut their activist teeth, as initially a support group for families of ISA detainees.[16]

When the *Reformasi* movement that birthed what became PKR and the Barisan Alternatif swept Malaysia in the late 1990s, that 'Mahafiraun' (the 'great pharaoh') resign was its most vociferous demand. (After Mahathir's new Bersatu had joined Pakatan Harapan, to hear party leaders – many of them, like Mahathir, fresh from UMNO – shout out 'Reformasi' at rallies could be distinctly discombobulating.) Among the ranks of today's opposition-party and CSO leaders are a not-insignificant number of individuals Mahathir's BN government previously detained, most frequently under the ISA, for their political activism or advocacy work.[17] But however improbably, by 2017, Mahathir had become the hoped-for saviour of the anti-BN opposition, not just among parties but also in civil society.

Driving that development were both Mahathir's savvy courtship of Pakatan-supporting civil society and the realities of competition, which shaped Pakatan Harapan's and Mahathir's respective (then conjoint) strategies. The alliance was one of mutual dependency/capture. Starting around mid-2015, well before Najib would be obliged to call elections (within five years of convening the parliament then in session), Mahathir started actively to woo support among the opposition mass base. However much the electoral justification for his joining Pakatan was to court rural Malays – and whether or not he intended from the outset to take the reins himself rather than simply propelling a better-than-Najib designee into office – he clearly preferred a solid, broad mandate. Most iconic was his presence in August 2015, together with his wife, at Bersih 4, the fourth in a series of episodic mass street protests since 2008, then his yellow-T-shirt-clad reappearance at Bersih 5 in November 2016, shortly after his break with UMNO. He had previously proscribed such events and fortified rules first introduced in the 1970s to prohibit students in particular from demonstrating. Now he seemed to recognize the utility of public protest to mobilize opposition to the regime.¹⁸ (Meanwhile, pro-Najib 'red shirts' rallied elsewhere in Kuala Lumpur, threatening aggressive disruption.) In court in March 2018, in a hearing about Bersih 4, Mahathir explained that his condemnation of Bersih 3 in 2012 as 'violent' and an attempt to foment chaos was his 'opinion', based on information from police – but that now his own subsequent participation revealed those impressions to be incorrect.¹⁹

Beyond Bersih, and perhaps even more starkly embodying Mahathir's deep dive into civil society, was a 2016 Citizens' Declaration, the drafting of which first really tested the depth and breadth of CSOs' willingness to trust and collaborate with this purportedly new-and-improved Mahathir. The Declaration, signed by fifty-eight representatives from CSOs and opposition parties, including Mahathir, centred on opposition to Najib as prime minister and a recounting of the 1Malaysia Development Berhad, or 1MDB, mega-scandal, but included claims about the weakness of institutions, lack of democracy and abuse of power generally, all of which issues later featured in Pakatan Harapan's GE14 manifesto. The Declaration's four central demands were the ouster of Najib 'through non-violent and legally permissible means'; the removal also of 'those who have acted in concert' with Najib; repeal of unconstitutional laws that undermine fundamental rights and 'policy choice'; and 'restoration of the integrity of the institutions that have been undermined' such as the police, central bank, Malaysian Anti-corruption Commission and Public Accounts Committee.²⁰

The drafting process saw perhaps the last keen flare-up of tension between Mahathir and his former deputy, Anwar Ibrahim. In 1999, Mahathir's government (with Mahathir's voluble acquiescence) had imprisoned Anwar for sodomy and related corruption, in a case widely presumed more politically motivated than substantive. In 2016, Mahathir had quit UMNO mere days earlier (and fellow signers soon to join Bersatu remained still in UMNO). Mahathir had not yet signalled intent to join Pakatan, noting, 'There's a difference between the citizens' agenda and party agenda'.²¹ But he had proposed cooperating with opposition parties and civil-societal leaders – comprising, in his words, 'a very strange group of people' with only citizenship in common²² – against Najib. (PAS officials joined the discussions over the Citizens' Declaration, but declined to support the core group.²³) Anwar, writing (melodramatically and at length) from prison, warned his Pakatan and affiliated colleagues to be careful in working with 'the most ruthless leader and the most corrupt ex-finance minister': Mahathir and Daim Zainuddin (a key architect of the political–business links that warp today's UMNO). He described the Declaration as 'essentially . . . Tun M[ahathir]'s document', narrowly focused on removing Najib and prosecuting 1MDB, with only some of 'our' concerns ('freedom and justice, rule of law, combating abuse of power and corruption and distributive justice') added at the 'insistence of civil society leaders', but 'clearly as embellishments'. Acknowledging the allure of a united front against Najib, Anwar urged, 'We must steer clear of the danger of falling into the games of the power elites and their skilful trickery to maintain an outdated system.'[24] In fact, the initiative predated Mahathir's involvement – though one of his go-to lines, that for Najib, 'Cash is King', does feature in the otherwise fairly staid document.[25]

Possibly smoothing Mahathir's path was the fact that Anwar Ibrahim had already made the same pilgrimage in 1998. Ousted from UMNO and the government, Anwar returned to his roots in civil society: he had gotten his start as a student activist at Universiti Malaya in the late 1960s, calling for Malay cultural rights and Islamization. Although committed opposition activists, particularly in political parties, had cause to doubt Anwar's commitment to reform, the massive Angkatan Belia Islam Malaysia (Malaysian Islamic Youth Movement, ABIM), which he had helped found in the early 1970s and with which he had remained close, embraced their former leader. Particularly as Anwar endured police abuse and threw himself into organizing opposition to Mahathir and his government, his Reformasi movement came to attract broader-based support among CSOs and opposition parties. As was the case for Mahathir nearly thirty years later, Anwar insinuated himself into an already-existing oppositional crowd, as its self-anointed leader. However transparently opportunistic the shift – unlike Anwar, Mahathir may not have planned initially to return to office, but for both, opposition politics offered a vehicle – their embrace of opposition, including with their own new parties, significantly restructured and re-pitched, as well as reinvigorating, this segment of the polity.

In Mahathir's case, his entry into Pakatan Harapan offered the coalition a wedge against an increasingly monochromatic Malay-vote-seeking UMNO (as described earlier). The architect of both pro-Malay, pro-Islamization policies in the 1980s and of Malaysia's developmentalist glory days of the 1980s–90s, Mahathir retained real clout among Malay voters. Having survived the Reformasi period largely unscathed, he stepped down voluntarily, *not* ignominiously, in 2003. Pakatan needed those Malay votes; Mahathir craved a bigger stage. Yet even so, the alacrity with which so many leaders within civil society embraced Mahathir and scions of his administration they previously roundly castigated – such as Daim or fellow former Cabinet minister Rafidah Aziz – was surprising. The best possible explanation is the inextricably intertwined nature of civil society with political parties, in shifting ranks of personnel, campaigns and strategies. CSOs active around issues of systemic reform (or stasis) have come to see their best route to success as running through elections (not unreasonably, given how central issues of government policy are to their objectives). Opinion-leading activists could recognize the instrumental benefit of Mahathir's entry, beyond the obvious decertification of the BN his turncoatism represented.

Moreover, to his credit, Mahathir appeared to have doffed his prior 'Mahathirism' – his 'political ideology, itself a composite of his core ideas of nationalism, capitalism, Islam, populism, and authoritarianism'[26] – particularly in his 'anti-authoritarian turn'. Political scientist Khoo Boo Teik suggested that if Mahathir 'recycles' some old positions, we should see that not as indication that it's all a façade, but simply the fact that he lacked 'the time to reinvent his ideology substantially'.[27] Still, not only does the confluence of parties and CSOs across camps make dramatic change harder to envision than where non-party influences are more monodirectional, as noted earlier, but, more to the point, Mahathir ran with a primarily reactive motive of ejecting an UMNO 'rotten at the core'. To 'resuscitate' from within had become impossible.[28] Pakatan party leaders' strategy in embracing Mahathir had everything to do with winning the election – an important first step for issue-advocates in civil society, as well, but not the end goal.

Pakatan's opponents then spun the coalition's progress as having moved too far in pursuing objectives beyond Mahathir's brief: challenging Malay rights, propounding religious liberty (or otherwise appearing to challenge Islam's primacy), loosening state controls on civil liberties (justified in the name of security and social peace) and so forth. Malay-rights activists aligned with these challengers nudged UMNO and PAS towards a 'right-wing' alliance and re-energized their base. Although mundane personalistic rivalries proved the proximate cause of the political upheaval that followed, that activism readied the ground.

The path ahead

Possible branches or switchbacks notwithstanding, Malaysia's path still looks more promising today than that of many states experiencing democratic regression. Given how low on the liberalism scale Malaysia started, backsliding per se is hardly an issue – rather, the transition in leadership in 2018 failed to consolidate. Activists and organizations from civil society played disproportionate roles in bringing about that transition, in determining progress towards subsequent reforms, *and* in facilitating Pakatan's fall to a right-wing Malay challenge in 2020.

Unless and until Malaysia's electoral system, parliamentary order and legal regime broadly are changed, Malaysia remains structurally competitive electoral authoritarian. Even had the Pakatan government passed more of the institutional reforms it proposed, the coalition still might well simply have supplanted the BN as a dominant party. Regardless, winning elections will remain the chief goal of parties in or out of power, an objective not necessarily requiring or even benefitting from liberalizing reforms. As Anwar put it, rather oddly, in his 2016 letter warning against playing nice with Mahathir, even his camp falls prey to 'nomological desperation. We are desperate for numbers—which is incidentally expedient in politics without scruples'.[29]

That balance suggests that, inasmuch as political parties may be unlikely to lead reformist change, or may feel pressed from below to institute changes not to the liking of key segments, civil society may feel ever more empowered and entitled to lead the charge in Malaysia, however institutionally channelled. At the same time, the thoroughgoing intermeshing of CSOs with the parties of Pakatan – so long previously in opposition, lacking resources or policymaking access, and thus functioning much like CSOs as they essayed to build support – facilitated rather dramatic co-optation. CSOs not only embraced erstwhile antagonist Mahathir as leader of 'their' administration but also many of the civil-societal leading lights are now Pakatan federal or state legislators, or Pakatan-appointed local councillors, or served on one of Pakatan's several prominent institutional-reform committees.

It is *not* the case that the 'Pakatan side' of civil society was thus silenced. We see concrete evidence of this persistence at the state level: particularly in Penang and Selangor, states it has controlled since 2008, Pakatan has continued both to cooperate and to spar with engaged CSOs. Activist networks have pushed Pakatan leaders to uphold their commitment to liberalization of local-government structures[30] – efforts Bersih and allied citizens' organizations continue to press[31] – but also to enact freedom of information laws, to institutionalize participatory and gender-responsive budgeting, and more. Then-Penang Chief Minister Lim Guan Eng, for example, however cognizant of CSOs' role in propelling his DAP towards electoral success and appreciative of the extent to which NGOs did collaborate with his administration, described his state government's relationship with civil society as 'ambivalent'. He complained of how 'stubborn' and 'with-us-or-against-us' Penang's engaged activist communities are, how many 'armchair elites'[32] they include, and of their propensity to assume the worst of government.[33]

Following GE14, progressive voices and media expressed concern with the slow pace of reform of civil liberties.[34] Dozens of organizations coalesced in a CSO Platform for Reform shortly after the election to monitor progress. Within mere weeks, the group had submitted a list of recommendations to the government-established Institutional Reform Committee (which itself included prominent activists and academics).[35] Especially heated were protestations at continuing evidence of BN-style nepotism and patronage in appointments to government-linked companies and awarding government contracts.[36] In addition, prominent human-rights group Suaram, for instance, offered a detailed and critical accounting of how the new government's progress stacked up in its first hundred days and through the end of the year, including specifically in relation to Pakatan's election manifesto. While they noted promising improvements, Suaram highlighted promises on which Pakatan had 'wavered' and noted a lack of clarity or direction on key human-rights issues.[37]

Pakatan Harapan was not impervious to these appeals. CSOs and the new government attempted to set a tone of collaboration at the outset with, for instance, a closed-door dialogue session between the CSO Platform and Pakatan backbenchers in June 2018.[38] However constrained to avoid scaring off loosely committed, merely anti-Najib/pro-Mahathir (rather than reform-seeking) voters, the new government showed signs of being at least moderately more responsive and transparent than its predecessor. Not least due to the rash of former rights-advocate leaders among the government's ranks, Pakatan *did* demonstrate a strong current of support for meaningful reform.

Yet in any polity, civil society needs to renegotiate its place after the ballots are counted and new leaders sworn in. Just as that new government seeks re-election above all, CSO allies seek policy access, progress towards their goals, and to keep those friendly parties in place, lest they be shut out anew. Malaysia's transition was not quite the same as a transition from below – replacement or even a negotiated transplacement, in Huntingtonian[39] terms – but a liberalizing electoral outcome, per Howard and Roessler's conceptualization.[40] Moreover, the civil-societal partners in that transition had long-standing relationships, entailing symbiotic epistemic or policy networks as well as close personal ties with parties in the new government, as did other CSOs with the ousted incumbents and additional challengers. We might not thus expect the extent of displacement of which scholars of transitions after mass protest (in Latin America, the Arab world, Southeast Asian neighbours) have written in the past. Malaysia's transition was no revolution or even closely comparable to the 'sudden breaks through mass mobilizations'[41] elsewhere, but electoral turnover; social protest played a role not in toppling the regime per se but in validating its institutions by mobilizing citizens for an electoral challenge. Even the parliamentary coup that followed, while unprecedented at the federal level (and requiring some constitutionally dubious manoeuvres[42]), followed state-level precedent, leaving relationships and networks reconfigured, but still largely in place.

CSOs – both Pakatan allies and antagonists – learned to navigate and even thrive in the institutional ecosystem that remained after 2018; they will surely regroup in the months ahead. Moreover, Pakatan and PN alike need those allies' capacity and moral certification; their challengers likewise must present a credible threat of mass displeasure and even unrest, should reforms stretch too far. As such, it seems likely that CSOs will continue to engage, polarized segments within civil society ultimately perhaps balancing each other out. However frustrating for activists in search of more speedy and substantial change, in whatever direction, the inertial status quo might be Malaysia's best way to ward off the increasingly tempestuous and illiberal politics of so many supposedly more firmly democratic contemporary states, and even to inch towards systemic reform.

Notes

1 Given Malaysian demographics – the constitution defines Malays legally as Muslim, and the vast majority of Malaysian Muslims are Malay – any Islamist party is essentially one by and for Malays. However, PAS had worked since the late 1990s to reassure reform-minded non-Malay/Muslim voters that it also had their back. That pretence faded once PAS exited Pakatan Rakyat.

2   Ibrahim Suffian and Lee T. D., 'How Malaysia Voted in 2018', in M. L. Weiss and Faisal S. Hazis (eds), *Toward a New Malaysia? The 2018 Election and Its Aftermath* (Singapore: NUS Press, 2020), 17–40.

3   S. Levitsky and L. A. Way, *Competitive Authoritarianism: Hybrid Regimes After the Cold War* (New York: Cambridge University Press, 2010), 3.

4   Ooi K. H., 'How Malaysia's Election Is Being Rigged', *New Naratif*, 19 March 2018, https://newnaratif.com/research/malaysias-election-rigged/ (accessed 2 July 2019); Wong C. H., 'Reconsidering Malaysia's First-Past-The-Post Electoral System: Malpractices and Mismatch', in Meredith L. Weiss and Faisal S. Hazis (eds), *Toward a New Malaysia? The 2018 Election and Its Aftermath* (Singapore: NUS Press, 2020), 211–45.

5   H. Washida, *Distributive Politics in Malaysia: Maintaining Authoritarian Party Dominance* (New York: Routledge, 2019), 182–3.

6   See M. L. Weiss, *Protest and Possibilities: Civil Society and Coalitions for Political Change in Malaysia* (Stanford: Stanford University Press, 2006), for an extended discussion of this symbiosis and the extent to which it enabled new opposition emphases, commitments and alliances.

7   See Weiss, *Protest and Possibilities*.

8   FMT Reporters, 'S4S to Contest Sarawak State Elections Next Year', *FMT News*, 14 February 2020. Available online: https://www.freemalaysiatoday.com/category/nation/2020/02/14/s4s-to-contest-sarawak-state-elections-next-year/ (accessed 16 August 2020).

9   We see similar pressures in Indonesia, where post-transition presidents tread warily amidst ratcheting-up Islamist mass mobilization in particular.

10 See, for instance, tan b. h., Maznah Mohamad and C. Ng, 'Still a Long Way to Go: GE14, Women and Political Representation', in F. Loh and A. Netto (eds), *Regime Change in Malaysia* (Penang, Aliran & Petaling Jaya: SIRD, 2018), 282–93; tan b. h., 'When More of the Same Is Not Enough: Making Policies Work for Women in Malaysia Baharu', *New Mandala*, 2 July 2019. Available online: https://www.newmandala.org/making-policies-work-for-women-in-malaysia-baharu/ (accessed 2 July 2019).

11 D. M. Stetson and A. G. Mazur, *Comparative State Feminism* (Thousand Oaks: Sage, 1995).

12 A dilemma not unique to Malaysia – see, for instance, J. S. Dryzek, 'Political Inclusion and the Dynamics of Democratization', *American Political Science Review* 90, no. 1 (1996): 475–87; P. Oxhorn, 'Where Did All the Protesters Go? Popular Mobilization and the Transition to Democracy in Chile', *Latin American Perspectives* 82, no. 21 (1994): 49–68.

13 I do not consider Malaysian politics to fit a strict definition of populism (M. L. Weiss, 'The Limits of "Populism": How Malaysia Misses the Mark and Why That Matters', *Journal of Current Southeast Asian Affairs*, 2020, http://dx.doi.org/10.1177/1868103420935555), but that pattern owes more to structural checks than to Mahathir's lack of trying.

14 Khoo B. T., 'Mahathir Mohamad Returns, but What of Mahathirism?' *ISEAS Perspective* 2018, no. 46 (2018): 5.

15 Kua K. S. 'Ops Lalang: The Worst Assault on M'sian Civil Society', *Malaysiakini*, 28 October 2017. Available online: https://www.malaysiakini.com/news/399846 (accessed 16 August 2020); Aliran, 'Operation Lalang Revisited', *Aliran*, n.d. Available online: https://aliran.com/oldsite/hr/js3.html (accessed 16 August 2020).

16 Called three decades later on his role as the Home Minister who oversaw Ops Lalang, Mahathir blamed his police chief, who advised him to sign the detention orders. However, he acknowledged in 2018 that he had then 'vilified' many of the people with whom he was now collaborating in order 'to win the elections', only to learn later that 'they're not as bad as I made them out to be then' ('Police Responsible for Ops Lalang, Mahathir Says', *Straits Times*, 28 October 2017. Available at: https://www.straitstimes.com/asia/se-asia/police-responsible-for-ops-lalang-mahathir-says (accessed 16 August 2020).).

17 One detainee, Mohd Yunus Lebai Ali, now deceased, was the husband of Bersih-leader-turned-Pakatan-MP, Maria Chin Abdullah.

18 'Dr M and Wife Make Surprise Visit at Bersih 4', *Malaysiakini*, 29 August 2015. Available online: https://www.malaysiakini.com/news/310411 (accessed 16 August 2020); 'Bersih Rally: Malaysia's Former Premier Mahathir Joins Calls to Oust 'Thieves'', *Straits Times*, 19 November 2016. Available online: https://www.straitstimes.com/asia/se-asia/berish-rally-malaysias-former-premier-mahathir-shows-up-in-support-of-protesters (accessed 16 August 2020).

19 I. Lim and K. Tee, 'Dr M Says Changed Mind about Bersih 2.0 after Attending "Peaceful" Rallies', *Malay Mail*, 7 March 2018. Available online: https://www.malaymail.com/news/malaysia/2018/03/07/dr-m-says-changed-mind-about-bersih-2.0-after-attending-peaceful-rallies/1592673 (accessed 16 August 2020).

20 Text available at 'Citizens' Declaration Spells Out Demands for Removal of Najib', *Malaysiakini*, 4 March 2016. Available online: https://www.malaysiakini.com/news/332750 (accessed 16 August 2020); see also T. Leong, 'Malaysia's Mahathir and Opposition Sign Declaration to Oust Najib', *Straits Times*, 4 March 2016. Available online: https://www.straitstimes.com/asia/se-asia/mahathir-and-opposition-sign-declaration-to-oust-najib (accessed 16 August 2020).

21 Quoted in A. Yunus and A. Tang, 'Mahathir Initiates Citizens' Declaration to Oust Prime Minister', *Nation* (Bangkok), 5 March 2016. Available online: https://www.nationthailand.com/news/30280813 (accessed 16 August 2020).

22 Quoted in Malaysiakini Team, 'Dr M: Strange Group, But All Agree Najib Must Go', *Malaysiakini*, 4 March 2016. Available at: https://www.malaysiakini.com/news/332716 (accessed 16 August 2020).

23 Leong, 'Malaysia's Mahathir and Opposition Sign Declaration to Oust Najib'.

24 Quoted in 'Anwar's "letter": Citizens' Declaration a Flawed Mahathir Document', *Malaysiakini*, 16 May 2016. Available online: https://www.malaysiakini.com/news/341735 (accessed 16 August 2020). After the election, his own pardon and release, and his entry into Parliament via a by-election,

and affirming a pluralist, progressive agenda under Pakatan, Anwar (Anwar Ibrahim, 'How Malaysia's Democratic Disruption Stands Apart in a Year of Populist Nationalism', *South China Morning Post*, 13 December 2018. Available online: https://www.scmp.com/comment/insight-opinion/asia/article/2177481/how-malaysias-democratic-disruption-stands-apart-year (accessed 16 August 2020)) wrote that given their known 'stormy relationship', for him to accept Mahathir's overtures 'required genuine forgiveness and a radical change in personal perspective, so that politics could move forward for the sake of the country'.

25 See 'Citizens' Declaration Spells Out Demands for Removal of Najib', *Malaysiakini*.

26 Khoo, 'Mahathir Mohamad Returns, but what of Mahathirism?', 2.

27 Khoo, 'Mahathir Mohamad Returns, but what of Mahathirism?'

28 Author's interview with Mahathir Mohamad, 10 October 2016, Putrajaya.

29 'Anwar's "letter": Citizens' Declaration a Flawed Mahathir Document', *Malaysiakini*.

30 G. Rodan, 'Civil Society Activism and Political Parties in Malaysia: Differences over Local Representation', *Democratization* 21, no. 5 (2014): 824–45.

31 For instance, a well-attended 13 January 2019 public forum on local-council elections in Kuala Lumpur brought together representatives from a range of local-government and governance-related organizations, along with MP Maria Chin Abdullah (former Bersih head) and a representative for the federal Minister for Housing and Local Government (who is sympathetic, but with a longer timeline, and lacks sure support from the rest of the Cabinet).

32 His framing was intriguingly redolent of Mahathir's reproving NGOs (including some of the same organizations with which Lim found himself jousting three decades on) as meddling 'intellectual elites' and 'thorns in the flesh' in the 1980s (M. L. Weiss, 'Malaysian NGOs: History, Legal Framework, and Characteristics', in M. L. Weiss and Saliha Hassan (eds), *Social Movements in Malaysia: From Moral Communities to NGOs* (London: RoutledgeCurzon, 2003), 36).

33 Interview with author, 3 January 2015, Butterworth, Penang.

34 See, e.g. Harapan Tracker: https://harapantracker.polimeter.org.

35 D. Jayasooria, 'SDGs as the Foundation for Reforms', *Malaysiakini*, 30 May 2018. Available online: https://www.malaysiakini.com/letters/427553 (accessed 16 August 2020).

36 J. D. Lovrenciear, 'Watchdog to Push for Reform of Government-Linked Companies Launched', *Aliran*, 24 January 2019. Available online: https://aliran.com/thinking-allowed-online/watchdog-to-push-for-reform-of-government-linked-companies-launched/ (accessed 16 August 2020).

37 Suaram, *Malaysian Human Rights Report* (Petaling Jaya: Suara Rakyat Malaysia (SUARAM), 2018).

38 J. Choong, 'In Closed-Door Meet, Groups Tell MPs What Issues They Want Addressed', *Malay Mail*, 27 June 2018. Available at: https://www.malaymail

.com/news/malaysia/2018/06/27/in-closed-door-meet-groups-tell-mps-what-issues-they-want-addressed/1646215 (accessed 16 August 2020).

39 S. P. Huntington, 'How Countries Democratize', *Political Science Quarterly* 106, no. 4 (1991): 579–616.
40 M. M. Howard and P. G. Roessler, 'Liberalizing Electoral Outcomes in Competitive Authoritarian Regimes', *American Journal of Political Science* 50, no. 2 (2006): 365–81.
41 D. Della Porta, *Where Did the Revolution Go? Contentious Politics and the Quality of Democracy* (New York: Cambridge University Press, 2016), 2.
42 Y. Tew, 'Malaysia's 2020 Government Crisis: Revealing the New Emperor's Clothes', *International Journal of Constitutional Law Blog*, 15 April 2020. Available at: http://www.iconnectblog.com/2020/04/malaysias-2020-government-crisis-revealing-the-new-emperors-clothes/ (accessed 16 August 2020).

References

Aliran. 'Operation Lalang Revisited'. *Aliran*, n.d. Available online: https://aliran.com/oldsite/hr/js3.html (accessed 16 August 2020).
'Anwar's "letter": Citizens' Declaration a Flawed Mahathir Document'. *Malaysiakini*, 16 May 2016. Available online: https://www.malaysiakini.com/news/341735 (accessed 16 August 2020).
Anwar Ibrahim. 'How Malaysia's Democratic Disruption Stands Apart in a Year of Populist Nationalism'. *South China Morning Post*, 13 December 2018. Available online: https://www.scmp.com/comment/insight-opinion/asia/article/2177481/how-malaysias-democratic-disruption-stands-apart-year (accessed 16 August 2020).
'Bersih Rally: Malaysia's Former Premier Mahathir Joins Calls to Oust "Thieves"'. *Straits Times*, 19 November 2016. Available online: https://www.straitstimes.com/asia/se-asia/berish-rally-malaysias-former-premier-mahathir-shows-up-in-support-of-protesters (accessed 16 August 2020).
Choong, J. 'In Closed-Door Meet, Groups Tell MPs What Issues They Want Addressed'. *Malay Mail*, 27 June 2018. Available at: https://www.malaymail.com/news/malaysia/2018/06/27/in-closed-door-meet-groups-tell-mps-what-issues-they-want-addressed/1646215 (accessed 16 August 2020).
'Citizens' Declaration Spells Out Demands for Removal of Najib'. *Malaysiakini*, 4 March 2016. Available online: https://www.malaysiakini.com/news/332750 (accessed 16 August 2020).
Della Porta, D. *Where Did the Revolution Go? Contentious Politics and the Quality of Democracy*. New York: Cambridge University Press, 2016.
'Dr M and Wife Make Surprise Visit at Bersih 4'. *Malaysiakini*, 29 August 2015. Available online: https://www.malaysiakini.com/news/310411 (accessed 16 August 2020).
Dryzek, J. S. 'Political Inclusion and the Dynamics of Democratization'. *American Political Science Review* 90, no. 1 (1996): 475–87.
FMT Reporters. 'S4S to Contest Sarawak State Elections Next Year'. *FMT News*, 14 February 2020. Available online: https://www.freemalaysiatoday.com/

category/nation/2020/02/14/s4s-to-contest-sarawak-state-elections-next-year/ (accessed 16 August 2020).

Howard, M. M. and P. G. Roessler. 'Liberalizing Electoral Outcomes in Competitive Authoritarian Regimes'. *American Journal of Political Science* 50, no. 2 (2006): 365–81.

Huntington, S. P. 'How Countries Democratize'. *Political Science Quarterly* 106, no. 4 (1991): 579–616.

Jayasooria, D. 'SDGs as the Foundation for Reforms'. *Malaysiakini*, 30 May 2018. Available online: https://www.malaysiakini.com/letters/427553 (accessed 16 August 2020).

Khoo, B. T. 'Mahathir Mohamad Returns, but what of Mahathirism?' *ISEAS Perspective* 2018, no. 46 (2018). https://www.iseas.edu.sg/images/pdf/ISEAS _Perspective_2018_46@50.pdf

Kua K. S. 'Ops Lalang: The Worst Assault on M'sian Civil Society'. *Malaysiakini*, 28 October 2017. Available online: https://www.malaysiakini.com/news/399846 (accessed 16 August 2020).

Leong, T. 'Malaysia's Mahathir and Opposition Sign Declaration to Oust Najib'. *Straits Times*, 4 March 2016. Available online: https://www.straitstimes.com/ asia/se-asia/mahathir-and-opposition-sign-declaration-to-oust-najib (accessed 16 August 2020).

Levitsky, S. and L. A. Way. *Competitive Authoritarianism: Hybrid Regimes after the Cold War*. New York: Cambridge University Press, 2010.

Lim, I. and K. Tee. 'Dr M Says Changed Mind about Bersih 2.0 After Attending "Peaceful" Rallies'. *Malay Mail*, 7 March 2018. Available online: https://www .malaymail.com/news/malaysia/2018/03/07/dr-m-says-changed-mind-about -bersih-2.0-after-attending-peaceful-rallies/1592673 (accessed 16 August 2020).

Lovrenciear, J. D. 'Watchdog to Push for Reform of Government-Linked Companies Launched'. *Aliran*, 24 January 2019. Available online: https://aliran .com/thinking-allowed-online/watchdog-to-push-for-reform-of-government -linked-companies-launched/ (accessed 16 August 2020).

Malaysiakini Team. 'Dr M: Strange Group, But All Agree Najib Must Go'. *Malaysiakini*, 4 March 2016. Available at: https://www.malaysiakini.com/news /332716 (accessed 16 August 2020).

Ooi, K. H. 'How Malaysia's Election Is Being Rigged'. *New Naratif*, 19 March 2018. https://newnaratif.com/research/malaysias-election-rigged/ (accessed 2 July 2019).

Oxhorn, P. 'Where Did All the Protesters Go? Popular Mobilization and the Transition to Democracy in Chile'. *Latin American Perspectives* 82, no. 21 (1994): 49–68.

'Police Responsible for Ops Lalang, Mahathir Says'. *Straits Times*, 28 October 2017. Available at: https://www.straitstimes.com/asia/se-asia/police-responsible -for-ops-lalang-mahathir-says (accessed 16 August 2020).

Rodan, G. 'Civil Society Activism and Political Parties in Malaysia: Differences over Local Representation'. *Democratization* 21, no. 5 (2014): 824–45.

Stetson, D. M. and A. G. Mazur. *Comparative State Feminism*. Thousand Oaks: Sage, 1995.

Suaram. *Malaysian Human Rights Report*. Petaling Jaya: Suara Rakyat Malaysia (SUARAM), 2018.

Suffian, I. and T. D. Lee. 'How Malaysia Voted in 2018'. In M. L. Weiss and Faisal S. Hazis (eds), *Toward a New Malaysia? The 2018 Election and Its Aftermath*, 17–40. Singapore: NUS Press, 2020.

Tan, B. H. 'When More of the Same is Not Enough: Making Policies Work for Women in Malaysia Baharu'. *New Mandala*, 2 July 2019. Available online: https://www.newmandala.org/making-policies-work-for-women-in-malaysia-baharu/ (accessed 2 July 2019).

Tan, B. H., M. Mohamad and C. Ng. 'Still a Long Way to Go: GE14, Women and Political Representation'. In F. Loh and A. Netto (eds), *Regime Change in Malaysia*, 282–93. Penang, Aliran & Petaling Jaya: SIRD, 2018.

Tew, Y. 'Malaysia's 2020 Government Crisis: Revealing the New Emperor's Clothes'. *International Journal of Constitutional Law Blog*, 15 April 2020. Available at: http://www.iconnectblog.com/2020/04/malaysias-2020-government-crisis-revealing-the-new-emperors-clothes/ (accessed 16 August 2020).

Washida, H. *Distributive Politics in Malaysia: Maintaining Authoritarian Party Dominance*. New York: Routledge, 2019.

Weiss, M. L. 'The Limits of "Populism": How Malaysia Misses the Mark and Why That Matters'. *Journal of Current Southeast Asian Affairs* (2020). http://dx.doi.org/10.1177/1868103420935555.

Weiss, M. L. 'Malaysian NGOs: History, Legal Framework, and Characteristics'. In M. L. Weiss and Saliha Hassan (eds), *Social Movements in Malaysia: From Moral Communities to NGOs*, 17–44. London: RoutledgeCurzon, 2003.

Weiss, M. L. *Protest and Possibilities: Civil Society and Coalitions for Political Change in Malaysia*. Stanford: Stanford University Press, 2006.

Wong, C. H. 'Reconsidering Malaysia's First-Past-The-Post Electoral System: Malpractices and Mismatch'. In Meredith L. Weiss and Faisal S. Hazis (eds), *Toward a New Malaysia? The 2018 Election and Its Aftermath*, 211–45, Singapore: NUS Press, 2020.

Yunus, A. and A. Tang. 'Mahathir Initiates Citizens' Declaration to Oust Prime Minister', *Nation* (Bangkok), 5 March 2016. Available online: http://www.nationmultimedia.com/detail/breakingnews/30280813 (accessed 16 August 2020).

6

People power in Putin's Russia

Social versus political protests

Laura A. Henry

In June and July 2018, Russia hosted the football World Cup. Almost three million foreigners visited the country to watch the football matches, and many of them were quoted in the press remaking on the warmth of their hosts and the high-quality infrastructure for the games. Those who had never visited Russia, and who had images of the grey gloom of empty shelves and a cowed populace from the Soviet era, were amazed to discover lively urban centres, a celebratory mood and more than 5,000 volunteers mobilized to help the event run smoothly. The BBC quoted a fan from the UK who said, 'I thank the Russian people for their hospitality.... Everything the British government has said about Russia is a lie. It's propaganda. Fair play to Putin. He's done a brilliant job with the World Cup.'[1] The Russian government had successfully brought the world's football fans to Russia, and emerged with a burnished reputation.

Even more than the 2014 Sochi Olympics, the 2018 World Cup was a triumph for the Russian government and marked a high point to the start of Vladimir Putin's fourth term as president. However, alongside the football games discontent simmered across the country in response to the Russian government's plan to raise the legal pension age from sixty to sixty-five for men and from fifty-five to sixty-three for women. A 2018 Levada Center poll showed that 89 per cent of Russians opposed the government's proposed pension reforms.[2] With male life expectancy hovering around sixty-seven, critics argued that a significant portion of the citizenry would not live to enjoy a retirement. In June 2018, the Moscow city government denied several applications for permits to allow protests on the issue of pension reform, citing the World Cup events, and protests were banned in other major cities as well.³ Still, by late June 2018, the newspaper *Vedmosti* reported that pension reform had prompted '100 applications for protests in 70 cities across the country and collected nearly 2.5 million signatures on an online petition'.⁴ According to the Interior Ministry approximately 6,500 people protested in Moscow in July 2018 and protests were organized in more than twenty-five cities in September.⁵

The joint timing of the global football competition and a controversial domestic reform proposal was likely not a coincidence. The games provided a feel-good moment for the Russian population and a useful distraction for the government from a controversial policy change. Nevertheless, the popularity ratings of both President Putin and the United Russia party fell markedly in reaction to the proposed pension reform.⁶ Although the public was happy to enjoy the World Cup circus while it was on offer, unsurprisingly the main concern of most Russian citizens remains the daily bread – income, living standards and quality of life issues.

Many observers have argued that during his first two terms in office Putin crafted an informal 'social contract' with a Russian public battered by the economic and political instability of the 1990s, when life savings were undermined by hyperinflation and the former superpower lost its international status.⁷ In contrast to this period of turmoil, President Vladimir Putin offered stability and prosperity, but with strings. In exchange for a growing economy and rising living standards, the public would acquiesce to an increasingly undemocratic political status quo with power centralized in the federal executive. Putin himself has led the Russian regime, directly or indirectly, since 1999 and other elected offices are mostly held by the United Russia party. The continuation of this political equilibrium depends in part on the Russian government's performance: the regime is legitimate because it has been able to deliver the goods of an improving quality of life. Putin has accepted the credit for Russia's economic successes since the turn of the century. However, this apparent bargain leaves the regime in a fragile position if its performance declines.

In this chapter, I draw a distinction between political protests that challenge the legitimacy of regime's political arrangements, the United Russia party and Putin personally and social protests around quality of life issues. I argue that the regime has identified multiple strategies to discredit protests orchestrated by the political opposition. The wave of protests for fair elections that erupted in response to fraud in the December 2011 parliamentary elections and continued sporadically until the March of Millions held on Putin's third inauguration as Russia's president in May 2012 raised hopes among observers that broad-based mobilization against the regime might prove to be its undoing. Yet in the wake of the 2011–12 protests, the regime has created conditions, both legal and rhetorical, that make a new wave of anti-Putin political protests even less likely. Selective repression by the regime has raised the costs of political protest, even as the discourse around patriotism has narrowed the range of acceptable political behaviour.

The weakness and constraint of *political* opposition does not mean that protest will not play a role in the fate of the current regime, however. A hybrid regime relying on performance legitimacy may be less vulnerable to political protests than to *social* protests focused on quality of life and governance issues, in part because the repressive apparatus that the regime has at its disposal is difficult to use again the 'average Ivan'. Social protests are more challenging to combat because they are not ideological, are more geographically and demographically diverse, and often use the language of patriotism to make demands. I will pay particular attention to protests on environmental issues as a variety of social protest often focused on good governance to illustrate the challenge to the regime.

Managing society under semi-authoritarian regimes

The challenges for the modern dictator are obvious as he (thus far, rarely she) governs in a world of instantaneous information exchange, easy travel and migration, global consumerism and highly mobile and fickle financial capital. With the possible exception of North Korea, it is virtually impossible to keep a population isolated from developments in the rest of the world, including withering critiques of one's own regime. Yet many authoritarian and hybrid regimes have proven surprisingly durable and have not succumbed to the 'inevitable' attraction of liberalism. In the past twenty years, scholars have devised new concepts – such as authoritarian stability, authoritarian resilience and authoritarian responsiveness – to explore the persistence of contemporary authoritarian regimes.[8]

To minimize opposition, an authoritarian leader must actively promote his popularity and offer a clear basis for the legitimacy of the regime. Legitimacy implies the consent of the governed.[9] According to Linz, legitimacy is 'the belief that in spite of shortcomings and failures, the political institutions are better than others that might be established and therefore can demand obedience'.[10] If the regime is not legitimated by a democratic political process, in accordance with Weber's rational legal authority, then it must deliver in other ways. This challenge is compounded in the absence of an ideological justification for undemocratic politics, such as Soviet communism. Without democratic procedures or ideology, legitimacy may be rooted in the provision of security, prosperity and certain basic public goods for citizens. In other words, some undemocratic regimes rely on performance legitimacy.

Authoritarian regimes also attempt to structure their state–society relations so as to persist in the long term. Regimes decide how to engage civil society actors – from the watchdog groups that monitor legal violations to noisy social groups unhappy with the effects of the regime's economic management. State repression of those who overstep the boundaries of state-sanctioned political participation is an option, but the use of coercive force is costly in terms of personnel, material and regime reputation. More often, the state looks for less costly techniques or attempts to co-opt civic activism. Indeed, contemporary authoritarian regimes are often hybrids – continuing to hold elections and voice rhetorical commitments to democracy while systematically violating political rights and civil liberties.[11] Hybrid regimes retain some of the trappings of democracy – elections, limited press freedom, associational life beyond the state – while still ensuring the dominance of a particular elite faction. Excessive control of citizen mobilization can lead to the problem of information. Without channels of representation, how can authoritarian leaders assess the public mood and determine which issues are provoking discontent?[12] However, the effort to balance control and response is uniquely challenging for hybrid regimes which retain a symbolic adherence to pluralism, even as the outcome of managed political competition is predictable.[13]

Authoritarian and hybrid regimes manage their interactions with society utilizing a dynamic and adaptable combination of carrots and sticks, coercion and responsiveness, a flexible approach that has made them more resilient than critics anticipated. Creating opportunities for popular participation is an important element of maintaining an undemocratic regime. Kendall and Taylor found that authoritarian regimes which seek to use repression in 'targeted and less-costly ways' can develop pseudo-democratic institutions prolong a regime's lifespan.[14] They develop incentive structures to encourage regime-supporting mobilization and discourage oppositional politics, combining repression and responsiveness to manage relations with social actors. For example, a number of scholars have studied how the Chinese Communist Party attempts to cultivate certain forms of activism while limiting others.[15] Similarly, scholars of Russia have examined the 'carrots and sticks' used to promote particular forms of mobilization.[16] We also see evidence of learning across authoritarian regimes, such as in the global wave of restrictions on international and domestic NGOs as a means to pre-empt social mobilization in states as diverse as Cambodia and Uganda.[17] Heiss argues that authoritarian regimes tend to take restrictive measures only under certain conditions, such as when regime stability is in doubt, or to prevent or in response to protests. These scholars broadly agree that authoritarian regimes can manipulate laws and resource availability to manage social mobilization.

Despite the strategic management of society, protest remains an ever-present threat to an authoritarian regime. Social movement theory suggests that protests are more likely to occur when institutionalized channels of political change are blocked or non-existent.[18] A closed political opportunity structure limits the space for interest groups to express their grievances or advance their policy goals using formal channels. Discontent builds over time. If activists frame 'what is the problem' and 'who is to blame' in a compelling way, people may take to the streets to express their dissatisfaction with the status quo.

Given constraints on social mobilization in an authoritarian regime, citizens may feel that they have few options for expressing themselves beyond protest.

Yet protest is difficult in a context with few resources and a closed political system in which the threat of repression is clear. In Russia, the challenges of protesters have been well documented by scholars. Debra Javeline showed how the difficulty of assigning clear blame for the problems of the post-Soviet period hindered Russian protesters.[19] Graeme Robertson identified patterns of protest under hybrid regimes depending on factors such as repertoire of protest, types of demands and characteristics of the protesters themselves.[20] Focusing in on protests around electoral fraud, Samuel Greene demonstrated how the choices and actions of political elites shape protest and Mischa Gabowitsch looks at the legacy of the protests for fair elections since 2012.[21] Alfred Evans examines an array of protests beyond political opposition to illustrate how property rights and a sense of ownership influence Russian protesters.[22] Tomila Lankina's construction and interpretation of a Russian protest event dataset provides evidence of the array of activism by Russian citizens despite the general depictions of public passivity.[23]

In this work, I focus on the elusive, but meaningful, distinction between two types of civic action: political protest and social protest. Political protesters who confront the regime directly, using the language of revolution or opposition to a leader, are often depicted as unpatriotic outsiders who do not speak for average citizens. In Russia, the political opposition frequently is portrayed as working in the interest of foreign powers. Social protesters – who are asking for the enforcement of existing laws, pleading for protection from negligent officials or for a better future for children, and who often articulate limited demands related to a single issue – are not so easily vilified. Yet the claims of social protesters may tarnish the regime's legitimacy even more effectively than direct opposition. Social protesters often present themselves as apolitical, cite problems that are widespread and attract a diverse array of participants. Repression is generally an undesirable response to social protesters, given the public sympathy that they evoke. Instead, the authoritarian regime could more self-consciously 'perform responsiveness'. A more concerted effort to appear sensitive to public concerns may pre-empt public outrage and bolster the popularity of the regime. Symbolic acts such as having the political leader accept public complaints, dress down lower-level officials for dereliction of duties and severely punish corruption are all ways of demonstrating responsiveness at the top of the regime. Yet these symbolic responses are unlikely to be effective in the face of persistent social problems.

Political protests in Russia

Since the 2004 Orange Revolution in Ukraine when a youth movement led citizens protesting a fraudulent election, the Russian regime has been acutely aware of the potential power of civil society. Russia has experienced periodic political protests in the past ten years, but with the exception of the 2011–12 protest against election fraud, most political protests have been fairly small and concentrated in a few urban centres. Following the 2011–12 events, the regime took steps to raise the costs of protesting both legally and rhetorically. Fully aware that political scientists have been spectacularly wrong in their predictions about the political trajectory of Russia (and the Soviet Union) in the past, the political opposition currently appears relatively weak – quite constrained and fragmented across ideological divides. In contrast, social protest in Russia appears to be on the rise and present a particular challenge to the regime, as described in the following.

Hybrid regimes have certain built-in vulnerabilities. Elections – even when the outcome is all but guaranteed – can be a flashpoint for opposition.[24] In Russia's December 2011 parliamentary elections, the pro-regime United Russia party purportedly received 49.3 per cent of the vote, winning 238 out of the 450 seats in the Duma. Many citizens were already disgruntled by Putin's announcement that he again would be running for president, swapping places in a so-called 'castling move' with his former prime minister and president from 2008 to 2012, Dmitri Medvedev. Protests broke out almost immediately when observers produced evidence of electoral fraud, launching the movement For Honest Elections (*Za chestnyi vybory*).[25] These protests were remarkable for their size and scale – the largest protests since the late Soviet period. Throughout December 2011 mass protests, starting in Moscow and spreading to cities and towns across Russia, attracted tens of thousands of citizens. At their height, protests in Moscow had 80,000 participants. Protesters spanned ideological divides, from leftists and liberals to nationalists, all united in their opposition to the United Russia as a hegemonic party, many chanting 'Russia without Putin'. Coordination across the movement was facilitated by an organizing committee and social media.[26] Protests continued intermittently until May 2012, when Putin was inaugurated in his third term as president of Russia after winning 63.6 per cent of the vote in elections that were viewed as generally fair. As a result of severe but selective repression of protesters and the clear continuation of the regime, the movement demobilized.

Smaller protests erupted two years later in response to Russia's annexation of Crimea and armed conflict in the Donbas region of Ukraine in 2014. In March 2014, the day before a referendum in Crimea on joining the Russian Federation, approximately 20,000 people participated in a Moscow march for peace. Then, in 2017, Aleksei Navalny, a well-known political opposition figure, called for anti-corruption protests in response to evidence that numerous officials – notably then Prime Minister Dmitri Medvedev – had enriched themselves while in office. Small but geographically widespread protests occurred March and June 2017. These protests were notable for attracting a number of young participants, including high school students, who follow Navalny's anti-corruption activism online. In June 2019 several thousand people rallied in Moscow to protest the detention of journalist Ivan Golunov on fabricated drug charges.[27]

The government has taken a hard line against protesters at all of these events. On the coercive side, the government has used forceful policing and arbitrary arrests to disrupt protests. Following the 2012 March of Millions, hundreds of people were detained and thirty – some active protesters and some bystanders – were prosecuted in what Amnesty International referred to as a 'show trial'.[28] Even Vladimir Lukin, the Russian human-rights ombudsman, argued that innocent people had been prosecuted.[29] Hundreds of young people – including minors – were detained by police following the anti-corruption protests led by Navalny and for the release of Golunov. Selective repression of protest participants is powerful because of its arbitrary nature. No one knows who will be targeted by the authorities. Protest organizers, fringe participants and even onlookers can be swept up and jailed. This serves as a powerful warning to people who may be on the fence about engaging in protest and who can be intimidated into staying at home.

The government also discredits protesters by portraying them as puppets of a foreign power – specifically the United States. Protesters are depicted as largely Moscow-based cosmopolitan elites out of touch with 'real' Russian citizens. During the 2011–12 protests, government officials claimed that protesters were being paid by the United States. In response, some protesters carried signs directed at the US Secretary of State, asking, 'Hillary, where is my money?' Portraying protesters as unpatriotic is a strategy that the government refined and used even more effectively against protesters opposing Russia's intervention in Ukraine. For example, in February 2012 a pro-regime, 'anti-Orange' rally attracted tens of thousands of demonstrators.[30] A leader onstage at the pro-regime rally shouted, 'We say no to the destruction of Russia! . . . We say no to Orange arrogance! We say no to the American embassy!'[31] This language of patriotism, and indeed nationalism, tied to traditional cultural and conservative values has been increasingly mobilized during President Putin's third and fourth terms as president.

In the aftermath of the 2011–12 protests, the State Duma passed a number of new laws, including rules on acquiring permits for a protest and vaguely written laws on extremism and blasphemy.[32] These laws were used to prosecute Pussy Riot, the feminist post-punk oppositional group, for example. The 2012 law on foreign agents lists new penalties for non-governmental organizations that engage in political activities and receive funding from foreign sources. Laws passed in 2014 raised the fine and detention period for repeatedly participating in protests, while a 2018 law made it illegal to encourage minors to protest. In 2016, a new National Guard was created, widely seen as a tool that could be used in suppressing domestic unrest. The 2016 Yarovaya package of laws increased the powers of law enforcement more broadly and mandates new rules for data collection and surveillance, among other measures. These new rules and penalties have decreased the space for anti-regime activism. They also are applied arbitrarily, with some NGOs labelled foreign agents on flimsy pretexts and other organizations seeming to escape scrutiny. Opposition figures also have faced harassment and intimidation, including physical violence.

Coercive measures and legal disincentives are important tools in raising the cost of opposition protest, but coercion is costly for the regime as well, both materially and in the potential loss legitimacy. For that reason, the Russian government has combined selective repression with incentives to encourage regime-supporting activities – including pro-regime protests – and patriotic social activism. The Russian government has supported pro-regime youth groups, such as Nashi, Molodaia Gvardiia, and the pro-regime youth summer camp at Lake Seliger. The government also has encouraged volunteerism as a model of civic engagement, facilitating youth support for veterans and modelling patriotic community improvement projects.[33] In 2015, the regime sponsored the creation of a 'Youth Army', which now has more than 500,000 participants to encourage 'comprehensive development of the personality of the young patriot'.[34] Moreover, as some NGOs have been designated 'foreign agents', other organizations have been identified as 'socially-oriented' and particularly worthy of government support through grants from the Presidential Fund and other government subcontracts for services.[35] Thus, even as some actors and issues are constrained, others are empowered.

Russia's 'political opportunity structure' is now consolidated to the point that the rules of the political game – imbalanced though they are – are clear. Regime-supporting activities by civil society actors are encouraged; regime-critical activities are discouraged. Major laws that govern aspects of citizen activism are sufficiently vague to allow for the selective prosecution of activists – and, through this prosecution, the intimidation of others. The regime has consolidated major elements to ensure its stability: the dominance of a hegemonic political party in United Russia; the cultivation of a 'systemic opposition' through other regime-sanctioned parties; the marginalization of the non-systemic opposition; the elimination of potential rivals to power, leading the public to see few alternatives; significant control of the media environment, most notably television; legal disincentives for protest; cultivation of a particular framing of political activism as not in the 'national interest' and the encouragement of patriotic forms of social mobilization, such as volunteerism. Not least of these among these sources of regime stability is the centralization of executive power and the personalization of authority in the figure of Vladimir Putin. As Andrei Kolesnikov, a senior fellow at the Moscow Carnegie Center, has said, 'When you ask Russians, "Do you approve of Putin?" it's the same as asking them, "Do you approve of your motherland?"'[36] However, sitting at the pinnacle of authoritarian power also has inherent vulnerabilities.

The challenge of social protests

At this point, it might seem that the only recourse aggrieved Russians have is a 'solitary picket' as the last form of protest available. Indeed, this approach of individuals holding a sign, each one in turn, in front of government office buildings has been widely used to protest the arrest of artists, journalists and others.[37] Yet while the political opportunity structure is highly unfavourable, protests do still occur in Russia, and indeed some kinds of protests seem to be increasing. In November 2018, the Center for Economic and Political Reforms announced that they had recorded '2,500 protests this year compared to under 1,500 nationwide' in 2017.[38] Most of these protests were not political actions that garner headlines in the Western media. Instead, these protests largely were inspired by socio-economic issues. For the purposes of this chapter, I am defining social protest as any protest that is directed at a single issue related to quality of life, broadly defined, and that is non-ideological, in contrast to protests in opposition to the regime or regime leaders.

If anti-Putin or anti-regime political protesters are easily discredited as a strident minority who do not have Russia's best interests at heart, protests on quality of life issues that directly affect the general public are more difficult for the regime to portray as either radical or self-interested.[39] These protests include 'average citizens' claiming the government's protection or enforcement of rights. Social protests may implicate the regime for its treatment of vulnerable citizens – children, the elderly, those in need of care. They are less easily discredited and attract widespread sympathy from citizens who face concerns similar to the protesters' demands. What is especially challenging is that social protesters frequently profess loyalty to the regime, express justified disappointment with the behaviour of lower-level officials and ask for the government simply to fulfil its promises.

Social protests appear to be growing more common. Graeme Robertson's research demonstrates a shift from the 1990s to 2000s in which issues inspiring protest moved from personal issues like the non-payment of wages to more societal issues such as justice and civil rights.[40] Following the 2011–12 political protests, Dmitriev found that survey respondents prioritized social concerns, summarizing, 'issues of housing and utilities came on top. Other priority demands included, apart from the demand for political change and complaints against corruption, problems of education, health care, personal security and the rule of law'.[41] We see evidence of these trends on the ground. Early Putin's second term in 2005–6, a reform to monetize pension benefits sparked protest by elderly citizens fearful of losing services formerly delivered for free.[42] From 2010 on, drivers in Moscow and other cities formed the 'Blue Bucket society' to mock government officials who disobeyed traffic laws while using flashing blue lights on their cars and protested the efforts of traffic police to extract fines from average drivers.[43]

In 2014–15, doctors and other medical staff protested the poor quality of health infrastructure and low salaries; these protests gained renewed momentum in 2018 and 2019.⁴⁴ Other actions include farmers protesting the confiscation of their land by agribusinesses and mortgage holders protesting the loss of the investment due to corrupt financial schemes.⁴⁵ Recent social issues that have led to protest are the decision to redevelop Moscow neighbourhoods,⁴⁶ domestic violence⁴⁷ and serious problems with waste disposal around the country. Sometimes these protests indirectly touch upon political issues. For example, protests by long-haul truckers about increased road tax pointed to Igor Rotenberg, the son of Arkady Rotenberg, who is one of Putin's oldest friends, as the direct beneficiary of the tax hikes. Indeed, willingness to protest due to social issues seems to be growing. A November 2018 Levada Center poll indicated a rising 'protest potential in Russia', with 30 per cent saying that they would take part in economic protests and 37 that it was 'quite possible' that they would participate.⁴⁸

A number of social protests have been linked to environmentalism broadly defined, including development plans that threaten green space and neighbourhoods and issues related to waste disposal. I review several of these protests in the following: the Khimki forest protests, a recycling effort that led to public outcry against trash incineration and protests against overflowing landfills near Moscow and planned landfills around Russia. Local, often unregistered, groups focused on concrete environmental problems have begun to use technology to publicize complaints and aggregate interests across a broader swathe of the population. The issues that these groups work on could be characterized as the 'environmentalism of daily life'. Angelina Davydova, a well-known environmental journalist, cites this type of environmentalism as the most energized wing of the movement.⁴⁹ These initiatives are focused on tangible problems that occur in close proximity to citizens, related to daily frustrations or threats to quality of life and public health. Citizens may feel empowered to do something to address these immediate local issues, a sentiment that they generally do not have in relation to broader national or transnational environmental issues such as deforestation, biodiversity loss or climate change.

The Khimki forest protests, from 2008 to 2011, are among the most well-known recent environmental action in Russia. The protest was initiated by Evgeniia Chirikova, a resident of a suburb northwest of Moscow. In 2007, Chirikova noticed some trees in the local forest marked for removal.⁵⁰ Local officials had failed to inform the public about plans for a new highway linking Moscow and St. Petersburg. When there was no response to her initial inquiries, Chirikova organized a number of meetings and demonstrations to try to save the forest, including a protest camp, eventually garnering attention in Moscow and beyond. In August 2010, the movement attracted several thousand protesters to a rally and protest concert.⁵¹ After this protest, then-President Medvedev halted the construction and called for a review of the plans,[52] but the construction resumed after several months.[53] Although ultimately unsuccessful, the fight for Khimki forest has reverberated as smaller protests to protect green space have occurred in many Russian communities, including the successful fight to preserve green space and oppose the construction of a new cathedral in Ekaterinburg in 2019.[54]

Separate Collection (*Razdel'nyi Sbor*) is an environmental network which has since grown into a registered organization in St Petersburg.[55] This group began as an initiative to organize recycling around St. Petersburg, in the absence of a public recycling option and organizes collection points in different neighbourhoods on the first Saturday of the month to gather recyclable materials which are then delivered to factories for reprocessing. These actions have grown from efforts to recycle mainly glass and paper to collections of ten different types of material, including plastics. In 2016, the organization won a presidential grant to carry out its collections. Yet over time Separate Collection also has united with several smaller initiatives around that arose in opposition to the construction of new waste incinerators. At public hearings, citizens challenged incinerator construction – asking, how were the locations selected (often in close proximity to residential neighbourhoods), why are they not using the newest technology and why are there few other options for waste management. When the authorities challenged residents attending public hearing for producing trash but not endorsing its disposal, the citizens became aligned with Separate Collection to promote recycling as an alternative to incineration. There are other similar movements addressing the issue of waste, including No More Garbage (*Bol'she Musora Net*) in Moscow and St. Petersburg and other cities.

Since 2015, local residents in the Moscow region have organized numerous protests related to landfills in at least five suburban towns. The biggest and most sustained garbage protests occurred in the town of Volokolamsk, site of the Yadrovo landfill.[56] For months, residents complained of foul smells, difficulty breathing and rashes. In early March 2018, local officials declared a state of emergency due to the release of gases from the dump. Then on March 21, more than fifty children were hospitalized with symptoms of poisoning, likely from hydrogen sulphide seeping out of the landfill. Official measurements showed that the chemical was at ten times the maximum allowable concentration. In response, 6,000 residents – more than a quarter of the Volokolamsk population – came out on the streets to demand that the landfill be closed. Protesters carried signs with slogans such as 'Stop poisoning us!' and 'Don't kill our children!' Officials promised to close the landfill, even as local businesspeople supporting the protesters were detained by the police. Similar protests have been sparked in other towns to oppose waste facilities that are expanded without stakeholder consultation – or even notification – and that endanger public health.

The dilemma of social protests and regime legitimacy

Why might it be more challenging for the regime to manage social protests than to repress and discredit political protesters? Numerous factors are at play, one of which is the regime's legitimation strategy. Given the high costs of repression, authoritarian leaders, particularly those without an ideological justification, need to deliver the goods in some way to stay in power – fulfilling the basic social contract to keep citizens safe and to keep the economy growing. When these promises are not kept – or when the coercive elements of authoritarianism grow too blatant – protests may erupt. If the regime can resolve the issues prompting social action quickly and effectively, then addressing protesters' concerns may even bolster the regime's performance. At a low level, protests may be useful at generating information for the regime about failed policies, official malfeasance or growing discontent.[57] However, in practice it can be challenging to rapidly resolve social complaints in a rigidly hierarchical system – especially in conditions of scarce resources.

The paradox of performance legitimacy heightens the power of social protests. As long as the economy is growing and living standards are improving, good performance alone may be sufficient to legitimize the regime. The public is less likely to take to the streets over how the country is governed as long as the outcomes are perceived as beneficial overall. In fact, cultivating dependence on state programmes and employment may increase public tolerance for undemocratic governance. But once performance slips, the regime is vulnerable to demands for good governance and greater responsiveness. Economic performance and delivery of social goods was an element of Soviet legitimacy strategy, and therefore familiar to Russians.[58] In post-Soviet Russia, performance legitimacy served Vladimir Putin well from 1999 until the economy slowed following the 2008 global financial crisis. After rebounding, the economy was again weakened by declining prices for oil and US and European sanctions following Russia's intervention in Ukraine in 2014. Russia no longer has budget surpluses to spend on social programmes. Having placed himself at the centre of the political system, President Putin enjoyed the credit for steady economy growth, but now seems vulnerable to receiving the blame for economic weakness. A December 2018 Levada poll showed that while 55 per cent of Russian surveyed gave the most credit for Russia's economic success and improvement in citizen's living standards, 55 per cent also identified Putin as 'primarily responsible for the country's problems and increasing cost of living'.[59]

Poor governance creates risks for the regime,[60] including protest. Characteristics of social protests heighten the challenge for the regime, such as the widespread relevance of issues raised by the protesters, the 'local patriotism' of protesters and the non-ideological nature of protesters' demands. Social protesters often eschew politics as a dirty business and declared themselves avowedly apolitical. However, over time these social protests have shown the potential to become politicized.

First, anecdotal evidence suggests that social protests tend to be more geographically widespread and the protesters themselves more demographically diverse than political protesters. Many social protests occur in regions far from Moscow and St. Petersburg, are not well publicized by Russian media and very rarely are covered by the international press. Protesters are not drawn only from the well-educated creative class and the under-40 demographic in major urban centres that the regime sees as a source of potential opposition. Living outside major urban centres, provincial and rural residents previously have been viewed as Putin's base. Yet recent research carried out by the Russian Institute of Regional Expertise showed that residents of villages and small towns in Russia feel that their problems are neglected, and they are forced to struggle with unresponsive local authorities.[61] The difficulty of replacing municipal and regional leaders in a system dominated by one political party means that protest is one of the few outlets for expressing dissatisfaction.

Protesters focus on social concerns that may be shared by a wide swathe of citizens across Russia – and government action may spread the grounds for protest even further. For example, in an effort to address public unrest around landfills, the Moscow municipal authorities began contracting with other regions to take the city's waste, including places as far away as Arkhangelsk, in Russia distant northwest. However, Arkhangelsk residents have themselves begun protesting the import of trash to their relatively pristine, forested region. In February and April 2018, thousands of people participated in a coordinated protest against poor management of waste, lack of information for residents and threats to air and water quality in a campaign they entitled 'Russia is not a dump!'[62] Protesters also have set up a camp near the construction site, and their protests have, at least temporarily, delayed construction at the site.[63]

Second, protesters focused on social issues often frame their actions as a form of patriotism. Instead of voicing opposition to the regime as a whole, or to Putin himself, citizens making social demands emphasize their love of country. However, their patriotism may be locally rooted – linked to a neighbourhood, city or region, ties that are important as a more diffuse national tie. Many social initiatives are based on a kind of civic pride – an explicit love of one's community. Beautiful St. Petersburg (*Krasivyi Peterburg*) originated as a way for citizens to make official complaints about illegal parking, unauthorized advertising, informal trading points and the misuse of public green space. Using Facebook and V Kontakte, citizens are able to send information, including photographs, to the relevant authorities, using their mobile phones. The network operates almost exclusively online, without legal registration, using volunteer labour and funds gathered through crowd-sourcing. This model of civic engagement has spread and similar 'beautiful city' networks have emerged in at least ten other locations, as the original group's leader has shared his technology and tips for organizing around civic issues.

Gabowitsch discusses how current protests in Russia – especially environmental protests– are tied to the personal affinities of the protesters.[64] These affinities may be attached to 'common-places', seemingly banal features of life that nevertheless elicit deep emotional attachment. Emotions are on display in protester's disappointment with current conditions and pessimism about their children's future. These are sentiments that run counter to the 'emotional regime' cultivated by the current government – a regime that prioritizes national unity above all.[65] Other Russian observers have noted the rise of 'regional patriotism' as citizens lose faith in the federal government's ability to deliver solutions.[66]

Third, protesters' demands for social change do not fall neatly into any one ideological camp. The organizers of these initiatives generally see 'politics' as a discredited space, and are avowedly apolitical.[67] A apolitical stance, at least initially, may attract a broader swathe of supporters as compared to overtly political projects. Their actions are not rooted in party affiliation, ideology or narrow opposition to the current government or President Putin. Evans has argued that social protests indicate that many Russians want more state protection, not less.[68]

But what happens when the government disappoints citizens who make demands around social issues by failing to respond effectively? A lack of demonstrated concern and unresolved problems can lead protesters to drift towards politics, despite their efforts to remain apolitical. What are at first modest and individual demands can cohere into broader sense of grievance. A leader of a St. Petersburg initiative notes that as the networks grows, participants are able to see that the problems they face are not just on their street or in their courtyard, but exist city-wide – and even across the country.[69] In some cases, the sense that 'our rights are being violated' has crept into the rhetoric of these groups. The St. Petersburg organizer commented that it has become clear that government officials are responsive not to citizens, but to those 'from above', who put them in their offices. Deputies are not influenced by elections, he lamented. Here we see apolitical activism drifting into a critique of the political system.

When the government does not provide necessary services, and citizens have resolved problems themselves, they begin to ask, what is the government for? Social protests have a tendency to cohere round a common theme: those situated closest to power have been able to enrich themselves. This type of mobilization pits the average citizen – just trying to get by, to protect his or her family, to ensure a dignified retirement – against an out-of-touch, corrupt elite. When the economy was growing and all boats were rising, it may have been easier to tolerate how the political elite enriched themselves. Now, it is seen as an insult.

There are several examples of protests that start out as apolitical becoming politicized over time. Protesters' language may invoke broader political themes as in the Moscow housing protests with slogans such as 'No to the demolition of the constitution!' and 'No to violation of the constitution and property law'.[70] The struggle for Khimki forest offers a dramatic example of politicization. Given the proximity to Moscow, the Khimki protests attracted the attention of several high-profile Russian opposition figures. In June 2011, opposition activists gathered at a protest camp in Khimki forest.[71] Chirikova and other Khimki protesters participated in the 2011–12 protests for fair elections and Chirikova several times ran for mayor of Khimki.[72] However, in 2015 after repeated harassment, including accusations of child neglect by a government agency, Chirikova fled to Estonia with her family.[73]

Government officials are left with few easy choices for addressing social protests. Protesters' demands may involve complex, long-term and costly changes to current governance strategies. One short-term strategy is to more visibly 'perform responsiveness'. The appearance of responsiveness is designed to bolster the popularity of the authoritarian leader and to prevent public expressions of outrage. Minimally, citizens can seek redress for problems by making complaints to government agencies at different levels, appealing above the heads of those seen as failing to resolve social issues.[74] In additional, state television frequently shows high-level officials, including the president, dressing down bureaucrats and elected officials lower down in the 'power vertical'. In an example peculiar to Russia, citizens can speak directly to President Putin in the annual Direct Line presidential call-in show.[75] In 2017, Yelena Mikhailenko called President Putin's annual programme to complain about noxious emissions from the Kuchino landfill which caused nausea and vomiting. 'Turning to you is our last hope', Mikhailenko told the president. Expressing sympathy, Putin ordered the Kuchino dump closed by presidential order. The quick resolution of the problem was covered favourably in the Russian media, but hardly represented a systemic response. In fact, Putin's recognition of 'the legitimate negative reaction of people' to problems with trash disposal may have emboldened protesters near other landfills to redouble their efforts.[76]

Is performing responsiveness enough? The Direct Line call-in show makes clear what many Russian citizens suspect: the only way to solve on-going social problems is to win sympathy from the federal centre – and preferably from the president himself. This pattern reveals the risks of an authoritarian regime rooted in both performance and personalism. The strength and popularity of a political leader can enhance regime stability, but if the leader's perceived effectiveness declines, the public can lose faith in the regime.[77] Some opinion polls show that trust in Putin is falling, even as his popularity remains high; other polls indicate that the president's popularity may be falling as well.[78] In response, in February 2019, President Putin announced a raft of new social programmes ranging from additional support for families to the modernization of Russia's health care and education systems.[79] Other strategies include increased monitoring. In July 2018, the federal government rolled out a new programme called 'Incident Management' to monitor social media for complaints about government officials in order to promote a faster response.[80] In 2020, the week-long public vote to endorse constitutional changes that would allow Putin two more terms as president, among other changes, was designed to elicit overwhelming public support.[81]

Repression may still be a necessary tool to address social protests, although it is fraught with risk for the regime's legitimacy. Following the government's pension reform proposal, forceful policing was used against protesters. Human Rights Watch issued a statement criticizing the Russian government for having 'arbitrarily detained hundreds of peaceful protesters, including older people and children' and injuring many on 9 September 2018, when many regions were holding local elections.[82] Repression inadvertently could have a radicalizing effect. Ekaterina Schulmann, a Russian political scientist, has identified Russian citizens desire for 'normal politics', not revolution. She stated, 'People want to be listened to, people want political participation and competition. They want to go to rallies and not get their skulls cracked by the National Guard, they want to go to vote and see candidates who represent them on the ballots. People want a party system that meets their needs, people want a public sphere, in which they can talk about what matters to them, not the "crimes of the Kyiv junta" committed some year or other.'[83]

Conclusion

Since the protests for fair elections in 2012, the Russian government effectively has limited the space for political opposition in the streets, raising the costs of protests through legal measures and painting political protesters as unpatriotic. However, protests around social issues appear to be on the rise during a period when the Russian government is dealing with greater budgetary constraints than in the early 2000s. New social challenges loom on the horizon. A notable example is the visible effects of ageing housing stock across the country. A 2019 explosion in an apartment building in Magnitogorsk may have been the result of the terrorist act, but some observers saw it as a sign of the mismanagement of the country's infrastructure.[84] New challenges, such as the Covid pandemic, and the regime's efforts to maintain authority in the regions are also flashpoints. Activists respond to the repression with innovation. Online networks of activists, such as those facilitated by Evgeniia Chirikova's website Activatica, share examples of common grievances and new strategies across Russia.[85]

While I have argued that social protests present a unique threat to the regime due to their widespread relevance, language of loyalty and non-ideological appeal, there are reasons to be cautious. Regimes are adaptable and may identify strategies either to address social problems or to demobilize protesters. After the upheaval of the 1990s, regime stability – even at lower living standards – retains broad appeal for Russians.[86] The

2020 Constitutional amendments featured a variety of new guarantees on pensions and welfare.[87] Moreover, social protests do not always show potential aggregate citizens across geography and may not inspire protesters to focus on the federal government or president as the source of blame.[88] Alternatively, political protests may rear their head again, with regional elections and Putin's declining popularity, despite the extension of his possible time in office until 2036, as vulnerable points for the regime. Finally, the regime could muddle through this period, waiting for oil prices to rise or sanctions to ease. In the meanwhile, however, citizens witnessing a slow erosion of the government's performance pose a quiet, but persistent, threat to the regime's legitimacy that is not easily addressed.

Notes

1. Steven Rosenberg, 'Is Russia the Real Winner of World Cup 2018?', 14 July 2018, https://www.bbc.com/news/world-europe-44812175.
2. Levada Center, 'Pensionnaia Reforma', 5 July 2018, https://www.levada.ru/2018/07/05/pensionnaya-reforma3/?utm_source=mailpress&utm_medium=email_link&utm_content=twentyten_singlecat_20920&utm_campaign=2018-07-05T06:30:56+00:00.
3. Interfax, 'Vlasti Moskvy otklonili zaiavki oppozitsii na aktsii protiv pensionnoi reformy', 21 June 2018, https://www.interfax.ru/moscow/617945.
4. Vladimir Ruvinskii, 'Chto delat' nizam, kogda verkhi molchat', 26 June 2018, https://www.vedomosti.ru/opinion/articles/2018/06/26/773746-chto-delat.
5. Novaya Gazeta, 'V Moskve proshel miting protiv povysheniia pensionnogo vozrasta', 28 July 2018, Available at: https://www.novayagazeta.ru/news/2018/07/28/143690-v-moskve-prohodit-miting-protiv-povysheniya-pensionnogo-vozrasta.
6. Levada Center, 'Approval Ratings', 22 October 2018, https://www.levada.ru/en/2018/10/22/approval-ratings-3/.
7. Linda J. Cook and Martin K. Dimitrov, 'The Social Contract Revisited: Evidence from Communist and State Capitalist Economies'," *Europe-Asia Studies* 69, no. 1 (2017): 8–26; Samuel A. Greene, 'From Boom to Bust: Hardship, Mobilization and Russia's Social Contract', *Daedalus* 146, no. 2 (2017): 113–27; Aleksei Makarin and Peter M. Oppenheimer, 'The Russian Social Contract and Regime Legitimacy', *International Affairs* 87, no. 6 (2011): 1459–74.
8. Martin K. Dimitrov, ed., *Why Communism Did Not Collapse: Understanding Authoritarian Regime Resilience in Asia and Europe* (Cambridge: Cambridge University Press, 2013); Milan W. Svolik, *Politics of Authoritarian Rule* (Cambridge: Cambridge University Press, 2012); Valerie Bunce and Sharon Wolchik, 'Defeating Dictators: Electoral Change and Stability in Competitive Authoritarian Regimes', *World Politics* 62, no. 1 (2010): 43–86.
9. Bruce Gilley, *The Right to Rule: How States Win and Lose Legitimacy* (New York: Columbia University Press, 2009).

10 Juan J. Linz, 'Legitimacy of Democracy and Socioeconomic Systems', in Mattei Dogan (ed.), *Comparing Pluralist Democracies: Strains on Legitimacy* (Boulder: Westview Press, 1988), 65.

11 Steve Levitsky and Lucan Way, *Competitive Authoritarianism: Hybrid Regimes after the Cold War* (Cambridge: Cambridge University Press, 2010).

12 Ronald Wintrobe, *The Political Economy of Dictatorship* (New York: Cambridge University Press, 1998).

13 Nikolay Petrov, Maria Lipman and Henry E. Hale, 'Three Dilemmas of Hybrid Regime Governance: Russia from Putin to Putin', *Post-Soviet Affairs* 30, no. 1 (2014): 1–26; Levitsky and Way, *Competitive Authoritarianism*.

14 A. Kendall-Taylor and E. Frantz, 'Mimicking Democracy to Prolong Autocracies', *Washington Quarterly* 37, no. 4 (2014): 71–84.

15 Jessica Teets, *Civil Society under Authoritarianism: the China Model* (Cambridge: Cambridge University Press, 2014); J. Hsu and R. Hasmath, eds, *The Chinese Corporatist State: Adaption, Survival and Resistance* (New York: Routledge, 2013); Christopher Heurlin, *Responsive Authoritarianism in China: Land, Protests, and Policy Making* (Cambridge: Cambridge University Press, 2016).

16 Elena Bogdanova, Linda J. Cook and Meri Kulmala, 'The Carrot or the Stick? Constraints and Opportunities of Russia's CSO Policy', *Europe-Asia Studies* 70, no. 4 (2018): 501–13.

17 Andrew Heiss and Judith G. Kelley, 'Between a Rock and a Hard Place: International NGOs and the Dual Pressures of Donors and Host Governments', *Journal of Politics* 79, no. 2 (April 2017); Andrew Heiss, 'Authoritarian Institutions and Restrictions on International Civil Society', Paper presented at the International Studies Association, February 2016; K. Dupuy, J. Ron, A. Prakash, 'Hands Off My Regime! Governments' Restrictions on Foreign Aid to Non-governmental Organizations in Poor and Middle-Income Countries', *World Development* 84 (August 2016): 299–311.

18 Sidney G. Tarrow, *Power in Movement: Social Movements and Contentious Politics*, 3rd edn (New York: Cambridge University Press, 2011); Doug McAdam, *Political Process and the Development of Black Insurgency, 1930-1970* (Chicago: University of Chicago Press, 1982).

19 Debra Javeline, *Protest and the Politics of Blame: The Russian Response to Unpaid Wages* (Ann Arbor: University of Michigan Press, 2003).

20 Graeme Robertson, *The Politics of Protest in Hybrid Regimes: Managing Dissent in Post-communist Russia* (Cambridge: Cambridge University Press, 2011).

21 Samuel A. Greene, *Moscow in Movement: Power and Opposition in Putin's Russia* (Stanford: Stanford University Press, 2014); Mischa Gabowitsch, *Protest in Putin's Russia* (Cambridge: Polity Press, 2017).

22 Alfred B. Evans, 'Protests in Russia: The Example of the Blue Buckets Society', *Demokratizatsiya* 26, no. 1 (2018): 3–24; Alfred B. Evans, 'Many Russians Aren't Protesting against Putin—They Want His Help', *Washington Post*, 21 August 2017, https://www.washingtonpost.com/news/monkey-cage/wp/2017

/08/21/many-russians-arent-protesting-against-putin-they-want-his-help/?utm_term=.a0331ab2b546.
23 See Political Mobilization and Democracy, available at: https://popularmobilization.net/.
24 Levitsky and Way, *Competitive Authoritarianism*.
25 For more information this movement, see Gabowitsch, *Protest in Putin's Russia* and Virginie Lasnier, 'Demobilisation and Its Consequences: After the Russian Movement Za chestnye vybory', *Europe-Asia Studies* 69, no. 5 (2017): 771–93.
26 Greene, *Moscow in Movement*.
27 BBC, 'Ivan Golunov Case: Moscow Protest Sees Hundreds Held', 12 June 2019, https://www.bbc.com/news/world-europe-48607317.
28 RFE/RL, '"Bolotnaya" Protester Released from Russian Prison after Serving Term', 26 June 2017, https://www.rferl.org/a/russia-bolotnaya-ushevsky-freed-prison-term/28640261.html.
29 Human Rights Ombudsman of the Russian Federation, 'Kommentarii Upolnomochennego', 29 June 2012, http://old.ombudsmanrf.org/ombudsman/document/zajavlenija/723-6-2012.
30 Orange is associated with Ukraine's pro-democracy or anti-Russian political movement. Regina Smyth, Anton Sobolev and Irina Soboleva, 'A Well-Organized Play', *Problems of Post-Communism* 60, no. 2 (2013): 24–39.
31 Simon Shuster, 'The Abominable Snow Protests of Russia: Moscow's New Cold War', *Time*, 7 February 2012, http://content.time.com/time/world/article/0,8599,2106275,00.html.
32 Geir Flikke, Conflicting Opportunities or Patronal Politics? Restrictive NGO Legislation in Russia 2012–2015'," *Europe-Asia Studies* 70, no. 4 (2018): 564–90; Saskia Brechenmacher, *Civil Society under Assault: Repression and Responses in Russia, Egypt, and Ethiopia* (Carnegie Endowment for International Peace, 18 May 2017).
33 Julie Hemment, *Youth Politics in Putin's Russia: Producing Patriots and Entrepreneurs* (Bloomington: Indiana University Press, 2015).
34 For more information, see IunArmiia. https://yunarmy.ru/.
35 Anna Tarasenko, 'Russian Non-profit Organisations in Service Delivery: Neoliberal and Statist Social Policy Principles Intertwined'," *Europe-Asia Studies* 70, no. 4 (2018): 514–30.
36 Pravda.ru, 'Rossiiu zakhlestnut protesty: narod vosstaet protiv pensionnoi reformy', 19 June 2018, https://www.pravda.ru/news/society/1386627-pensia/; Amy MacKinnon, 'In Russia, Plan to Raise Pension Age Draws Protests', *Foreign Policy*, 1 July 2018, https://foreignpolicy.com/2018/07/01/in-russia-plan-to-raise-pension-age-draws-protests/.
37 The Moscow Times, 'Dozens Protest Russian Investigative Reporter's Arrest in Moscow', 7 June 2019, https://www.themoscowtimes.com/2019/06/07/dozens-protest-russian-investigative-reporters-arrest-in-moscow-a65932; Lucian Kim, '"Solitary Picket" Is One of the Last Forms of Legal Public Protest in Russia', *NPR*, 23 October 2018, https://www.npr.org/2018/10/23/659988709/solitary-picket-is-one-of-the-last-forms-of-legal-public-protest-in-russia.

38 Tsentr ekonomichestkikh i politicheskikh reform, 'Protesty 2017-2018: rost protestnoi aktivnosti naseleniia', 8 November 2018, http://cepr.su/2018/11/08/protests-2017-2018/.

39 I would like to thank Alfred B. Evans for several important conversations on this topic.

40 Robertson, *The Politics of Protest in Hybrid Regimes*.

41 Mikhail Dmitriev, 'Lost in Transition? The Geography of Protests and Attitude Change in Russia', *Europe-Asia Studies* 67, no. 2 (March 2015): 224–43, 233.

42 Susanne Wengle and Michael Rasell, 'The Monetisation of l'goty: Changing Patterns of Welfare Politics and Provision in Russia', *Europe-Asia Studies* 60, no. 5 (2008): 739–56.

43 Evans, 'Protests in Russia'.

44 Nataliia Chernova, 'Vrach Naroda', *Novaya Gazeta*, 16 October 2018, https://www.novayagazeta.ru/articles/2018/10/16/78209-unizhenie-nevynosimee-nischety.

45 Evans, 'Many Russians Aren't Protesting against Putin'.

46 Regina Smyth, 'How the Kremlin Is Using the Moscow Renovation Project to Reward and Punish Voters', *PONARS*, March 2018, http://www.ponarseurasia.org/memo/kremlin-using-moscow-renovation-project-reward-punish-voters.

47 Meduza, 'Petersburg Residents Protest against Domestic Violence under Heavy Police Surveillance as Khachaturyan Case Continues', 5 August 2019, https://meduza.io/en/feature/2019/08/05/petersburg-residents-protest-against-domestic-violence-under-heavy-police-surveillance-as-khachaturyan-case-continues.

48 Levada Center, 'Otsenka tekushchego polozheniia del v strane', n.d. Available at: https://www.levada.ru/indikatory/polozhenie-del-v-strane/.

49 Personal communication with the author, October 2017.

50 Alfred Evans, 'Protests and Civil Society in Russia: The Struggle for the Khimki Forest', *Communist and Post-Communist Studies* 45, nos. 3–4 (2012): 233–42; Elizabeth Plantan, 'Mass Mobilization in China and Russia: From Unexpected Victories to Unintended Consequences', *Russian Politics* 3, no. 4 (2018): 513–47.

51 *RIA Novosti*, 'Iurii Shevchuk na mitinge-kontserte v zashchitu Khimkinskogo lesa', 23 August 2010, https://ria.ru/photolents/20100823/268068268.html.

52 *Kommersant*, 'Dmitrii Medvedev priostanovil vyrubku Khimkinskogo lesa', 26 August 2010, https://www.kommersant.ru/doc/1493287.

53 Andrei Kozenko, 'Khimkinskii les srubili v sude', *Kommersant*, 11 July 2011, https://www.kommersant.ru/doc/1677036.

54 Matthew Luxmoore, 'Thousands Protest Proposed Church for Third Day in Russia's Yekaterinburg', *RFE/RL*, 15 May 2019.

55 For more information, see Razdel'nyi Sbor, http://rsbor.ru/.

56 Darko Janjevic, 'Volokolamsk: Russians Protest Toxic Landfills Near Moscow', *Deutsche Welle*, 3 April 2018, https://www.dw.com/en/volokolamsk-russians-protest-toxic-landfills-near-moscow/a-43239740.

57 Peter L. Lorentzen, 'Regularizing Rioting: Permitting Public Protest in an Authoritarian Regime', *Quarterly Journal of Political Science* 8, no. 2 (2013): 127–58.

58 S. White, 'Economic Performance and Communist Legitimacy', *World Politics* 38, no. 3 (1986): 462–82; see also 'socialist citizenship' in G. Distelhorst and D. Fu, 'Performing Authoritarian Citizenship: Public Transcripts in China', *Perspectives on Politics* 17, no. 1 (2019): 106–21.

59 Levada Center, 'Protest Potential', 14 December 2018. Available at: https://www.levada.ru/en/2018/12/14/protest-potential/.

60 Vladimir Gel'man, *'Nedostoinoe Pravlenie': Politika v sovremennoi Rossii* (St. Petersburg: European University Press, 2019).

61 Institute of Regional Expertise, 'Protestnoe Pole v Rossii: Formaty i Praktika', n.d., http://irex.group/uploads/article/pdf/108/%D0%9F%D1%80%D0%BE%D1%82%D0%B5%D1%81%D1%82__.pdf.

62 Nikita Girin and Anna Shuliat'eva, 'Russkii Sever i musornyi Iug', Novaya Gazeta, 13 December 2018, https://www.novayagazeta.ru/articles/2018/12/13/78928-russkiy-sever-i-musornyy-yug; RFE/RL, 'Thousands Participate In "Russia Is Not A Dump" Protests', 3 February 2019, https://www.rferl.org/a/thousands-participate-in-russia-is-not-a-dump-nationwide-protests/29748950.html.

63 Thomas Nilsen, 'Moscow Garbage Sparks Mass Protest across Northwest-Russia', *The Barents Observer*, 6 December 2018, https://thebarentsobserver.com/en/ecology/2018/12/moscow-garbage-plan-sparks-mass-protest-across-arkhangelsk-region.

64 Gabowitsch, *Protest in Putin's Russia*, 24.

65 Gabowitsch, *Protest in Putin's Russia*, 71.

66 Elena Mukhametshina, 'V Rossii podnimaetsia tret'ia volna regional'nogo patriotisma', *Vedomosti*, 20 May 2019, https://www.vedomosti.ru/politics/articles/2019/05/19/801760-rossii-tretya-volna.

67 Tom Balmforth, 'Moscow's Plan To Raze "Khrushchyovki" Sparks Anger, Confusion Ahead of Elections', *RFE/RL*, 6 May 2017, https://www.rferl.org/a/russia-moscow-khrushchyovki-demolition-housing-controversy-elections/28471341.html.

68 Evans, 'Protests in Russia'.

69 Personal communication with author, St. Petersburg, Russia, October 2017.

70 'Protests in Moscow at Plan to Tear Down Soviet-era Housing in Affluent Areas', *The Guardian*, 14 May 2017, https://www.theguardian.com/world/2017/may/14/people-protest-moscow-plans-to-tear-down-housing.

71 Julia Ioffe, 'Anti-Seliger', *The New Yorker*, 20 June 2011, http://www.newyorker.com/news/news-desk/anti-seliger.

72 *RFE/RL*, 'Prominent Russian Environmentalist to Run for Khimki Mayor', 20 August 2012, https://www.rferl.org/a/russia-khimki-mayor-chirikova/24682176.html.

73 Associated Press, 'Russia's Leading Environmentalist Fees to Estonia', *The Guardian*, 20 April 2015, https://www.theguardian.com/environment/2015/apr/20/russias-leading-environmentalist-flees-to-estonia.

74 Laura A. Henry, 'Complaint-Making as Political Participation in Contemporary Russia', *Communist and Post-Communist Studies* 45, nos. 3–4 (2012): 243–54.

75 Susanne Wengle and Christine Evans, 'Symbolic State-Building in Contemporary Russia', *Post-Soviet Affairs* 34, no. 6 (2018): 384–411.

76 RBC, 'Putin potreboval ne pooshchriat' sozdaniie svalok riadom s zhil'em', 27 November 2017, https://www.rbc.ru/politics/27/11/2017/5a1bf1709a79475263a148ff.

77 Regina Smyth, 'The Putin Factor: Personalism, Protest, and Regime Stability in Russia', *Politics & Policy* 42, no. 4 (2014): 567–92.

78 Fond Obshchestvennoe Mnenie, 'V. Putin: reiting, otnoshenie, otsenki raboty', 24 January 2019, https://fom.ru/Politika/10946; Levada Center, 'Odobrenie institutov vlasti', 31 January 2019, https://www.levada.ru/2019/01/31/odobrenie-institutov-vlasti-9/.

79 'President's Address to the Federal Assembly', 20 February 2019, http://kremlin.ru/events/president/news/59863.

80 RBK, 'Kak Kreml' budet reagirovat' na zhaloby v cotssetiakh', 23 July 2018, https://www.rbc.ru/politics/23/07/2018/5b50d1579a7947c62c195e8b?from=main.

81 Andrew Higgins, 'The Theatrical Method in Putin's Vote Madness', *New York Times*, 1 July 2020.

82 Human Rights Watch, 'Russia: Police Crush Peaceful Protests', 9 September 2018, https://www.hrw.org/news/2018/09/13/russia-police-crush-peaceful-protests.

83 Ekaterina Schulmann, 'Zapros est' takoi, shto zakruchennye gaechki nemnogo potriakhivaet', Znak.com, 9 January 2019, https://www.znak.com/2019-01-09/kakoy_dolzhna_byt_vlast_v_rossii_i_chego_zhdet_narod_lekciya_ekateriny_shulman.

84 Mariia Zheleznova, 'Bezalabernost' protiv terrorizma', 9 January 2019, https://www.vedomosti.ru/opinion/articles/2019/01/09/790940-bezalabernost-protiv-terrorizma.

85 See Activatica at http://activatica.org/.

86 Aleksandar Matovskii, 'It's the Stability, Stupid! How the Quest to Restore Order after the Soviet Collapse Shaped Russian Popular Opinion', *Comparative Politics* 50, no. 3 (2018): 347–90.

87 Gosudarstvennaia Duma RF, 'Kak novaia konstitutsiia zashchitit sotsial'nyi pravy grazhdan', 19 March 2020. http://duma.gov.ru/news/48041/.

88 Katerina Tertytchnaya and Tomila Lankina, 'Whom Do Russian Protesters Blame (and Why It Matters)?', *Political Mobilization and Democracy*, 20 September 2018, https://popularmobilization.net/2016/09/20/whom-do-russian-protesters-blame-and-why-it-matters/.

References

Bogdanova, Elena, Linda J. Cook and Meri Kulmala. 'The Carrot or the Stick? Constraints and Opportunities of Russia's CSO Policy'. *Europe-Asia Studies* 70, no. 4 (2018): 501–13.

Brechenmacher, Saskia. *Civil Society under Assault: Repression and Responses in Russia, Egypt, and Ethiopia*. Carnegie Endowment for International Peace, 18 May 2017.

Bunce, Valerie and Sharon Wolchik. 'Defeating Dictators: Electoral Change and Stability in Competitive Authoritarian Regimes'. *World Politics* 62, no. 1 (2010): 43–86.

Chernova, Nataliia. 'Vrach Naroda'. *Novaya Gazeta*, 16 October 2018.

Cook, Linda J. and Martin K. Dimitrov. 'The Social Contract Revisited: Evidence from Communist and State Capitalist Economies'. *Europe-Asia Studies* 69, no. 1 (2017): 8–26.

Dimitrov, Martin K., ed. *Why Communism Did Not Collapse: Understanding Authoritarian Regime Resilience in Asia and Europe*. Cambridge: Cambridge University Press, 2013.

Dmitriev, Mikhail. 'Lost in Transition? The Geography of Protests and Attitude Change in Russia'. *Europe-Asia Studies* 67, no. 2 (March 2015): 224–43, 233.

Dupuy, K., J. Ron and A. Prakash. 'Hands Off My Regime! Governments' Restrictions on Foreign Aid to Non-governmental Organizations in Poor and Middle-Income Countries'. *World Development* 84 (August 2016): 299–311.

Evans, Alfred B. 'Many Russians Aren't Protesting against Putin—They want His Help'. *Washington Post*, 21 August 2017.

Evans, Alfred B. 'Protests and Civil Society in Russia: The Struggle for the Khimki Forest'. *Communist and Post-Communist Studies* 45, nos. 3–4 (2012): 233–42.

Evans, Alfred B. 'Protests in Russia: The Example of the Blue Buckets Society'. *Demokratizatsiya* 26, no. 1 (2018): 3–24.

Flikke, Geir. 'Conflicting Opportunities or Patronal Politics? Restrictive NGO Legislation in Russia 2012–2015'. *Europe-Asia Studies* 70, no. 4 (2018): 564–90.

Gabowitsch, Mischa. *Protest in Putin's Russia*. Cambridge: Polity Press, 2017.

Gel'man, Vladimir. *'Nedostoinoe Pravlenie': Politika v sovremennoi Rossii*. St. Petersburg: European University Press, 2019.

Gilley, Bruce. *The Right to Rule: How States Win and Lose Legitimacy*. New York: Columbia University Press, 2009.

Girin, Nikita and Anna Shuliat'eva. 'Russkii Sever i musornyi Iug'. *Novaya Gazeta*, 13 December 2018.

Greene, Samuel A. 'From Boom to Bust: Hardship, Mobilization and Russia's Social Contract'. *Daedalus* 146, no. 2 (2017): 113–27.

Greene, Samuel A. *Moscow in Movement: Power and Opposition in Putin's Russia*. Stanford: Stanford University Press, 2014.

Heiss, Andrew. 'Authoritarian Institutions and Restrictions on International Civil Society'. Paper presented at the International Studies Association, February 2016.

Heiss, Andrew and Judith G. Kelley. 'Between a Rock and a Hard Place: International NGOs and the Dual Pressures of Donors and Host Governments'. *Journal of Politics* 79, no. 2 (April 2017): 732–41.

Hemment, Julie. *Youth Politics in Putin's Russia: Producing Patriots and Entrepreneurs*. Bloomington: Indiana University Press, 2015.
Henry, Laura A. 'Complaint-Making as Political Participation in Contemporary Russia'. *Communist and Post-Communist Studies* 45, nos. 3–4 (2012): 243–54.
Heurlin, Christopher. *Responsive Authoritarianism in China: Land, Protests, and Policy Making*. Cambridge: Cambridge University Press, 2016.
Higgins, Andrew. 'The Theatrical Method in Putin's Vote Madness'. *New York Times*, 1 July 2020.
Hsu, J. and R. Hasmath, eds. *The Chinese Corporatist State: Adaption, Survival and Resistance*. New York: Routledge, 2013.
Ioffe, Julia. 'Anti-Seliger'. *The New Yorker*, 20 June 2011.
Janjevic, Darko. 'Volokolamsk: Russians Protest Toxic Landfills Near Moscow'. *Deutsche Welle*, 3 April 2018.
Javeline, Debra. *Protest and the Politics of Blame: The Russian Response to Unpaid Wages*. Ann Arbor: University of Michigan Press, 2003.
Kendall-Taylor, A. and E. Frantz. 'Mimicking Democracy to Prolong Autocracies'. *Washington Quarterly* 37, no. 4 (2014): 71–84.
Lasnier, Virginie. 'Demobilisation and Its Consequences: After the Russian Movement Za chestnye vybory'. *Europe-Asia Studies* 69, no. 5 (2017): 771–93.
Levitsky, Steve and Lucan Way. *Competitive Authoritarianism: Hybrid Regimes after the Cold War*. Cambridge: Cambridge University Press, 2010.
Linz, Juan J. 'Legitimacy of Democracy and Socioeconomic Systems'. In Mattei Dogan (ed.), *Comparing Pluralist Democracies: Strains on Legitimacy*, 65–11. Boulder: Westview Press, 1988.
Lorentzen, Peter L. 'Regularizing Rioting: Permitting Public Protest in an Authoritarian Regime'. *Quarterly Journal of Political Science* 8, no. 2 (2013): 127–58.
MacKinnon, Amy. 'In Russia, Plan to Raise Pension Age Draws Protests'. *Foreign Policy*, 1 July 2018.
Makarin, Aleksei and Peter M. Oppenheimer. 'The Russian Social Contract and Regime Legitimacy'. *International Affairs* 87, no. 6 (2011): 1459–74.
Matovskii, Aleksandar. 'It's the Stability, Stupid! How the Quest to Restore Order After the Soviet Collapse Shaped Russian Popular Opinion'. *Comparative Politics* 50, no. 3 (2018): 347–90.
McAdam, Doug. *Political Process and the Development of Black Insurgency, 1930–1970*. Chicago: University of Chicago Press, 1982.
Petrov, Nikolay, Maria Lipman and Henry E. Hale. 'Three Dilemmas of Hybrid Regime Governance: Russia from Putin to Putin'. *Post-Soviet Affairs* 30, no. 1 (2014): 1–26.
Plantan, Elizabeth. 'Mass Mobilization in China and Russia: From Unexpected Victories to Unintended Consequences'. *Russian Politics* 3, no. 4 (2018): 513–47.
Robertson, Graeme. *The Politics of Protest in Hybrid Regimes: Managing Dissent in Post-communist Russia*. Cambridge: Cambridge University Press, 2011.
Rosenberg, Steven. 'Is Russia the Real Winner of World Cup 2018?' 14 July 2018. https://www.bbc.com/news/world-europe-44812175.
Ruvinskii, Vladimir. 'Chto delat' nizam, kogda verkhi molchat', 26 June 2018. https://www.vedomosti.ru/opinion/articles/2018/06/26/773746-chto-delat.

Smyth, Regina. 'How the Kremlin Is Using the Moscow Renovation Project to Reward and Punish Voters'. *PONARS*, March 2018.

Smyth, Regina. 'The Putin Factor: Personalism, Protest, and Regime Stability in Russia'. *Politics & Policy* 42, no. 4 (2014): 567–92.

Smyth, Regina, Anton Sobolev and Irina Soboleva. 'A Well-Organized Play'. *Problems of Post-Communism* 60, no. 2 (2013): 24–39.

Svolik, Milan W. *Politics of Authoritarian Rule*. Cambridge: Cambridge University Press, 2012.

Tarasenko, Anna. 'Russian Non-profit Organisations in Service Delivery: Neoliberal and Statist Social Policy Principles Intertwined'. *Europe-Asia Studies* 70, no. 4 (2018): 514–30.

Tarrow, Sidney G. *Power in Movement: Social Movements and Contentious Politics*. New York: Cambridge University Press, 2011.

Teets, Jessica. *Civil Society under Authoritarianism: The China Model*. Cambridge: Cambridge University Press, 2014.

Wengle, Susanne and Christine Evans. 'Symbolic State-Building in Contemporary Russia'. *Post-Soviet Affairs* 34, no. 6 (2018): 384–411.

Wengle, Susanne and Michael Rasell. 'The Monetisation of l'goty: Changing Patterns of Welfare Politics and Provision in Russia'. *Europe-Asia Studies* 60, no. 5 (2008): 739–56.

White, S. 'Economic Performance and Communist Legitimacy'. *World Politics* 38, no. 3 (1986): 462–82.

Wintrobe, Ronald. *The Political Economy of Dictatorship*. New York: Cambridge University Press, 1998.

7

How the party-state harnessed people power in China

Diana Fu

People power in an illiberal era

When China's top leader Xi Jinping abolished presidential term limits in 2018,[1] the Western media declared him as a new emperor. Since taking power in 2012, Xi Jinping has joined a global consortium of authoritarian 'strongman leaders',[2] including Putin (Russia), Erdogan in Turkey, Duterte in the Philippines, Fattah al-Sisi in Egypt, Viktor Orban in Hungary and others. The rise of these leaders has ushered in a renewed era of global authoritarianism, with 55 per cent of countries in the world considered to be not free or partly free in 2018.[3]

In this illiberal era, has 'people power' – the power of the masses to mobilize against the state – dissipated? What has become of the collective power of people taking to the streets to oust authoritarian incumbents? In the case of China, the world's largest and most powerful authoritarian regime, the ruling party has been able to continue successfully harnessing people power. In doing so, it has drawn up on a traditional repertoire of cultural governance, exploitation of class conflict and overt state propaganda. By flexibly wielding these techniques for over seventy years, the Chinese government has been able to harness the power of the masses (*qunzhong*) to advance the state's interests.

Under the current leader Xi Jinping, the party-state has also retooled a traditional repertoire of power accompanying China's emergence as a global power. Composed of a mix of the old and the new, this repertoire has been re-invented for the new era of tech-savvy, high-capacity authoritarianism. Specifically, the party-state has infused traditional emotional governance with legal rhetoric. This is clearly manifest in the anti-corruption campaign and the anti–civil society campaign in which the familiar theatrics of public confessions are framed in the language of the law. Second, the party has supplanted exploiting class conflict with mobilizing citizens against external, foreign enemies. Finally, censorship is now coupled with public opinion guidance.

This chapter briefly reviews the historical importance of 'people power' in China. It examines the traditional repertoire through which the Chinese Communist Party sought to harness people power through the Tiananmen Democracy Movement in 1989. It then turns to how the contemporary party-state under Xi has transformed these three traditional techniques to turn the power of the masses to the Party's advantage. This new repertoire stands out in its deployment of teched-up deception and the rule of law to hide the state's intervention.

Mobilizing the people via traditional repertoire

Harnessing people power has been an integral part of Chinese governance even before the founding of the People's Republic in 1949. Every leader from Mao Zedong to Xi Jinping has mobilized the masses to advance the party-state's most transformative political campaigns. This traditional repertoire included 'cultural governance',[4] exploiting social classes, and overt state propaganda.

During the revolutionary era in the 1920s, the Chinese Communist Party deftly mobilized the proletariat through what has been termed 'cultural governance'.[5] In this early period, mobilization relied on the charisma and ingenuity of the communist leaders. Specifically, the Chinese Communist Party mobilized workers through 'cultural governance' – the deployment of symbolic resources as an instrument of political authority'.[6] Mao, along with his comrades Liu Shaoqi and Li Lisan, drew upon a range of traditional cultural resources, including textbooks, dramas, songs and lectures to persuade the workers at Anyuan – the birthplace of communism – to join in the party's revolutionary efforts.[7] This cultural mobilization resulted in a party-led workers' movement in Anyuan that eventually precipitated a Communist revolution nationwide. The party channelled these early experiences of cultural mobilization and emotional manipulation into political campaigns after the establishment of the People's Republic of China in 1949.

In addition to cultural mobilization and emotional manipulation, the party-state also strategically deployed another instrument – mobilizing different classes against each other. Perhaps no other political campaign exhibited this as visibly as during the Cultural Revolution (1967–76). This state-led mobilization was characterized by both high degrees of visibility in terms of the supreme leader's involvement and the exploitation of class differences. Under Mao's directions, the Communist party directly mobilized groups of workers in Beijing and Shanghai to do the state's bidding in confronting increasingly intractable student-led red guard factions.[8] Worker propaganda teams were sent onto university campuses to educate the students on Mao's latest directives via traditional tools of loudspeaker broadcasts, posters, mass forums and meetings.[9] In the eight years following the state-led workers' counter-protests, the proletariat class held sway over higher education, effectively taking control over college curriculum and campus activities.[10] Through rallying the workers to confront the students, the state pitted the people (*renmin*) against each other, thus creatively exploiting class differences to achieve the supreme leader's political objectives.

The 1989 Tiananmen Democracy Movement marked another turning point in which the state exploited class differences to harness people power. During the student-led movement, Chinese workers and students supported each other[11] but also diverged in their grievances and ideologies. These differences prompted workers to form the Beijing Workers' Autonomous Association (*Gongzilian*), an act that expressed 'an unabashed working-class trade-union mentality' and a spirit of anti-elitism.[12] At the peak of the movement, the party-state took advantage of the split between workers and students to quell the latter. In Beijing and Shanghai, the party mobilized the proletariat, including peasants and rural cadres in Beijing, to suppress the raucous students through staging counter-protests, rallies and demonstrations in support of political stability. However, the party's involvement was initially more disguised than during Mao's intervention in the Cultural Revolution. The party-state in Shanghai sought to hide its hand in organizing the workers via work units only to make it evident soon afterwards that they had been mobilized by the state.[13]

In conjunction with cultural governance and exploiting class conflict, the party also overtly deployed propaganda to establish thought control. In the Mao era, China was decidedly a propaganda state. The party used a range of tools to directly steer the masses' thoughts. These included both productive and coercive tools. On the productive side, the party created study groups and model citizens, as well as sent propaganda teams.[14] In the 1950s, it established a nationwide network of loudspeakers that could channel the party's voice into every neighbourhood.[15] Propaganda was disseminated via highly visible and dramatic mass gatherings, including public rallies, demonstrations, big-letter posters, study sessions and the like. The party-state was quite bold in showing its hand; it did not care to disguise its intervention in getting the masses out. On the coercive end, the party-state incarcerated individuals for the purposes of brainwashing and placed monitors in society to keep track of public discourse.[16]

No matter the method, the party guided the propaganda and was literally the voice behind the loudspeakers.

In short, since the revolutionary period, the Chinese Communist Party has deftly harnessed people power for the purposes of state control. From the lead-up to the Chinese Communist revolution in 1949 through the 1989 Tiananmen Democracy Movement, the party-state has repeatedly turned to a similar repertoire for rallying the masses. This repertoire included, but was not limited to, drawing upon traditional cultural arts, exploiting the divisions between social classes, and propaganda.

The new and the old under Xi Jinping

Much has changed since the era of crowd-rallying via loudspeakers and big-letter posters. The party-state under Xi Jinping is now a global power, actively disseminating its governance model and capital investment abroad.[17] Accordingly, the party-state has strategically retooled the traditional repertoire for harnessing people power. This retooled repertoire is composed of a mix of the new and the old. Specifically, cultural governance and emotional manipulation have been infused with a legal-rational justification for repression. Domestic class struggle has been supplanted by warfare against external, foreign enemies. Overt propaganda has been coupled with censorship and public opinion guidance. This new repertoire combines traditional strategies with novel elements that only a high-capacity authoritarian state could deliver.

Most notably, the retooled repertoire has manifested in three overlapping political campaigns under Xi Jinping: the anti-corruption campaign, the anti–civil society campaign and the online propaganda campaign. All three campaigns exhibited elements of the transformed repertoire that has elements of the old and the new. Through examining these three campaigns, it is possible to deduce to how the contemporary party-state has adapted its methods of harnessing people power in China. These developments are in keeping with the broader pattern of Chinese governance, which 'meanders' like water, constituting 'a multi-stranded process which privileges nimbleness, mutability, and openness'.[18] This re-invention is a part of China's tradition of adaptive governance.[19]

Coupling the emotional with the legal

Xi Jinping's administration has revived a traditional repertoire of emotional manipulation with a new twist. Specifically, the cultural practice of public confessions has been infused with a discourse on governance by law (*yifa zhiguo*), which was introduced under a previous leader, Jiang Zemin.[20] Most notably, Xi Jinping's resuscitation of public confession is reminiscent of political theatre during the Cultural Revolution (1966–76), in which targets of political campaign were paraded on the streets wearing tall hats and were made to confess to a denouncing crowd.[21] This form of political theatre sought to manipulate the emotions of 'the people' by mobilizing social groups to actively participate in the spectating, denouncement and punishment of 'political enemies'. At its core, this practice shares common characteristics with spectacles of torture and public executions at the scaffold which were common in historical Europe.[22] Whereas this 'gloomy festival of punishment' was phased out in Europe by the beginning of the nineteenth century,[23] contemporary authoritarian regimes, including the former communist states in Eastern Europe, North Korea and Iran, have used or continue to stage public trials and televised confessions.[24]

Xi Jinping brought back public confessions early during his administration in the anti-corruption campaign, one of his landmark political projects. The anti-corruption campaign, memorably termed 'catching tigers and flies',[25] began in 2013 during Xi's first year in office and has since sprawled to over 300,000 investigations of officials for corruption charges, according to official figures.[26] The Central Commission for Discipline Inspection (CCDI) has implicated some 2 million officials on corruption charges.[27] This constitutes about 2 per cent of 89 million members of the Chinese Communist Party, which also include non-state officials.[28]

Beyond its scale, this campaign is also remarkable in its dual deployment of political theatre infused with the rule of law. Specifically, this involves producing and disseminating a number of televised confession trials and anti-graft-themed television dramas that feature both the affective and the rational. The party-state not only sentenced the 'tigers and the flies', they also mobilize the masses to spectate and participate in the punishment of wayward party members. They do this through publicizing the trials of officials on China Central Television (CCTV), clips of which are then circulated on Chinese social media.[29]

The airing of these emotionally charged confessions exhibits a long tradition of the party's 'emotion work' – a part of a 'conscious strategy of psychological engineering' perfected during mass campaigns, including the Land Reform, the Great Leap Forward and the Cultural Revolution.[30] Departing from the Mao-era goals of public confessions of self-transformation and redemption, the Xi administration is using it to exert 'affective sovereignty' – bolstering the party's own image and moral legitimacy.[31]

Televised confessions of corruption trials elicit emotional reactions of the viewing public while also serving as a pedagogical tool for the law. In 2016, the state produced an eight-part documentary series, 'Always on the Road', showcasing seventy-seven officials investigated for corruption.[32] The series was a hit, attracting millions of viewers. Its production and dissemination exhibit the party-state wielding 'emotional governance'[33] at its best. One of the front-runners whose on-air confession performance was emotionally resonated with WeChat viewers was Li Chuncheng, former deputy party chief of Sichuan province. Appearing unable to restrain his emotions, Li broke down on camera, uttering apologies to both the party and to the people:

> This is all my fault *(inhales, shakes his head, takes off his glass and wipes tears)*. I really feel sorry to the party *(looks into his palm)*, sorry to the people, and even more sorry to *(sobs)* those cadres in Chengdu who followed my lead . . . *(sobs continuously)* I'm supposed to influence their values. What kind of thing have I done?[34]

By visually showcasing the 'tigers and the flies' expressing contrition for their deviance and apologizing to the people (*renmin*), the party-state is turning to a well-crafted tool of emotional manipulation. Moreover, the authorities used the online social media platform WeChat (ubiquitously used by Chinese mobile users) to invite the masses to vote on the best confession. The state-monitored WeChat posted the following question to the public: 'If you were the party-secretary of the disciplinary commission, who would pass?'[35] These manoeuvres ensure that the public is actively participating in the state's political theatre, not just passive consumers of propaganda.

This traditional method of manipulating peoples' emotions is coupled with an emphasis on the rule of law. It is evident that the party-state is also using confessions as a form of legal mobilization and education. This type of mobilization seeks to garner public support for the party-state's project to govern by the law (*yifa zhiguo*). China's rule of law reform began in the 1990s when 'ruling the country in accordance with the law' was incorporated into the 1999 constitution.[36] Since then, the rule of law has suffused the governing rhetoric of the party-state. The Chinese government has launched numerous legal education campaigns to disseminate basic legal knowledge to the population.[37] Governance by law remains a basis of state legitimacy under Xi Jinping, who has made judicial reform a top priority.[38]

By infusing traditional political theatre with legal rhetoric, the party-state is trying to shore up popular support for its legal campaigns, which is important to solidifying its rule. Whereas previous administrations in the 1990s and 2000s have tolerated bottom-up experimentation with legal reforms, Xi Jinping has sought to recentralize judicial control.[39] This means minimizing local officials' roles in the judiciary and closing up spaces for local experimentation. Such a centralization of judicial power needs to be accompanied by popular support. Airing confessions replete with references to the law is an attempt by the party to invigorate the masses into buttressing a state that gets tough on criminals and corrupt officials alike.

From internal to external enemies

The party has also sought to harness people power by re-directing internal class conflict towards external enemies. In previous eras, the party-state orchestrated class conflict, mobilizing workers to quell extremist student groups. In the Xi era, the party has sought instead to mobilize people against foreign, external enemies whom they blame for staging domestic unrest. While this tactic is hardly new, it has become ever more prominent in the contemporary period. Instead of pitting social groups against each other, the party-state tries to direct the people's wrath against a common enemy – the conspiring West and its liberal democratic values.

Nowhere is this more ironically manifested than in the state's response to Marxist students allying with striking workers. In August of 2018, some fifty students from several different elite universities decided to join migrant workers in the southern city of Huizhou to demand the formation of an independent labour union, forbidden under Chinese law. Chanting the Internationale and carrying portraits of Mao, the students sought to rally to the side of migrant workers and to fulfil their true calling as members of leftist Marxist societies.[40] Inspired by what they believed to be true Marxist-Leninist values, the students broke ranks with their apolitical classmates to champion proletarian causes. Not only that, student leader Yue Xin also wrote an open letter addressed to Xi Jinping, listing several demands on behalf of the Jasic workers.[41]

This show of people power, although negligible compared to the 1989 democracy movement, shook the party-state. Under the previous administration, labour activists in China engaged in mobilizing without the masses, a form of organized, but individualized, contention that had limited cross-class alliances.[42] In contrast, this new form of collective action exhibited a rare cross-class alliance between the intelligentsia and the proletariats. Moreover, this collective action challenged the party-state's monopoly on defining Marxism. It is one thing for workers to demand material compensation such as higher wages and social insurance. The authorities can quell such demands through a combination of repression and concessions. But when workers start to ally with students to demand independent unionizing, this directly challenges the party's ideological legitimacy. To the party-state, this is seen as outright defiance and rejection of the state-led socialism. It is these two factors – the alliance of students with workers – and their ideological challenge to the state – that strike fear in the ruling power.

The authorities first raided the meeting of about forty students and then disappeared a number of student leaders in August 2018. Among the disappeared was Yue Xin, who penned the open letter to Xi.[43] Later, the police snatched the student leader of the Marxist society at Beijing University while on his way to celebrate the great Chairman's birthday in December of 2018.[44] And most recently, the authorities compelled four of the detained students to confess their 'crimes', circulating the confession video to university students.[45] The police also flew in students' parents to Guangzhou[46] in a classic exercise of 'relational repression' – putting pressure on activists via their social ties.[47]

Elements of this repressive repertoire clearly depart from the traditional method of pitting social groups against each other. The party could have, for instance, rallied workers from other factories to swarm the students, defying their apparent show of cross-class solidarity. Instead, the authorities attributed blame towards an external enemy – illegal organizations supported by the West. According to testimonies given by students who had watched the confession video (which is not openly circulated), the four student activists confessed to 'spreading false information', founding subversive organizations and conspiring with foreign media. In particular, Yue Xin, who had previously campaigned Beijing University to release information on a rape case, also allegedly admitted to foreign interference on that act as well.[48] Like the confessions of other activists,[49] the students' confessions reveal a transcript that the party-state dictated, one of attributing domestic activism to Western interference.

In addition to blaming domestic woes on foreign enemies, the current regime's repressive tactics are also less visible than its predecessors. It deploys repression in a camouflaged manner in order to pre-empt further collective action. Whereas Mao openly admitted to empowering workers to swarm university campuses, Xi disappeared the vociferous student leaders. If Mao's intent was to squash undesirable people power with state-sponsored collective action, Xi's goal is to snuff out any restive social actors by erasing them from the public consciousness. In the era of maintaining social stability, the party-state cannot afford to rally different social classes against one another, for fear of stoking the flames of social unrest. It can, however, resort to under-the-radar repression such as disappearing activists. Such tactics are hardly new or unique to the contemporary era, but they have been deployed with increased fervour under a regime that is keen to keep social unrest at bay.

Despite the current regime's efforts to step up pre-emptive control, contentious collective action is still prevalent domestically in Mainland China. One of the most indicative types of social unrest is labour activism. Under Xi, labour protests have become smaller in size, averaging less than one hundred participants, but they have become more broadly distributed geographically.[50] Moreover, the demands of workers have shifted since 2008 from defensive claims such as requesting wage arrears to offensive claims such as higher compensation, better working conditions and respect.[51]

Bucking the trend towards small-scale activism, both blue-collar and white-collar workers have taken large-scale collective action in recent years. In June 2018, tens of thousands of truck drivers across China reportedly went on strike in June 2018 against rising fuel prices and low pay.[52] This large-scale collective action took place in the midst of censorship as officials sought to delete related posts on social media and banned official media form reporting it.[53] In 2014, thousands of teachers in Northeast China went on strike against low salaries and mandatory payments to pension plans.[54] Teachers are part of an increasingly vociferous middle class taking collective action to demand a clean environment,[55] fair education policies[56] and stricter regulation of the financial industry.[57] The party-state has, thus far, been able to harness these manifestations of people power through repression and censorship. However, the fact that large-scale collective action has persisted in an era of consolidated control and heighted surveillance suggests that people power cannot be fully harnessed, even by a high-capacity authoritarian state.

Pairing censorship with positive propaganda

A third tactic that has been adapted from the traditional repertoire is state propaganda. Propaganda serves the same purposes it did under Mao as it does under Xi, which is to convince the public of the legitimacy of the Chinese Communist Party's rule. However, the current party-state is attempting to influence public opinion through indirect means. Public support is so important to the current regime that Xi Jinping told his Politburo colleagues that 'winning or losing public support is an issue that concerns the CCP's survival or extinction'.[58] Accordingly, it is of utmost importance for the party-state to guide public opinion. This, too, can be seen as a means through which the authorities attempt to harness people power. In mobilizing the public to participate in the public shaming of state officials, the party is channelling the masses away from popular protests that could get out of hand.

The virtual world is a contentious sphere, with netizens using social media and other platforms to organize online and offline collective action.[59] Accordingly, the party-state closely monitors online content via a combination of censorship and propaganda.[60] However, unlike the Mao era in which propaganda was blatantly broadcast by the party, Xi's mode of propaganda is characterized by disguise. Mass gatherings and public rallies have been replaced with paid online commentators and cyberspace mobilization.[61]

The state's revamped propaganda machine seeks to hide, rather than reveal, the speaker behind the mouthpiece. Instead, it relies on third parties including paid online commentators and private companies to whom the party-state outsources public opinion guidance (*yuqing gongzuo*). Doing so allows the state to manage people power manifested in virtual collective action.

This nouveau propaganda is created and disseminated under the disguise of third parties. This includes paid online commentators as well as the network of private companies to whom the state outsources public opinion guidance work.[62] The party-state is hiring online commentators, pejoratively named the 'fifty-cent party' because they were reportedly paid fifty cents per positive commentary. A recent study estimates that in 2013, the paid commentators generated 448 billion posts on social media annually, accounting for one out of every 178 posts on commercial websites.[63] Moreover, these fabricated posts appeared in bursts coinciding with major political events during which collective action potential is high.[64] This means that the party-state pre-emptively *de-mobilizes* people during periods of potential unrest.

By disguising its presence behind voices of ordinary netizens, the party-state is able to create a spectre of choice for consumers of information. Unable to verify which posts are fabricated by government agents and which are genuine expressions, netizens believe that they are actively choosing to consume whichever posts they prefer. While one had no choice but to listen to state broadcast during the pre-reform era, the contemporary citizen has the 'choice' of which posts to pay attention to. Accordingly, the state's 'thought work' is much more concealed.

Disguised propaganda is accompanied by hidden censorship. Netizens may notice when their posts are deleted from websites or when they can't find certain banned websites, but they are less likely to know for certain if their posts have been censored. Social media users are often unaware of the state's hand in filtering their messages to friend circles. Recent studies show that images that were filtered may not be obvious to WeChat users.[65] Users are not given any notices that the images they posted were censored; the image simply does not appear on the receivers' end.[66] Thus, the state's intervention on social media is again masked.

The combination of indirect propaganda and hidden censorship and has kept people power in check in contemporary China. The state is able to harness people power without the people noticing. Not only are activists unable to organize online without being detected, it has also become more difficult for them to disseminate information about their activism, even via images.[67] For instance, it was discovered that a number of images related to the '709' crackdown on human-rights lawyers had been blocked on group chats when using a domestic Chinese account. These included profile sketches of lawyers and relatives as well as people holding placards with subversive slogans.[68] Internet surveillance has also enabled the police to track the locations of activists in real time,[69] presumably allowing them to arrive at the site of collective action at the same time as protesters. As a result, the people power that could have been unleashed via internet mobilization has been significantly undermined.

Global China: Harnessing people power

Will the party-state's re-designed toolkit of control keep people power in check in the long term both domestically and in its territorial frontiers? The China case is interesting because it is a live experiment in social control by a *global* authoritarian power. Before 2013, China was arguably a partial, rather than a global, power. Today, China has been deemed by the West as a 'sharp power'.[70] This is a type of authoritarian power that seeks to 'pierce, penetrate, or perforate' free societies while using censorship and control to limit information to its domestic audience.[71] What the West has called 'sharp power' Xi Jinping has termed 'the Chinese dream'. Encapsulating many aspects, the Chinese dream has come to signal at its core the rejuvenation of the Chinese nation. This narrative of rejuvenation is not new, but the fact that it is projecting Chinese values beyond its boards is of great importance.

As a global power, the Chinese regime is applying its repertoire of control both inside and outside of Mainland China.[72] It is concerned not only with keeping people power in check at home but also with mobilizing people to stand up for 'Chinese' political values in its frontiers and also abroad.

According to a recent report by the Hoover Institute, Chinese influence operations in the United States 'have moved beyond their traditional United Front focus on diaspora communities to target a far broader range of sectors in Western societies, ranging from think tanks, universities, and media to state, local and national government institutions'.[73] The repertoire of control tactics that the regime is deploying domestically is also being adapted to project Chinese political values and ideologies abroad. There is emerging evidence of China exporting its digital repression technologies to other countries.[74] For instance, China has hosted various seminars on cyberspace management for countries along the Belt Road Initiative. Chinese private companies have also been providing high-tech surveillance tools that use artificial intelligence and facial recognition to identify 'threatening' people.[75]

The Chinese government's efforts to harness people power has already met resistance in one of its frontiers – Hong Kong. The territory of Hong Kong was ceded to the British colonial government in 1841 after a humiliating defeat in the first Opium War.[76] It was handed back to Beijing in 1997 in accordance with the 1984 Sino-British Joint Declaration. The declaration set out a 'one country, two systems' governing principle under which Hong Kong was entitled to enjoy certain political and social freedoms that are not granted to citizens of Mainland China for fifty years. Among these included the freedom of speech, assembly and protest, all protected under the Basic Law, which serves as a mini-constitution governing the territory.[77]

Since the 1997 handover, the Chinese government has sought repeatedly to wrest autonomy from Hong Kong, each time meeting fierce opposition from the Hong Kong people. Among such notable opposition was the 2014 umbrella movement, so named for protesters' use of umbrellas as a tool to block the police's pepper spray. This seventy-nine-day-long show of people power on the part of Hong Kong residents was triggered by Beijing's decision to prescribe a selective pre-screening for candidates of the 2017 election for Hong Kong's top leader.[78] Although the protests eventually subsided, it had 'galvanized a generation of young Hong Kongers' to take to the streets to defend their political and civil liberties.[79]

In the aftermath of the 2014 umbrella movement, the Chinese government stepped up repression of civil society in Hong Kong, arresting activists and booksellers and pressuring businesses to side with Beijing.[80] This culminated in May 2020, when the National People's Congress in Beijing took a decisive manoeuvre which would impinge upon the autonomy of Hong Kong: the passing of a National Security Law in the territory.[81] This law was passed directly through Beijing and not through Hong Kong's local legislative council.[82] It was in direct response to months of unrest in Hong Kong starting in the summer of 2019, as hundreds of thousands of Hong Kongers engaged in some of the largest mass demonstrations in the territory's history to demand the retraction of an extradition law proposed by Beijing.

Rather than capitulating to people power in Hong Kong with the Hong Kong government's withdrawal of the extradition bill,[83] Beijing's fist came down much harder than anticipated following the 2019 demonstrations. The 2020 Hong Kong national security law embodies Beijing's efforts to harness people in its frontiers and beyond. The law is sweeping in nature, criminalizing four broad categories of actions: succession, subversion, terrorism, collusion with foreign forces. Those charged with these actions can be sentenced to a maximum of life sentence.[84] Remarkably, the law extends to those outside of China's national borders. Article 38 of the law states that the law shall apply to offences committed outside of Hong Kong, which asserts 'extraterritorial jurisdiction' to anyone, anywhere in the world.[85] This means that in addition to Hong Kong people, foreigners could also be prosecuted under the law upon entering China's territories, should they be found guilty of activities that constitute the four broadly defined actions deemed illegal under the law.[86] This is a marked change in terms of the global reach of the Chinese Communist Party. Once a state that concerned itself primarily with maintaining domestic social stability, the party-state is now a global power attempting to control political behaviour outside off its borders.

It is too early to sound the gong on how the National Security Law will affect people power in Hong Kong and globally. Beijing has tried to reassure people that the law is meant to target only a handful of troublemakers in Hong Kong, not the broad population. A spokesperson for the government in Hong Kong called the law a 'sharp sword hanging over people's heads', emphasizing its deterrence effect.[87] Nonetheless, the effects on Hong Kong's pro-democracy social movement has been visibly chilling. Leading pro-democracy activists have pre-emptively disbanded their pro-democracy organizations, while others have fled.[88] Hong Kong protesters have had to adopt creative tactics, such as holding up blank pieces of paper to their faces to express self-censorship.[89] However, the tactics that the party-state have deployed to both tame and manipulate people power in Mainland China in the past few decades carry certain lessons for Hong Kong. Over time, they may take lessons from their counterparts in Mainland China who have learned to disguise collective action,[90] tell control parables[91] and engage in performative social media activism.[92]

These developments warrant close study from a comparative perspective. This chapter has traced how repertoires for harnessing people power have been adapted from the Mao era for the contemporary era. Looking forward, it will be important to examine the extent to which domestic tools for controlling dissent are exported abroad and to what effect. As a disseminator of control technologies and non-democratic values, China's domestic politics of control carries global implications in an era of illiberalism.

Notes

1 https://www.nytimes.com/2018/03/10/world/asia/china-xi-jinping-term-limit-explainer.html.

2   http://time.com/5264170/the-strongmen-era-is-here-heres-what-it-means-for-you/.
3   https://freedomhouse.org/report/freedom-world/freedom-world-2018.
4   E. Perry, 'Cultural Governance in Contemporary China: "Re-Orienting" Party Propaganda', in V. Shue and P. Thornton (eds), *To Govern China: Evolving Practices of Power* (Cambridge: Cambridge University Press, 2017).
5   Perry, 'Cultural Governance in Contemporary China', 29.
6   Perry, 'Cultural Governance in Contemporary China', 29.
7   Perry, 'Cultural Governance in Contemporary China', 10–11.
8   E. Perry and X. Yan, 'Suppressing Students in the People's Republic of China: Proletarian State-Mobilized Movements in 1968 and 1989', in E. Perry, G. Ekiert and X. Yan (eds), *Ruling by Other Means: State-Mobilized Movements* (New York: Cambridge University Press).
9   Perry and Yan, 'Suppressing Students in the People's Republic of China'.
10 Perry and Yan, 'Suppressing Students in the People's Republic of China'.
11 D. Zhao, *The Power of Tiananmen: State-Society Relations and the 1989 Beijing Student Movement* (Chicago: The University of Chicago Press, 2001).
12 A. Walder and X. Gong, 'Workers in the Tiananmen Protests: The Politics of the Beijing Workers' Autonomous Federation', *The China Journal* 29 (1993): 4–5.
13 Perry and Yan, 'Suppressing Students in the People's Republic of China'.
14 D. Shambaugh, 'China's Propaganda System: Institutions, Processes and Efficacy', *The China Journal* 57 (2007): 25–58.
15 D. Lynch, *After the Propaganda State: Media, Politics, and 'Though Work' in Reformed China* (Stanford: Stanford University Press, 1999).
16 Shambaugh, 'China's Propaganda System', 26.
17 For China's global capital investments, see Ching Kwan Lee, *The Specter of Global China: Politics, Labor, and Foreign Investment in Africa* (Chicago: University of Chicago Press, 2018).
18 V. Shue and P. Thornton, eds, 'Introduction', in *To Govern China: Evolving Practices of Power* (Cambridge: Cambridge University Press), 22.
19 S. Heilmann and E. Perry, 'Embracing Uncertainty: Guerrilla Policy Style and Adaptive Governance in China', in S. Heilmann and E. Perry (eds), *Mao's Invisible Hand: The Political Foundation of Adaptive Governance in China* (Cambridge, MA: Harvard University Asia Center Press, 2011), 1–29.
20 http://press-files.anu.edu.au/downloads/press/n2374/pdf/forum03.pdf.
21 F. Dikotter, *The Cultural Revolution: A People's History, 1962-1976* (New York: Bloomsbury Press, 2017), 21.
22 M. Foucault, *Discipline and Punish: The Birth of the Prison* (London: Penguin, 1991), 7–8.
23 Foucault, *Discipline and Punish*, 8–9.
24 G. Hodos, *Show Trials: Stalinist Purges in Eastern Europe, 1948-1954* (New York: Praeger, 1987); E. Abrahamian, *Tortured Confessions: Prisons and*

Public Recantations in Modern Iran (Berkeley: University of California Press, 1999); A. Fifield, 'The Strange Ways North Korea Makes Detainees Confess on Camera', *Washington Post*, 29 February 2016.

25 The 'tigers' refer to high-ranking state officials while the 'flies' refer to lower-ranked officials investigated for corruption.

26 http://www.chinafile.com/infographics/visualizing-chinas-anti-corruption-campaign.

27 http://www.chinafile.com/infographics/visualizing-chinas-anti-corruption-campaign.

28 https://www.nytimes.com/2018/11/27/business/jack-ma-communist-party-alibaba.html.

29 J. Wang, 'What's Wrong with Corruption? Messages from Confessions in China', *Crime Law Social Change* 69 (2018): 447–63.

30 Perry, 'Cultural Governance in Contemporary China', 39.

31 C. Sorace, 'Extracting Affect: Televised Cadre Confessions in China', *Public Culture* 31, no. 1 (2018): 145–71.

32 https://www.bbc.com/news/world-asia-37695109; https://qz.com/820427/and-the-award-for-best-corruption-confession-by-a-chinese-official-goes-to/.

33 Perry, 'Cultural Governance in Contemporary China'.

34 https://qz.com/820427/and-the-award-for-best-corruption-confession-by-a-chinese-official-goes-to/.

35 https://mp.weixin.qq.com/s?__biz=MzA3MDM2NTIwMA==&mid=2651079079&idx=1&sn=d630b0dfaca8d5ddf664399f5a5fdd78&chksm=84cd18d8b3ba91cee3733edb7f7e9f9fcce0dd040e3aabaceed3ce8f06eeb4a2e0eaacfbcdb6&mpshare=1&scene=1&srcid=1027FKOoN2b0YOZ0pRfHpciZ#rd.

36 Y. Wang, *Tying the Autocrat's Hands: The Rise of the Rule of Law in China* (New York: Cambridge University Press, 2015).

37 C. Minzner 'Legal Reform in the Xi Jinping Era', *Asia Policy* 20 (2015): 4–9; D. Stockmann and M. Gallagher, 'Remote Control: How the Media Sustain Authoritarian Rule in China', *Comparative Political Studies* 44, no. 4 (2011): 436–67; H. Fu and R. Cullen, 'Weiquan (Rights Protection) Lawyering in an Authoritarian State: Building a Culture of Public-Interest Lawyering', *The China Journal* 59 (2008): 111–27.

38 Minzner, 'Legal Reform in the Xi Jinping Era', 4–9.

39 Minzner, 'Legal Reform in the Xi Jinping Era'.

40 J. Hernandez, 'China's Leaders Confront an Unlikely Foe: Ardent Young Communists', *The New York Times*, 28 September 2018.

41 https://zhichigongyou.github.io/gkx01/.

42 D. Fu, *Mobilizing Without the Masses: Control and Contention in China* (New York: Cambridge University Press, 2018).

43 https://www.cnn.com/2018/11/13/asia/china-student-marxist-missing-intl/index.html; https://chinadigitaltimes.net/2018/08/no-one-can-resist-the-tides-of-history-detained-activist-yue-xin-on-the-jasic-workers/; https://uk.reuters.com

/article/uk-china-labour-protests/student-activists-disappear-in-southern-china-after-police-raid-idUKKCN1L90XZ.

44 https://www.cnn.com/2018/12/26/asia/china-marxist-mao-peking-university-intl/index.html.

45 https://www.scmp.com/news/china/politics/article/2173090/chinese-campus-crackdown-young-marxist-activists-expands-major; https://www.nytimes.com/2019/01/21/world/asia/china-marxist-students.html.

46 https://uk.reuters.com/article/uk-china-labour-protests/student-activists-disappear-in-southern-china-after-police-raid-idUKKCN1L90XZ.

47 Y. Deng and K. O'Brien, 'Relational Repression in China: Using Social Ties to Demobilize Protesters', *China Quarterly* 215 (2013): 533–52.

48 https://www.reuters.com/article/us-china-rights-confessions/at-a-top-chinese-university-activist-confessions-strike-fear-into-students-idUSKCN1PF0RR.

49 For an analysis of other dissident confessions, see Fu, *Mobilizing Without the Masses*.

50 https://clb.org.hk/content/state-labour-relations-china-2018.

51 M. Elfstrom and S. Kuruvilla, 'The Changing Nature of Labor Unrest in China', *Industrial & Labor Relations Review* 67, no. 2 (2014): 453–80.

52 https://clb.org.hk/content/china's-truck-drivers-strike-over-stagnant-pay-high-fuel-costs-and-arbitrary-fines; https://clb.org.hk/content/state-labour-relations-china-2018.

53 https://www.rfa.org/english/news/china/strike-06112018112639.html; https://www.scmp.com/news/china/policies-politics/article/2152196/road-warriors-strike-back-why-protests-chinas-truck.

54 https://www.nytimes.com/2014/12/02/world/asia/teachers-strikes-spread-across-northeast-china.html.

55 https://www.economist.com/china/2017/03/02/chinas-citizens-are-complaining-more-loudly-about-polluted-air.

56 https://foreignpolicy.com/2017/02/06/chinas-middle-class-anger-at-its-education-system-is-growing-gaokao-quota-protest-resentment-study-abroad/.

57 https://www.scmp.com/business/banking-finance/article/2158533/police-thwart-protest-rallies-victims-chinas-underground.

58 Xi quoted in https://www.theatlantic.com/international/archive/2017/05/what-china-wants/528561/.

59 G. Yang, *The Power of the Internet in China: Citizen Activism Online* (New York: Columbia University Press, 2009).

60 M. Roberts, *Censored: Distraction and Diversion Inside China's Great Firewall* (Princeton: Princeton University Press, 2018).

61 R. Han, *Contesting Cyberspace in China: Online Expression and Authoritarian Resilience* (New York: Columbia University Press, 2019).

62 R. Hou, 'Neoliberal Governance or Digitalized Autocracy? The Rising Market for Online Opinion Surveillance in China', *Surveillance and Society* 15, nos. 3–4 (2017): 418–24.

63 G. King, J. Pan and M. Roberts, 'How the Chinese Government Fabricates Social Media Posts for Strategic Distraction, Not Engaged Argument', *American Political Science Review* 111, no. 3 (2017): 484–501.

64 King, Pan and Roberts, 'How the Chinese Government Fabricates Social Media Posts for Strategic Distraction, Not Engaged Argument', 488.

65 WeChat is China's dominant chat application and the fourth largest in the world.

66 https://citizenlab.ca/2018/08/cant-picture-this-an-analysis-of-image-filtering-on-wechat-moments/.

67 Users used to bypass text-based censoring by circulating images instead.

68 https://citizenlab.ca/2018/08/cant-picture-this-an-analysis-of-image-filtering-on-wechat-moments/.

69 https://www.scmp.com/comment/blogs/article/1083025/hu-jia-explains-why-mobile-apps-make-activism-spooky.

70 https://www.foreignaffairs.com/articles/china/2017-11-16/meaning-sharp-power.

71 https://www.ned.org/sharp-power-rising-authoritarian-influence-forum-report/.

72 Lee, *The Specter of Global China*.

73 https://www.hoover.org/research/chinese-influence-american-interests-promoting-constructive-vigilance.

74 https://freedomhouse.org/report/freedom-net/freedom-net-2018/rise-digital-authoritarianism.

75 https://freedomhouse.org/report/freedom-net/freedom-net-2018/rise-digital-authoritarianism.

76 https://www.britannica.com/topic/Opium-Wars.

77 https://www.theatlantic.com/international/archive/2020/02/hong-kong-berlin-protest-china/606211/.

78 J. Wasserstrom, *Vigil: Hong Kong on the Brink* (New York: Columbia Global Reports, 2020).

79 Wasserstrom, *Vigil*, 58.

80 Wasserstrom, *Vigil*, 58–61.

81 https://www.theguardian.com/world/2020/may/28/china-vote-npc-national-security-laws-hong-kong-us-protest.

82 https://npcobserver.com/2020/05/22/2020-npc-session-npcs-imminent-decision-on-national-security-in-hong-kong-explained/.

83 https://www.bbc.com/news/world-asia-china-50150853.

84 https://www.bbc.com/news/world-asia-china-52765838.

85 https://thechinacollection.org/hong-kongs-national-security-law-first-look/.

86 https://www.nytimes.com/2020/06/30/world/asia/hong-kong-security-law-explain.html.

87 https://www.nytimes.com/2020/06/30/world/asia/hong-kong-security-law-explain.html.

88 https://www.reuters.com/article/us-hongkong-protests-wong/hong-kong-democracy-activist-group-led-by-joshua-wong-disbands-idUSKBN2410C6; https://www.cbc.ca/news/world/political-exile-nathan-law-china-1.564053.
89 D. Fu and S. Liu, 'China's Activists Mourn the Loss of Hong Kong's Glimmer of Hope', *The Diplomat*, 16 June 2020.
90 D. Fu, 'Disguised Collective Action in China', *Comparative Political Studies* 50, no. 4 (2017): 499–527.
91 Rachel E. Stern and Jonathan Hassid, 'Amplifying Silence: Uncertainty and Control Parables in Contemporary China', *Comparative Political Studies* 45, no. 10 (2012): 1230–54.
92 D. a. S. L. Wang, 'Performing Artivism: Feminists, Lawyers, and Online Legal Mobilization in China', *Law and Social Inquiry* 45, no. 3 (2020): 678–705.

References

Abrahamian, E. *Tortured Confessions: Prisons and Public Recantations in Modern Iran*. Berkeley: University of California Press, 1999.

Deng, Y. and K. O'Brien. 'Relational Repression in China: Using Social Ties to Demobilize Protesters'. *China Quarterly* 215 (2013): 533–52.

Dikotter, F. *The Cultural Revolution: A People's History, 1962-1976*, 21. New York: Bloomsbury Press, 2017.

Elfstrom, M. and S. Kuruvilla. 'The Changing Nature of Labor Unrest in China'. *Industrial & Labor Relations Review* 67, no. 2 (2014): 453–80.

Foucault, M. *Discipline and Punish: The Birth of the Prison*, 7–8. London: Penguin, 1991.

Fu, D. 'Disguised Collective Action in China'. *Comparative Political Studies* 50, no. 4 (2017): 499–527.

Fu, D. *Mobilizing Without the Masses: Control and Contention in China*. New York: Cambridge University Press. 2018.

Fu, D. 'Repression Via Confession: Televised Confession Scripts in China'. Working paper, 2020.

Fu, D. and S. Liu. 'China's Activists Mourn the Loss of Hong Kong's Glimmer of Hope'. *The Diplomat*, 16 June 2020.

Fu, H. and R. Cullen. 'Weiquan (Rights Protection) Lawyering in an Authoritarian State: Building a Culture of Public-Interest Lawyering'. *The China Journal* 59 (2008): 111–27.

Han, R. *Contesting Cyberspace in China: Online Expression and Authoritarian Resilience*. New York: Columbia University Press, 2018.

Heilmann, S. and E. Perry. 'Embracing Uncertainty: Guerrilla Policy Style and Adaptive Governance in China'. In S. Heilmann and E. Perry (eds), *Mao's Invisible Hand: The Political Foundation of Adaptive Governance in China*, 1–29. Cambridge, MA: Harvard University Asia Center Press, 2011.

Hodos, G. *Show Trials: Stalinist Purges in Eastern Europe, 1948–1954*. New York: Praeger, 1987.

Hou, R. 'Neoliberal Governance or Digitalized Autocracy? The Rising Market for Online Opinion Surveillance in China'. *Surveillance and Society* 15, nos. 3–4 (2017): 418–24.

King, G., J. Pan and M. Roberts. 'How the Chinese Government Fabricates Social Media Posts for Strategic Distraction, Not Engaged Argument'. *American Political Science Review* 111, no. 3 (2017): 484–501.

Lee, C. K. *The Specter of Global China: Politics, Labor, and Foreign Investment in Africa*. Chicago: University of Chicago Press, 2018.

Lynch, D. *After the Propaganda State: Media, Politics, and 'Though Work' in Reformed China*, 24. Stanford: Stanford University Press, 1999.

Minzner, C. 'Legal Reform in the Xi Jinping Era'. *Asia Policy* 20 (2015): 4–9.

Perry, E. 'Cultural Governance in Contemporary China: "Re-Orienting" Party Propaganda'. In V. Shue and P. Thornton (eds), *To Govern China: Evolving Practices of Power*. Cambridge: Cambridge University Press, (2017): 29–55.

Perry E. and X. Yan. 'Suppressing Students in the People's Republic of China: Proletarian State-Mobilized Movements in 1968 and 1989'. In E. Perry, G. Ekiert and X. Yan (eds), *Ruling by Other Means: State-Mobilized Movements*. New York: Cambridge University Press, (2020): 55–85.

Roberts, M. *Censored: Distraction and Diversion Inside China's Great Firewall*. Princeton: Princeton University Press, 2018.

Shambaugh, D. 'China's Propaganda System: Institutions, Processes and Efficacy'. *The China Journal* 57 (2007): 25–58.

Shue, V. and P. Thornton, eds. 'Introduction'. In *To Govern China: Evolving Practices of Power*, 22. Cambridge: Cambridge University Press.

Sorace, C. 'Extracting Affect: Televised Cadre Confessions in China'. *Public Culture* 31, no. 1 (2018): 145–71.

Stern, Rachel E. and Jonathan Hassid. 'Amplifying Silence: Uncertainty and Control Parables in Contemporary China'. *Comparative Political Studies* 45, no. 10 (2012): 1230–54.

Stockmann, D. and M. Gallagher. 'Remote Control: How the Media Sustain Authoritarian Rule in China'. *Comparative Political Studies* 44, no. 4 (2011): 436–67.

Walder, A. and X. Gong. 'Workers in the Tiananmen Protests: The Politics of the Beijing Workers' Autonomous Federation'. *The China Journal* 29 (1993): 4–5.

Wang, D. and S. Liu. 'Performing Artivism: Feminists, Lawyers, and Online Legal Mobilization in China'. *Law and Social Inquiry* 45, no. 3 (2020): 678–705.

Wang, J. 'What's Wrong with Corruption? Messages from Confessions in China'. *Crime Law Social Change* 69 (2018): 447–63.

Wang, Y. *Tying the Autocrat's Hands: The Rise of the Rule of Law in China*. New York: Cambridge University Press, 2015.

Wasserstrom, J. *Vigil: Hong Kong on the Brink*. New York: Columbia Global Reports, 2020.

Yang, G. *The Power of the Internet in China: Citizen Activism Online*. New York: Columbia University Press, 2009.

Zhao, D. *The Power of Tiananmen: State-Society Relations and the 1989 Beijing Student Movement*. Chicago: The University of Chicago Press, 2001.

8

Caught between Kemalist and Islamist authoritarianisms

The masses as auxiliary power in Turkey, 1923 to present

Azat Zana Gündoğan

Introduction

Turkish democracy has fallen from grace. In 2010, Western circles celebrated President Recep Tayyip Erdoğan's moderate conservatism and pro-EU, pro-market orientation as an antidote to Islamic fundamentalism and a role model for the Middle East. Indeed, as part of the EU accession process, a series of constitutional amendments had abolished the death penalty, introduced affirmative action, brought about minor changes in the penal code and anti-terror laws, and reduced the power of the military over civilian rule.[1] These steps were tactical performances of a 'protracted process of a "trench warfare" against the old regime',[2] which would only be resolved by a 'constitutional coup'.[3] Erdoğan's coronation as Executive President in July 2018 enabled him to monopolize all political power in his office. In a sense, through the effective use of the tools, institutions and discourses of the political establishment, Erdoğan and his *Adalet ve Kalkınma Partisi* (AKP, Justice and Development Party) masterfully transformed the vestiges of nominal democracy, founded by Kemalists and developed under military tutelage, into a civilian autocracy. This all happened through successive elections, which further reinforced the AKP's popular mandate. However, when faced with diminishing popularity and criticism, Erdoğan refused to be intimidated and instead resorted to a polarizing discourse and violence against dissidents. Where, then, does authoritarianism stop and democracy start?

A single-party regime until 1946 and a multiparty constitutional democracy ever since, Turkey has been at least a nominal democracy with a more-or-less functioning competitive election system overseen by the military. Recent analyses of the AKP regime have emphasized a sharp turn to authoritarianism.[4] Borrowing concepts from Levitsky and Way[5] some call it 'competitive authoritarianism'[6] or 'delegative democracy'[7] while others define it as 'electoral authoritarianism'[8] and highlighted Turkish democracy's 'hybridity,' emphasizing its potential to either consolidate into a liberal democracy or degenerate towards competitive authoritarianism.[9] Though of significant value, these neologisms only account for the reconfiguration of judicial, executive and legislative structures without considering the connections between the political and economic spheres or Turkey's unique experience with democracy and authoritarianism in the past.

Despite the distinctive characteristics of the AKP regime (e.g. its welfare regime and social policies, and undermining military tutelage), the current form of authoritarianism does not mark an abrupt turn from Turkish democracy. On the contrary, it represents a continuation of some of the distinctive features of the actually existing Turkish democracy, which has historically oscillated between coups d'état and civil rule of populist right-wing parties – albeit under the close supervision of the military and its political offices prior to the rise of the AKP. AKP authoritarianism has distinguished itself by capitalizing on the conservative lineage of the Turkish political-party system as well as the cultural and ideological touchstones of Turkish society (namely, Turkish nationalism, Sunni-Islam, primacy of the state, etc.). I argue that, these innovations notwithstanding, an incessant *state of exception* has undergirded modern Turkish political life in one authoritarian continuum between the Kemalists and the Islamists. It is a story of two authoritarianisms locked in a hegemonic contest, with the masses caught in-between and sometimes marginalized, subjugated, or excluded from the political sphere. I further posit that narrow analyses of the cleavage between secularists and Islamists conceal their broad agreement on the foundational version of Turkish nationalism, the survival and continuity of the state (*devletin bekası*), a pro-market economic orientation and the utility of ascribing an auxiliary role to the masses.

Tracing the ebb and flow of authoritarianism across a nearly century-long process of state formation may be daunting, but it is necessary. Conceptualizing the masses as *auxiliary power* and situating them within this long history without neglecting either their agency in opposing the establishment or the cultural and ideological influences on mass behaviour manifest in mass violence or mass mobilizations presents no less of a challenge. This chapter undertakes the task of providing a long-term, diachronic historical-sociological account of Turkish authoritarianism that considers both the political economy of regime change and the role of official ideologies in mobilizing the masses, structured as a three-axis narrative.

The first narrative axis follows shifts in the political regime between Kemalist-secularist military tutelage and populist authoritarianism against the background of fluctuations in the country's economic regime (i.e. étatism, liberalism, import-substitution and neoliberalism). Each of the subsections of the chapters corresponds to periodization along this axis: the single-party regime laid the foundational ideologies of the Republic in 1923, persisting until 1945; the subsequent multiparty regime ended with the execution of the democratically elected, populist prime minister by the military in 1960; mass mobilizations and three coups d'état characterized the 'long '68' period which followed between 1960 and 1980; and the first phase of neoliberal era spanning 1980 to 2002 witnessed the so-called post-modern coup against the first Islamist-conservative coalition government in 1997. Finally, in the post-2002 era the AKP has been able to turn the tables against military tutelage both by democratic means, such as elections-turned-plebiscites, and by undemocratic means legitimized by populist, polarizing discourses. This current phase of neoliberalization also witnessed the 2016 attempted coup.

The second axis of this narrative tracks the place of the masses during regime-change events, as their role developed into what I call *auxiliary power*. Modern Turkish political history has followed a peculiar pattern. Since the foundation of the Republic the masses had acted either as a pool of electoral clients, as was often the case during times of 'normalcy', or as violent force in its own right, prepared to mobilize against fellow citizens during times of crisis. The 'masses', it seems, tended to occupy auxiliary roles during both the Kemalist era and the period of Islamists rule since 2002.

This chapter's final narrative axis concerns the characteristics of the mass action. The history of mass action in Turkey has alternated between mass violence and episodic mobilization. Mass violence has taken the form of pogroms (1957, 1978, 1993), as well as active and inactive support of or participation in wars within and beyond Turkey's borders (e.g. occupation of Cyprus in 1974, the low-intensity war with the Partiya Karkeren Kürdistan (PKK) in the 1990s or the Operation Euphrates in the Syrian War). Mass mobilization, however, indicates episodes of socialist or democratic claim making and protests against state authority (e.g. the long 1968 or the Gezi Park protests in 2013). In order to highlight the auxiliary role of the masses, I focus on top-down organization or sponsorship of mass violence and collective actions that work to the advantage of the ruling elite or their competitors in the hegemonic rivalry. As *auxiliary power*, masses remain compliant when they are dormant and contribute to populist agendas as electorates. When they are active or mobilized, as the emblematic cases in each of the sections reveal, the masses can be ruthless, brutal and destructive. These tragic moments of sheer violence in a super-polarized sociopolitical setting reflect the cultural and ideological themes that Turkish authoritarianism has drawn upon to legitimize itself: Turkish nationalism, Sunni-Islam and market capitalism.

1923–50: The origins of Turkish authoritarianism and mass violence

Nineteenth-century Ottoman reforms had worked to modernize the bureaucracy, military and fiscal structure of the state, thereby centralizing state power over the polyglot and multicultural Islamic empire. The relationship between that state power centre and the people that it claimed to represent shifted during the rule of the Committee of Union and Progress (CUP) (1913–18), a consequence of the de-territorialization of the *ancien régime* following the Balkan Wars, the re-territorialization of a nation-state in Anatolia and efforts to stitch together a unified nation from the ethnoreligious patchwork of the late Ottoman Empire. Their Young Turk ideology advocated progress through national unity, which they believed was possible only under the leadership of the military and/or the ruling elite. In an effort to realize this vision, they cultivated an ideal of a people bound together by their love of state, nation and land; a modern and Western-minded, yet Turkish and Muslim, people. The Young Turks further exhibited distaste for the traditionalism of the Muslim population from which they sought to carve their modern nation *a la Européenne*, as well as for what they saw as its 'reactionary' and 'ignorant' tendencies.

Once in power, the CUP cadres designed and executed violent state practices during their short rule (1913–18). Young Turks in the post-1908 period – and their Kemalist successors after 1923 – had imagined an economic order that would be based on the state's ability to generate capital accumulation and thus a national bourgeoisie.[10] Eventually, they eradicated non-Muslim existence through genocide and forced migration, wealth and property appropriation, and reallocation of those resources among Muslims of Turkic origin. By the time Mustafa Kemal and his cadres emerged as the new leaders in a political power vacuum in 1918 and set out to mobilize the Muslim masses, the CUP had already left them a solid ground in the reterritorialization process. The War of Independence was as much fought to save the sultanate and caliphate from European powers as it was to purge the desired territory of its native non-Muslim populations (primarily Greeks). Up until the late 1930s, the Republic was still involved in both security and bureaucracy formation. The Kurdish region was the scene of a series of uprisings until 1937–8. In these years, the Turkish military's indiscriminate mass extermination of Kurdish combatants and civilians of the Dersim region ended the constant turbulence of the early republic. Meanwhile, Kemalists adopted a secular constitution, Western-style trade laws, standardization of property laws and other reforms that directly penetrated people's everyday lives.

The sheer oppression that undergirded the étatist model had a significant impact on the historical origins of authoritarianism in Turkey, the creation of a classless mass and the political economy of nation-building and ethnicist, exclusive Turkish nationalism. Accompanying the dominant corporatism of the early Republican single-party regime, exclusive nation-building deeply resonated with the fascist zeitgeist of the time. For instance, the industrial bourgeoisie–bureaucracy alliance assured the suppression of labour rights and wages. The 1942 Capital Tax (*Varlık Vergisi*) and the formation of labour battalions (1941–2) amounted to anti-minority measures.[11] Those who could not pay the excessive taxes were sent to these battalions. Following these injustices in taxation, about 30,000 Jewish and 20,000 Orthodox Christians, all citizens of Turkey, left the country.[12]

The new nation-state had also worked to erase the relics of a multi-ethnic geography and history through toponymical policies and the destruction of religious sites and buildings.[13] Alongside official historical origin narratives and Turkification policies,[14] these practices eventually gave way to the collective suppression of the memory of violence against Christians and Kurds, and later to denial of their existence.[15] The oppressive state further funnelled wealth to a select minority, creating the basis for a clientelist relationships in the decades to come and grounding populist discourses in official Turkish nationalism. This still serves as the root-language of various versions of nationalisms today, including the Islamist nationalism[16] that the AKP has embraced and mobilized.

1950–60: The Democrat Party era and the dawn of populism

This period is illustrative of the dual themes of this chapter – the continuity of authoritarianism and the masses as auxiliary power in Turkey – and significant to the contemporary political climate in Turkey in that Erdoğan has repeatedly claimed the legacy of Democrat Party (DP), the first populist party in modern Turkish history. With the defeat of fascist totalitarianisms in the Second World War, the single-party regime opted for a shift to multiparty rule. Although neither fair nor free, the first multiparty elections were held in 1946. The founders and the guardians of the republican regime, the Kemalist civil bureaucracy and military, were toppled with the second free elections in 1950, from which the DP emerged as the victor. Eventually, the fledgling rural and commercial bourgeoisie under the wings of a statist bureaucratic-military establishment challenged its creators. The DP's conservative-liberal position helped it build a hegemonic front against the established Republican People Party (RPP)-led Kemalist coalition between the urban industrial bourgeoisie, civil bureaucracy and military, and secularist intelligentsia.[17]

Allied with the West and equipped with the post-war global discourse of democracy, the DP built a bastion of populism, and of its subsequent majority tyranny, from popular Islam and the traditionalism of those who were suppressed by the Kemalist republicans. Populist policies, patron–client relations, improvements in economic indicators and American economic aid (i.e. the Marshall Plan) polished the DP's electoral victory but also made way for its civil authoritarianism. The DP organized a censorship campaign against the press, arrested journalists, banned newspapers and started a communist witch-hunt. By doing so, the DP inherited many of the founding premises of the Republic (nationalism, authoritarianism and, a pro-market, anti-left stance) while challenged others such as its strict étatism and radical secularism in everyday life. From its electoral victory to its demise following the coup in 1960, the party not only became the catalyst for a resentment of those social sectors that were left behind socio-economically and suppressed ideologically under the Kemalists' top-down modernization but also mobilized these masses against non-Turkish, non-Muslim minorities when it deemed such violence necessary. This, however, was only the first swing of the pendulum between populist authoritarianism and recurrent coup d'états.

The Istanbul Pogrom of September 6–7, 1955

One emblematic case that exemplifies the auxiliary character of the masses-in-the-making in this period of majoritarian authoritarianism and populism was the Istanbul Pogrom in September 1955. Weeks before the pogrom, and in relation to the dispute over Cyprus, nationalist anti-Greek sentiments were induced in the masses. The simmering anti-Greek mood erupted upon Istanbul newspapers reporting a fake bombing of the Turkish Consulate complex that included Kemal Ataturk's birth house. During the '*Kristallnacht* in Constantinople', writes the Greek-American historian Speros Vryonis, Jr., the pogrom:

> delivered a fatal blow to the Hellenism of Constantinople in seven hours. Well planned (for some years), masterfully carried out in a well-organized manner by the Turkish government, the Turks destroyed 71 churches, 41 schools, 4,008 stores, the offices and printing presses of eight newspapers, and approximately 2,100 dwellings, all the property of the Greeks and their communities. The Turks killed 28 Greeks and also carried out the rapes of Greek women. They profaned and soiled the Greek Orthodox religious vessels; they smashed and dug up the graves in Greek cemeteries, throwing out the bones and remains of the dead; they effected circumcisions on some elderly priests on the streets.[18]

The government declared martial law in the city. Although around 6,000 people were detained, the government and press blamed the communists.[19] During the trials of the Prime Minister Adnan Menderes and Foreign Minister Fatin Rüştü Zorlu in 1961, it was revealed that the explosion was a plot by Turkish agents used to rouse 'national sentiments'. The agent provocateur in Salonika later occupied high positions in the Turkish state following the pogrom.[20] Moreover, the two student unions of the time – the National Turkish Students Union (NTSU) and the Cyprus is Turkish Society – played an ancillary role in inciting nationalist sentiments weeks before and during the pogrom. It is worth noting that the NTSU functioned as the incubator of future cadres of the Islamist movement, some of whom occupied the highest offices of the Republic during the AKP regime, including president Erdoğan; former president Abdullah Gül; former prime minister Ahmet Davudoğlu; former president of the assembly Bülent Arınç and former ministers Mehmet Ali Şahin, Cemil Çiçek, Beşir Atalay, Abdülkadir Aksu, Hüseyin Çelik and Numan Kurtulmuş.

Since the beginning of Kemalist rule, these ultra-nationalist 'civil' organizations acted as articulation points between the state and society and were utilized for extra-legal operations during the state's legitimacy crisis. The perpetrators of such operations have usually been protected from legal trials.

1960–80: The long '68 and the demands of the masses

Following the Second World War, the state elite sided with the Western bloc and ended étatism and the corporatist single-party regime, giving preference to liberalization of the economy. The Democrat Party era of 1950–60 was one of rapid integration into world capitalism and the further development of the capitalist classes, the consequences of which were twofold. First, a development in the industrial working class triggered a class struggle after 1965 and throughout the 1970s. Second, the absorption of Anatolia into a capitalist economy accelerated in the 1950s and onwards. The socio-economic transformations included urbanization, geographical mobility, migration, population growth in urban areas and eventually the dissolution of the agricultural way of life. These groups felt the ups and downs of the economic crises acutely during DP rule, and their 'national sentiments' were eventually provoked against the Christian minorities during the Istanbul Pogrom in 1955.[21]

While Turkey further integrated into global capitalism during this period, it was also swept by the tides of the Global '68. As a developmentalist Third World state with a record of broken promises to its youth, its newly urban industrial proletariat, its peasantry and its Kurdish population, Turkey's new generation of activists had a lot to demand from their government. Students, peasants and labourers were politically active in many different organizations ranging from student clubs to labour unions to political associations. They staged boycotts, meetings, protests, labour strikes and occupations of factories, faculties or land . However, the range of political mobilization was not solely limited to 'progressives'. The ultra-nationalist and conservative groups mobilized as well, forming organizations like the Grey Wolves (*Ülkü Ocakları*), which became instrumental in the governments' covert and overt operations against the rising left, particularly in the 1970s and onwards. The cadres of these ultra-nationalist and anti-communist groups would later take positions in the state establishment.

On the state level, regime change was both a reflection of and a reason for popular activism. The coup d'état on 27 May 1960 ended DP rule with the execution of Prime Minister Adnan Menderes. The junta responsible for the coup did not content itself with simple regime change, aiming instead for a complete restructuring of the political establishment. Although it initially announced that the 'revolution' was not directed against any group, the main targets of the army were the groups that had gained economic and political power under the Democrats. In essence, the struggle was within the capitalist class itself, mainly between the petit bourgeoisie (small capitalists and the trade bourgeoisie) and the industrial bourgeoisie.[22] The latter had chaffed at the unplanned populist economic policies of the DP and desired a new system of accumulation led by the state using principles of planning. Therefore, the basis of the May 27 coup d'état was the gradual strengthening of the industrial bourgeoisie and its imperative to defend its own interests against those of the other sectors of the bourgeois class that had become dominant under the DP. In other words, the urban-based coalition of the army-bureaucracy-industrial bourgeoisie established a new system of accumulation (i.e. import-substitution industrialization) based on two premises: (1) the allocation of scarce economic resources through political mechanisms and the promise of redistribution of wealth aimed at providing a social appeasement, and (2) the creation and maintenance of an internal market.[23]

The 1961 Constitution brought collective negotiations and, thus, collective agreements. More importantly, it guaranteed the right to strike.[24] Prior to a second coup in 1980 the labour movement in modern Turkey carried out the largest collective actions, strikes and marches in the streets and in the regions where industrial investments had intensified. Groups whose interests were once represented by the DP kept their silence for a time, but the Justice Party (JP), the heir to the DP, eventually emerged as the voice of these excluded groups in opposition to the Constitution. In the same year, the results of the general election seemed to verify the results of the referendum. The parties that claimed the legacy of the DP gained the majority of the votes and hence the majority of the deputy and senate seats, while the RPP drifted towards a centre-left position. The centre-right JP government, now divided within itself, could not hold out against the political pressure of the organized masses. The military issued a memorandum on 12 March 1971, the second military intervention in Turkey. A wave of martial law in urban and Kurdish regions followed. Hundreds of students, leftists, liberal-democrats, academics and intellectuals were detained and tortured. Labour strikes were banned. In the next couple of years, the legitimacy crisis of the regime escalated. It was during this crisis another pogrom was instigated.

Anti-Alevi pogroms in Maraş in 1978

State-provoked and state-sponsored mass violence often arose when the Turkish regime went through a legitimacy crisis. A week-long pogrom in Alevi neighbourhoods in the south-eastern city of Maraş serves as this period's emblematic case of the masses as auxiliary power under an authoritarian regime. This time the provocation took the form of a 19 December 1978 movie theatre bombing during the screening of a nationalist movie. A group of ultra-nationalists riled up the religious-conservative audience by spreading a rumour that it had been a communist attack. The crowd attacked the local branches of the RPP and a left-leaning teachers' association, where two teachers were murdered. During the thirty-six hours that followed, over 100 people were brutally murdered, their houses burnt and destroyed by right-wing groups. Among the chants heard that long day were 'Maraş is going to be the grave of Alevis!' and 'Muslim Turkey'. Official statistics state that 120 people were massacred and more than 200 houses and stores were burnt down.[25] Witness accounts of the survivors attest to the brutality of mass violence:

> On 23 December 1978, Saturday, at around 3 pm, attackers came to our house holding axes, clubs, and shotguns. [. . .] they mowed down the house. (Yeter İşbilir)
>
> . . .
>
> From morning till mid-afternoon, they burned all of the houses. They burned a little boy in a caldron. They pillaged everything. We were in the basement in knee-deep water; the floor was wooden. Burning woods were all falling on us. We were eight people. They didn't know we were in the basement. They left. (Meryem Polat)[26]

During the massacres, state forces did not intervene. On 26 December 1978, martial law was declared in thirteen provinces. According to journalistic accounts based on then Prime Minister Bülent Ecevit's personal archives, the masterminds of the massacre were the leader of the ultra-nationalist Nationalist Movement Party and his father-in-law, the legal adviser for the National Intelligence Agency. Some 500 perpetrators were indicted following an investigation that was kept classified by the government. All three of the joint attorneys determined to follow the trials were assassinated during the course of 1979 and 1980. The agent provocateurs were never identified.[27]

1980–2002: The dawn of neoliberal authoritarianism

By 1977 the growth model based on a sensitive balance between all social classes had proved to be unsustainable due to the limits of the import-substitution model, dependency on foreign currency, high inflation rates, increasing public and foreign debt, and insufficient foreign credit opportunities. In such a crisis environment, however, increasing demands on organized labour accompanied by the aforementioned social and political crises culminated in yet another coup d'état in September of 1980.

Reminiscent of Chile's coup in 1973, a sister coup in Turkey on 12 September 1980 brought about a 'structural adjustment' programme.[28] Restructuring the Turkish economy meant a total makeover of political architecture over the next three decades beginning with a spiral of recession, crises and militarization of society throughout the 1990s. During this period, progressive and unionized labour movements were suppressed, and in only a couple of years, the shock doctrine[29] accomplished its mission of redressing a new hegemony by combining a political shock (the coup) with ensuing fear and torture tactics. In the following decades, oppression and economic crisis ensured that structural adjustment occurred without protest, even without public awareness. Redressed by the powers of a majority rule and securitized environment, Turgut Özal's Motherland Party (in Turkish acronym, ANAP) set to restructure the Turkish economy by reducing labour costs through disciplining the working class, privatizing state-owned enterprises and financialization of the economy.[30]

Concurrently, the Turkish polity was characterized by an authoritarian constitutional regime and its state that was founded on a military core and the National Security Council (NSC) whose iron hand drew the boundaries of policymaking with extreme measures throughout the 1990s. The NSC became the shadow government behind the civilian façade and securitized all aspects of life.[31] This heavy-handed *roll-back* phase of neoliberalization refers to a shift in the developmental agenda and preoccupation with destruction and the discrediting of constitutional and progressive forces, state services, social expenditures, institutions and regulations obstructing 'free' operation of market forces.[32] The new regime and its constitution allowed anti-union practices, macro-economic factors such as privatization of state enterprises, decrease in employment rates in the public sector, forms of flexible employment, an increase in unemployment rates, and weakened unionization and union-led labour movements.[33]

The new power bloc consisted of a military-bureaucracy ensuring order and security for capitalist circles unsettled by labour activism, along with conservative politicians and some privileged segments of society. Excluded from this alliance were the rural and urban labourers and salaried civil servants. On the ideological plain, the neoliberal era brought about practices against Kurdish and Alevi minorities justified by exclusionary discourses. The Kurdish issue became the hotbed of the 'state of exception'[34] during the 1990s. As economic and political restructuration was underway, armed conflicts between the Turkish army and the PKK (Kurdistan Workers' Party) informed nationalist discourse with leitmotifs of Kurdish 'separatism' (*bölücülük*) and a 'national unity', The Turkish state's internal security measures – both legal and extra-legal – marked the 1990s as a period hostile to human rights, the right to life and freedom of expression. It was a decade of political-party closures, extrajudicial killings, unidentified murders and forced evacuations of Kurdish villages.

Under these circumstances, the 1990s became an era of severe economic and political crises. The neoliberal restructuring of the economy and bureaucracy fuelled corruption and state-led allocation of public resources between pro-market forces. Devoid of any type of public accountability, ruling elites used state resources in a populist-clientelist setting to fight a two-front battle against counter-hegemonic forces challenging the Kemalist establishment and its military tutelage, thereby deepening its legitimacy crisis in the 1990s. The first of these was fought against the Kurdish movement, which had been on the rise since 1965, radicalized in the 1970s and led by the PKK from the 1980s onwards. The second was the multi-sect Islamist movement from which the current AKP regime emerged.

The Islamists succeeded in seizing the opportunities created by the post-1980 regime crisis, capitalizing on the Kemalist establishment's age-old repression of the traditionalist segments of the society and the lack of a general leftist agenda. In time Islamists, and the Welfare Party (RP) in particular, were able to form an alliance between the small- and medium-scale bourgeoisie, especially pious provincial capitalists who demanded more share from export-oriented economy, and conservative Sunni-Muslim electorates. It was within this context of increased militarism, conservatism and nationalism that once again the state resorted to the masses as auxiliary power in 1993.

Sivas massacre in July 1993

On 2 July 1993, thousands of people blockaded a hotel in downtown Sivas, a central Anatolian town 220 miles east of Ankara. Dozens of artists, actors, authors, poets and other accompanying people who were in town to attend a festival commemorating Alevi culture were trapped in the building under a hail of stone and brick for eight hours. No police, army forces or emergency workers intervened in the situation throughout the duration of the massacre, even as it was broadcast live on national television. The mob eventually set fire to the building and killed thirty-five of those trapped within. Among the attendants was the left-wing intellectual Aziz Nesin, who was at the hotel to give a talk. An ardent communist, then seventy-seven years old, Nesin had already been a target of both state forces and conservatives for decades. He had been detained, put on trial and imprisoned numerous times. In 1993, he was once again targeted by the growing Islamist groups for his attempt to publish Salman Rushdie's *The Satanic Verses*. His participation in the festival gave provocateurs a pretext to attack the crowd gathered at the hotel. The *New York Times* reported on the massacre and mentioned Nesin:

> The man who was apparently the target of the attack, in which 145 people were reported wounded, was a newspaper editor who was staying at the hotel and who was accused by the militants of spreading atheism. The rampage was the worst outburst so far of fundamentalist violence in Turkey, a Muslim nation with a secular government.[35]

Two days before the massacre, pamphlets circulated in the city, condemning Nesin and his recent attempt to publish Rushdie's controversial novel in Turkish translation. On that day, following the Friday prayer, hundreds marched downtown, chanting, 'Sivas will be the grave of seculars', 'Sharia will arrive; oppression will end', and 'Army of Islam; fear of seculars'. According to the governor's report, at 6 pm 15,000 people could gather in front of the hotel without facing any intervention by state forces.[36]

An agent of the Department of Special Operations – a unit conducting extrajudicial operations – later gave an interview admitting the state's role in the massacre and the decades-old narrative of 'national sensibilities'. He stated that 'Turkish people have a specific frailty. Turkish people get to their feet when you shout "in the name of *Allah* and the prophet." Turkish military abused this eloquently'.[37] The then mayor of Sivas talked to the mob and hailed them by saying, 'may your cause be blessed.' Later he was elected to parliament. Only 124 attackers were detained. Some of their lawyers subsequently held high offices in the Islamist governments beginning in the late 1990s. One later became the Minister of Justice in the Islamist-Conservative coalition government in 1996; another held the post of Minister of Customs and Trade during the AKP's second term between 2011 and 2014. Two others were elected to parliament. Following many trials and appeals, in 2012, the case was dropped based on a statute of limitations, despite the fact that it had been a crime against humanity.[38]

2000s: Revisiting the 'turn to authoritarianism'

The regime crisis during the Islamist-conservative coalition reached its peak with the so-called post-modern coup when the military issued a memorandum during the NSC meeting on 28 February 1997. The list of demands imposed on the government included measures against *irtica* (religious reactionism) such as eight years of compulsory primary education, shutting down many religious schools and the abolition of *tarikats* (religious orders). This was a radical secularist throwback attempting to reverse the post-1980 'neo-republican' practices of incorporating Islamic elements into public life 'to provide a moral basis, ideological unity, and some certainty in the face of global capitalism'.[39] Turkey's crisis in the late 1990s was due to growing pains of neoliberalization, which now required further restructuration that was not possible with the unwieldy, oppressive, militaristic state formation. In other words, the rolled-back capitalism of the 1990s needed to roll out in a new fashion. The 2001 and 2002 financial crises and constituents' resentment and frustration following two decades of unstable coalition governments brought about a two-party parliament led by the secularist RPP and conservative AKP.

Political, economic and ideological turmoil, along with the Kemalist military core's turn to radical secularism with the 1997 memorandum, provided the AKP with an ideal environment to form a single-party government in 2002 and to further consolidate its hegemony in the decade to come. The AKP's emergence from within the radical political Islamist Welfare Party and its subsequent victory with nearly two-thirds of the seats was an answer to this new phase of neoliberalization in Turkey. Yet, prior to 2007, the AKP was careful not to Islamize everyday life, in contrast to the fears of hard-line secularist circles and in spite of the desires of certain radical Islamists in Turkey, in particular its Welfare Party predecessors. At home, the party successfully reunited civil society and political society,[40] constructing a centrist hegemony in an environment rife with short-lived coalition governments and a legitimacy crisis which created a discourse of stability-cum-consensus in the late 1990s.[41] In international affairs, the leading figures of the AKP even paid homage to Turkey's Western allies, the United States, the EU, and NATO, and their 'conservative democracy' emphasized liberal values of limited government, a free-market economy, strong civil society, human rights, dialogue and toleration.[42] Polished by liberal intellectuals and equipped with the electoral support of conservative, right-wing and even centrist voters, the AKP enjoyed successive electoral victories accompanied by economic growth.

Since 2002, the populist party has won the five most recent national elections (2007, 2011, June 2015, November 2015 and 2018). It held the majority of parliamentary seats until the June 2015 election, and regained its parliamentary majority shortly thereafter in the snap election in November 2015. In the 2018 election, it lost its majority, if not the leadership. Moreover, the AKP was the leader in the 2004, 2009 and 2014 local elections. The leader of AKP, Recep Tayyip Erdoğan, is currently the incumbent President of Turkey.

The AKP was also able to unite the fractions of the Turkish bourgeoisie, namely Istanbul-based industrial capital and small and medium business circles as well as its conservative Muslim segment. The former had traditionally fallen under the aegis of the Republican establishment; the latter had been excluded from the alliance. Additionally, upper segments of the middle classes could jump on the wagon in an expanding economy. According to Akça:[43]

These various fractions of the bourgeoisie were united by the AKP's neoliberal economic policies, based on financial capital inflows and its financial accumulation strategy, privatization, the reduction of real wages, especially in manufacturing, and the legalization and extensive use of subcontracting.

As for the 'masses', with AKP rule they became the bastion of its success and, later, its authoritarianism. AKP's neoliberal social policy regime followed World Bank–sponsored poverty alleviation programmes and included social security reforms and social policies (social aid, conditional cash transfer, municipality aid, etc.) which targeted the subaltern segments of society. Thus, within civil society, the party was able to master an Islamic solidarity and aid mechanism. In this hegemony formation, state-led urban renewal projects have commodified urban space, functioned as a wealth creation and allocation mechanism among propertied groups while dispossessing subaltern communities which were forced to react to urban renewal.[44] Eventually, the rural and urban poor gave their consent to AKP policies, which essentially rendered poverty sustainable rather than vanishing.

All in all, the AKP's welfare regime allowed the party to implement macro-economic reforms required by neoliberalization (further privatization, anti-labour arrangements, financing of housing and mortgage markets, etc.) while minimally extending welfare to groups that had been excluded from social protection programmes in previous decades. For instance, in the realm of labour reform and social policy, the AKP regime defamed the notion of full-time, formal employment and effectively pitted public sector workers who the AKP portrayed as privileged against the precariat that the party capitalizes on. As Özden[45] pointed out, the already hierarchical and inegalitarian social welfare regime became the context within which the AKP built its populism. In order to conserve the parameters of this neoliberal, populist economic and political setting, the AKP devised a specific discourse that is built upon certain themes of the 'root ideology' of the regime.

AKP's hegemony over civil and political societies is a successful articulation of neoliberalism, authoritarianism and conservatism. Named 'Turkish-Islamic Synthesis', this post-1980 ideology of the Kemalist establishment circulated through the educational and religious state apparatus up until the 2000s. In its attempt to legitimize the neoliberal social order, AKP administrations invoked the symbols and codes of an idealized Islamic and Ottoman past, for instance by reviving a kitsch version of Ottoman and Islamic architecture and symbolism[46] and routinizing public celebrations of Islamic and national festivals as part of a politics of Ottoman nostalgia. Meanwhile, AKP leadership employed polarizing discursive strategies to justify authoritarian urban renewal practices, portraying squatters and migrants as 'undeserving occupiers', and stigmatizing the urban poor along ethno-religious lines.[47]

Successive AKP governments were certainly able to dismantle the Kemalist state's neoliberal military core, yet rather than enlarging the boundaries of civil, democratic politics, the AKP replaced the military with the police and a judiciary-centred security state.[48] This new neoliberal 'security state'[49] meant that the state can act pre-emptively in the face of potentially dangerous individuals and groups. Within the context of weakening hegemonic power and a perceived threat to state authority after 2008, this security state formation has enabled Erdoğan's government to intervene harshly in the Turkish political and social spheres. Three important moments are indicative of the hyper-concentration of state power and its devastating effects: the Gezi Uprising in 2013, Kurdish protests in October 2014 and pro-government mobilization on two occasions – mass mobilization right after the Gezi Uprising and pro-AKP demonstrations after the attempted coup in 2016.

Clash: Masses as auxiliary power versus masses as demanders

The Gezi Uprising in the summer of 2013 was particularly remarkable as it was an entirely bottom-up reaction against the rising authoritarianism of the AKP. As a seemingly spontaneous collective action, Gezi drew on resentment of increasing conservatism, control of women's bodies, Islamization of education and relentless urban renewal at the expense of the environment and commons. What started as a civil defence of trees that the municipality had planned to uproot on 28 May 2013 escalated into dissident action. Three and a half million people took to the streets in solidarity with the Gezi protesters in close to 5,000 demonstrations across Turkey. The Gezi Uprising represented a major blow to Erdoğan's authority, and caused a shift in the regime's hegemonic discourse from a Turkish centre-right style of populism to a more Islamist discourse directed towards mobilizing Erdoğan's supporters.

Erdoğan's turn to his base is indicative of the authoritarian-populists' tried-and-tested method of resorting to the auxiliary power of the masses. The more support he harvested, the more authoritarian he became. This was apparent in the state's violence against its own Kurdish citizens following their street protests in Kurdish cities on 6–7 October 2014. Thousands of Kurdish people protested the Turkish government's active backing of radical Islamist groups in Syria and supported their brethren in Kobane fighting against ISIS (Islamic State of Iraq and Syria). The police killed fifty people. Not only was this a harbinger of the end of the so-called Peace Process between the PKK and the AKP government but also the beginning of anti-Kurdish military attacks and curfews in the Kurdish cities, justified in the name of war against terror, in 2015 and 2016. Between August 2015 and August 2016, there were at least 111 officially confirmed, open-ended and round-the-clock curfews in at least thirty-five districts of nine cities in southeastern Turkey.

Masses were also activated in support of the government following the 15 July 2016 attempted coup. A group within the military announced that the army had seized power and had instated a national curfew and martial law. Among the reasons cited for the attempted coup were an erosion of secularism, elimination of democratic rule and disregard for human rights.[50] The two suspension bridges of Istanbul were closed, and the Turkish Parliament was bombarded by fighter jets while more than fifty deputies were in session. Also, an assassination attempt was curbed while President Erdoğan was on vacation. He later went on live television to call on the Turkish people to take to streets, squares and airports in support of the government and in reaction to the coup. The masses listened and responded accordingly by taking part in protests. More than 300 people, 104 of whom were pro-coup personnel, were killed. The rest is history: massive purges in the military, judiciary, academia, media and other public offices, and an expansion of executive power free from checks and balances. In other words, even the nominal character of Turkish 'democracy' was lost but this is hardly an abrupt turn.

Conclusion

The objective of this chapter has been to question claims that the AKP's current authoritarianism is a break or an exit from democracy and a sharp turn from its earlier (2002–10) democratic stance. In agreement with Tansel,[51] who claims that the transformation of Turkish politics on the basis of 'two competing, temporally bound images of the AKP is problematic, I have shown that the AKP's recently surfaced authoritarianism is the product of a long-term authoritarian continuum running through modern Turkish history. This claim is based on an epistemological stance that does not dissociate the economic sphere from the political one. In other words, a political-economic viewpoint enables us to situate these political regime changes into the context of changes in the regimes of accumulation, and, production and distribution of wealth. Repeated 'authoritarian' turns in Turkish politics are neither aberrations of a normally democratic state of affairs nor simply due to the irrational practices of charismatic populist leaders or politicians capable of harvesting popular support like Adnan Menderes or Recep Tayyip Erdoğan of the right and Bülent Ecevit of the centre-left. This chapter demonstrates the converse, what Karaveli calls a paradox: 'the dynamics of Turkish capitalist development have ensured that the [political] right is dominant, but they have also made it unstable.'[52] Indeed, internal conflicts of the capitalist classes regularly ended with coups, executions or imprisonment of right-wing representatives. However, from the first coup in 1960 to the last (failed) coup in 2016, the history of Turkish politics has traversed a continuum of radical secularism, military tutelage, populism and resultant authoritarianism. Yet, contrary to dominant narratives of 'military tutelage vs. civilian populists', all but the last of these coups have one thing in common: they all restored order to the benefit of capitalist development and to the detriment of the masses that are always forced to choose between two evils. These coups opened the way for industrial capital (1960), suppressed popular left and working class (1971 and 1980) or dealt with the representatives of Islamic capital (1997). Yet another common point of these interventions in civilian politics is that they all suppressed democracy, human rights and the left, eventually enabling the ruling elite and their economic allies to silence calls for unalienated labour, equitable welfare provisions, peaceful coexistence of different ethnicities and religious sects, tolerance and gender equity. Instead, in the long history of state-making in Turkey, the horizons of political imagination have been limited by a troubled, introverted, self-acclaimed Turkish identity, an intolerant version of Islam, xenophobia and toxic masculinity. These constitute the cultural hotbed of authoritarianism in Turkey.

Moreover, the masses, as this chapter claims, have been caught in these intra-class conflicts and hegemonic rivalry between the Kemalists and Islamist-conservative populists over political society. Depending on historical contingencies, the masses have been abused as auxiliary power and cast as the bastion of authoritarian policies. They were provoked to the point of slaughtering their own neighbours during the legitimacy crises of the polity or were rendered dependent clients of the politicians who exchanged benefits and services for their votes.

Acknowledegement

I thank Ege Özen, Nilay Özok-Gündoğan, Nathan Stoltzfus and Chris Osmar for comments that greatly improved the chapter.

Notes

1 Aslı Bâli, 'Turkey's Constitutional Coup', *MERIP Reports* 48, no. 3 (2018): 2–9; İsmet Akça, 'Hegemonic Projects in Post-1980 Turkey and the Changing Forms of Authoritarianism', in İsmet Akça, Ahmet Bekmen and Barış Alp Özden (eds), *Turkey Reframed: Constituting Neoliberal Hegemony* (London: Pluto Press, 2014), 14–46.

2 Kumru Toktamış, 'Now There Is, Now There Is Not: The Disappearing Silent Revolution of AKP as Re-Entrenchment', *British Journal of Middle Eastern Studies* (2019): 2.

3 Bâli, 'Turkey's Constitutional Coup'.

4 Seyla Benhabib, 'Turkey's Authoritarian Turn', *The New York Times*, 3 June 2013. https://www.nytimes.com/2013/06/04/opinion/turkeys-authoritarian-turn.html.

5 Steven Levitsky and Lucan A. Way, 'Elections Without Democracy: The Rise of Competitive Authoritarianism', *Journal of Democracy* 13, no. 2 (2002): 51–65; Steven Levitsky and Lucan A. Way, *Competitive Authoritarianism: Hybrid Regimes after the Cold War* (New York: Cambridge University Press, 2010).

6 Berk Esen and Şebnem Gümüşçü, 'Rising Competitive Authoritarianism in Turkey', *Third World Quarterly* 37, no. 9 (2016): 1581–606; Ergun Özbudun, 'Turkey's Judiciary and the Drift toward Competitive Authoritarianism', *The International Spectator* 50, no. 2 (2015): 42–55.

7 Ergun Özbudun, 'AKP at the Crossroads: Erdoğan's Majoritarian Drift', *South European Society and Politics* 19, no. 2 (2014): 155–67; Hakkı Taş, 'Turkey– from Tutelary to Delegative Democracy', *Third World Quarterly* 36, no. 4 (2015): 776–91.

8 Bâli, 'Turkey's Constitutional Coup'; Ayhan Kaya, 'Islamisation of Turkey under the AKP Rule: Empowering Family, Faith and Charity', *South European Society and Politics* 20, no. 1 (2015): 47–69.

9 Ziya Öniş, 'Turkey's Two Elections: The AKP Comes Back', *Journal of Democracy* 27, no. 2 (2016): 141–54.

10 Korkut Boratav, *Türkiye Iktisat Tarihi, 1908–2007*, 12th edn (Ankara: İmge, 2008).

11 Ayhan Aktar, *Varlık vergisi ve "Türkleştirme" politikaları* (İstanbul: İletişim Yayınları, 2000); Sait Çetinoğlu, 'The Mechanisms for Terrorizing Minorities: The Capital Tax and Work Battalions in Turkey during the Second World War', *Mediterranean Quarterly* 23, no. 2 (2012): 14–29; Ali Tuna Kuyucu, 'Ethno-Religious "unmixing" of "Turkey": 6–7 September Riots as a Case in Turkish Nationalism*', *Nations and Nationalism* 11, no. 3 (2005): 361–80.

12 Kuyucu, 'Ethno-Religious "unmixing" of "Turkey"'.

13 Joost Jongerden, 'Resettlement and Reconstruction of Identity: The Case of the Kurds in Turkey', *The Global Review of Ethnopolitics* 1, no. 1 (2001): 80–6; Kerem Öktem, 'The Nation's Imprint: Demographic Engineering and the Change of Toponymes in Republican Turkey', *European Journal of Turkish Studies. Social Sciences on Contemporary Turkey*, no. 7 (2009).

14 Heath W. Lowry, *The Islamization & Turkification of the City of Trabzon (Trebizond), 1461–1583* (İstanbul: Isis Press, 2009); Erol Ülker, 'Contextualising 'Turkification'. Nation-Building in the Late Ottoman Empire. 1908–1918', *Nations and Nationalism* 11, no. 4 (2005): 613–36.

15 For a seminal work on the foundational quality of the civil and state-level denial of violence against Armenians in late-Ottoman and Republican periods, see Fatma Müge Göçek, *Denial of Violence: Ottoman Past, Turkish Present, and Collective Violence, 1789-2009* (New York: Oxford University Press, 2015).

16 Tanıl Bora, 'Nationalist Discourses in Turkey', in Ayşe Kadıoğlu and Fuat Keyman (eds), *Symbiotic Antagonisms in Turkey: Sources, Discourses and Changing Nature of Turkish, Kurdish and Islamic Nationalisms* (Salt Lake City: University of Utah Press, 2011).

17 Çağlar Keyder, *State and Class in Turkey: A Study in Capitalist Development* (London: Verso, 1987).

18 Gregory Pappas, 'On This Day September 6–7, 1955: Krystallnacht in Constantinople', *The Pappas Post* (blog), 8 September 2018. https://www.pappaspost.com/on-this-day-september-6-7-1955-krystallnacht-constantinople/.

19 Kuyucu, 'Ethno-Religious "unmixing" of "Turkey"', 362.

20 Alfred de Zayas, 'The Istanbul Pogrom of 6–7 September 1955 in the Light of International Law', *Genocide Studies and Prevention: An International Journal* 2, no. 2 (2007): 138.

21 Kuyucu, 'Ethno-Religious "unmixing" of "Turkey"'.

22 Çağlar Keyder, *State and Class in Turkey: A Study in Capitalist Development* (London: Verso, 1987).

23 Keyder, *State and Class in Turkey*, 202.

24 Tevfik Çavdar, *Türkiye'nin demokrasi tarihi: 1950'den günümüze* (İmge Kitabevi, 2008), 132.

25 *Milliyet*, 27 December 1978.

26 http://bianet.org/bianet/toplum/103785-maras-katliami-ni-hatirlamak-bir-arada-yasami-savunmak.

27 David McDowall, *A Modern History of the Kurds* (I. B. Tauris, 2004), 415.

28 Erinç Yeldan, *Küreselleşme sürecinde Türkiye ekonomisi: Bölüşüm, birikim ve büyüme* (İletişim, 2001).

29 Naomi Klein, *The Shock Doctrine: The Rise of Disaster Capitalism* (Macmillan, 2007).

30 Korkut Boratav, *Türkiye İktisat Tarihi 1908–2009*. (15. Baskı) (Ankara: İmge Kitabevi, 2011; Yeldan, *Küreselleşme sürecinde Türkiye ekonomisi*.

31 Ali Bayramoğlu, *Asker ve Siyaset* (Ankara: Birikim Yayınları, 2004); Çavdar, *Türkiye'nin demokrasi tarihi*.

   Seydi Çelik, *Osmanlı'dan günümüze: devlet ve asker: askeri bürokrasinin anayasal sistem içerisindeki yeri* (Salyangoz Yayınları, 2008); Ümit Cizre Sakallioğlu, 'The Anatomy of the Turkish Military's Political Autonomy', *Comparative Politics* (1997): 151–66.

32 Jamie Peck and Adam Tickell, 'Neoliberalizing Space', *Antipode* 34, no. 3 (2002): 380–404.

33 Fikret Adaman, Ayşe Buğra and Ahmet İnsel, 'Societal Context of Labor Union Strategy: The Case of Turkey', *Labor Studies Journal* 34, no. 2 (2009): 168–88; Özün Millioğulları, 'Türkiye'de 1960-1980 ve 1980–2005 Dönemlerinde Grev Hareketlerinin Karşılaştırılması'. Master's Thesis, Ankara: Ankara University, 2007, 142.

34 Giorgio Agamben, *State of Exception* (University of Chicago Press, 2002).

35 https://www.nytimes.com/1993/07/03/world/40-killed-in-a-turkish-hotel-set-afire-by-muslim-militants.html.

36 https://bianet.org/bianet/toplum/176469-kafka-nin-dava-si-utanc-ve-sivas-madimak-katliami.

37 https://www.sabah.com.tr/gundem/2011/07/02/bu-kadarini-biz-bile
-beklemiyorduk.
38 https://web.archive.org/web/20130218064532/http://www.todayszaman.com/
news-274125-sivas-massacre-case-drops-due-to-statute-of-limitations.html.
39 Umit Cizre-Sakallioglu and Menderes Cinar, 'Turkey 2002: Kemalism,
Islamism, and Politics in the Light of the February 28 Process', *South Atlantic
Quarterly* 102, no. 2 (2003): 312.
40 Cihan Tuğal, *Passive Revolution: Absorbing the Islamic Challenge to
Capitalism* (Stanford: Stanford University Press, 2009).
41 Simten Coşar, 'Turkish Nationalism and Sunni Islam in the Construction of
Political Party Identities', in Ayşe Kadıoğlu and Fuat Keyman (eds), *Symbiotic
Antagonisms in Turkey: Sources, Discourses and Changing Nature of Turkish,
Kurdish and Islamic Nationalisms* (Salt Lake City: University of Utah Press,
2011), 162–96.
42 Ergun Özbudun, 'From Political Islam to Conservative Democracy: The Case
of the Justice and Development Party in Turkey', *South European Society &
Politics* 11, nos. 3–4 (2006): 543–57.
43 Akça, 'Hegemonic Projects in Post-1980 Turkey and the Changing Forms of
Authoritarianism', 31.
44 Azat Zana Gündoğan, 'Divergent Responses to Urban Transformation Projects
in Turkey: Common Sense and State Affinity in Community Mobilization',
Urban Geography 40, no. 7 (2019): 893–217.
45 Barış Alp Özden, 'The Transformation of Social Welfare and Politics in Turkey:
A Successful Convergence of Neoliberalism and Populism', in İsmet Akça,
Ahmet Bekmen and Barış Alp Özden (eds), *Turkey Reframed: Constituting
Neoliberal Hegemony* (London: Pluto Press, 2014), 157–73.
46 Bülent Batuman, 'Minarets without Mosques: Limits to the Urban Politics
of Neo-Liberal Islamism', *Urban Studies* 50, no. 6 (2013): 1097–113; Alev
Çınar, *Modernity, Islam, and Secularism In Turkey: Bodies, Places, and
Time* (Minneapolis: University of Minnesota Press, 2005); Jeremy F. Walton,
'Practices of Neo-Ottomanism: Making Space and Place Virtuous in Istanbul',
in Deniz Göktürk, Levent Soysal, and İpek Türeli (eds), *Orienting Istanbul:
Cultural Capital of Europe?* (London: Routledge, 2010), 88–103.
47 Neslihan Demirtaş-Milz, 'The Regime of Informality in Neoliberal Times
in Turkey: The Case of the Kadifekale Urban Transformation Project',
International Journal of Urban and Regional Research 37, no. 2 (2013):
689–714; Gülçin Erdi Lelandais, 'Space and Identity in Resistance against
Neoliberal Urban Planning in Turkey', *International Journal of Urban and
Regional Research* 38, no. 5 (2014): 1–22.
48 Akça, 'Hegemonic Projects in Post-1980 Turkey and the Changing Forms of
Authoritarianism', 38; Özlem Kaygusuz, 'Authoritarian Neoliberalism and
Regime Security in Turkey: Moving to an 'Exceptional State' under AKP',
South European Society and Politics 23, no. 2 (2018): 281–302.
49 İsmet Akça, Ahmet Bekmen and Barış Alp Özden, 'Introduction', in İsmet
Akça, Ahmet Bekmen and Barış Alp Özden (eds), *Turkey Reframed:*

Constituting Neoliberal Hegemony (London: Pluto Press, 2014), 1–9; Kaygusuz, 'Authoritarian Neoliberalism and Regime Security in Turkey'.

50 Drew Kinney, 'Civilian Actors in the Turkish Military Drama of July 2016', *Eastern Mediterranean Policy Note*, no. 19 (2016): 1–12.

51 Cemal Burak Tansel, 'Authoritarian Neoliberalism and Democratic Backsliding in Turkey: Beyond the Narratives of Progress', *South European Society and Politics* 23, no. 2 (2018): 2.

52 Halil Magnus Karaveli, *Why Turkey Is Authoritarian: From Atatürk to Erdoğan* (Pluto Press, 2018), 116.

References

Adaman, Fikret, Ayşe Buğra and Ahmet İnsel. 'Societal Context of Labor Union Strategy: The Case of Turkey'. *Labor Studies Journal* 34, no. 2 (2009): 168–88.

Agamben, Giorgio. *State of Exception*. Chicago: University of Chicago Press, 2002.

Akça, İsmet. 'Hegemonic Projects in Post-1980 Turkey and the Changing Forms of Authoritarianism'. In İsmet Akça, Ahmet Bekmen and Barış Alp Özden (eds), *Turkey Reframed: Constituting Neoliberal Hegemony*, 14–46. London: Pluto Press, 2014.

Akça, İsmet, Ahmet Bekmen and Barış Alp Özden. 'Antinomies of Authoritarian Neoliberalism in Turkey: The Justice and Development Party Era'. In Cemal Burak Tansel (eds), *States of Discipline: Authoritarian Neoliberalism and the Contested Reproduction of Capitalist Order*, 189–209. London: Rowman & Littlefield, 2017.

Akça, İsmet, Ahmet Bekmen and Barış Alp Özden. 'Introduction'. In İsmet Akça, Ahmet Bekmen and Barış Alp Özden (eds), *Turkey Reframed: Constituting Neoliberal Hegemony*, 1–9. London: Pluto Press, 2014.

Aktar, Ayhan. *Varlık vergisi ve "Türkleştirme" politikaları*. İletişim Yayınları, 2000.

Bâli, Aslı. 'Turkey's Constitutional Coup'. *MERIP Reports* 48, no. 3 (2018): 2–9.

Batuman, Bülent. 'Minarets without Mosques: Limits to the Urban Politics of Neo-Liberal Islamism'. *Urban Studies* 50, no. 6 (2013): 1097–113.

Bayramoğlu, Ali. *Asker ve Siyaset*. Ankara: Birikim Yayınları, 2004.

Benhabib, Seyla. 'Turkey's Authoritarian Turn'. *The New York Times*, 3 June 2013. https://www.nytimes.com/2013/06/04/opinion/turkeys-authoritarian-turn.html.

Bora, Tanıl. 'Nationalist Discourses in Turkey'. In Ayşe Kadıoğlu and Fuat Keyman (eds), *Symbiotic Antagonisms in Turkey: Sources, Discourses and Changing Nature of Turkish, Kurdish and Islamic Nationalisms*. Salt Lake City: University of Utah Press, 2011.

Boratav, Korkut. *Türkiye İktisat Tarihi, 1908–2007*, 12th ed. Ankara: İmge, 2008.

Boratav, Korkut. *Türkiye İktisat Tarihi 1908–2009* (15. Baskı). Ankara: İmge Kitabevi, 2011.

Çavdar, Tevfik. *Türkiye'nin demokrasi tarihi: 1950'den günümüze*. İmge Kitabevi, 2008.

Çelik, Seydi. *Osmanlı'dan günümüze: devlet ve asker: askeri bürokrasinin anayasal sistem içerisindeki yeri*. Salyangoz Yayınları, 2008.

Çetinoğlu, Sait. 'The Mechanisms for Terrorizing Minorities: The Capital Tax and Work Battalions in Turkey during the Second World War'. *Mediterranean Quarterly* 23, no. 2 (2012): 14–29.

Çınar, Alev. *Modernity, Islam, and Secularism in Turkey: Bodies, Places, and Time*. Minneapolis: University of Minnesota Press, 2005.

Cizre-Sakallioglu, Umit and Menderes Cinar. 'Turkey 2002: Kemalism, Islamism, and Politics in the Light of the February 28 Process'. *South Atlantic Quarterly* 102, no. 2 (2003): 309–32.

Coşar, Simten. 'Turkish Nationalism and Sunni Islam in the Construction of Political Party Identities'. In Ayşe Kadıoğlu and Fuat Keyman (eds), *Symbiotic Antagonisms in Turkey: Sources, Discourses and Changing Nature of Turkish, Kurdish and Islamic Nationalisms*, 162–96. Salt Lake City: University of Utah Press, 2011.

Demirtaş-Milz, Neslihan. 'The Regime of Informality in Neoliberal Times in Turkey: The Case of the Kadifekale Urban Transformation Project'. *International Journal of Urban and Regional Research* 37, no. 2 (2013): 689–714.

Esen, Berk and Şebnem Gümüşçü. 'Rising Competitive Authoritarianism in Turkey'. *Third World Quarterly* 37, no. 9 (2016): 1581–606.

Göçek, Fatma Müge. *Denial of Violence: Ottoman Past, Turkish Present, and Collective Violence, 1789–2009*. New York: Oxford University Press, 2015.

Gündoğan, Azat Zana. 'Divergent Responses to Urban Transformation Projects in Turkey: Common Sense and State Affinity in Community Mobilization'. *Urban Geography* 40, no. 7 (2018): 893–17.

Jongerden, Joost. 'Resettlement and Reconstruction of Identity: The Case of the Kurds in Turkey'. *The Global Review of Ethnopolitics* 1, no. 1 (2001): 80–6.

Karaveli, Halil Magnus. *Why Turkey Is Authoritarian: From Atatürk to Erdoğan*. London: Pluto Press, 2018.

Kaya, Ayhan. 'Islamisation of Turkey under the AKP Rule: Empowering Family, Faith and Charity'. *South European Society and Politics* 20, no. 1 (2015): 47–69.

Kaygusuz, Özlem. 'Authoritarian Neoliberalism and Regime Security in Turkey: Moving to an "Exceptional State" under AKP'. *South European Society and Politics* 23, no. 2 (2018): 281–302.

Keyder, Çağlar. *State and Class in Turkey: A Study in Capitalist Development*. London: Verso, 1987.

Kinney, Drew. 'Civilian Actors in the Turkish Military Drama of July 2016'. *Eastern Mediterranean Policy Note*, no. 19 (2016): 1–12.

Klein, Naomi. *The Shock Doctrine: The Rise of Disaster Capitalism*. New York: Metropolitan Books, 2007.

Kuyucu, Ali Tuna. 'Ethno-Religious "unmixing" of "Turkey": 6–7 September Riots as a Case in Turkish Nationalism*'. *Nations and Nationalism* 11, no. 3 (2005): 361–80.

Lelandais, Gülçin Erdi. 'Space and Identity in Resistance against Neoliberal Urban Planning in Turkey'. *International Journal of Urban and Regional Research* 38, no. 5 (2014): 1–22.

Levitsky, Steven and Lucan A. Way. *Competitive Authoritarianism: Hybrid Regimes after the Cold War*. New York: Cambridge University Press, 2010.

Levitsky, Steven and Lucan A. Way. 'Elections Without Democracy: The Rise of Competitive Authoritarianism'. *Journal of Democracy* 13, no. 2 (2002): 51–65.

Lowry, Heath W. *The Islamization & Turkification of the City of Trabzon (Trebizond), 1461–1583*. Istanbul: Isis Press, 2009.
McDowall, David. *A Modern History of the Kurds*. London: I. B. Tauris, 2004.
Millioğulları, Özün. 'Türkiye'de 1960-1980 ve 1980–2005 Dönemlerinde Grev Hareketlerinin Karşılaştırılması.' Master's Thesis, Ankara: Ankara University, 2007.
Öktem, Kerem. 'The Nation's Imprint: Demographic Engineering and the Change of Toponymes in Republican Turkey'. *European Journal of Turkish Studies. Social Sciences on Contemporary Turkey*, no. 7 (2009).
Öniş, Ziya. 'Turkey's Two Elections: The AKP Comes Back.' *Journal of Democracy* 27, no. 2 (2016): 141–54.
Özbudun, Ergun.'AKP at the Crossroads: Erdoğan's Majoritarian Drift'. *South European Society and Politics* 19, no. 2 (2014): 155–67.
Özbudun, Ergun. 'From Political Islam to Conservative Democracy: The Case of the Justice and Development Party in Turkey'. *South European Society & Politics* 11, no. 3–4 (2006): 543–57.
Özbudun, Ergun. 'Turkey's Judiciary and the Drift toward Competitive Authoritarianism'. *The International Spectator* 50, no. 2 (2015): 42–55.
Özden, Barış Alp. 'The Transformation of Social Welfare and Politics in Turkey: A Successful Convergence of Neoliberalism and Populism'. In İsmet Akça, Ahmet Bekmen and Barış Alp Özden (eds), *Turkey Reframed: Constituting Neoliberal Hegemony*, 157–73. London: Pluto Press, 2014.
Pappas, Gregory. 'On This Day September 6–7, 1955: Krystallnacht in Constantinople'. *The Pappas Post* (blog), 8 September 2018. https://www.pappaspost.com/on-this-day-september-6-7-1955-krystallnacht-constantinople/.
Peck, Jamie and Adam Tickell. 'Neoliberalizing Space'. *Antipode* 34, no. 3 (2002): 380–404.
Sakallıoğlu, Ümit Cizre. 'The Anatomy of the Turkish Military's Political Autonomy'. *Comparative Politics* 29, no. 2 (1997): 151–66.
Tansel, Cemal Burak. 'Authoritarian Neoliberalism and Democratic Backsliding in Turkey: Beyond the Narratives of Progress'. *South European Society and Politics* 23, no. 2 (2018): 197–217.
Taş, Hakkı. 'Turkey–from Tutelary to Delegative Democracy'. *Third World Quarterly* 36, no. 4 (2015): 776–91.
Toktamış, Kumru. 'Now There Is, Now There Is Not: The Disappearing Silent Revolution of AKP as Re-Entrenchment'. *British Journal of Middle Eastern Studies* 46, no. 5 (2019): 735–51.
Tuğal, Cihan. 2009. *Passive Revolution: Absorbing the Islamic Challenge to Capitalism*. Stanford: Stanford University Press.
Ülker, Erol. 'Contextualising "Turkification": Nation-Building in the Late Ottoman Empire. 1908–1918'. *Nations and Nationalism* 11, no. 4 (2005): 613–36.
Walton, Jeremy F. 'Practices of Neo-Ottomanism: Making Space and Place Virtuous in Istanbul.' In Deniz Göktürk, Levent Soysal and İpek Türeli (eds), *Orienting Istanbul: Cultural Capital of Europe?*, 88–103. London: Routledge, 2010.
Yeldan, Erinç. *Küreselleşme sürecinde Türkiye ekonomisi: Bölüşüm, birikim ve büyüme*. Istanbul: İletişim, 2001.
Zayas, Alfred de. 'The Istanbul Pogrom of 6–7 September 1955 in the Light of International Law'. *Genocide Studies and Prevention: An International Journal* 2, no. 2 (2007): 137–54.

9

1989 inverted

Transformative authoritarian memory and the rise of populism in Poland and Hungary

Michael Bernhard

Introduction

The year 1989 was a pivotal moment in the global expansion of democracy. It marked the collapse of communism in Europe, the end of the Cold War and the democratization of a number of the countries in the former Soviet Bloc. Yet thirty years later, the two countries that sparked that process, Poland and Hungary, have lapsed into periods of democratic backsliding under illiberal populist governments. At the centre of this change of fortune is a transformation of the political significance of 1989 in both countries. I argue that the study of democratization in political science has been ill-equipped to make sense of such developments because of a failure to understand that the meaning of momentous events like 1989 is susceptible to change, and, when it does, it has critical ramifications for the politics of the countries that experienced them.

In comparison to other social sciences, such as sociology and anthropology, or the humanities, political science has less extensively studied the impact of historical memory on contemporary developments. This chapter shows that sometimes the analytic tools of political science by omitting actors' shifting understandings of the past can miss developments of great consequence for subsequent political outcomes. I revisit the theory of modes of transition as a structural frame to help explain how the democratic successes of 1989 in Poland and Hungary left particular legacies that subsequently contributed to democratic backsliding in the long term. In this process the very notion of '1989' as a watershed democratic breakthrough has been called into question.

I do not adopt the notion of 'modes of transition' uncritically because it can entail the teleological assumption that the fall of authoritarianism put countries on a path to democracy.[1] While such optimism may have seemed realistic in periods of widespread democratization in Southern Europe, Latin America and East-Central Europe, they seem far less sanguine following the dissolution of the Soviet Union, ongoing regime instability in Africa or the Arab Spring. We are now acutely aware that the end of one form of authoritarianism can just as easily inaugurate a novel form of authoritarianism. For that reason, I reconceptualize the process as 'extrication from authoritarianism' to capture the uncertainty of it ultimate outcome.

In this chapter I will (1) review the literature on modes of transition with respect to its understanding of the role of elites and masses, (2) discuss the extrication processes of Poland and Hungary and how they do not fit easily into the conceptual scheme of the modes literature, (3) discuss how attention to the discursive spaces created by extrications from authoritarianism helps us to understand the contribution of specific actors to democratic backsliding in both countries and (4) discuss the role of civil society actors in both perpetuating and resisting the populist attack on democracy in both countries. In doing so I hope to show how the integration of the politics of memory into conventional political science allows us to re-evaluate important concepts, understand their limitations and provide insight into the unexpected episodes of democratic backsliding in Poland and Hungary.

The modes of transitions literature

The Third Wave of global democratization encompassed a large number of nonviolent transitions that involved negotiations between authoritarian incumbents and their democratic opponents.[2] The foundational literature provided a set of ad hoc categories to think of different kinds of transition based on a series of terms that emerged in the discussion of the Spanish and Latin American cases. These included *reforma*, where elites took the lead in the process; *ruptura*, where elites lost control and opposition groups took the lead; and *reforma pactada* or *ruptura pactada*, where the terms of democratization were the product of a negotiated 'pact' between the two sides. The focus on this novel and widespread aspect, the negotiation of pacts between incumbents and their opponents, sometimes came at the expense of overlooking the importance of contentious processes of mass mobilization. There was an early consensus that the essential ingredient for democratic success was an explicit understanding between the soft-line faction of authoritarian incumbents and the moderate wing of their oppositional challengers, who each would control either the hardliners or radicals from their own camps.[3]

The modes of transition approach broke with the singular focus on elites by paying attention to 'the identity of the actors who drive the transition and the strategies they employ'.[4] Terry Karl was the first to innovate in this way, distinguishing between those processes that were elite controlled vs. those which included contentious political actions by the masses. To this she added whether transition was accomplished by compromise or force. This led to four distinct modes: (1) pact (compromise with elites ascendant), (2) reform (compromise with masses ascendant), (3) imposition (force with elite ascendant) and (4) revolution (force with masses ascendant).[5]

Munck and Leff further refined Karl's theory, introducing a greater degree of variation in the actor dimension by adding an intermediate category in which both elites and masses play an important role in the transition. In the strategic dimension they change the terminology somewhat but still capture the way in which the outcome is decided – involving accommodation or confrontation or some combination of the two.[6] While they draw it as a property space with a largely undemarcated central area, it effectively functions as a 3X3 (as depicted in Table 9.1) because of the adding of the intermediate categories in the two dimensions that define mode.

They illustrate the utility of their typology with cases from Latin America and Eastern Europe. In Poland, they characterize the process as reform through transaction, an accommodation between incumbent and oppositional elites. The strength of the regime incumbents and uncertainty over Soviet

TABLE 9.1 *Typology of Modes of Democratic Transition*

	Identity of Agent of Change		
Strategy	*Incumbent*	*Both*	*Counter-elite*
Confrontation	Revolution from Above Bulgaria	Reform through Rupture Czechoslovakia Argentina	Social Revolution
Combination of Confrontation and Accommodation		Reform through Extrication Hungary	
Accommodation	Conservative Reform	Reform through Transaction Poland Brazil	Reform from Below Chile

intentions led Solidarity to enter Roundtable talks with the regime and sign an agreement for partially free competitive elections.[7] In Hungary they characterize the mode as reform through extrication. While there were also Roundtable Negotiations in Hungary, they did not result in a final agreement, and those issues unsolved were solved contentiously via referendum.[8]

The aim of all this typological work was to determine the consequences of these different paths to democracy for its subsequent development. In this regard the introduction of the contentious dimension into the consideration of patterns of extrication did not overturn the elitist bias of the foundational literature on transition. Munck and Leff's final words on the subject was that that if transition was conducive to fostering elite cooperation rather than confrontation, then the chances of long-term democratic success or what the discipline then referred to as democratic consolidation was much more likely.[9]

Paths of extrication and democracy

I also see the process of extrication as having durable legacies, but proceed more explicitly from a historical institutionalist perspective. I conceptualize the extrication from communism as a critical juncture for regime formation which created twenty to twenty-five years of democratic stability in both Poland and Hungary which was disrupted in the 2010s. In this discussion I will focus explicitly on the impact of the mixture of contention and accommodation in their extrications from communism, thus building on, but not fully adopting, the insights of the modes of democratization literature as well as more recent work on paths of extrication from authoritarianism discussed in the following. With hindsight I will show that the long-term legacy of this mixed path does not accord with the predictions of either literature, and here the incorporation of the politics of memory into the account will show that the meaning of 1989 changed for the actors engaged in the struggle for power, and this had important ramifications for the durability of post-communist democracy.

In thinking about the enduring legacies of extrication from authoritarian regimes, there have been different schools of thought on the ramifications of contentious versus accommodative extrication. The centrality of elites and their ability to cooperate following accommodative processes of regime change continued to dominate political science thinking on the subject for a substantial period of time. For instance, in their influential work Burton, Gunther and Higley argued that negotiated elite settlements led to consolidated democracy by creating consensus on norms and rules, promoting legitimacy, limited government, moderation and the effective channelling of popular demands.[10] In a somewhat more tempered argument, Casper and Taylor argued that highly consensual negotiations lead to weak or abortive democratization, whereas difficult negotiations characterized by strong demands by the opposition help to resolve substantive differences between the two sides and thus stood a better chance of sustaining democracy. Failing that, the incumbents would be able to structure institutions to their advantage and impede the full emergence of democracy.[11]

Not until recently has a school of contending thinkers who have argued for the positive effects of contentious extrication for long-term democratic development questioned the tenets of this democratic elitism. Haggard and Kaufmann show that in cases where democratic transition includes distributional conflict the quality of democracy improves in the long term.[12] This parallels Fishman's paired comparison of democratization in Spain and Portugal, where Portugal's revolution has led to a higher degree of egalitarianism than Spain's elite bargaining.[13] Brancati demonstrates the size of democratic protests has a salutary effect on the depth of democratic reform.[14] Both della Porta and Bernhard argue that popular participation and contention in episodes of democratization create better odds for success and better democratic outcomes.[15] What all these studies stress is how a mobilized citizenry blocks the ability of elites to channel reforms in ways that allow them to either maintain authoritarian privilege or convert it to new forms of privilege following transition.

All of these works, despite differences over whether contention or accommodation is conducive for democracy, argue that the circumstances by which regimes come into being have critical ramifications for democracy's viability and durability. Whether explicitly or implicitly, these theories adhere to historical institutionalist assumptions on regime formation. New regimes come into being during critical junctures when the ability of the existing system of institutions to enforce order falters, and actors, under conditions of enhanced agency, create new institutions and inaugurate a new regime. Assuming sufficient actor buy-in such institutions can become self-regulating and stable, and establish institutional lock-in or path-dependence.[16] In this account I also treat 1989 as a critical juncture, but argue that that there has been disruption of path-dependence in both cases, and that we are now in a period of regime change. In both cases I will also show that the previous critical juncture left legacies that have helped to weaken liberal democracy in the last decade. Most unexpectedly, in the ideational dimension, I will also show that central to this destabilization has been the inversion of the meaning of 1989 via an aggressive memory politics by the populist actors who are now dismantling democracy.

The combination of accommodation and contention in the Polish and Hungarian extrications

Munck and Leff see Poland as a case of 'reform through transaction' and Hungary as a case of 'reform through extrication'. While both processes included both authoritarian incumbents and the opposition as important actors, they see the Hungarian process as involving both confrontation and accommodation, whereas the Polish process is dominated by accommodation. My assumption is that they see this as a function of the successful conclusion of the Roundtable Talks in Poland leading to the partially free elections of 1989, whereas in Hungary the Roundtable Talks did not settle all issues and some issues had to be settled by referendum due to recalcitrance by elements in the opposition.

In contrast I stress the similarity of the patterns of extrication in both countries, and, if anything, see the Polish case as slightly more contentious. First, the initiation of negotiations with the ability to affect real change was a function of the strength of the Polish opposition. The Solidarity opposition that negotiated with the Polish United Workers' Party (PZPR) in 1989 could trace its emergence back to 1976, even prior to the emergence of Solidarity, its sixteen months of legal existence in 1980–81 and its persistence as an underground opposition from 1981 until its relegalization.

Second, the Roundtable in Poland was part of a more extended extrication process. The event that led to the Roundtable Negotiations was a strike wave in 1988, which signified that the regime's efforts to stabilize the country and its economy in the post–Martial Law era had failed. In order to draw Solidarity into the reform process the regime relegalized the union and entered into negotiations in March 1989. These were successfully concluded in April with a pact that fell far short of full democratization. Under its terms, elections were scheduled for June but entailed substantial guarantees for the ruling communists and its allies. The PZPR, the United Peasant Party (ZSL) and the Democratic Party (SD) were guaranteed two thirds of the 360 seats in the Sejm, with one third subject to contestation, including by Solidarity. A second chamber, a Senat, was created and its 100 mandates were subject to full contestation. The accord also created an executive president to be elected by the membership of the two houses meeting jointly as a National Assembly. Given the apportionment of seats, the first president and prime minister were expected to be chosen by the communists and their allies.

The plan misfired. All contested seats, save one in the Senat, were won by Solidarity-backed candidates and many seats reserved for the communists were left unfilled because of insufficient positive votes. Ultimately, the weakness of the PZPR's performance led their coalition partners, the ZSL and the SD, to defect from efforts to form a government. A second ad hoc compromise was then negotiated where a national unity government was formed under a Solidarity Prime Minister, Tadeusz Mazowiecki, in return for allowing the PZPR leader General Wojciech Jaruzelski to assume the presidency.

Once the terms of the Roundtable were breached, this led to splits within Solidarity and the process got highly contentious again. Many activists continued to push against the remaining guarantees for the communists that stood in the way of full democratization. A cadre of activists left out of the government, centred on Solidarity's leader, Lech Wałęsa, continued to push for full democratization, whereas the Mazowiecki government felt bound to honour the previously negotiated agreements. The pressure brought by the former proved too much to resist and a second set of negotiations led to direct election of a new president in 1990, a contest won by Wałęsa. This, in turn, led to the replacement of the Mazowiecki government and calling of fully competitive legislative elections in 1991, completing the democratization process.

The extrication in Hungary was similarly contentious, but temporally compact. As the second country to move the Hungarians faced less uncertainty about Soviet intentions. While there was a political opposition in Hungary, it was not as developed as its Polish counterpart. It supported an alternative uncensored public space, but was more modest in its outreach to society at large. However, late in the tenure of the communist regime it did show an increasing capacity to demonstrate and stage other public events on national anniversaries and issues such as ecological destruction, the rights of the Hungarian diaspora and peace. It was divided between a more liberal/social-democratic Budapest-based and a more provincial Christian-democratic wing. These two wings crystalized into competing parties – the Alliance of Free Democrats (SzDSz) and the Hungarian Democratic Forum (MDF). Another important actor was the more libertarian student milieu organized as the Alliance of Young Democrats (FiDeSz). Of particular importance to the democratic breakthrough in Hungary was the symbolic reburial of Imre Nagy, the leader of the Revolution of 1956, who was executed in secret in 1958. In June 1989 Nagy was rehabilitated by the party and was given a burial of honour in Budapest on the 31st anniversary of his execution. The funeral turned into an opposition demonstration of a quarter million people. Young Viktor Orbán of FiDeSz exploded onto the scene with a speech in which he called for the Soviets to withdraw from Hungary.

Capable of reading the writing on the walls, the ruling Hungarian Socialist Workers' Party (MSzMP), which had a sustained history of reformism, took a proactive stance after the removal of long-time leader János Kádár. They made contact with the opposition and tried to draw them into the process of reform from a position of strength. Their leading figure, Imre Pozsgay, had good relations with the MDF and tried to draw them into a cross-camp alliance in hope of maintaining his position. The Roundtable Negotiations in Hungary were unable to reach a resolution on the timing of presidential and parliamentary elections and other contentious issues. Pozsgay, as the most well-known and popular politician in the country, and his allies hoped for direct presidential elections prior to parliamentary elections and in this way to endow the presidential office with direct democratic legitimacy and greater executive power. This was opposed by SzDSz and FiDeSz and ultimately resolved by referendum to their satisfaction. In the parliamentary elections that followed in March 1990 the MDF triumphed and formed a government with two smaller parties: the Christian Democrats (KDNP) and the Smallholders (FkGP). The parliament then elected Árpád Göncz of SzDSz, who went to jail for his activity in 1956, as president.

The legacy of extrication: Revisionist discursive space and the emergence of memory warriors

So in hindsight, both the Polish and Hungarian extrication processes included contentious opposition movements who engaged in negotiation with the party-state. The ability of the communist incumbents to negotiate and abide by the results of those processes showed that they still had the ability to evolve and respond to the uncertainty of events. Their ability to do so combined with the resource advantages they enjoyed as ruling party successors allowed them to expunge hard-line elements, take on new allies and remake themselves as reformist social-democratic parties.[17] Their effectiveness in doing so is attested to by their ability to rebound, win elections and form governments soon after their initial removal from power in both states.

After taking the largest share of votes in the parliamentary election of 1993, the successor party to the PZPR, the Democratic Left Alliance (SLD), participated in a government under Waldemar Pawlak of the Polish People's Party (PSL) from 1993 to 1995. After the Pawlak government fell, the next two governments were led by SLD Prime Ministers, Józef Oleksy and Włodzimierz Cimoszewicz, until the parliamentary elections of 1997. The comeback of the party was epitomized by the victory of Aleksander Kwaśniewski over Lech Wałęsa in the presidential elections of 1995.

The MSzP triumphed decisively in the parliamentary elections of 1994, winning an outright majority of seats in parliament (209 of 386) on the basis of a plurality of just over 30 per cent of the vote. It nevertheless formed a coalition government with the Free Democrats under MSzP Prime Minister Gyula Horn. The thought was that including a former opposition party in the government would soften the shock of their rapid return to power.

On the opposition side of the political spectrum, once extrication was complete, politics became more competitive. Specifically, the need for solidarity across different political currents against the regime was no longer a question of survival. With this, opposition parties worked hard to distinguish themselves programmatically from each other both to win elections and to establish their claim to lead governments. In both countries this led to alternation between post-communist and opposition-led governing coalitions in the short term.

The nature of contentious but negotiated extrications led to the creation of a marginal, but durable, right-wing discursive space from which it was easy to attract constituencies that were disenchanted with aspects of the post-communist political, social and economic transformation. It became connected with a form of memory politics that increasingly criticized 1989 as a failed opportunity to end communism. Further, when post-communist liberal democracy was threatened by the sequential crises of global financial meltdown and the refugee influx, the discourse it spawned acquired a greater resonance with the electorate and became the basis for an expansive populist backlash against liberal democracy.

There are four aspects of the Polish and Hungarian pattern of extrication that gave rise to this discursive space. First, its negotiated episodes made it possible to cast the settlements of 1989 as corrupt bargains between elements of the opposition and the communists. In this narrative, post-communist liberal democracy is depicted as an incomplete revolution which instead of creating 'true' democracy protected the communists and allowed them to convert their political privilege under the old system into material privilege. Second, with the fracturing of unified opposition following founding elections, the articulation of more radical positions was no longer a liability, but became possibly the best option for weaker political parties on the right. This provided them with a programme which both explained the renewed success of recently defeated communist successor parties and attributed it to the collusion of the more moderate and successful parts of the opposition camp with whom they were in competition. Third, the emergence of viable post-communist social democratic parties and the pattern of alternation in power by post-communist and post-opposition groups of parties also lent some plausibility to the narrative of the rotten deal. Further, given that the reformist programmes of both camps – market-oriented growth and joining the EU and NATO – were very similar, this provided fodder for claims that political choices were not fully free and constrained by the rotten deal. Fourth, given the repertoires of contentious political engagement that emerged in both countries under late communism and which carried over into the post-transition period,[18] learned capacities for contentious politics became another way in which these actors pursued their agenda.

For these actors 1989 ceased to be a moment of national liberation but the origin of everything that went wrong with liberal democratic post-communism. This narrative came to colour their view of politics and their thoughts for how to address the future. In work co-authored with Jan Kubik, we describe these actors as taking the stance of 'mnemonic warriors'. Such actors pursue a course of action which is predicated on the assumption that the issues that presently face the nation 'cannot be effectively addressed unless the whole polity is set on the proper foundation, constructed according to the "true" version of history'.[19] Herein lies the very roots of populism in the two countries, by which liberal democracy is delegitimized by portraying it substantively as a sell-out of the people, which necessitates measures to counteract its theft by a corrupt elite. In inverting 1989 the memory warriors turned 1989 from a moment of liberation into one of national betrayal.[20]

In Hungary, the actor which eventually came to occupy this space was FiDeSz. The path by which it came to occupy this space was more convoluted than that of its Polish counterpart. It began as a party of liberal youth, then the dominant party of centre-right and the MSzP's major rival, then finally drifting further to the right over time. In Poland, PiS, and the parties of the Solidarity right that preceded it, often took part in the post-Solidarity party coalitions that alternated in power with the SLD. Until recently, they generally enjoyed less electoral success than their liberal and centrist competitors from the Solidarity, such as Freedom Union (UW) and Civic Platform (PO). Over time, the discourse of PiS and FiDeSz has grown more ethno nationalist, even rehabilitating anti-communist activists who collaborated with Nazi Germany. They have tried to minimize national responsibility for participation in the Holocaust despite active state collaboration in Hungary and by elements in Polish society. The rehabilitation of past anti-democratic right-wing traditions, dismissal of liberal democracy as an outmoded form of rule and outright attacks on Western traditions of tolerance have become increasingly common in the discourse of both countries. And finally, they caricature the EU as new form of tyranny which constrains national sovereignty as perniciously as the Soviet Union.

The paths that the parties took to becoming illiberal populists were quite different. PiS in some sense lived in the discursive space of 'revolution betrayed' since its outset. Its origins go back to the period of the 'war at the top' in Solidarity over whether the union should challenge Jaruzelski's legitimacy to hold the presidency. The Kaczyński brothers, Jarosław and Lech, founded the Center Compact (PC) party, which strongly supported Wałęsa's efforts to unseat Jaruzelski. After the first free parliamentary election in 1991 PC was the lead party in the coalition that supported the Olszewski government (December 1991 to June 1992) which unsuccessfully attempted to weaponize the secret police archives and rapidly fell from power.

PC also participated in the Solidarity Electoral Alliance (AWS) that supported Prime Minister Jerzy Buzek (1997–2001). Late in his term, the AWS began to decompose into competing factions and parties, and the Kaczyński brothers created Law and Justice (PiS). Following a final round of SLD rule, PiS emerged as the strongest party in the elections of 2005 and formed two short-lived governments from 2005 to 2007. This election marked the eclipse of the SLD which found itself fully discredited by corruption scandals. Since then electoral politics in Poland has been dominated by post-Solidarity political forces.

In early elections in 2007 PiS lost to their more moderate liberal competitors, the PO. The PO went on to rule successfully from 2008 to 2015, the first party to win two consecutive parliamentary elections in Poland. It was during this period that PiS began to fully try to discredit the memory of 1989, in particular the Roundtable Negotiations. As I have documented elsewhere with Jan Kubik, this was not an effective strategy for returning to power at first.[21]

In Hungary, the transformation of FiDeSz into an illiberal party that has crippled Hungarian democracy has followed a convoluted path. Unlike PiS and its predecessors, it was the most successful post-opposition party in Hungary. Whereas SzDSz and MDF faded early, FiDeSz transformed itself into a catchall centre-right party that challenged the post-communist MSzP from the late 1990s throughout the 2000s. Initially, the stolen revolution discursive space in Hungary was occupied by the Hungarian Justice and Life Party (MIÉP). That party's highpoint came in 1998 when it won 5.5 per cent of the vote and secured representation in the parliament before fading into obscurity. Since losing the election of 2006, FiDeSz has moved steadily to the right and emerged as a hegemonic party winning three consecutive elections.

Orbán's first stint as prime minister came in 1998 and was followed by two close losses to the MSzP in 2002 and 2006, when the MSzP became the first party to win re-election in post-communist Hungary. The year 2006 was a turning point. During the campaign Prime Minister Gyurcsány lied about the state of the economy, presenting an optimistic picture despite a negative prognosis. When Gyurcsány was taped publicly acknowledging his dishonesty, this led to an extensive campaign of protest by FiDeSz supporters and right-wing youth. It was during this period that the previously marginal ultra-right Jobbik also began to gain strength and prominence and FiDeSz began to move more aggressively to the right and assume the stance of a mnemonic warrior.

Dual crisis, right civil society mobilization and populist success

The path to populist forms of illiberal rule was not the inevitable product of the discursive space on the right that I have argued was a product of the path of extrication from communism in both countries. PiS had long occupied this space and FiDeSz came to occupy it over time, but it by no means guaranteed a path to power. Two external shocks to the liberal democratic equilibrium of both countries made this space considerably more valuable. These were the world financial crisis of 2008 and the subsequent great recession, and the influx of large numbers of Muslim refugees from failed states such as Syria, Libya, Iraq and Afghanistan into Europe in the summer of 2015. It is important to say at the outset that economic crisis played a much larger role in Hungary than it did in Poland. The narratives of failed revolutions in 1989 gained credence as liberalism failed to protect the world from a deep financial crisis and the entry of millions of refugees into the Schengen area. The rehabilitation of ethno-national xenophobia and arguments for protecting citizens against the uncertainties of the market gave both parties solid governing majorities that have allowed them to undertake their illiberal agendas.

The illiberalism of the present is thus a product not only of the discursive space that created comfortable niches for FiDeSz and PiS to contest power prior to the late 2000s as a legacy of 1989 but also of the existential uncertainty created by the financial and security failures from which European liberalism could not protect itself. Thus the dual crisis of European economy and security helped to validate that narrative of the partial and corrupt transformation of 1989 and made radical responses to it more attractive to voters.

An additional structural factor that needs to be taken into account is that prior to joining the European Union in 2004, right-wing movements were more modest players in both Poland and Hungary. The explanation here is that the existence of such movements would have been seen as evidence that a candidate country was not yet ready for membership. Following accession in 2004, both countries were less subject to pressures to keep right rhetoric and activists under control. Certainly the cost of flouting EU norms was not nearly so high after accession.[22]

The dual crises allowed both PiS and FiDeSz to focus on discontent and utilize popular mobilization to change their electoral fortunes. The economic crisis in Hungary and FiDeSz' move to right-wing populism began earlier than the global economic crisis. The revelation that Prime Minister Gyurcsány lied about the state of the economy led to over a month of protests beginning in mid-September 2006. These protests centred on Parliament in Budapest and involved frequent fighting between the police and youthful protesters from FiDeSz, Jobbik, and more extreme groups. The highpoints of protest involved tens of thousands of protesters and spread to several cities beyond Budapest. On 23 October, the fiftieth anniversary of the outbreak of the Revolution of 1956, FiDeSz and its allies held a separate commemoration from the government and drew a crowd of 100,000. The party's ability to maintain this level of protest was not a case of spontaneous outrage, but the direct product of longer-term investment in its own network of Civic Circles following its electoral defeat in 2002.[23]

While the Gyurcsány government survived these protests, economic slowdown in 2007–8 and recession in 2009 brought its resignation and its replacement by a caretaker government under Gordon Bajnai, composed of MSzP and independent ministers. The full inversion of the meaning of 1989 came on the celebration of the 53rd anniversary of the Revolution on 23 October 2009, twenty years after reburial of Imre Nagy. There were three separate commemorations: one official hosted by the government, one held by Jobbik and one by FiDeSz. The official government commemoration was sombre, and sparsely attended, with members of the government laying a memorial wreath at the statue of Nagy, then on Martyr's Square. The energy and intensity of the oppositional commemorations of 1956 matched that of the commemoration twenty years earlier in 1989. Both the Jobbik and FiDeSz commemorations literally obliterated the memory of 1989 as liberation. The transition of 1989 was reconfigured as continuity with the restoration of order by János Kádár and the Soviets in 1956. The year 1989 had changed nothing, but had been a continuation of the communist past. The MSzP as the successor to the communists was painted as unfit to hold power, and not even as a legitimate participant in national politics. The upcoming general election of 2010 was not seen as normal, but as a continuation of the national uprising of 1956.[24] And when FiDeSz won the election they described it as a 'revolution at the polling booth'.

FiDeSz won a crushing victory in the general election of 2010 in coalition with the Christian Democrats (KDNP). While they only won a bare majority of votes in the first round, the nature of the Hungarian electoral system gave them over two thirds of the seats in the parliament, a majority sufficient to change the constitution. Jobbik also made a strong showing, placing third after the fading MSzP. With their constitutional majority, FiDeSz embarked on its illiberal turn, curtailing the independence of the judiciary and other independent regulatory parties, reconfiguring the electoral system to their advantage and curtailing the autonomy of civil society groups.[25]

In 2014 despite these advantages FiDeSz only gained a plurality victory, though its legal manipulation still delivered a constitutional majority victory in terms of seats. Faced with this loss of popularity Orbán again moved to the right yet again. In the summer of 2014 he delivered his famous illiberal democracy speech in Băile Tuşnada, in which he attacked the West and its decadence, declared civil society to be an enemy of the nation and looked to 'strong states' such as Turkey, Russia and China as models for the future.[26] Despite tacking even further to the right, FiDeSz continued to lose popularity in public opinion polling as well as some highly visible by-elections to Jobbik in 2015.[27]

This trend was reversed by the European refugee crisis of 2015. Hungary was on the transit route from the Balkans to northern Europe, and a large number of refugees streamed through the country that summer. Capitalizing on the fears of his population about an influx of impoverished Muslim refugees, Orbán ordered the construction of a border fence to control the influx and attacked EU policy on resettlement. With this, the popularity of both Orbán and FiDeSz rebounded. This carried FiDeSz on to a third electoral victory in 2018 and further consolidation of its illiberal rule with extension of control over higher education and the private media.

In Poland, economic crisis has been less of a driver of populism. During the great recession it continued to grow at a healthy rate, though the state of the global economy was cause for concern. If there is anxiety over the economy in Poland it is over the rapid pace of social change that three decades of uninterrupted rapid growth has wrought. This is particularly unsettling for those parts of Polish society that are highly religious and traditional.[28]

After PiS was denied re-election in 2007, the party met with tragedy in 2010 when the plane carrying President Lech Kaczyński and those accompanying him to the commemoration of the 70th anniversary of Katyń massacre of Polish Officers crashed outside Smolensk. Kaczyński was replaced by the Speaker of the Sejm Bronisław Komorowski of PO. In the period prior to his death, PO and PiS had been engaged in a dispute over the meaning of 1989 coinciding with the twentieth anniversary of the Roundtable Agreement and elections of June 1989. PiS positioned itself as a memory warrior and depicted the Roundtable Agreement as a corrupt bargain between the communists and a part of the Solidarity elite which left the communists with too much power especially in the economy. PO, for its part, stayed out of it, and celebrated the elections of June 1989 fulsomely as a breakthrough.[29] As in Hungary, the meaning of 1989 has been inverted by PiS. Instead of being seen the breakthrough moment in which communism was replaced by democracy, it was instead depicted as, at best, a partial break from the past. PiS used the purported failure of 1989 to make a decisive break with the past to justify the necessity of its return to power and extraordinary measures to set things right.

PiS finally regained power in 2015, following two consecutive PO governments. PO's reputation was damaged prior to the elections by the release of illegally taped conversations between a number of its leaders, which cast them as power hungry, cynical and opportunistic. The election season also coincided with the refugee crisis – the presidential election came in May at its onset and parliamentary elections at its height in October. The government of Prime Minister Ewa Kopacz was unable to come up with a consistent message on the topic, both supporting the humanitarian impulses of the EU and at the same time pushing back on higher quotas for Poland.[30] Her opponents in PiS and the forces further to the right were strongly opposed to refugees and attacked the government unceasingly on the subject.

Like FiDeSz in Hungary, while in opposition, PiS developed an extensive protest and mobilization capacity. Beyond local discussion clubs associated with the party, there was also extensive growth in conservative religious and even far-right activism in this period. The religious activists strongly defend traditional values against feminism, LGBTQ+ equality and other forms of difference. It is during this campaign that PiS joined this so-called campaign against 'gender ideology' launched by far-right and conservative Church circles in 2013–14.[31] Far-right activists stigmatize and engage in periodic violent actions against ethnic, religious and sexual minorities. While it would be patently wrong to attribute the most extreme of this activity to PiS, they sometimes benefit from it and often overlook or make excuses for extremist action.[32]

With PO losing popularity and traction, in the May presidential election incumbent Bronisław Komorowski came in a surprise second in the first round to PiS candidate Andrzej Duda, and lost in the second round. In the parliamentary elections that followed in October, PiS won a plurality of the popular vote which was enough for it to secure a majority of seats in both houses of the Polish Parliament. In the period since it has moved to undermine the independence of the judiciary and turned the state-run media into a propaganda arm of the ruling party. It has been illiberal but not nearly as successful as FiDeSz. It lacks the constitutional majority from which its Hungarian counterpart has benefitted and it has faced more significant countervailing contention than the FiDeSz government.[33]

In 2019 and 2020, PiS reinforced its hold on power winning both parliamentary and presidential elections. In the parliamentary elections of 2019 PiS again won a majority of seats in the Sejm. It did, however, lose control of the Senat, though this body really only has minimal power to obstruct the legislative agenda of a majority in the Sejm. In the presidential election in July 2020, which functioned as a kind of referendum on PiS rule, President Duda won re-election by a narrow margin (51%–49%) over Warsaw Mayor Rafał Trzaskowski, the PO candidate.

The PiS electoral campaigns were marked by a strong renewal of attacks on 'gender ideology' as an assault on the traditional family and the Catholic Church which are presented by the right as fundamental attributes of Polishness. The recent presidential campaign included a dangerous escalation of rhetoric by President Duda, who characterized the promotion of LGBTQ+ equality as an 'ideology worse than communism'. This went beyond rhetoric, and included campaign promises specified in a 'Family Charter' that pledges to prevent gay marriage or adoption of children by gay couples, and a prohibition on teaching about LGBTQ+ issues in school. This builds on a grassroots movement that has declared a number of localities in Poland gay-free zones (covering over 30 per cent of the country's territory), and escalating anti-gay violence, such that met the first equality march in the city of Bialystok in July 2019.

The success of these illiberal populists has further highlighted the potential importance of the contentious participation of the masses in politics. Both FiDeSz and PiS, as noted previously, built up civil society organizations as part of their strategy for vying for power, and this has been an important part of their electoral success by cementing strong ties with local activist communities while they were out of power. But beyond that, both parties have weakened the mechanisms of horizontal accountability built into democratic systems, by undermining judicial independence and regulatory watchdogs, and turning large parts of public mass media into propaganda outlets for the ruling party. Thus the only force defending any notion of democratic accountability has been contentious protests organized by civil society.

The scope of resistance has been more extensive in Poland. Because of their constitutional mandate, the Hungarian authorities have been able to throw up more legal roadblocks to civil society organizations and funding, as well as protest.[34] Still major protests have continued into the present and in the last few years demonstrations were organized to resist the decertification of Central European University from 2017 to 2019, the introduction of a draconian overtime law in 2019, against a major increase in taxes on the internet in 2014 and the assertion of political control over the Hungarian Academy of Sciences in 2019.[35]

In Poland, the resistance has been more intense. The Committee for Defense of Democracy (Komitet Obrony Demokracji) was organized in 2015 and has been very active in protesting the attempts of the regime to undermine rule of law and the independence of the judiciary. Its first large demonstration on 12 December 2015 brought 50,000 people onto the streets of Warsaw, and in smaller numbers in other large Polish cities.[36]

Polish women's and feminist movements have also been quite active in protesting attempts to further narrow their reproductive rights. Notable in this regard were the Black Protests (Czarny Protest) which ran from 2016 to 2018. These were organized initially in the big cities by the 'Together' Party (partia Razem) and a range of civil society actors. The most notable of these protests was 'Black Monday' (3 October 2016) organized by the All-Poland Women's Strike (Ogólnopolski Strajk Kobiet [OSK]) in opposition to legislation that would have led to a total ban on abortion, including in cases of incest, rape and when the life of the mother was threatened. Between 100,000 and 200,000 people participated, including at least 50,000 women dressed in black in 150 separate localities in Poland and in major international centres. The legislation was subsequently withdrawn by PiS.[37]

Conclusion

On balance, mass mobilization and the contention of ruling authority should be empowering and should enhance democracy. Recent studies on the impact of an engaged civil society conducted under the auspices of the Varieties of Democracy project supports such a contention.[38] And, indeed, the symbolic depiction of the events of 1989–91 in Central and Eastern Europe as the falling of a row of dominoes provoked by the popular mobilization of the people against long-standing unjust and illegitimate authority is a powerful trope. And it is undeniable that the end of communism began in Poland because it was the home of an unprecedented social movement that was able to claim the loyalty of 10 million people out of a population of just over 30 million. Poland and Hungary were the first movers in the collapse of the Soviet Bloc because of the mobilization and organizational capacities of the assertive civil societies and the vibrant alternative public spheres they created in the end phase of communism. The experience of these events was integrated into the contentious repertoires of the Color Revolutions of the 1990s as well.[39]

This seemed like an obvious pattern for success, and for many years both Poland and Hungary were seen as the poster children for liberal democracy, until they weren't. In understanding this reversal of fortune, there is a cautionary tale with regard to popular mobilization. Faced with the dual crisis of European liberalism posed by the great recession and the influx of refugees, both polities contained opportunistic political forces prepared to use the crisis to subvert democracy to extend their grip on power. In both cases, the reactionary political space was an effective frame and the forces that occupied it had developed popular mobilization capacities that helped them to exacerbate the crisis and to take power electorally. Having attained that, they have used the state to advance their illiberal agendas. The Hungarians have gone much further than the Poles, and it is important to note that Polish mobilization against PiS has been stronger in the early phases of its rule. This reminds us that popular mobilization can also function as a kind of firewall against democratic backsliding. Ultimately, popular mobilization has no intrinsic democratic value independent of the motivation of those mobilizing.

One last point that is worth mentioning is that the political science literature on democratic transition reviewed at the onset of this contribution saw the effect of mode as a kind of structural condition that strongly affected the prospects for democracy. This account also sensitizes us to the importance of the ideational component of politics. The authoritarian populists who currently rule in both Poland and Hungary, as a critical step on their path to power, worked to reinterpret the meaning of critical events of 1989. They undermined their valuation as democratic breakthroughs and replaced them with a narrative of the people betrayed, which they in turn used in their own narratives to justify their rule on a more authoritarian basis when conditions enabled their return to power.

Notes

1 Thomas Carothers, 'The End of the Transition Paradigm', *Journal of Democracy* 13, no. 1 (2002): 5–21.

2 Samuel P. Huntington, *The Third Wave* (Norman: University of Oklahoma Press, 1991).

3 Guillermo O'Donnell and Philippe C. Schmitter, 'Tentative Conclusions about Uncertain Democracies', in Guillermo O'Donnell et al. (eds), *Transitions from Authoritarian Rule* (Baltimore: The Johns Hopkins University Press, 1986), 1–72; and Adam Przeworski, *Democracy and the Market* (Cambridge: Cambridge University Press, 1991).

4 Gerardo L. Munck and Carol Skalnik Leff, 'Modes of Transition and Democratization: South America and Eastern Europe in Comparative Perspective', *Comparative Politics* 29, no. 3 (1997): 343.

5 Terry Lynn Karl, 'Dilemmas of Democratization in Latin America', *Comparative Politics* 23, no. 1 (1990): 9.

6 Munck and Leff, 'Dilemmas of Democratization', 344.

7 Munck and Leff, 'Dilemmas of Democratization', 349–50.

8 Munck and Leff, 'Dilemmas of Democratization', 352–3.

9 Munck and Leff, 'Dilemmas of Democratization', 345.

10 Michael Burton, Richard Gunther and John Higley, 'Introduction: Elite Transformations and Democratic Regimes', in John Higley and Richard Gunther (eds), *Elites and Democratic Consolidation in Latin America and Southern Europe* (Cambridge: Cambridge University Press, 1992), 1–37.

11 Gretchen Casper and Michelle M. Taylor, *Negotiating Democracy, Transitions from Authoritarian Rule* (Pittsburgh: Pittsburgh University Press, 1996), 164–6.

12 Stephan Haggard and Robert Kaufman, *Dictators and Democrats: Elites, Masses, and Regime Change* (Princeton: Princeton University Press, 2016).

13 Robert Fishman, 'How Civil Society Matters in Democratization: Setting the Boundaries of Post-Transition Political Inclusion', *Comparative Politics* 49, no. 3 (2017): 391–409.

14 Dawn Brancati, *Democracy Protests: Origins, Features and Significance* (New York: Cambridge University Press, 2016).

15 Donatella Della Porta, *Mobilizing for Democracy* (Oxford: Oxford University Press, 2014) and Michael Bernhard, 'The Moore Thesis: What's Left after 1989?' *Democratization* 23, no. 1 (2016): 118–40.

16 James Mahoney, 'Path Dependence in Historical Sociology, *Theory and Society* 29, no. 4 (2000): 507–48, and Giovanni Capoccia and R. Daniel Kelemen, 'The Study of Critical Junctures: Theory, Narrative, and Counterfactuals in Historical Institutionalism', *World Politics* 59, no. 3 (2007): 341–69.

17 Anna Grzymala-Busse, *Redeeming the Communist Past: The Regeneration of Communist Successor Parties* (Cambridge: Cambridge University Press, 2002).

18 Grzegorz Ekiert and Jan Kubik, 'Contentious Politics in New Democracies: Hungary, the former East Germany, Poland and Slovakia', *World Politics* 50, no. 4 (1998): 547–81.

19 Jan Kubik and Michael Bernhard, 'A Theory of the Politics of Memory', in Michael Bernhard and Jan Kubik (eds), *Twenty Years After Communism, The Politics of Memory and Commemoration* (New York: Oxford University Press, 2014), 15.

20 This is congruent with the definition of populism as 'a thin-centered ideology that considers society to be ultimately separated into two homogenous and antagonistic groups, "the pure people" versus "the corrupt elite," and which argues that politics should be an expression of the . . . general will . . . of the people'. Cas Mudde, 'The Populist Zeitgeist', *Government and Opposition* 39, no. 4 (2004): 542–63.

21 Michael Bernhard and Jan Kubik, 'Roundtable Discord: The Contested Legacy of 1989 in Poland', in Michael Bernhard and Jan Kubik (eds), *Twenty Years After Communism, The Politics of Memory and Commemoration* (New York: Oxford University Press, 2014), 60–85.

22 R. Daniel Kelemen, 'Europe's Other Democratic Deficit: National Authoritarianism in Europe's Democratic Union', *Government and Opposition* 52, no. 2 (2017): 211–38.

23 Béla Greskovits and Jason Wittenberg, 'Civil Society and Democratic Consolidation in Hungary in the 1990s and 2000s' (Unpublished Manuscript, 27 February 2016); Bela Greskovits, 'Rebuilding the Hungarian Right through Conquering Civil Society: The Civic Circles Movement', *East European Politics* 36, no. 2 (2020): 247–66; Csepeli György et al., 'Vizsgálati jelentés a 2006.

szeptember–októberi fővárosi demonstrációkkal, utcai rendzavarásokkal és rendfenntartó intézkedésekkel kapcsolatos eseményekről' [Investigative report on the events of September–October 2006 in capital city demonstrations, street disturbances and policing], Budapest, 2 February 2007, http://www.gonczolbizottsag.gov.hu/jelentes/gonczolbizottsag_jelentes.pdf (4 June 2019); Anna Seleny, 'Revolutionary Road: 1956 and the Fracturing of Hungarian Historical Memory', in Michael Bernhard and Jan Kubik (eds), *Twenty Years After Communism, The Politics of Memory and Commemoration* (New York: Oxford University Press, 2014), 48; and Karl Benziger, *Imre Nagy, Martyr of the Nation: Contested History, Legitimacy and Popular Legitimacy, and Popular Memory in Hungary* (Lanham: Lexington Books, 2008), 62–3.

24 Seleny, 'Revolutionary Road', 50–2, 55–6.

25 Miklós Bánkuti, Gábor Halmai and Kim Lane Scheppele, 'Hungary's Illiberal Turn: Disabling the Constitution', *Journal of Democracy* 23, no. 3 (2012): 138–46.

26 'Full text of Viktor Orbán's speech at Băile Tuşnad (Tusnádfürdő) of 26 July 2014', Budapest Beacon, 29 July 2014, trans. Czaba Toth, https://budapestbeacon.com/full-text-of-viktor-orbans-speech-at-baile-tusnad-tusnadfurdo-of-26-july-2014/.

27 Kristóf Szombati, 'Why Hungarian Voters Are Turning away from Fidesz and towards Jobbik?' *Heinrich Böll Stiftung*, 2 June 2015, https://www.boell.de/en/2015/06/02/why-hungarian-voters-are-turning-away-fidesz-and-towards-jobbik.

28 Joanna Fomina and Jacek Kucharczyk, 'Populism and Protest in Europe', *Journal of Democracy* 27, no. 4 (2016): 66.

29 Bernhard and Kubik, 'Roundtable Discord', 65–7, 71–5.

30 'Prime Minister Ewa Kopacz: I won't let the Europe's Migration Crisis Affect Poles' Life', 14 September 2009, https://www.premier.gov.pl/en/news/news/prime-minister-ewa-kopacz-i-wont-let-the-europes-migration-crisis-affect-poles-life.html.

31 Agnieszka Graff and Elżbieta Korolczuk, '"Worse than Communism and Nazism Put Together": War on Gender in Poland', in Roman Kuhar and David Paternotte (eds), *Anti-gender Campaigns in Europe: Mobilizing against Equality* (New York: Rowman and Littlefield 2017), 175–94.

32 Yasuko Shibata, *Discrimination for the Sake of the Nation, The Discourse of the League of Polish Families against 'Others', 2001-2007* (Frankfurt-Am-Main: PL Academic Research, 2013); Marcin Ślarzyński, 'Rola klubów *Gazety Polskiej* w sukcesie politycznym Prawa i Sprawiedliwości w 2015 roku. Aktorzy lokalni czy actor ogólnokrajowej sfery publicznej III RP?' *Przegląd Socijogiczny* 67, no. 2 (2018): 139–58; and Daniel Płatek and Piotr Płucienniczak, 'Civil Society and Extreme-Right Collective Action in Poland 1990–2013', *Revue d'études comparatives Est-Ouest*, no. 47 (2016): 117–46.

33 Kerstin Jacobsson and Elżbieta Korolczuk, 'Preface', in Kerstin Jacobsson and Elżbieta Korolczuk (eds), *Civil Society Revisited, Lessons from Poland* (New York: Berghahn Books, 2017), vii–ix.

34 Balázs Majtényi, Ákos Kopper and Pál Susánszky, 'Constitutional Othering, Ambiguity and Subjective Risks of Mobilization in Hungary: Examples from the Migration Crisis', *Democratization* 26, no. 2 (2019): 173–89.

35 Zoltan Enyedi, 'Democratic Backsliding and Academic Freedom in Hungary', *Perspectives on Politics* 16, no. 4 (2018): 1067–74; Krizstina Than and Marton Dunai, 'Hungary's Orban puts Internet Tax on Hold after Huge Protests', *Reuters*, 1 November 2014, https://www.reuters.com/article/us-hungary-internet-tax/hungarys-orban-puts-internet-tax-on-hold-after-huge-protests-idUSKBN0IK0MM20141101; Marc Santora and Benjamin Novak, 'Protesting "Slave Law," Thousands Take to Streets in Hungary', *The New York Times*, 5 January 2019, https://www.nytimes.com/2019/01/05/world/europe/hungary-protests-slave-law.html; and Marton Dunai, 'Hungarians Protest over Government Overhaul of Academic Bodies', *Reuters*, 2 June 2019, https://www.reuters.com/article/us-hungary-scientists-protests/hungarians-protest-over-government-overhaul-of-academic-bodies-idUSKCN1T30KE.

36 Ireneusz Paweł Karolewski, 'Protest and Participation in Post-transformation Poland: The Case of the Committee for the Defense of Democracy (KOD)', *Communist and Post-Communist Studies* 49, no. 3 (2016): 255–67.

37 Elżbieta Korolczuk, 'Explaining Mass Protests against the Abortion Ban in Poland: The Power of Connective Action', Zoon *Politikon* 7 (2016): 91–113, and Bogumila Hall, 'Gendering Resistance to Right-Wing Populism: Black Protest and a New Wave of Feminist Activism in Poland?' *American Behavioral Scientist* 63, no. 10 (September 2019): 1497–515.

38 Michael Bernhard et al., 'Parties, Civil Society, and the Deterrence of Democratic Defection', *Studies in Comparative International Development* 55, no. 1 (2020): 1–21.

39 Valerie Bunce and Sharon Wolchik, *Defeating Authoritarian Leaders in Postcommunist Countries* (New York: Cambridge University Press, 2011).

References

Bánkuti, Miklós, Gábor Halmai and Kim Lane Scheppele. 'Hungary's Illiberal Turn: Disabling the Constitution'. *Journal of Democracy* 23, no. 3 (2012): 138–46.

Benziger, Karl. *Imre Nagy, Martyr of the Nation: Contested History, Legitimacy and Popular Legitimacy, and Popular Memory in Hungary*. Lanham: Lexington Books, 2008.

Bernhard, Michael. 'The Moore Thesis: What's Left after 1989?' *Democratization* 23, no. 1 (2016): 118–40.

Bernhard, Michael and Jan Kubik. 'Roundtable Discord: The Contested Legacy of 1989 in Poland'. In Michael Bernhard and Jan Kubik (eds), *Twenty Years After Communism, The Politics of Memory and Commemoration*. New York: Oxford University Press, 2014.

Bernhard, Michael, Allen Hicken, Christopher Reenock and Staffan I. Lindberg. 'Parties, Civil Society, and the Deterrence of Democratic Defection'. *Studies in Comparative International Development* 55, no. 1 (2020): 1–26.

Brancati, Dawn. *Democracy Protests: Origins, Features and Significance*. New York: Cambridge University Press, 2016.

Bunce, Valerie and Sharon Wolchik. *Defeating Authoritarian Leaders in Postcommunist Countries*. New York: Cambridge University Press, 2011.

Burton, Michael, Richard Gunther and John Higley. 'Introduction: Elite Transformations and Democratic Regimes'. In John Higley and Richard Gunther (eds), *Elites and Democratic Consolidation in Latin America and Southern Europe*, 1–37. Cambridge: Cambridge University Press, 1992.
Capoccia, Giovanni and R. Daniel Kelemen. 'The Study of Critical Junctures: Theory, Narrative, and Counterfactuals in Historical Institutionalism'. *World Politics* 59, no. 3 (2007): 341–69.
Carothers, Thomas. 'The End of the Transition Paradigm'. *Journal of Democracy* 13, no. 1 (2002): 5–21.
Casper, Gretchen and Michelle M. Taylor. *Negotiating Democracy, Transitions from Authoritarian Rule*. Pittsburgh: Pittsburgh University Press, 1996.
Ekiert, Grzegorz and Jan Kubik. 'Contentious Politics in New Democracies: Hungary, the former East Germany, Poland and Slovakia'. *World Politics* 50, no. 4 (1998): 547–81.
Enyedi, Zoltan. 'Democratic Backsliding and Academic Freedom in Hungary'. *Perspectives on Politics* 16, no. 4 (2018): 1067–74.
Fishman, Robert. 'How Civil Society Matters in Democratization: Setting the Boundaries of Post-Transition Political Inclusion'. *Comparative Politics* 49, no. 3 (2017): 391–409.
Fomina, Joanna and Jacek Kucharczyk. 'Populism and Protest in Europe'. *Journal of Democracy* 27, no. 4 (2016).
Graff, Agnieszka and Elżbieta Korolczuk. '"Worse than Communism and Nazism Put Together": War on Gender in Poland'. In Roman Kuhar and David Paternotte (eds), *Anti-gender Campaigns in Europe: Mobilizing against Equality*, 175–94. New York: Rowman and Littlefield, 2017.
Greskovits, Béla. 'Rebuilding the Hungarian Right through Conquering Civil Society: The Civic Circles Movement'. *East European Politics* 36, no. 2 (2020): 247–66.
Greskovits, Béla and Jason Wittenberg. 'Civil Society and Democratic Consolidation in Hungary in the 1990s and 2000s' (Unpublished Manuscript, 27 February 2016).
Grzymala-Busse, Anna. *Redeeming the Communist Past: The Regeneration of Communist Successor Parties*. Cambridge: Cambridge University Press, 2002.
Haggard, Stephan and Robert Kaufman. *Dictators and Democrats: Elites, Masses, and Regime Change*. Princeton: Princeton University Press, 2016.
Hall, Bogumila. 'Gendering Resistance to Right-Wing Populism: Black Protest and a New Wave of Feminist Activism in Poland?' *American Behavioral Scientist* 63, no. 10 (September 2019): 1497–515.
Huntington, Samuel P. *The Third Wave*. Norman: University of Oklahoma Press, 1991.
Jacobsson, Kerstin and Elżbieta Korolczuk. 'Preface'. In Kerstin Jacobsson and Elżbieta Korolczuk (eds), *Civil Society Revisited, Lessons from Poland*. New York: Berghahn Books, 2017.
Karl, Terry Lynn. 'Dilemmas of Democratization in Latin America'. *Comparative Politics* 23, no. 1 (1990): i–v.
Karolewski, Ireneusz Paweł. 'Protest and Participation in Post-transformation Poland: The Case of the Committee for the Defense of Democracy (KOD)'. *Communist and Post-Communist Studies* 49, no. 3 (2016): 1–21.

Kelemen, R. Daniel. 'Europe's Other Democratic Deficit: National Authoritarianism in Europe's Democratic Union'. *Government and Opposition* 52, no. 2 (2017): 211–38.

Korolczuk, Elżbieta. 'Explaining Mass Protests against the Abortion Ban in Poland: the Power of Connective Action'. *Zoon Politikon* 7 (2016): 91–113.

Kubik, Jan and Michael Bernhard. 'A Theory of the Politics of Memory'. In Michael Bernhard and Jan Kubik (eds), *Twenty Years After Communism, The Politics of Memory and Commemoration*. New York: Oxford University Press, 2014.

Mahoney, James. 'Path Dependence in Historical Sociology'. *Theory and Society* 29, no. 4 (2000): 507–48.

Majtényi, Balázs, Ákos Kopper and Pál Susánszky. 'Constitutional Othering, Ambiguity and Subjective Risks of Mobilization in Hungary: Examples from the Migration Crisis'. *Democratization* 26, no. 2 (2019): 173–89.

Mudde, Cas. 'The Populist Zeitgeist'. *Government and Opposition* 39, no. 4 (2004): 541–63.

Munck, Gerardo L. and Carol Skalnik Leff. 'Modes of Transition and Democratization: South America and Eastern Europe in Comparative Perspective'. *Comparative Politics* 29, no. 3 (1997): 343–62.

O'Donnell, Guillermo and Philippe C. Schmitter. 'Tentative Conclusions about Uncertain Democracies'. In Guillermo O'Donnell et al. (eds), *Transitions from Authoritarian Rule*, 1–72. Baltimore: The Johns Hopkins University Press, 1986.

Płatek, Daniel and Piotr Płucienniczak. 'Civil Society and Extreme-Right Collective Action in Poland 1990–2013'. *Revue d'études comparatives Est-Ouest*, no. 47 (2016): 117–46.

Porta, Donatella Della. *Mobilizing for Democracy*. Oxford: Oxford University Press, 2014.

Przeworski, Adam. *Democracy and the Market*. Cambridge: Cambridge University Press, 1991.

Shibata, Yasuko. *Discrimination for the Sake of the Nation, The Discourse of the League of Polish Families against 'Others', 2001–2007*. Frankfurt-Am-Main: PL Academic Research, 2013.

Ślarzyński, Marcin. 'Rola klubów *Gazety Polskiej* w sukcesie politycznym Prawa i Sprawiedliwości w 2015 roku. Aktorzy lokalni czy actor ogólnokrajowej sfery publicznej III RP?' *Przegląd Socijogiczny* 67, no. 2 (2018): 139–58.

Szombati, Kristóf. 'Why Hungarian Voters Are Turning away from Fidesz and towards Jobbik?' 2 June 2015. https://www.boell.de/en/2015/06/02/why-hungarian-voters-are-turning-away-fidesz-and-towards-jobbik (accessed 1 June 2019).

10

Protesting democracy in Africa

Popular movements and political transformation

Zachariah Mampilly

In December 2018, two of Africa's largest countries, the Democratic Republic of Congo and Sudan, faced concurrent political crises. In Congo, misruled by the Kabila family since 1996, President Joseph Kabila allowed national elections to take place after years of delay. In Sudan, under the reign of the despotic Omar al-Bashir since 1989, a popular movement broke out across the country. Juxtaposed against each other, the countries represent two possible trajectories for popular politics in the contemporary moment.

In Congo, opposition parties and other civil society actors, including several new youth-led popular movements, patiently played along with the electoral process even as Kabila excluded key opposition figures. Shortly after the election was held and despite the widespread exclusion of millions of voters, the Catholic Church, which had deployed 40,000 election observers around the country, leaked that the outcome was an overwhelming victory for the opposition candidate Martin Fayulu. Kabila, whose favoured candidate mustered only about a fifth of the vote, surprised everyone when he announced that a third candidate, Felix Tshisekedi, had won the election. The Constitutional Court soon confirmed Tshisekedi's victory and the international community quickly acquiesced after initially expressing concern. Shocked and dismayed, voters across the country were left with little recourse despite Fayulu's exhortation to engage in peaceful resistance to the blatant theft.

Meanwhile, in Sudan, protesters took to the streets following an increase in bread prices. Beginning in the once-industrial town of Atbara, the protests quickly spread to other small towns before eventually arriving in Khartoum, the capital. In 2015, Bashir had been re-elected by an overwhelming 94 per cent of the vote, an outcome that the African Union Election Observation Mission quickly confirmed reflected 'the expression of the will of the voters of Sudan'.[1] Yet, just three years later, ordinary Sudanese demonstrated their disgust by risking their lives to call for the overthrow of the regime through non-electoral means. Six months on, protesters remain in the street despite a brutal military crackdown and the forced removal of Bashir. While a final resolution remains far from clear, by refusing the leave the streets, the movement has succeeded where its Congolese counterparts could not, forcing the regime to resort to violence and make concessions that actually threaten its hold on power.

How do we interpret these two events? Does Congo represent democratic progress for the first peaceful transition of power despite the rigged election? Is Sudan a case of democratic backsliding considering the inability of both sides to agree on an electoral timeline?

Globally, scholars and policymakers have rued the 'democratic backtracking' they perceive as unfolding as right-wing populists chip away at the rule of law from the United States to India, and from Brazil to Turkey. Freedom House, which provides an influential measure of global democracy, titled its 2019 report 'Democracy in Retreat', for example. Africa has not been immune to such analyses. *Foreign Affairs*, a leading US-based journal, captured this tendency recently in an essay entitled 'The Retreat of African Democracy', by Nic Cheeseman and Jeffrey Smith.

But is Africa actually experiencing a decline in democracy? And how would we know if it was? In this chapter, I argue that rather than a devolution of democracy, many African countries are actually experiencing a democratic deepening as popular movements supplant political parties as the primary outlet for oppositional energies. In this reading, the audacious and undeniable theft of formal democratic elections does not suggest a decrease in African democracy itself. Rather, it is better understood as the inevitable by-product of the narrow form of electoral competition bequeathed upon African countries by often well-meaning international actors after the last major convulsion of popular energies. Bereft of any substantive engagements with the popular will, electoral democracy has revealed itself as little more than a means through which entrenched political and economic elites rig the system in their favour while garnering support for their actions from a disinterested and disengaged liberal world order.

Yet, while elections are often stolen or manipulated either openly or through other means, popular movements are surging, even in some of Africa's most autocratic environments. To accept that democracy in Africa is in retreat, we have to believe that people participating in popular movements at a higher rate than they have since at least the 1990s are insignificant for

Africa's overall democratic trajectory.[2] This is hard to square if we accept that protest should be understood as an expression of two of the most fundamental democratic rights – a right to free speech and the right of free association – alongside voting which is the only metric generally considered sacrosanct by the international community.

By 'protesting democracy', what I mean to highlight is the way in which electoral politics is no longer the route to political change in the African context. Incumbents have become too adept at manipulating electoral outcomes and so there is little popular faith in elections as the endpoint of political competition. Yet elections remain important, less for the predetermined outcome at the ballot box, but more because they provide opportunities for other forms of political mobilization, especially popular protest. By this standard, rather than a democratic retreat, Africans are rejecting the electoral mode of democracy imposed by outsiders in favour of a democracy of the street, one that has the potential to more accurately reflect the democratic orientation of most people on the continent who remain overwhelmingly in support of government for, by and of the people.

Third termism as a manufactured crisis

That Africa is facing a crisis of democracy makes sense only if you accept the narrative that holding elections, no matter how flawed, is the key indicator of democratization. 'Third Termism' refers to the tendency that international observers decry as being evidence of this crisis, as long-standing incumbents seek to subvert constitutions to extend their time in office. Yet this focus on undemocratic third terms is warranted only if you assume that the first and second terms were legitimate in the first place.

For example in Uganda, Yoweri Museveni was first elected to the presidency in 1996, ten years after first coming to power. In 2005, facing a constitutional limit of two terms, he easily had the restriction removed winning his third term in 2006. He was elected to his fifth term in 2016. In Rwanda, Paul Kagame first held an election in 2003, nine years after coming to power. He won with 95 per cent of the vote. In the 2010 election, his share of votes dipped slightly to 93 per cent, before rebounding to a triumphant 99 per cent in the 2017 election. To overcome the two-term limit, Parliament passed a special bill which then went to a popular referendum during which 98 per cent of voters supposedly decided to lift the limit, but only as an exception for Kagame, who was also given the option of running for two additional five-year terms.

Even in countries that do better on global indicators of democracy, ruling parties are rarely threatened. In South Africa and Tanzania, analysts have taken to critiquing the decline of democracy under Jacob Zuma and John Magufuli, respectfully. But in the post-colonial histories of both countries, the candidates were put forth by parties, the African National Congress and the Chama Cha Mapinduzi, that have never ceded power to opposition parties.

To appreciate how elections in Africa became so divorced from the democratic will, it is necessary to look back at the last major convulsions that shook the continent during the tail end of the Cold War. In 1985, a series of popular protests broke out in Sudan and quickly spread across much of the continent. Between the mid-1980s and the early 1990s, mass protests took hold in numerous African countries, with fourteen affected in 1990 alone. These protests, a response to brutal austerity measures imposed upon African states by the World Bank and the International Monetary Fund, led to a flowering of elections across the continent (Bratton and Van de Walle). With only three countries holding competitive elections prior to the protests, by the mid-1990s more than a third of African countries could claim to be at least partially free by the standards of Freedom House and other Western agencies that measure democracy globally, with numerous more holding elections.

But how did the protesters demands for revolutionary transformation get translated into a narrow call for elections? Opposition parties, often founded and controlled by former members of the ruling elite, successfully corralled popular energies into a narrow demand for electoral competition, from which they stood to gain the most. Across Africa, participants in the second protest wave (following the first wave of the 1940s–60s which led to independence) found their legitimate demands for reform replaced with empty talk of multipartyism. As Thandika Mkandawire wrote at the time, for too many African states, the democratic reforms of the early 1990s amounted to little more than 'choiceless democracies', assuaging the energies of protesters but denying them what they truly sought: political and economic transformation.

The issue is not simply that elections are often meaningless. It is that even where elections lead to a change in the ruling party, it rarely amounts to a substantive transformation of political and economic conditions. The neoliberal turn that accompanied Africa's ostensible democratic wave rendered opposition parties merely symbolic artefacts rather than genuine opponents to existing power dynamics. As numerous opposition parties entered the African political space, they were quickly transformed into vehicles of existing political elites who called for elections even as they embraced the prevailing economic consensus centring on austerity, privatization and liberalization. Even the vaunted African National Congress in South Africa, still an official member of the Socialist International, could not escape these trends.

Opposition parties in the African context occasionally do present a new face at the pinnacle of political power. But nowhere in Africa do they represent a genuine challenge to the prevailing neoliberal economic consensus nor do they respect the rights of free assembly and free speech necessary for civil society to function and democracy to flourish. Considering that many of the loudest oppositional were once former card-carrying radicals, the disciplining of Africa's unruly oppositional energies in the post–Cold War era has been remarkable. Yet, this result is not surprising. Many left-leaning

African intellectuals predicted this outcome in the 1990s. Scholars like Malawi's Thandika Mkandawire, Egypt's Samir Amin and Tanzania's Issa Shivji loudly critiqued the neoliberal consensus shared by Africa's ruling and oppositional parties, even as they found themselves increasingly marginalized within their countries' new, ostensibly democratic political dispensations.

Two decades later, African countries rank among the most unequal in the world. This holds true whether we look at income, consumption or wealth. For example, seven of the ten countries with the highest Gini coefficients in the world (the standard measure of income inequality) are African Union members. This includes both middle-income countries like Botswana and South Africa and some of the poorest countries in the world such as Sierra Leone and the Central African Republic.

In short, the Western-backed liberal order that solidified in the aftermath of the Cold War entrenched the equation of democracy with the holding of semi-regular elections. But elections are not democracy. Democracy is a process, not an event. Central to its consolidation are respect for two basic principles that define the relationship between a government and society: the right to free assembly and the right to free speech. These are the basic needs for any popular movement to function and any government that holds elections while restricting protest should not be treated as democratic. Yet while the international community celebrated Africa's democratic turn in the 1990s and now rues its democratic backsliding, at no point have popular movements been treated as elemental indicators of democracy, neither by African governments nor by the so-called advocates for global democracy abroad.

Measuring and promoting democracy in Africa: The role of the international community

A large part of this tendency to omit protest as an elementary component of democratization has to do with what constitutes democracy and who gets to makes that distinction. Freedom House, a non-profit organization funded overwhelmingly by the US government, has been at the forefront of measuring democracy globally. Yet its measures, supposedly derived from the Universal Declaration of Human Rights and hence beyond political partisanship, instead reflect the values and interests of Western states. As Diego Giannone notes, Freedom House 'developed to respond to political ideological motives, in line with the rise, over the 1970s, of a new hegemonic paradigm, neoliberalism, developed in leading Western countries and aimed at strengthening their power in international relations'.[3]

Its 2019 report, for example, suggests that we are in the thirteenth year of consecutive years of global democratic decline. Its method is to assign every country in the world 'between 0 and 4 points on a series of 25 indicators, for an aggregate score of up to 100'. Based on its score, each country is then assigned the designation of 'free', 'partially free' or 'not free'. Aggregated, they tell the story of world increasingly shifting from democracy to more authoritarian forms of rule. But dig a little deeper and it is not clear what this seemingly rigorous methodology actually has to do with the relatively abstract concept of democracy. Indeed, like most such measures, Freedom House emphasizes electoral competition over other indicators of democratization, directly at the expense of popular movements.

For example, of the 100 available points, fully 28 are awarded based on various electoral dimensions such as the nature of the electoral process and the space for opposition parties. Freedom of expression, which is combined with the freedom of religion, is given just 16 points. Associational rights, which include the right to protest, are included alongside the right to form non-governmental organizations (NGOs) and unions and assigned only 12 points.[4] None of the measures are designed to capture the frequency or scale of popular protests themselves, which, according to numerous sources, have been increasing globally as well as in Africa.[5]

Beyond the numerical values assigned to each, Giannone, like many others, points out that such measures favour formal over substantive rights and state-centric over society-centric understandings of democracy. For example, while in early iterations, Freedom House asked, 'Do the people organize freely in different political parties . . .', in 2002, the language was changed to, 'Do the people *have the right to* organize freely in different political parties . . .' While seemingly a minor addition, the shift in language changes the emphasis away from whether people are actually able to organize freely to whether they have the formal right to do so (whether or not they are actually able to enjoy it).

More problematically, earlier versions asked directly about a right to free association asking simply: 'Is there freedom of assembly and demonstration?' In 2002, this was changed to: 'Is there freedom of assembly, demonstration, *and open public discussion*?' Relatedly, the question on free speech was amended from 'Is there open *public discussion* and free private discussion?' in earlier versions to 'Is there open and free private discussion?' In both instances, straightforward questions designed to capture the degree to which people are able to protest were amended to include other activities that are only tangentially related.

Despite its limitations, Freedom House's measures are widely used as the basis for academic studies of democratization. 'Democratic consolidation', through which developing countries are assessed by the degree to which they resemble idealized Western democracies, became a buzzword in the Western academy and policy circles shortly after the fall of the Soviet Union. As Steven Friedman notes, this approach 'created the democracy scoring index which gave scientific credibility to the consolidation approach by ranking democracies and then assigning them a numerical score or a ranking in an index'.[6] This vast literature rarely takes a critical look at the assumptions undergirding these measures.

While popular movements do not earn their due respect in leading indicators or academic studies of democracy, they are at least granted a degree of recognition. In contrast, policymakers rarely, if ever, champion popular movements beyond innocuous statements of support, preferring instead to reinforce the status quo. Activists from Congo's Lucha movement were repeatedly told to avoid protesting ahead of the 2018 elections by Western diplomats. Their concern, it was claimed, was that protesters would only trigger violence from the regime and could have the effect of delaying the election, already two years late, even further. This antipathy towards popular movements was reflected in the official US government response to Kabila's blatant electoral theft. Despite initially promising that the 'the U.S. Government will hold accountable those who . . . impede the democratic process',[7] two weeks later, the State Department changed its tune congratulating 'President Joseph Kabila's commitment to becoming the first President in DRC history to cede power peacefully through an electoral process'.[8]

The role of popular movements in deepening democracy

But there is hope. The ongoing third wave of African protest began in the mid-2000s in Ethiopia and has included large popular protests in every region of Africa. Since 2005, there have been protests in over forty African countries, including the so-called Arab Spring. Often triggered by electoral or economic crises, many of these movements have quickly evolved into broader critiques of the broader political and economic system. While some, such as those in Senegal, Burkina Faso, Tunisia and more recently Algeria and Sudan, have achieved considerable success, others have been crushed violently by African governments. Yet new popular movements keep emerging, often in response to economic or electoral crises.

In fact, it is only when elections are accompanied by large-scale street protests do they seem to lead to meaningful change. Y'en a Marre in Senegal, a popular movement started by musicians and journalists, successfully prevented former president Abdoulaye Wade from running for an illegal third term in 2012. In Burkina Faso, protesters drove out the long-running dictator, Blaise Compaoré, after twenty-seven years in power, in 2014 (including four electoral victories). In Ethiopia, recurring popular protests helped lead to the ascension of the new Prime Minister who has already begun to open the political landscape after years of repression, despite the lack of a national election. Most recently, in Algeria the announcement that the president would run for an unprecedented fifth term led to the protests that ultimately led to his downfall. The list goes on.

This begs the question, is it the holding of elections – even when those elections are widely acknowledged as manipulated by elites rather than representing the popular will – that should be the favoured measure of democracy? Or should the presence of broad-based popular movements demanding political change whether through the ballot box or the downfall of the regime altogether be understood as the better indicator of the health of democracy?

There are several reasons why popular movements provide a stronger measure of democracy than elections. Democracy is concerned with extending opportunities for political participation to the citizenry, but elections are often shaped as much by who they exclude. Most directly, governments may exclude vast portions of eligible voters from casting their ballots through deception or outright theft, as was the case in the recent Congolese elections. Even in so-called consolidated democracies, political parties often fight to deny the franchise to the public. In the United States, struggles over the voting rights of non-property holders, women or African Americans historically find resonance in efforts to reinstate the franchise for formerly incarcerated people today. The attack on the Voting Rights Act shows that the extension of the franchise does not always progress in a unilinear fashion. Beyond explicit attempts to curtail the number of people eligible to vote, political elites frequently work to limit the number of voters by imposing harsh standards on what constitutes a vote, how much time people are given to cast their vote or spreading misinformation on basic voting procedures and rights.

In contrast, protests are relatively open and non-exclusionary spaces in which anyone able and willing to participate are welcome. This extends to those who are not given the franchise, such as undocumented migrants or youth who form an integral part of a political community but are rarely afforded the right to cast a vote. Certainly, the risk to protesters may dissuade certain populations, such as women, the disabled or other visible minorities, from joining the crowds. Yet, the relative safety of a protest itself is an indicator of the degree to which governments support the right to free assembly or not (by providing protesters protection rather than viewing them as a threat).

Popular movements are also a more organic expression of public sentiments than political parties. Political parties, especially in two-party systems, rarely capture the range of public opinion. Instead, ordinary citizens often view both ruling and opposition parties as two faces of the same beast, one that represents a relatively limited range of acceptable public opinion. As discussed earlier, many of Africa's leading opposition figures tamed their political views once co-opted by an electoral system in which once popular viewpoints were abandoned in exchange for incorporation into multiparty elections. The result is a deep distrust of political parties that frequently seek to co-opt the energies of popular movements without championing the issues that drove people to the streets in the first place.

As protests may emerge around a wide array of issues and often encompass a panoply of differing agendas, they are often derided as undisciplined or lacking the focus of the formalized platforms put forth by political parties. While this may affect the ability of popular movements to effect political change especially of the incremental sort, as discussed below, it does not negate the reality that they are understood as legitimate venues for articulating a wider array of popular opinions than the more constrained platforms offered by political parties.

Elections are also by necessity episodic affairs. Whether spaced two, four, five or seven years apart, they cannot respond to rapidly shifting political and environmental contexts. This is a fundamental feature of representative democracy, where the public is expected to live with the consequences of an election, even if an elected representative is manifestly incapable of performing his or her duties or engages in actions directly in opposition to their pre-election promises. Globally, forms of 'direct democracy', in which voters are given the capacity to participate more regularly in political and economic decision-making, are exceedingly rare and generally limited to issues of great national import. Democracy promotion efforts in Africa almost never champion direct democracy despite widespread disillusionment with the behaviour of elected representatives across the continent.

Protests, in contrast, are contingent and dynamic events, emerging whenever and wherever people seek to articulate their opinions in a public fashion. Again, critiques that this is a less efficient method for bringing political and economic change do not negate their superiority as a form of (informal) direct democracy compared to elections.

Finally, and related to the previous point, treating democracy as multiparty elections limits the scope of political possibility. Popular movements have the potential to articulate a different, more people-centric form of democracy that is more in line with the lived experiences of the marginalized.[9] Elections, in contrast, are about working within the system rather than transforming the system itself, the goal of many social movements. The state will always attempt to co-opt the powerful energies of a movement so as to deactivate its politics. Being co-opted into the state by supporting a political party or accepting appointments into state bureaucracies undermines the disruptive role that all social movements must play in order to be effective. As the Congolese philosopher Ernest Wamba-dia-Wamba, has put it, 'It is not possible to achieve a democratic state, i.e. a state that is transparent to, rather than destructive of, people's viewpoints, if people only 'think' state, internalize state and thus self-censor themselves.'

Challenges of protest democracy

While it is important to centre popular movements in our understanding of democracy and political change, it is also essential to assess the challenges they confront with a critical eye. Three in particular deserve attention: the tension between civil and political society, the difficulty of organizing in urban and rural settings simultaneously, and, finally, the temptations of armed struggle. This section discusses each and assesses them through an examination of the ongoing struggle in Sudan between the Forces for Freedom and Change and the Transitional Military Council.

Within political liberalism, civil society denotes an open and voluntary space for political action that is distinct from both the market (private sector) and the government (public sector). It is idealized as the site of autonomous, civilian-led political action that has the capacity to pressure the state to live up to its obligations while remaining free of the profit motive that defines that private sector. Yet the concept of civil society is often a poor fit to describe societies that do not meet the standards of advanced capitalist Western democracies. In response, scholars like Partha Chatterjee,[10] writing about India, and Michael Neocosmos, in South Africa, have sought to problematize the concept, especially as it relates to the actions of the poor and other marginalized populations.

For Chatterjee in particular, civil society is best understood as referring to the space of formal political action within a liberal rights-based framework generally adhered to by legally sanctioned not-for-profit NGOs. These organizations, omnipresent throughout the developing world, are most commonly treated as the African analogues of the more organic variants of civil society in the West. Chatterjee suggests that 'civil society' be limited to describing this domain, the 'actually existing arena of institutions and practices inhabited by a relatively small section of the people whose social locations can be identified with a fair degree of clarity'.[11] According to Chatterjee, civil society encompasses all members of a society who claim to be citizens with equal rights. But what of those populations, as is the case in much of the developing world, who suffer under no illusions that their claims to citizenship are politically meaningful, and who hence have little faith in rights-based forms of political action?

For Chatterjee, political society consists of those segments of the population who do not relate to the state through the rights-based approach favoured by civil society. Instead, marginalized by economic or other social locations, they must engage in varying forms of political action that do not adhere to the middle-class niceties emphasized by civil society. Political society relies on contestation and negotiation with state agencies in order to advance their political objectives, often in ways that appear unruly, devoid of clear messaging and reliant on violence or its threat to enable political transformation.

Chatterjee's insights provide a useful method for describing the fundamental divide between two forms of protest in much of Africa. The first, undertaken by actors ensconced within formally defined civil society organizations, works through existing institutions with the intention of placing pressure on the state to comply with its obligations as defined by law. Civil society protest adopts the pre-existing playbook for nonviolent action. Organized and led by civil society, non-governmental organizations and opposition parties work to pressure regimes to honour their stated commitment to democracy by facilitating multiparty elections. Even as civil society relies on the participation of ordinary people to make its demands resonant, it is political and economic elites that stand to gain the most by winning political offices through the electoral process. In this version, protest is simply one step towards securing the real objective, the holding of multiparty elections. Once safely ensconced in their new political positions, the same opposition figures rarely pay attention to the issues articulated by the broader protest movement. Instead, a return to 'normal' politics with its excuses for a lack of transformative change quickly follows.

In contrast, political society protest is an articulation of democracy from below. The key difference between political society and civil society protest is that the latter works within existing systems in order to make incremental change. It is fundamentally a top-down and reformist project, one that places great faith in existing institutions and elites to fulfil their duties, despite the sheer contempt for democratic life they regularly demonstrate. In contrast, political society, already accustomed to the hypocrisy and corruption that characterizes 'democratic' rule in much of Africa, places little faith in existing institutions or elites to take actions that would ensure the promise of democracy for all. As such, political society protest is often radical in its politics calling for the overthrow of corrupt systems rather than reform.

Yet political society protest often struggles to translate its ability to motivate large crowds of ordinary people into actual political change. Without a clear template for how to move forward following large-scale protests, political society may often appear adrift with no clear direction for a future politics that provides ordinary people a central role in a truly democratic dispensation. This lack of clarity also leaves open the door for counterrevolutionary forces to undermine social movements either through factionalization or through outright repression.

Many of these dynamics are in evidence in the two cases mentioned at the outset of this chapter: the Democratic Republic of Congo and Sudan. In Congo, social movements that drew their strength from political society despite middle-class leadership like Lucha and Filimbi played an integral role in challenging the Kabila family's grip on power. These movements attracted large numbers of young people from the urban poor and the country's peripheral towns and rural areas. Despite differences in their demands, social location and class position, these political society–led popular movements worked alongside formal civil society actors, which in DRC refers to organized political parties and the Catholic Church, to effectively pressure the regime to hold long-overdue elections. When national elections were finally held in late 2018 after two years of delay, it appeared for a brief moment that the convergence of civil and political society had successfully brought down a regime in power since 1996. Yet when the winner was announced, rather than crowning the overwhelming victor, opposition candidate Martin Fayulu, a third candidate, who received far fewer votes, was declared president. The international community quickly acquiesced to this outright theft. Having placed faith in a doomed electoral process, both civil and political society were left adrift.

About 1,500 miles away in Sudan, protesters also took to the streets. Beginning in the once-industrial town of Atbara, the protests over rising bread prices quickly spread to other small towns before eventually reaching the capital Khartoum. Importantly, and in contrast to Congo, the protest movement clearly began within political society before civil society organizations, most prominently the Sudan Professional Association, a collection of doctors, lawyers, teachers and others, joined the movement. Once again, the convergence of civil and political society proved effective. In May, after failing to crush the uprising and with support in the military waning, Bashir was forced out.

Once Bashir was gone, protesters in Sudan faced a difficult choice – support efforts by the country's sclerotic parties for a quick election overseen by the still in power military regime or continue to pressure the regime into ceding power to a civilian-led transition process. Despite entreaties by opposition-party figures and other civil society leaders, protesters, most with roots in political society, rejected what they considered a flawed approach. Instead, they maintained their encampments in Khartoum and elsewhere. In June, after almost six months of pressure on the regime, the counterrevolutionary forces struck, slaughtering over 100 protesters and breaking up the camps. Despite the brutality, protesters have not given up and negotiations continue. The unwillingness of the Sudanese protesters to accept a superficial transition to democracy under the control of the military reflects their deep mistrust of the ways in which elections are easily manipulated to favour those already in power.

The Sudanese protesters also successfully overcame another of the major challenges to popular movements in Africa – the divide between urban and rural populations. Many African countries remain predominantly rural, and they feature their own political movements and electorates, far from the street politics of urban life. This is a legacy of the colonial period, during which urban spaces were structured as multi-ethnic spaces due to the need for cheap labour. In contrast, rural areas were given over to traditional authorities, who were empowered by both colonial and post-colonial regimes through a politics of ethnic patronage. This legacy has created a yawning chasm between urban and rural life despite the increased migration between the two over the past two decades, a phenomenon that is rapidly increasing the share of Africa's population that lives in cities.

In Sudan, the fact that the protests started in a peripheral town and initially gained steam in small towns and villages before arriving in the Khartoum megalopolis gave the protests a truly national character from the start. This forced the regime to attempt to repress the protest in multiple sites simultaneously, making it far more difficult for it to even control Khartoum despite decades of investment to protest-proof the city. It also meant that when the crackdown came, the protesters were far more able to withstand the regime's brutality by moving the movement underground and out of the capital.

While movements in DRC and Sudan have yet to achieve success by their own standards, by refusing to cede leadership to established political parties and other civil society institutions, the political society–led Sudanese protesters remain far more vibrant and politically relevant than their civil society–led Congolese counterparts. Yet both movements confront a moment of truth around the question of violence.

It is important to draw a distinction between varying forms of political violence. While civil society rejects all forms of violence outright – a function of the privileged position of its members – many in political society have far more fraught relationships to violent politics. On one side, political society protest itself can often turn violent as protesters lack the discipline or moral preoccupation to abstain from violent actions. While most political society protesters do not seek to use violence, they are frequently more willing to tolerate violent actors within their ranks and may even sympathize with their actions. This is why political society protest is often dismissed by regimes as nothing more than violent insurrection or ignored by the international community as little more than rioting.

But beyond the character of a specific protest action, political society–based popular movements face a more existential conundrum. Many of the participants of such movements rely upon are simultaneously recruited by organized violent groups, whether rebel organizations or criminal mafias. Ensuring that protesters remain committed to a collective popular movement rather than more violent options that promise more immediate individual rewards is an acute challenge.

In Congo, political figures have openly spoken about a violent insurrection to challenge the Kabila regime, standing down only when confronted by the overwhelming military advantage of the Congolese regime. In Sudan, numerous violent groups in the country's peripheries have thus far deferred to the leadership of the movement while retaining the ability to use force at their own discretion. As the crackdown on protesters escalated, a recurring concern among organizers was the ethics of asking the often young and poor participants to continue taking to the streets knowing the likelihood of repression. Furthermore, without the resources available to formal civil organizations, political society has few resources, whether legal aid or international donors, to draw on to support protesters injured, killed or arrested by the regime. But the movement can remain relevant only if the masses participate, an increasingly challenging proposition when faced with repression and the easy opportunity to join groups willing to deploy violence.

Conclusion

What is the role of Africa's burgeoning social movements? Bereft of genuinely oppositional parties, abandoned by nominally pro-democratic forces in the West and lacking a genuine economic alternative as formerly socialist countries deepen their embrace of capitalism, social movements represent the only viable alternative to the prevailing economic and political consensus.

While it is understandable that international observers decry a crisis of democracy, this presupposes that democracy in Africa is best measured by whether elections are held regardless of their quality. However, Africans have come to see through this elite charade that characterizes electoral politics in Africa. Even where elections seem to bring about a change in the ruling party, as in Congo currently, there is little change in the political and economic elites that dominate national politics. Even as elites turn away from even the semblance of democracy, all hope is not lost. Popular movements demanding genuine political and economic transformation have emerged in most African countries. How governments and the international community react to such movements will determine the future of African democracy.

But the trajectory of African social movements should not be of concern only to Africans. Amid the many questions African activists have centred among their recent agitations is the appropriate role of the political party in popular liberation. During the first wave of African protest when Africans threw off the shackles of colonial domination, the decision to form political parties was understood as a necessary tool in the pursuit of national liberation. Even during the massive uprisings that shook the continent during the 1980s and 1990s and led to its formal democratization, political parties were understood as potentially progressive forces and the natural focus of any political agitation.

Yet two decades of misrule have led to disillusionment with the conflation of democracy with the existence of relatively homogenous political parties. The ongoing wave of African protests are suspicious of the role of political parties. In Sudan, for example, activists have met opposition leaders' efforts to engage with the protests with disinterest or outright hostility. In Senegal, activists have decried the increasing authoritarian tendencies of the opposition leader–turned-President Mackey Sall, despite their central role in helping him capture the presidency in the first place. Much like elsewhere, ordinary Africans are increasingly disillusioned with party-centric representative democracy and are exploring new forms of political action that promise to deepen the meaning of democracy for us all.

Notes

1 https://reliefweb.int/report/sudan/african-union-election-observation-mission-april-2015-general-elections-republic-sudan.
2 Adam Branch and Zachariah Mampilly, *Africa Uprising: Popular Protest and Political Change* (London: Zed Books, 2015), ACLED.

3 Diego Giannone, 'Political and Ideological Aspects in the Measurement of Democracy: The Freedom House Case', *Democratization* 17, no. 1 (2010): 68–97.
4 https://freedomhouse.org/report/methodology-freedom-world-2018.
5 See, for example, Thomas Carothers and Richard Young, 'The Complexities of Global Protests', Carnegie Endowment for International Peace, 2015. Major event databases such as ACLED provide empirical evidence for this trend both globally and in Africa. In Africa specifically, see Branch and Zachariah Mampilly, *Africa Uprising* and Lisa Mueller, *Political Protest in Contemporary Africa* (Cambridge: Cambridge University Press, 2018).
6 Steven Friedman, 'Democracy by the Numbers', *Africa's a Country*, 2019, https://africasacountry.com/2019/02/democracy-by-numbers.
7 https://www.state.gov/r/pa/prs/ps/2019/01/288417.htm.
8 https://www.state.gov/r/pa/prs/ps/2019/01/288532.htm.
9 Michael Neocosmos, *Thinking Freedom in Africa: Toward a Theory of Emancipatory Politics* (Johannesburg: Wits University Press, 2018).
10 Partha Chatterjee, *The Politics of the Governed Reflections on Popular Politics in Most of the World* (New York: Columbia University Press, 2004).
11 Chatterjee, *The Politics of the Governed Reflections on Popular Politics in Most of the World*, 38.

References

Branch, Adam and Zachariah Mampilly. *Africa Uprising: Popular Protest and Political Change*. London: Zed Books, 2015.
Carothers, Thomas and Richard Young. 'The Complexities of Global Protests', Carnegie Endowment for International Peace, 2015.
Chatterjee, Partha. *The Politics of the Governed Reflections on Popular Politics in Most of the World*. New York: Columbia University Press, 2004.
Friedman, Steven. 'Democracy by the Numbers'. *Africa's a Country*, 2019.
Giannone, Diego. 'Political and Ideological Aspects in the Measurement of Democracy: The Freedom House Case'. *Democratization* 17, no. 1 (2010): 68–97.
Mueller, Lisa. *Political Protest in Contemporary Africa*. Cambridge: Cambridge University Press, 2018.
Neocosmos, Michael. *Thinking Freedom in Africa: Toward a Theory of Emancipatory Politics*. Johannesburg: Wits University Press, 2018.

11

Populism in Latin America as global history

Federico Finchelstein

In this era of global populisms, an initial question to think about is the relationship between populism and dictatorship. I would argue that populism is in fact the opposite of dictatorship: a form of democracy that is nonetheless authoritarian. This dual dimension of populism made it historically different from both communist and fascist dictatorships. It also made it distinctive from constitutional forms of democracy on a global scale.

Historically, populism has been often a democratic result of the fall of dictatorships rather than the creator of new dictatorships. This has been the case in two key historical turning points, 1945 and 1989, that resulted in the surge of new forms of populism. Both the fall of Berlin and the fall of the Berlin Wall were events with major geopolitical implications across the world. They led to a global increase of democracies but also populist regimes.

Let me start with the second turning point, that of 1989. An important question regarding the fall of the Berlin Wall is whether this fall had relatively symmetrical consequences on both sides of the Atlantic and in particular with regard to the political development of populisms that have reached power in recent years. Was 1989 the beginning of these major changes in the political spectrum? Although the answer seems to be more affirmative for the cases of European countries that had experienced dictatorships and therefore contexts in which populism as a form of democracy could not have developed before, the 1989 rupture was not so important, or at least it was not the main cause that would explain the explosion of current populisms in Western Europe, the United States, Africa, Asia and Latin America as a whole. Populism as a political movement has existed since the end of the nineteenth century and as a power regime since the late 1940s. From its beginnings, populism was a global phenomenon. For this reason, it is especially important to consider the first turning point, marked by the demise of fascism in 1945. By focusing on the rupture that created the context for the populisms in power, I would like to stress the importance of transnational phenomena, exchanges and appropriations in the history of populism. How much do 1945 and 1989 differ from one another? More generally, how much transfers and synchronicities influenced the development of populism in the course of its national and global histories? What is clear is that after the global event of 1989, right-wing populisms in Europe experienced a renaissance but their transnational dimensions preceded them and also explain them historically in the long term. In this text I propose that 1945 is the major breaking point in the history of populism, and I present a first approximation to think of the history of populist globality.

Global populisms

If we start by the end, or, to put it differently, if we begin with Trumpism, which is the most recent chapter in the history of populism, it is clear that the European tours of 'Trump's former brain' Steve Bannon confirmed the globalizing character of current populisms. And yet, this does not mean, as is often implied, that this international story is new in America. It also does not mean that Europopulism was created after the fall of the Berlin Wall. This historical globality of populism seems to be a paradox because the new populist ideologues and leaders are precisely the ones that accuse their enemies of being 'globalists'. Seemingly contradicting is the fact that those who likewise present themselves as retuning their countries to a golden past, and at the same time state that they lack historical antecedents or that they represent a new chapter in the history of the world; a new era that the leader of the White House has immodestly called 'the age of Trump'. In theory, the new populists are extreme nationalists who say they want to put their countries above everything and everyone else. In practice, these nationalists form a new international right-wing bloc, based on the similarity of their politics of xenophobia. In other words, they share a common enemy in the democratic legacies of the enlightenment. None of this is new in the history of populism. The now-classical populism of Juan Domingo Perón tried (and failed) to present their third way beyond liberalism and socialism as the solution to the problems of the world, particularly the bipolar world of the Cold War. More recently, Venezuelan Chavismo tried to make its leader, the architect, the symbol of a new way of doing politics.[1] Before them, fascism, the original proponent of a third way, had also tried to generate a 'fascist international' of nationalisms. Specifically, fascism crossed the Atlantic and also went beyond Latin America, in places like China, India or Syria. After the global defeat of fascism, former fascists and militants of dictatorships tried to follow the anti-liberal tradition by reformulating it through democratic means. This began the birth of populism as a new way of governing the nation. And this populist foundations were global and transnational from the very beginning.

Populism is not fascism. Historically, fascism has been adequately contextualized as, above all, a form of political dictatorship. It often emerges in democracy and destroys it from within. Historically, populism has done the opposite. It has often emerged from other authoritarian experiences, including dictatorship, and in most cases it has distorted democracies, minimizing their qualities, while never, or almost never, destroying them.

Populism is a form of democracy that is based on the notion of a leader who, without institutional mediations, equates his or her voice with that of the people. This idea of unifying the people and the leader is central. It has authoritarian implications, but it starts with a democratic premise: establishing a closer relationship between those in power and the people.

As a movement, populism is presented as an attempt at achieving a more direct form of democracy. In other words, populists portray themselves as bypassing the representational and institutional mediations of traditional politics. After starting with this anti-politics premise of bringing the people to power when it is in the opposition, when/if it reaches power populism in fact narrows representation and even replaces it with delegation. In power the leader does not create a more direct form of democracy. In fact, the leader ('the voice of the people') does what he wants and does not consult anyone. The crisis of representation is not reduced but often increased. The leader speaks on behalf of the people and decides for them.

What is populism then? Populism is historically a form of authoritarian and anti-liberal democracy. In this sense, populism cannot be explained only by the changes that occurred after the fall of the wall in Europe and/or Trumpism in the United States because it belongs to a global and long-term history. In my work I propose a historical understanding of what populism has constituted in history. After studying many cases, I found a couple of patterns that prevailed over time in this vertical rethinking of democracy. To begin with, populism implies an authoritarian understanding of democracy that reformulated the legacy of fascism after 1945 to combine it with different democratic procedures. Populism in power is a form of post-fascism that reformulates fascism for democratic times. In other words, it is fascism adapted to democratic times.[2]

It was in Latin America that modern democratic populism became for the first time a regime in history and was originally constituted as a post-fascist response to the left. However, it was not a radical break with the past, and populism was not generated outside of a historical continuum. In the period from the end of the nineteenth century to the interwar years, previous forms and proto-forms of populism emerged in places like the United States, Russia, Mexico, Argentina, Brazil and France. These movements and leaders spoke on behalf of the people as a single and homogeneous entity. From the left and from the right, they opposed the oligarchies and the elites, but in general they did not oppose liberal democracy in its entirety. The absolute rejection of democracy came after the First World War, when fascism merged the pre-populist tendencies of left and right with an anti-liberal and anti-communist extremist ideology. After 1945, in a radically changed context, modern populism returned to its pre-fascist roots, but without forgetting the lessons of the experience of fascism.

As a post-fascism, populism emerged as a form of authoritarian democracy for the Cold War world. Populist wanted to adapt the totalitarian version of politics to the hegemony of post-war democratic representation and to give rise, once more, to supranational political alliances against constitutional democracy. This transformation was first predominant in Latin America after the global fall of fascism in 1945, and much later it became generalized in Europe after the fall of real socialism after 1989. Populism began with the recognition that fascism had ended and was part of the past, not the present. For General Perón, fascism was 'an unrepeatable phenomenon, a classic style to define a precise and determined epoch'. As much as Perón lamented the loss of 'poor Italy' and Mussolini's fascism, he did not want to imitate the defeated past. He wanted to free Perónism from the accusation of fascism and the result was a version of post-fascist, authoritarian and anti-liberal democracy.[3] Like the Argentine leader, but many years later, the Italian neo-fascists came to a similar conclusion. Thus, Gianfranco Fini, the leader of the neo-fascist Movimento Sociale Italiano (MSI), tried to transform it into a populist formation and argued in 1993 that fascism was irreversibly part of the past: 'Like all Italians, we are not neo-Fascists, but post-Fascists.'[4]

While populism as a political regime often curtailed political rights, it also sometimes extended social rights; at the same time, it placed limits on the most radical emancipatory combinations of both. This specific post-fascist historicity of populism is often lost in various theoretical reconfigurations, including those approaches that are in favour or against the populist phenomenon. In addition, these theoretical visions present a subject without a history. They also impose Eurocentric opinions or the idea of the absolute exceptionality of the United States. Against these ahistorical ideas and the stereotypical visions of populism as an exclusive European or American phenomenon that exists only after the fall of the wall, it is necessary to present a global reading of its varied historical itineraries and global conceptions.

Close encounters of the third position

'I did not go to Italy to see the Leaning Tower [of Pisa]. I went because of more important things that were going on there.' According to General Juan Perón, the real reasons for his visit to that country in 1939 were Benito Mussolini and fascism. The same reasons apply to his admiration for Adolf

Hitler and his trip to Nazi Germany. 'Nor did I go to Berlin only to see the Brandenburg Gate.' In fact, these visits as a young Argentine officer, and his personal observations of fascism in power, were key in his reformulation of fascism, which led to the creation of the first populist regime in history. As for Mussolini, Perón would invent a personal encounter with the Duce. In fact, he had only observed Mussolini from a distance, while the Italian dictator was giving an important speech of war from the balconies of the Palazzo Venezia.

Nonetheless, Perón created a myth of origins where the Italian dictator handed him the baton of the global struggle against liberalism. According to Perón's foundational story, Mussolini improbably walked towards him: 'I went straight to his office, where he was writing, looked up at me with attention and came to say hello.' In this fictional account of a meeting between colleagues, Perón was the first speaker. The Duce just listened to him: 'I told him that, knowing his gigantic work, I would not have been happy to my country without having shaken his hand.'

This personal fantasy encounter that Perón recounted many years later in the 1970s is significant precisely because it shows the fascist genealogies of the first populist regime, but it is also important because it signals its critical differences. Among so many possible genealogies, why at the end of his life, the Argentine leader would return in his memory to fascism as a form of genealogical legitimation?

Perón showed a similar admiration for Nazi Germany: 'In all that time that I lived in Germany I had the feeling of a witnessing a huge machinery that worked with marvelous perfection and where even a small screw was not missing.' For Perón, Nazi organization was something formidable. A new social phenomenon had been unleashed with the Nazis: 'It was national socialism, in the same way that fascism triumphed in Italy.' For the first time 'popular organizations' had an 'effective representation' in the 'national life, from which the people had always been separated'. Thus, for the first populist president, it was under the leadership of Hitler and Mussolini that the people were first represented in power.

In the fascist dictatorships, Perón saw an admirable anti-liberal form of political representation. It was a new form of popular legitimacy. A sovereignty that combined corporate technocratic planning with hierarchical leadership. Perón concluded that even if the means of execution could have been defective, the phenomenon of fascism represented a powerful third supranational position between US capitalism and Soviet socialism. The leader brought these lessons from fascism to Latin America thinking that the role of people, the leader and the state in fascism would influence the 'political form of the future'. In the eventually defeated fascism Perón had seen an object of study to think about 'true social democracy'. After Hitler and Mussolini had died, Perón made it clear that 'popular democracy' no longer existed 'in the West': 'That is what I discovered when I went to study the old European institutions and when returning to my country I said to myself "We are not going back to the XIX century with the capitalist imperialist democracies: we are going to the XX century with the social democracies".[5] In his peculiar understanding of social democracy the Argentine leader did not have in mind the European social-democratic forms of the past, but a new combination of social nationalism: 'and this is how I created (my) social doctrine and launched it towards the 21st century.'

Undoubtedly, Perón was not the first Latin American to visit the Nazi and Fascist regimes. There were many transnational fascists who shared their global dictatorial projects to dominate the world, but, unlike these fascists, the Argentine conductor learned a very different lesson. At the end of the war, Perón was the first to create an electoral democracy that turned out to be very different from the original fascist model. Populism reformulated fascism to the extent that, as in the case of Argentine Perónism, it became a totally differentiated 'ism'; a regime that was, and is, at the same time rooted in electoral democracy and that also shows a tendency to reject democratic diversity and tolerance.

Populism is the opposite of pluralism in politics. It talks in the name of an imagined majority and dismisses all views that it considers part of the minority. Especially on the right, its enemies often include actual religious and ethnic minorities and always involve the independent press. Perón spoke in the name of the people and imagined himself as the opposite of the elites. Like Le Pen, Wilders, Trump and many other contemporary leaders, the Argentine general set his own persona against politics as usual. He represented 'anti-politics' and conceived his own role in messianic terms. He was tasked with radically changing Argentina, giving it a new historical foundation at a time of terminal crisis. Perón presented his movement as having transnational dimensions. Populism existed without borders. This was not specific to Argentina or Latin America, but rather a general condition of populism in its history and its theory. Populism is a way of thinking about universal politics that, while being conceived in a nationalist way, gives answers to a global situation. It presents national anti-liberal solutions to the universal problem of the crisis of representation in democracy. For the populists there is no contradiction between nationalism and supranational ties. In fact, by turning transnational fascism into a post-fascist transnational phenomenon, the first populist regime in history attempted to create a new third global position.

Populism without borders

In 1951, Perón announced that 'the hour of the people' was coming and warned that there were was an alternative to the bipolar world of communism and capitalism. There was a third option, which was the government of the people by its true representative: Perónism, that is to say, himself. Both capitalism and communism were 'imperialist systems of human exploitation'. Only Perónism, and its global peers, represented social justice for the people and their 'liberation'. Against the two systems ('usurpers of power'), the 'third position' guaranteed economic independence and political sovereignty for all nations and their peoples. This third way marked a global 'evolution'. The people finally 'take the government into their hands'. Perón thought that this populism would see the light in Europe two decades later than in Latin America. Argentina had always followed after Europe, but in the new postwar context the populist leader Argentina wanted to lead the way. Populists needed to be ready and show the way to others. 'We are going to move forward and do what is necessary so that when the announced political and social events take place in Europe, we will be already firm in our ideology.'[6]

Perónism promoted its model at the international level, achieving a questionable success and limited results.[7] But even if Perónism tried to be the anchor of a new international movement and its leader emphasized the need for Latin American continental integration and a world liberation of both communism and 'plutocracy', Perón, however, was ambivalent in the face of the possibility of playing the main role in this confrontation. The populist leader later acknowledged that when he was in power he approached related regimes such as Getulio Vargas in Brazil, but also emphasized links with Franco's dictatorship in Spain. But despite the alliance with Franco, the dictatorship was not part of the new political wave that Perón had imagined. For Latin America Perón even claimed that 'borders are not needed".[8]

After 1945, the fascist globalization continued, but first in Latin America – and much later in Europe and in particular after 1989, it was reformulated as post-fascist. However, the transnational attempts of classical Latin American populisms (the Perónism between us and Varguism in Brazil or the first Venezuelan populism) denied the dictatorship and racism. Perón dreamed of similar movements in post-war Europe in countries such as France and Italy. The peoples were 'in a life of uncertainty, they raise their shoulders and wait, while their governments act dominated by the same pressure as in South America'. Post-war Germany was 'divided, occupied and mocked, only can think of its release'. In short, at the time when it became a regime, populism was conceived as the global movement of the future. It was a new third position between capitalism and communism that was also being adopted 'without saying so' in India. Countries like Iran, Iraq, Pakistan and Afghanistan followed the example of India. In addition, the 'idea' of the third position beyond capitalism and communism 'through the Red Sea seems to reach Africa'. The Arab world was no exception, but presented a central role: 'Sixty million Arabs' they are in the wave.' On a global scale, Perón saw expanding 'a clear and courageous third position'. Perónism was the first step but 'Every day more countries appear in the position of the people'. This time of the peoples, thought as a definitive historical break, was going to be 'affirmed about the spoils of governments and nations that did not have faith in the "voice of God".'

Perón stressed that his third position represented a new supranational resurgence against 'demoliberalismo' and communism which he regarded as the natural outcome of the former. His was a global reaction against the victors of the Second World War. It was a symptomatic early response to the triumph of liberalism and communism and a call for new global third position against them. The peoples had reacted against those that had seized their power or merely had wanted to represent them. Perónism and kindred regimes of power had finally returned to the people. People in Latin America, Europe, Asia and Africa started their pathway to freedom.

Perón even thought that American liberalism and Russian communism were going to be overwhelmed by this new political progression. In a context in which he was convinced of a forthcoming Third World War, Perón assured his listeners that liberal democracy and communism were fighting for their survival. He said that when they were 'united they were dangerous but their weakness would be the outcome of their confrontation'. The peoples of the world were opposed to these two imperialisms. While Russia and the United States represented governments opposed to the will of the people, in 1946, Argentina had 'announced to the world that its government will do what the people wants'. Perón observed similar 'continuadores' in Brazil where Vargas was 'the authentic representative of the Brazilian people' as well as in Bolivia, Chile, Venezuela, Guatemala and Puerto Rico where there was a 'similar fight between peoples and governments'.[9]

Perón's vision of a new global hegemony for what we now know as classical populism, of course, never materialized, but this messianic vision of a moment of breakthrough and momentous change in the history of politics is an important key for thinking about populist historical ruptures. While in 1989, the fall of the wall cemented the foundations of future European populisms, especially in Central and Eastern Europe, and also reformulated the Latin American populist tradition through the emergence of the new neoliberal populisms in Argentina, Brazil, Peru, Ecuador and other countries; the populist rupture of 1945 left a major imprint on the path followed by the first populisms of the twenty-first century in Latin America. In this regard, Hugo Chávez declared: 'Well, Perón said we were at the hour of the peoples. Unfortunately those battles dissipated, but they were not lost, it is one thing to cut out momentarily, and another thing is that they were lost forever.' Chávez stressed the centrality of the supranational dimensions of Latin American classic populism and identified that Perónist wave with the 'new wave'. If the past had been cut from the present, he hoped that the new situation will last forever and like Perón he also connected populist global politics with the divine:

> I take my General Perón, by remembering him here in Buenos Aires and say that I hope this new wave will forever mark the peoples. But it depends on us (the peoples) that yes, this will be the time, as the bible says, 'everything that is going to happen under the sun has its time'. Bolivar also said 'the hour or the great day of South America has not arrived yet.' I wish this is it.[10]

If Perón was the epitome of twentieth-century populism and Chávez his disciple and early twenty-first-century version, the new trend of European and American right represents the new wave of populism. This time, however, populism returns to some fascist themes that Perón, Vargas and other predecessors had mostly rejected. While fascist violence and racism represented the past, the future would be different. As Perón said in 1945 before being elected and in clear rejection of political violence, 'You do not win with violence, you defeat with intelligence and organization.' Populism was an electoral form of authoritarian democracy that was inspired but at the same time rejected the fascist dictatorship. After 1945, this historical relationship between fascism and populism created the first post-fascist notions of authoritarian anti-liberal democracy.

The new European and American right-wing strain represents populism's new wave for the new century. This time, however, populism returns to some fascist themes that Perón had mostly rejected. Trumpism and its European counterparts, such as the French Marine Le Pen, Bolsonaro in Brazil, the Italian League or the AFD in Germany, return to xenophobia in a way that the Latin American driver could never have imagined. In Europe one can speak of a true populist international, while in Latin America the 'Bolsonaro effect' begins to appear in both the traditional neoliberal right and the populist one.[11]

Past and presents

The new right-wing populist global alliances, which often include the fascists, show how the most recent populism on the right is reducing the post-fascist dimensions of post-war populism. Historically, the populists wanted to distance themselves from the 'methods' of fascism. But, for example, in Trumpism, the National Front, Bolsonarism or the Italian populists, it is possible to observe a coalition of neo-fascist supporters with populist leaders. These relations are both national and supranational.

The new populisms present a rupture with their post-fascist predecessors from the classical populists to Hugo Chávez and his 'new wave'. Things have changed in Trump's time. In that sense, the breaking point of 2016 is of greater influence than that of 1989 in the global history of populism.

In the present time, the populists are also racists. At present, we are experiencing a new globalization of xenophobia and anti-politics. On one of his quasi-triumphal tours of Europe, Bannon spoke in March 2018 in France at the convention of the National Front. In that context he told his listeners that they were all enrolled in 'a world movement bigger than France, than Italy, Hungary or Poland'. He asked them: 'Let them call them racist, xenophobic or whatever. Wear it as a medal of honor.' What was previously perceived as an insult is now thought of as a programme. Among the post-fascist listeners in France was its leader Marine Le Pen (who had come second in the French presidential elections of 2017) and who in turn had celebrated the triumph of trumpismo as part of 'a global revolution'.

At that time, at the end of 2016, when populism reached its historic and global peak in the White House, other populists echoed the transnational proportions of that victory of anti-politics. The Italian populist Beppe Grillo then argued that Trump's victory was a turning point in world history: 'This is a wide-ranging fuck off. Trump has pulled off an incredible V-Day.' For Le Pen the victory of Trump was the triumph of the will of the people over the elites. Like Trump and many others, Le Pen identified her own position with that of the true patriots: 'The division is no longer between right and left [but] between patriot and globalist.'[12]

Just as Rome and Berlin became models for the fascists, or Buenos Aires or Caracas for the populists of Latin America, the xenophobic presidential campaign and the administration of Donald Trump (2017–2021) became a source of validation for the right-wing populists of all the world. Washington lit a beacon that illuminated the populist universe. Populist leaders of the far right such as Salvini, Le Pen, Bolsonaro, as well as some populists calling themselves left but in fact located between the right and the left as the Italian 5-star movement, praise the Trumpist voters for opposing traditional forms of democratic representation. They are part of a new global reaction against deliberative democracy and populist politics based on the repudiation of those who are, look or think differently.

Notes

1 'Hugo Chávez and the Diffusion of Bolivarianism', *Democratization* 24, no. 7 (2017) and also Routledge Handbook of Global Populism A Populist International?: ALBA's Democratic and Autocratic; Promotion, texto con nadia.

2 Federico Finchelstein, *From Fascism to Populism in History* (Oakland: University of California Press, 2017).

3 Juan Domingo Perón, *Memorial de Puerta de Hierro* (Buenos Aires: Honorable Congreso de la Nación, 2001), 65.

4 Cited Roger Griffin, 'Interregnum or Endgame? The Radical Right in the "post-fascist" era', in Cas Mudde (ed.), *The Populist Radical Right* (London: Routledge, 2017), 15. On post-fascism and Peronism, see Federico Finchelstein, *Transatlantic Fascism* (Durham: Duke University Press, 2010). For Europe, see also the recent work by Enzo Traverso, New Faces of fascism.

5 Juan Domingo Perón, *Yo, Juan Domingo Perón* (Barcelona: Planeta, 1976), 27–9.

6 Juan Domingo Perón, *Artículos de Descartes* (Buenos Aires, 1951), 203–8; *Yo, Juan Domingo Perón*, 27–9.

7   Ver Loris Zanatta, *La internacional justicialista* (Buenos Aires: Sudamericana, 2013) and Ernesto Semán, *Ambassadors of the Working Class* (Durham: Duke University Press, 2017).
8   Perón, ANTE UNA DELEGACIÓN UNIVERSITARIA BRASILERA, 66. 'Y soy todavía más atrevido en esto, porque en todas las oportunidades he sostenido que en esta parte del mundo las fronteras están de más'.
9   Perón, *Artículos de Descartes*, 203–8.
10 Conferencia de Prensa del Comandante Presidente Hugo Chávez Frías, 1 de febrero, 2005, http://www.todochavez.gob.ve/todochavez/3594-conferencia-de-prensa-del-comandante-presidente-hugo-chavez-frias.
11 For Europe, see Duncan McDonnell and Annika Werner, *International Populism: The Radical Right in the European Parliament* (London: Hurst, 2019); Andrea Mammone, 'Why the European Union Must Respond to the Italian Election', *Washington Post*, 13 March 2018.
12 Finchelstein, *From Fascism to Populism in History*, 158.

References

Finchelstein, Federico. *From Fascism to Populism in History*. Oakland: University of California Press, 2017.
Finchelstein, Federico. *Transatlantic Fascism*. Durham: Duke University Press, 2010.
Griffin, Roger. 'Interregnum or Endgame? The Radical Right in the "post-fascist" Era'. In Cas Mudde (ed.), *The Populist Radical Right*. London: Routledge, 2017: 15, 21.
Mammone, Andrea. 'Why the European Union must Respond to the Italian Election'. *Washington Post*, 13 March 2018.
McDonnell, Duncan and Annika Werner. *International Populism: The Radical Right in the European Parliament*. London: Hurst, 2019.
Perón, Juan Domingo. *Artículos de Descartes*. Buenos Aires: 1951.
Perón, Juan Domingo. *Yo, Juan Domingo Perón*. Barcelona: Planeta, 1976.
Perón, Juan Domingo. 'Discurso ante una delegación universitaria brasileña'. In Autor, *Obras completas (Vol. 2)*. Buenos Aires, Argentina: Biblioteca del Congreso de la Nación, 2016.
Semán, Ernesto. *Ambassadors of the Working Class*. Durham: Duke University Press, 2017.
Torre, Carlos de la. 'Hugo Chávez and the Diffusion of Bolivarianism'. *Democratization* 24, no. 7 (2017).
Zanatta, Ver Loris. *La internacional justicialista*. Buenos Aires: Sudamericana, 2013.

12

Why Trump is not the problem

Andrew J. Bacevich

In 1955, the writer James Baldwin observed that 'In America, life seems to move faster than anywhere else on the globe and each generation is promised more than it will get: which creates in each generation, a furious bewildered rage, the rage of people who cannot find solid ground beneath their feet'.[1]

In the aftermath of the so-called Age of Trump, the diagnosis that Baldwin offered several decades back remains remarkably apt. That is, the essential problem we confront in our present crisis is the difficulty Americans have in finding something solid to stand on, with many of our fellow citizens expressing their furious bewildered rage by electing Donald Trump president back in 2016.

In short, however much members of the American intelligentsia may fixate on Trump, he is not the problem. He is merely symptom or consequence of several problems that formed long before he appeared on the political scene and that developments in recent decades have served to exacerbate. An unfortunate irony of the Trump presidency, with its daily dose of outrages and inanities, was that it provided an excuse for ignoring those problems or giving them short shrift.

Let me suggest that in general Americans pay way too much attention to what presidents say and do. That statement certainly applies – indeed, especially applies – to the forty-fifth president. For too long, a veritable cult of the presidency has provided an excuse for treating politics as a melodrama, staged at four-year intervals and centring on hopes of another Roosevelt or Kennedy or Reagan appearing as agent of American deliverance. Donald Trump's ascent to the office once inhabited by such worthies should demolish such fantasies once and for all.

My own bet is that historians will classify Trump as the least significant president in recent memory. I fully understand that such an assumption is a nontrivial one. But given that he managed to steer clear of an apocalyptic armed conflict, Donald Trump will prove to be what Millard Fillmore was to the nineteenth century and Warren G. Harding to the twentieth.[2]

To be sure, in the meantime Trump routinely said (or tweeted) innumerable things that qualified as inane or inflammatory or downright reprehensible, to put it mildly.[3] This was true whether he was spouting off about climate change or guns or immigrants from south of the border or Covid-19. And he did or proposed to do more than a few things that were wrongheaded. But little of what he actually did is irreversible. As soon as he took office, Trump's successor wasted little time in repairing much of the damage that Trump had wreaked.

Note that most of the horrors forecast by Trump's critics did come to pass. The constitutional order remained intact. Press freedom was rarely exercised with comparable vigour and passion. In the streets, ordinary citizens assembled, spoke their minds and raised their voices in protest. Those so inclined worshipped as they see fit. Despite frequent references to fascism, that belief system remained distinctly unfashionable. Running for office as a fascist in America today is not a recipe for electoral success.[4]

One of the most striking aspects of the Trump presidency was the gap between rhetoric and action. Such a gap exists with any administration. With Trump, it reached unusually large proportions, exacerbated further by subversive subordinates.[5] Indeed, one distinguishing attribute of the Trump presidency was the yawning gap between what the president vowed (or threatened) to do and what in most cases actually ensued.

Trump liked to pose as a bold leader making big decisions that will Make America Great Again. In practice, however, his decisions tended to fall well short of momentous. As a leader, he was weak one day and capricious the next. Whenever possible, Trump dodged the central issue or offloaded responsibility onto Congress or to the military. Or insubordinate subordinates stymied his declared intentions.[6]

We got a hint of this early in his presidency when Trump announced that he intended to organize a grand parade down Pennsylvania Avenue that would flaunt American military might. The Pentagon responded to this clear-cut directive from the commander-in-chief by announcing that it would take the matter under consideration. Months passed. Various inflated price tags were floated. In the end nothing happened.[7]

So it was time and again, especially on matters related to national security. With his notoriously short attention span, Trump either lost interest or simply forgot about the issue.

Consider NATO. As a candidate, Trump announced that it was time for European nations to assume responsibility for their own security.[8] Yet despite his anti-NATO posturing, the United States remains a member of the alliance, having affirmed Article V, which commits us to Europe's defence even as wealthy European countries like Germany continue to underinvest in their own defence.

Indeed, despite Trump's putative bromance with Vladimir Putin, the Pentagon increased the US military presence in Eastern Europe, thereby offering increased security assurances to nations that feel most threatened by Russia. The US Army now has a mechanized brigade stationed in Poland. USAF warplanes patrol Baltic airspace. US national guard troops train in Lithuania.[9]

Or consider the Afghanistan War, the longest in our country's history. Candidate Trump denounced the war and promised to win it or get out. As president, he repeatedly announced his intention to end US participation in this endless war.[10] His subordinates have responded by either contradicting or ignoring the boss. The Afghanistan War continues.

Much the same applies to Syria. Trump's predecessor ordered US forces to intervene in Syria without bothering to get congressional authorization. Trump announced that he intended to terminate US involvement in that conflict forthwith.[11] Members of Congress from both parties immediately protested. The president soon thereafter revised his position.[12] Count on US forces to remain in Syria in some capacity for some time to come.

Whatever the central theme of the Trump administration's approach to national security, it was clearly not the isolationism that his recurring references to 'America First' seem to imply.

More than a few of Trump's critics feared that he was leading us down the path to fascism. But that was never going to happen. Doing so would require a sense of purpose that he does not possess. Say what you will about fascists or other totalitarian ideologues. They at least have a worldview and convictions. They adhere to a theory of history. Trump has none of these. Trump is not a Hitler or a Mussolini. He's not even a Franco or a Peron.

Hence, my expectation that he will ultimately prove to be an insignificant figure, notwithstanding the hysteria that enveloped much of the country since the day of his election. History is likely to judge Trump as less disruptive than he now appears (and wishes to appear) and as more of a transitory figure who simultaneously embodied and laid bare the accumulating contradictions of American life.

What then actually explains the rage of the people who cannot find solid ground beneath their feet and expressed their dismay by electing Donald Trump president? Well, blame sexism, Fox News, James Comey, Russian meddling and Hillary's failure to visit Wisconsin all you want, but a more fundamental explanation is this: The election of 2016 constituted a de facto referendum on the course of recent US history. It was a de facto plebiscite.

That plebiscite rendered a definitive judgement: The underlying consensus informing basic US policy since the end of the Cold War has collapsed. Premises for basic policy that members of the policy elite have long treated as self-evident and sacrosanct no longer command the backing or assent of the American people. To repurpose an expression credited to James Carville back when he was first trying to get Bill Clinton elected president: It's the ideas, stupid. Or to put it another way, a specific set of ideas marketed in the wake of the Cold War as defining our future and the future of humankind had been thoroughly tried and found sadly wanting.

So those who imagine that Trump's removal will put things right – such would seem to be the view of the *New York Times, Washington Post* and other prominent media outlets – are deluding themselves. To persist in thinking that Trump himself defines the problem is to commit an error of the first order.

To understand what I am getting at, consider this second quote: 'Without the Cold War, what's the point of being an American?'[13]

As the long twilight struggle was finally winding down, Harry 'Rabbit' Angstrom, novelist John Updike's late-twentieth-century Everyman, pondered that question. In short order, Rabbit got an answer to his question. So, too, did his fellow citizens, albeit after only perfunctory consultation.

The end of the Cold War offered cause for celebration – on that point just about everyone agreed, me very much included. Yet just about everyone also agreed that the passing of this era of continuing tension and occasional great danger did not require reflection nor regret nor repentance on the part of the United States. This, I have come to believe, was a grave mistake.

As to what would come next – well, on such matters, policy elites professed to have matters well in hand. On that score, Rabbit Angstrom was told that he could rest easy. People much smarter than he was had the answers.

The dawning era, these elites believed, summoned Americans to look not to the past but to the future, exploiting vast opportunities that were now presenting themselves. No longer obliged to fret about Communist takeovers or the risks of nuclear Armageddon, Americans could throw caution to the winds.

In 1989, a hitherto obscure political scientist named Francis Fukuyama rocketed to worldwide fame by penning an essay announcing that history itself had ended.[14] Fukuyama's 'end of history' hypothesis caught fire not because it was true, but because it was exquisitely timed. It captured the mood of the moment. And it played directly to a conceit that Americans had been nursing ever since the very founding of the Republic, if not before.

With the end of the Cold War, that conceit came roaring back in full force. Its essence can be simply stated: We are God's new Israel.[15] We represent the Alpha and the Omega of the human story. We define the aspirations and destiny of all others. We stand for freedom, even if our reigning conception of what freedom requires, allows, or forbids continually evolves and occasionally veers sharply in a different direction.

So with the fall of the Berlin Wall and a 'sole superpower' – a popular phrase of the day – now positioned to call the shots, utopia beckoned just around the corner. That's the way things looked back at the dawn of the 1990s. All that was needed was for the United States to demonstrate the requisite confidence and resolve to usher that utopia into existence.[16]

Three specific propositions comprised the elite consensus that coalesced during the initial decade of the post–Cold War era. According to the first, the globalization of corporate capitalism held the key to wealth creation on a hitherto unimaginable scale. According to the second, jettisoning norms derived from what we might broadly call Judeo-Christian religious traditions held the key to the further expansion and indeed the perfection of personal autonomy. And autonomy became synonymous with freedom. According to the third, muscular global leadership exercised by the United States held the key to promoting a stable and humane international order.

Unfettered neoliberalism *plus* the unencumbered self *plus* unabashed American assertiveness: These defined the elements of the post–Cold War consensus that formed during the first half of the 1990s – these plus what enthusiasts were already calling the information revolution. The miracle of that 'revolution', gathering momentum just as the Soviet Union was going down for the count, provided the secret sauce that infused the emerging consensus with a sense of historical inevitability.

Now the Cold War itself, running from the late 1940s to the end of the 1980s, had fostered notable improvements in computational speed and capacity. During those decades, new modes of communication appeared along with new techniques for storing, accessing and manipulating information. Yet however impressive these developments, only as the Cold War receded did they move from background to forefront.

For true believers, information technology served a quasi-theological function, promising answers to life's ultimate questions. Although God might be dead, with it Americans found in Bill Gates and Steve Jobs nerdy, but nonetheless compelling, idols. More immediately, in the eyes of the policy elite, the information revolution meshed with and reinforced the new policy consensus.

For those focused on the political economy, it greased the wheels of globalized capitalism, creating vast new opportunities for trade and investment. Information would accelerate the movement of capital, goods, ideas and people. The world itself would be flat, open and accessible to all.

For those looking to shed constraints on personal freedom, information promised empowerment, making identity itself something to choose, discard or modify according to individual preference.

For members of the national security apparatus, the information revolution seemed certain to endow the United States with unassailable military capabilities. Properly employed, armed force itself would become more precise, more decisive and even more humane. As employed by the best-trained, best-equipped, most capable forces the world had ever seen, violence could become a means for countering evil and promoting good – not to be held in reserve but to be put to use.

That these various enhancements would combine to improve the human condition more generally was taken for granted; that they would in due course align everybody from Afghans to Zimbabweans with American values and the American way of life seemed more or less inevitable.

The three presidents of the post–Cold War era – Bill Clinton, George W. Bush and Barack Obama – put these several propositions to the test. Now politics-as-theatre requires us to pretend that our forty-second, forty-third and forty-fourth presidents differed in fundamental ways. In practice, however, their similarities greatly outweighed any of those differences.

Taken together, the administrations over which they presided collaborated in pursuing a common agenda, each intent on proving that the post–Cold War consensus could work, notwithstanding mounting evidence to the contrary.

To be fair, that consensus did work for some. 'Globalization' did make some people very rich indeed. In doing so, however, it greatly exacerbated inequality, while doing nothing to alleviate the condition of the American working class and underclass. We are, after all, a nation in which members of the top 1 per cent control more wealth than the bottom 90 per cent.[17] I'm not sure what's more shocking – the statistics that describe economic inequality or that fact that those statistics are widely reported and then essentially shrugged off.

The abandonment of traditional moral norms upended long-established social hierarchies. The resulting emphasis on diversity and multiculturalism *did* improve the status of groups long subjected to discrimination. Yet these advances have done remarkably little to reduce the alienation and despair pervading a society that suffers from an epidemic of chronic substance abuse, morbid obesity, teen suicide and similar afflictions. Throw in the world's highest incarceration rate, a seemingly insatiable appetite for pornography, urban school systems stuck in permanent crisis and mass shootings that occur with metronomic regularity and what you have is something other than the profile of a healthy society.

The 'good old days' of my youth were not good. Racism, sexism, nativism and other forms of prejudice remain a blot on the American story that can never be eradicated. Yet in my judgement we are not yet in a position to look down our noses at our benighted forebears. We have our own sins to attend to.

As for militarized American global leadership, it did indeed result in various bad actors such as Saddam Hussein and Muamar Ghaddafi meeting richly deserved fates. Yet it also embroiled the United States in a series of costly, senseless, unsuccessful and ultimately counterproductive wars.

US forces today are unquestionably the best military in all of history. Of that I have not the slightest doubt. But what is the purpose of war? It is to accomplish the essential political objectives of the state, when all other means have been exhausted or are unavailable. Victory means achieving stated political objectives, conclusively and at a reasonable cost. By that standard, US forces rarely win, even when allowed years to accomplish their mission.

As for the vaunted information revolution, let me confess here that you are reading an essay written by someone who doesn't own a smart phone, doesn't use social media and doesn't tweet. Even so, I am prepared to argue that the impact of the information technology that envelops our lives is ambiguous at best, even if those with eyeballs glued to their personal electronic device can't tolerate being offline long enough to assess the actual costs of being perpetually connected.

Here's my point: In the election of November 2016, Americans who not without reason consider themselves ill-served by the post–Cold War consensus signalled that they had had enough. Voters who concluded that neoliberal economic policies were not working to their benefit provided the crucial margin in electing Donald Trump president. So too did voters who found little to admire in a culture that seemingly takes its motto from the Outback steakhouse chain: 'No rules, just right.' So too did still others who found nothing to celebrate in the conversion of the US military into a global police force that is permanently at war – especially when it is their sons and daughters who serve repeated tours in places like Iraq and Afghanistan with little to show as a result.

This is what Trump wrought. His ascent to the presidency made it impossible to ignore any longer the shortcoming of the post–Cold War policy consensus. In his own bizarre way, he gave voice to millions who see themselves, not without reason, as dispossessed, abused and forgotten.

I am not suggesting that this was Trump's conscious purpose. He had no purpose other than self-aggrandizement.

Should we dismiss Trump voters as ignorant or stupid or bigoted – in the notorious characterization of Hillary Clinton, as mere 'deplorables'?[18] I would caution against doing so. After all, they are our fellow citizens. And they are both numerous and more than slightly pissed off. Their claims and concerns deserve as much attention as yours and mine.

And how has the political establishment responded to this extraordinary repudiation – for that's what it is, a repudiation of both major parties? Thus far at least, the establishment response amounts to a declaration of its own bankruptcy.

To the limited extent that the Republican Party retains any recognizable principles, he clings to the notion that reducing taxes, cutting government red tape, restricting abortion, curbing immigration, protecting gun rights and increasing military spending will alleviate all that ails the country.

To judge by the promises contained in their already forgotten 'Better Deal' that Democratic leaders not long ago unveiled as their new platform, their party believes that raising the minimum wage, capping the cost of prescription drugs and creating apprenticeship programmes for the unemployed will return their party to the good graces of the American electorate.[19]

In both parties embarrassingly small-bore thinking prevails, with Republicans and Democrats, equally bereft of fresh ideas. Let me add this caveat: The proposed 'Green New Deal' offered by left-wing Democrats does indeed qualify as bold and innovative.[20] Yet it remains to be seen whether this initiative will gain political traction anywhere other than among a minority of self-described progressives.

I am by temperament a conservative and a traditionalist, wary of revolutionary movements that more often than not end up being hijacked by nefarious plotters more interested in satisfying their own ambitions than in pursuing high ideals. Yet even I am prepared to admit that the status quo appears increasingly untenable. Incremental change will not suffice. The challenge of the moment is to embrace radicalism without succumbing to irresponsibility.

Perhaps the only good thing we can say about the presidency of Donald Trump is this: To borrow an image from Thomas Jefferson, it should serve as a fire bell in the night, curing Americans once and for all from the illusion that from the White House comes redemption. By now we ought to have had our fill of de facto monarchy.

By extension, Americans should come to see as intolerable the meanness, corruption and partisan dysfunction so much in evidence at the opposite end of Pennsylvania Avenue. We need not wax sentimental over the days when Lyndon Johnson and Everett Dirksen presided over the Senate to conclude that Mitch McConnell and Chuck Schumer represent something other than progress. If Congress continues to behave as contemptibly as it has in recent years it will, by default, allow the conditions that produced Trump and his cronies to prevail.

So it's time to take another stab at an approach to governance worthy of a democratic republic. Where to begin? I submit that Rabbit Angstrom's question offers a place to start: *What's the point of being an American?*

There are many ways of answering Rabbit's query. My own answer is rooted in an abiding conviction that our problems are less quantitative than qualitative. Rather than simply more – yet more wealth, more freedom, more attempts at bending the global order to suit our preferences – the times call for different.

In my view, the point of being an American is to participate in creating a society that strikes a balance between wants and needs, that exists in harmony with nature and the rest of humankind, and that is rooted in an agreed-upon conception of the common good – that last a phrase from my youth that has all but disappeared from political discourse.

People of goodwill are likely to differ on *how* to fulfil such aspirations. But therein lies the basis for an interesting debate, one that is essential to prospects of stemming the accelerating decay of American civic life. Yet the real beginning of wisdom, I submit, lies in recognizing that Trump is not cause, but consequence.

A post–Cold War consensus that promoted transnational corporate greed, mistook libertinism for liberty and embraced militarized neo-imperialism as the essence of enlightened statecraft created the conditions that handed Trump the presidency.

Many Americans celebrate his departure from office, much as they celebrated the fall of the Berlin Wall just over a quarter-century ago. But as was the case back then, the real question is this one: What should come next? In that instance, the answers we embraced, informed by an extraordinary bout of hubris, were deeply defective. Perhaps this time around, chastened by the events of the recent past, we may be able to do at least slightly better.

Notes

1 James Baldwin, *Collected Essays* (New York: Library of America, 1998), 52. This volume collects Baldwin's nonfiction to include *Notes of a Native Son*.
2 A recent survey of political scientists ranked Fillmore and Harding as 38th and 39th respectively out of 45. Donald Trump came in dead last. Brennan Weiss, 'Ranked: The Greatest US Presidents, According to Political Scientists', *Business Insider*, 18 February 2019.
3 For a running compendium of those tweets, see https://twitter.com/realDonaldTrump.
4 In 2018, a neo-Nazi did win an uncontested Republican primary in the 3rd Congressional District of Illinois. In the general election, he was crushed by a margin of three to one. Elyssa Cherney, 'Holocaust-Denier Arthur Jones Loses in Illinois 3rd District, but Still Gets More than 25 Percent of the Vote', *Chicago Tribune*, 7 November 2018.
5 (Anonymous), 'I Am Part of the Resistance inside the Trump Administration', *New York Times*, 5 September 2018.
6 According to the Mueller Report, for example, 'The President's efforts to influence the investigation were mostly unsuccessful, but that is largely because the persons who surrounded the President declined to carry out orders or accede to his requests', *Report on the Investigation Into Russian Interference in the 2016 Presidential Election* (March 2019), 370.
7 Eileen Sullivan, Helene Cooper and Michael D. Shear, 'Citing Costs, Trump Retreats From Massive Military Parade in Capital', *New York Times*, 17 August 2018.
8 Ben Jacobs, 'Donald Trump Reiterates He will Only Help Nato Countries That Pay "Fair Share"', *The Guardian*, 28 July 2016.
9 Eric Schmitt, 'In Eastern Military, U.S. Military Girds Against Russian Might and Manipulation', *New York Times*, 27 June 2018.
10 Jacob Pramuk, 'What Trump Said about Afghanistan before He Became President', *CNBC News*, 21 August 2017.
11 Mark Landler, Helene Cooper and Eric Schmitt, 'Trump to Withdraw U.S. Forces from Syria, Declaring "We Have Won against ISIS"', *New York Times*, 19 December 2018.
12 Mark Landler and Helene Cooper, 'In Latest Shift, Troop Agrees to Leave 400 Troops in Syria', *New York Times*, 22 February 2019. The actual number is several times larger.

13　John Updike, *Rabbit at Rest* (New York: Alfred A. Knopf, 1990), 442.
14　Francis Fukuyama, 'The End of History?' *The National Interest* (Summer 1989), 3–18.
15　For a classic example, see John Winthrop's 1630 sermon 'A Model of Christian Charity', https://history.hanover.edu/texts/winthmod.html (accessed 28 April 2019).
16　For a pugnacious expression of this view, see Charles Krauthammer, 'The Unipolar Moment', *Foreign Affairs* (America and the World 1990 Issue).
17　Elena Holodny, 'The Top 0.1% of American Households Hold the Same Amount of Wealth as the Bottom 90%', *Business Insider*, 23 October 2017.
18　'Read Hillary Clinton's "Basket of Deplorables" Remarks about Donald Trump Supporters', *Time*, 10 September 2016.
19　For details, see 'A Better Deal', https://abetterdeal.democraticleader.gov/ (accessed 28 April 2019).
20　Salvador Rizzo, 'Fact Checker: What's Actually in the "Green New Deal" from Democrats', *Washington Post*, 11 February 2019.

References

Baldwin, James. *Collected Essays*. New York: Library of America, 1998.
Cherney, Elyssa. 'Holocaust-Denier Arthur Jones Loses in Illinois 3rd District, but Still Gets More than 25 Percent of the Vote'. *Chicago Tribune*, 7 November 2018.
Fukuyama, Francis. 'The End of History?' *The National Interest*, Summer 1989.
Holodny, Elena. 'The Top 0.1% of American Households Hold the Same Amount of Wealth as the Bottom 90%'. *Business Insider*, 23 October 2017.
Jacobs, Ben. 'Donald Trump Reiterates He will only Help Nato Countries That Pay "Fair Share"'. *The Guardian*, 28 July 2016.
Krauthammer, Charles. 'The Unipolar Moment'. *Foreign Affairs* (America and the World 1990 Issue).
Landler, Mark and Helene Cooper. 'In Latest Shift, Troop Agrees to Leave 400 Troops in Syria'. *New York Times*, 22 February 2019.
Landler, Mark, Helene Cooper and Eric Schmitt. 'Trump to Withdraw U.S. Forces from Syria, Declaring "We Have Won Against ISIS"'. *New York Times*, 19 December 2018.
Rizzo, Salvador. 'Fact Checker: What's Actually in the "Green New Deal" from Democrats'. *Washington Post*, 11 February 2019.
Schmitt, Eric. 'In Eastern Military, U.S. Military Girds against Russian Might and Manipulation'. *New York Times*, 27 June 2018.
Sullivan, Eileen, Helene Cooper and Michael D. Shear. 'Citing Costs, Trump Retreats From Massive Military Parade in Capital'. *New York Times*, 17 August 2018.
Weiss, Brennan. 'Ranked: The Greatest US Presidents, According to Political Scientists'. *Business Insider*, 18 February 2019.

INDEX

Abdullah, Maria Chin   122
abolition   27–8, 45
abortion   220, 261
Act on Protection against Coronavirus (Hungary)   32
Afghanistan   4, 29, 215, 249, 257, 261
African National Congress   230
African Union   42, 228, 231
agents provocateur   3, 47, 96–7, 104, 189–90
al-Banna, Hassan   84
al-Bashir, Omar   41–2, 227–8, 238
Alevis   189–92
Algeria   34, 41, 81–2
    demonstrations in   3, 41, 73, 233
Alliance of Free Democrats (Hungary)   211–12, 215
All-Poland Women's Strike   220
Al-Sisi, Abdel Fattah   83, 163
alternative for Germany   251
Amin, Samir   231
Amnesty International   143
Andreyev, Yuriy   102
anti-corruption campaign (China)   13, 164, 166–7
anti-Semitism   62
Antipersonnel Mine Convention   79
Anyuan   164
Aquino, Benigno   32, 45
Aquino, Corazon   32, 45
Arab Spring   3, 10, 14, 22, 25, 27, 34–41, 48, 73–85, 120, 206, 233
    failures of   34, 44–5, 48
    generalizations about   35
Arkhangelsk   149
Armenia   22, 42–3

Argentina   16, 45, 245, 248, 250
Asian Financial Crisis   117
Assad, Bashar   40
Atbara   228, 238
authoritarianism, mischaracterization as 'dictator'   37–8, *see also* extrication from authoritarianism
    characteristics of new authoritarianism   33–4
    hybrid authoritarian regimes   139–42
    in multiethnic states   28–9
Azarov, Mykola   100
Azerbaijan   42–3
Aziz, Rafidah   126

Bahrain   34, 36–7, 40, 42, 73
Băile Tușnada   217
Bajnai, Gordon   216
Baldwin, James   255
Balkan Wars   184
Bannon, Steve   244, 251
Barisan Nasional   11, 115–19, 121–2, 124, 126–7
Beautiful St. Petersburg   149
Beijing   165, 169, 173
Beijing Workers' Autonomous Association   165
Belarus   45
    demonstrations in   1, 22, 44, 48
Belgium, occupation of the Ruhr   25
Belt Road Initiative   173
Ben Ali, Zine El Abidine   75, 77, 83
Berlin Wall   3, 243, *see also* Soviet bloc, collapse of
Berman, Sheri   57

Bermeo, Nancy   56–7
Bernstein, Eduard   2
Bersih   119, 121–5, 128
Besant, Annie   45
Bialystok   219
Black Lives Matter
   demonstrations   5, 44, 45, 74
Black Protests (Poland)   220
Blue Bucket Society   145
Bolivar, Simon   250
Bolivia   250
Bolsonaro, Jair   251–2
Bosnia   29
Botswana   231
Bouazizi, Mohamed   12, 34, 75, 77
Bourguiba, Habib   75, 77
Bouteflika, Abdelaziz   3, 41
Brazil   31, 207, 228, 245, 249–51
Brexit   6, 30
Budapest   211, 216
Bulgaria   207
bureaucracy, as a political force   10, 83–5, 184–6, 190–1
Burkina Faso   233
Bush, George H. W.   55
Bush, George W.   4, 260
Buzek, Jerzy   214

caliphate   184
Cambodia   140
Canetti, Elias   2
Carville, James   257
Catholic Church   54, 61–2, 219, 227, 237
   and Polish identity   63, 219
Center Compact party (Poland)   214
Central African Republic   231
Chama Cha Mapinduzi   230
Charter 77   54
Chatterjee, Partha   236
Chávez, Hugo   244, 250–1
Chemerys, Volodymyr   96, 103
Chenoweth, Erica   24–5, 46
Chile   190, 207, 250
China   80, 163–74, 217, 244
   and censorship   171–2
   demonstrations in   10, 47, 169–70
   and Hong Kong   43–4, 173–4
   propaganda campaign within   163–72
   and public confessions   13, 164, 166–70
   repression of opposition in   169–70, 173–4
China Central Television   167
Chinese Communist Party   2, 140, 164–7, 171, 174
Chirikova, Evgeniia   146, 151–2
Christian Democrats (Hungary)   211–12, 217–18
Cimoszewicz, Włodzimierz   212
Civic Platform (Poland)   214, 217–19
civil resistance   22–4, 29–30, 35–48, see also demonstrations
   conceptualization of   23
   bottom-up movements   74, 76–9
   as key component of democracy   228, 231, 233–5, 239–40
   organized movements   74, 76, 78, 82–5
   repression of   35–7, 90, 95–8, 105, 142–4, 152
   women and   10, 22, 45–7, 79–82, 90, 100, 104, 220, 234
civil rights movement   45
civil society   11, 53–65, 75, 119–23, 144, 193–4, 219–20, 227, 230, 235–7
   conservative civil society   58–9
   democratizing influence of   55–6
   pillarization of   53–65
   as threat to democracies   56–8
Civil Society Organizations   116–17, 120–9, 144, 187–8, 217, 219–20, 236, 238–9
   women's participation in   120, 122–3, 220
class conflict   7, 13, 163–5, 168–9, 187–8
Clinton, Bill   257, 260
Clinton, Hillary   143, 257, 261
Codur, Anne-Marie   45–6
Cold War consensus   16–17, 257–61
Colonialism   45, 238
Comey, James   257

Committee for the Defence of
    Democracy (Poland) 64,
    219–20
Committee of Union and Progress 184
Compaoré, Blaise 233
corruption 55, 119, 123, 125, 141,
    191, 214, 237, 262, *see also*
    anti-corruption campaign
    (China)
  demonstrations against 3, 23,
    41–2, 98, 117, 142–3, 145
Covid pandemic 5, 8, 31–2, 43, 152,
    256
Crimea 142
Croatia 29
Cullors, Patrice 45
Cultural Revolution (China) 13,
    164–7
culture wars 5, 6, 14, 58, 65
Cyprus 183
Czechoslovakia 24, 54, *see also*
    Velvet Revolution
  1968 occupation of 24, 40
  collapse of communism in 3–4,
    24, 207
Częstochowa 62

Dagalo, Hamdan 42
Davao City 33
Davies, Thomas 36
Davydova, Angelina 146
Democratic Action Party
    (Malaysia) 117, 120–1, 128
Democratic Left Alliance
    (Poland) 212, 214
Democratic Party (Poland) 210
Democratic Party (Turkey) 185–8
Democratic Party (United
    States) 261–2
Democratic Republic of Congo 15,
    227–8, 233–5, 237–40
  demonstrations in 227, 233
  repression of opposition 233
demonstrations, repression of 7, 11,
    13, 47, 105–6, 142–4, 152,
    173–4, *see also* civil resistance
  vilification as foreign plot 10, 11,
    13, 35, 40, 98, 141, 143, 164,
    169–70

violence in the context of 90,
    103–4, 239
  women in 10, 22, 45–7, 79–82,
    90, 100, 220, 234
Dersim 184
Diamond, Larry 55
Dirksen, Everett 262
Donbas 142
Duda, Andrzej 218–19
Duterte, Rodrigo 32–3, 163
  and comparison with Trump 33

Ecevit, Bülent 189, 196
Ecuador 250
Egypt 12, 25, 34–42, 47, 73–85, 163
  and electoral quotas for
    women 81
elections, as catalyst for popular
    mobilization 100, 138,
    141–2, 227–9, 233
  choiceless elections 228–35, 240
  real and imagined interference
    in 30, 33, 47, 99, 118–19,
    138, 227, 233–4, 257
  as vehicle for empowering
    people 28
Enabling Act 7
'end of history' 3–5, 22, 27–30,
    258
Eng, Lim Guan 128
Ennahda party 38, 76–7, 80, 84
environmentalism 23, 48, 54, 139,
    146–7, 149, 151, 195, 211,
    261
Erdogan, Recep Tayyip 9, 163,
    181–2, 185, 187, 193,
    195–6
Essebsi, Beji Caid 77, 84
Estonia 151
Ethiopia 42, 233
EuroMaidan demonstrations 11, 12,
    90–1, 101–6
European Union 30, 65, 101, 181,
    193, 214, 216–18
  and Brexit 6, 30
  Hungarian accession to 213, 216
  Polish accession to 60–1, 213, 216
  Turkish accession process 181
Evans, Alfred 141

extrication from
 authoritarianism 206–10,
 212, 214–16

Facebook 102, 149
Fanon, Franz 81
fascism 1–2, 7–9, 15, 57, 243–9, 251
 collapse as catalyst for
  development of
  populism 243–6, 250
 influence on Turkey 185
 as a 'third way' 244, 247
 in the United States 256–7
Fayulu, Martin 227, 237
FiDeSz 6, 14, 211, 213–19
Filimbi 237
Fillmore, Millard 256
financial Crisis of 2008, 5, 14, 148,
 213, 215, 220
Fini, Gianfranco 246
Floyd, George 44
Forces of Freedom and Change
 (Sudan) 41–2
For Honest Elections movement
 (Russia) 142
France 80, 245, 249, 251
 demonstrations in 10
 occupation of the Ruhr 25
Franco, Francisco 249, 257
Freedom House 3, 15, 228, 230–2
freedom of assembly 9, 14, 229–32
freedom of movement 33
freedom of speech 229–32
freedom of the press 1, 9, 14, 248,
 256
Freedom Union (Poland) 214
Friedman, Steven 232
Fukuyama, Francis 4, 28, 258

Gabowitsch 141
Gabungan Parti Sarawak 121
Garza, Alicia 45
Gates, Bill 259
Gazeta Polska 64
Gellner 55
Georgia 22
German Democratic Republic 40
 collapse of communism in 3–4

Germany 2, 7–8, 214, 246–9, 251,
 256
 1923 Franco-Belgian occupation of
  the Ruhr 25
Gezi Uprising 183, 195
Ghaddafi, Muamar 260
Ghonim, Wael 76
Giannone, Diego 231
Gilets jaunes 10
Gliński, Piotr 63–4
globalization 4, 30, 244, 259–60
Goering, Hermann 7
Golan Heights, occupation of 25
Golunov, Ivan 142–3
Göncz, Árpád 212
Gongadze, Heorhiy 95
Gorbachev, Mikhail 3–4
Gramsci, Antonio 55
Great Depression 7
Great Leap Forward (China) 167
Greco-Persian Wars 26
Green, Samuel 141
Green New Deal 261–2
Grey Wolves (Turkey) 188
Grillo, Bepee 252
Guangzhou 169
Guatemala 250
Gyurcsány, Ferenc 215–16

Habermas, Jürgen 55
Harding, Warren G. 256
Havel, Václav 5, 54
Helsinki Human Rights Union 96
Hindenburg, Paul von 7
Hitler, Adolf 2, 7–9, 13, 106, 246–8,
 257
Hoffmann, Stanley 58
Holocaust memory 214
Hong Kong 1, 5, 14, 22, 43–4, 47,
 173–4
Horn, Gyula 212
Hromadskyi sector 104
Huizhou 169
Human Rights Watch 152
Hungarian Civic Alliance, *see* Fidesz
Hungarian Democratic Forum 211,
 215
Hungarian Justice and Life Party 215

Hungarian Socialist Workers'
    Party   211
Hungary   14, 31–2, 47, 60, 163,
    205–21, 251
    confrontation and
        accommodation   210–15
    constitutional amendment   217
    demonstrations in   216, 219
    transition to democracy   32
Huntington, Samuel   57
Hussein, Saddam   260

Ibrahim, Anwar   125–7
illiberal democracy   31–4
immigration, as political issue   30, 32,
    34, 62, 261
Independence Marches (Poland)   63
India   54, 228, 236, 244, 249
Indian National Congress   45
institutions, erosion of   3, 8, 14,
    217–19
    in multiethnic states   28
International Monetary Fund   230
Iran   167, 249
Iraq   4, 10–11, 29, 38, 48, 73, 215,
    249, 261
Islamic State of Iraq and Syria   195
Islamist political parties   74
Israel   54
    occupation of Golan Heights   25
Istanbul   187, 193, 196
Italian League   251
Italy   57, 246–9, 251

Janjaweed militias   42
Jaruzelski, Wojciech   210, 214
Javeline, Devra   141
Jefferson, Thomas   262
Jiang Zemin   166
Jobbik   14, 215–17
Jobs, Steve   259
Johnson, Boris   31
Johnson, Lyndon   262
Jordan   34, 41, 73
journalism, and fact checking   31
    fragmentation of   59
    intimidation or repression of
        journalists   65, 95, 142, 145
    state influence over   63–4, 218–19

support of popular
    mobilizations   96, 99–100,
    102
Justice and Development Party
    (Morocco)   76, 78, 84
Justice and Development Party
    (Turkey)   181–3, 185, 188,
    191, 193–6

Kabila, Joseph   15, 227, 233, 237,
    239
Kaczynski, Jaroslaw   63, 214
Kaczynski, Lech   214, 217
Kádár, János   211, 216
Kagame, Paul   229
Karl, Terry   207
Karman, Tawakkol   80
Katyń massacre   217
Kemal, Mustafa   184
Kemalism   181–5, 191, 193–5, 197
Kharkiv   93
Khartoum   42, 228, 238
Khimki forest protests   146–7, 151
King, Mary   45–6
Klitchko, Vitaliy   105
Kobane   195
Kolesnikov, Andrei   144
Kolesnikova, Maria   45
Komorowski, Bronisław   217–18
Kopacz, Ewa   218
Kosovo   29, 47
Kuala Lumpur   125
Kuchma, Leonid   95–8, 100
Kuchmizm   98–9
Kurdistan Workers' Party   183, 191,
    195
Kurds   182–5, 187, 189, 191, 195–6
Kurski, Jaroslaw   65
Kwaśniewski, Aleksander   212
Kyiv   93, 99, 103

La Boétie, Étienne de   25–7, 47, 48
Lai, Jimmy   1
Lam, Carrie   43–4
Lankina, Tomila   141
Law and Justice (party in Poland), *see*
    PiS
Lebanon, demonstrations in   2
    and the 'Cedar Revolution'   35

Le Bon, Gustav 2
Leff, Carol 207-9
Leninist organizing 10, 75-7
Le Pen, Marie 248, 251-2
LGBTQ policy 218-19
Libya 29, 34, 36, 40, 73, 215
Li Chuncheng 167-8
Li Lisan 164
Lithuania 257
    demonstrations in 1
Liu Shaoqi 164
Lucha movement 233, 237
Lukashenko, Alexander 1, 44, 45
Lukin, Vladimir 143
Lutsenko, Yuriy 96
Luxembourg, Rosa 2
Lux Veritas Foundation 61
Lviv 93

McConnel, Mitch 262
Maduro, Nicholás 6
Magnitogorsk 152
Magufuli, John 229
Mahfouz, Asmaa 12
Maidan Nezalezhnosty 93, 96, 99, 103
Malaysia 11, 115-29
    demonstrations in 115-16, 124, 129
    elections in 117
Mao Zedong 164-5, 170-1
March of Millions (Russia) 138, 143
Marcos, Ferdinand 45
Marx, Karl 55
Mazowiecki, Tadeusz 210-11
Medvedev, Dmitri 142, 146
memory politics 205-6, 208, 212-18, 220-1
Menderes, Adnan 188, 196
Mexico 245
Mikhailenko, Yelena 151
military, defection of 13, 24, 36, 46
    intervention following a mass mobilization 75, 78, 83, 103
Mill, John Stuart 28
Minneapolis 44
Mkandawire, Thandika 230-1
modes of transition 206-8

Mohamad, Mahathir 11, 116, 118, 120-7
Mohammed VI of Morocco 78, 80
Molodaia Gvardiia 144
Montaigne, Michel de 26
Morocco 22, 34, 41, 74-85
Moroz, Oleksandr 95
Morsi, Mohammed 78-9, 85
Moscow 142-3, 145-7, 149
Motherland Party (Turkey) 190
Mothers of the Plaza del Mayo 45
Movimento Sociale Italiano 246
Mubarak, Hosni 25, 77-8, 83
Mubarak, Suzanne 80-1
Munck, Gerardo 207-9
Museveni, Yoweri 229
Muslim Brotherhood 10, 39, 75, 76, 78-9, 81, 84
Mussolini, Benito 246-8, 257
Mykolaiv 91

Nagorno-Karabakh 42-3
Nagy, Imre 211, 216
Nashi 31, 144
Nasser, Gamal Abdel 74, 83
National Institute of Freedom (Poland) 64
nationalism 33
    in Poland 61-4
    in Turkey 182, 184-5, 189, 191
Nationalist Movement Party (Turkey) 189
National self-determination 28
national socialism 57, 214, 247-8, *see also* fascism
NATO 29, 36, 193, 213, 256
Navalny, Aleksei 142-3
Nayem, Mustafa 102
Neocosmos, Michael 236
Nezim, Aziz 192
Nida Tounes 77, 84
No More Garbage 147
non-governmental organizations 56, 59-60, 79, 98, 128, 140, 143, 232, 236
nonviolent resistance 24, 26, 36, 46, 47, 90, 92, 97, 100, 104, 122, 125, 206, 236
Nord, Philip 58

Northern Ireland 47
North Korea 139, 167

Obama, Barack 260
Odessa 91
Oleksy, Józef 212
Olszewski, Jan 214
Oman 73
Operasi Lalang 124
Operation Euphrates 183
opposition, suppression of 9
Orange Revolution 11, 90, 97–101, 141
Orbán, Viktor 32, 33, 163, 211, 215, 217
organized popular mobilizations 10–12
Ottoman Empire 184, 194
Özal, Turgut 190

Pakatan Harapan 11, 115–29
Pakistan 249
Pakatan Rakyat 117
Pan-Malaysian Islamist Party 117–19, 121, 125, 127
Parasiuk, Volodymyr 106
Parti Amanah Nasional 117
Parti Keadilan Rakyat 117–18, 124
Parti Pejuang Tanah Air 118
Parti Pribumi Bersatu Malaysia 118
Parti Warisan Sabah 121
Pashinyan, Nikol 42–3
Pawlak, Waldemar 212
Pearl Roundabout 37
Penang 128
Perikatan Nasional 115, 121, 128
Perón, Juan 16, 244, 246–52, 257
Peru 250
Philippines 31–3, 45, 47, 163
PiS 6, 14, 54, 61, 63–4, 214–21
Poland 6, 14–15, 53–4, 60–5, 205–21, 251, 257
   collapse of communism in 3–4
   confrontation and accommodation 210–14
   demonstrations in 63, 218–21
   pillarization of civil society in 60–5
   repression of dissent 210, 219
   transition to democracy 53, 60
Polish National Foundation 64
Polish People's Party 212
Polish United Workers' Party 210, 212
political ju-jitsu 23–4, 35–6
political society 193–4, 197
   tensions between political and civil society 235–9
Polityka 64
populism 16, 30–1, 40, 47, 58, 243–52
   conceptualization of 245, 248
   and the crisis of representation 244, 248
   and "fake news" 40
   and nationalism 244, 248
   and pillarized civil society 58
   similarities with fascism 8, 16, 243–5, 247–8
   and sloganeering 33
   as a 'third way' 244, 248–51
   as transnational phenomenon 244–5, 248–51
   in the west 30–1
Portugal 209
Pozsgay, Imre 211
Proshenko, Petro 99, 107
protests, *see* civil resistance; demonstrations
public sphere 55
Puerto Rico 250
Pussy Riot 143
Putin, Vladimir 9, 11, 40, 137–8, 142–6, 148–53, 163
   and his 'social contract' with the public 138, 148, 151, 257
Putnam, Robert 55, 57–8

Rada Maidanu 104–5, 107
Radio Maryja 61–2
Razak, Najib 117, 123–6, 128
Reformasi movement 117–18, 124
refugee crisis 3, 5–6, 14, 32, 34, 37, 62–3, 213, 215, 217–18, 220, 256
Reichstag 7–8
Republican Party (Untied States) 261

Republican People Party 185, 188–9, 193
Revolution on the Granite 11, 90, 92–5
Revolutions of 1989, *see* Soviet bloc, collapse of
Riley, Dylan 57
Robertson, Graeme 141, 145
Romania 57
Rosary on the Borders 62
Rotenberg, Arkady 146
Rotenberg, Igor 146
Roundtable Talks 208, 210–11, 214, 217–18
Rukh 93
Rumsfeld doctrine 38
Rushdie, Salman 192
Russia 31, 60, 80, 137–53, 163, 217, 245, 257
  demonstrations in 10, 11, 143–53
  pension reforms in 137–8, 152–3
  repression of opposition in 13, 142–4, 152
Rwanda 229

Sabah 121
Saeed, Khaled 12
Saint Petersburg 146–7, 149–50
Saleh, Ali Abdullah 38
Sall, Mackey 240
Sarawak 121
Sargsyan, Serzh 42
Saudi Arabia 34, 37, 42, 73, 77
Schmitter, Phillipe 58
Schulmann, Ekaterina 152
Schumer, Chuck 262
Seattle 74
Selangor 128
Senegal 233, 240
Separate Collection 147
Serbia 22, 29
Shanghai 165
Sharp, Gene 23–4, 29
Shistdesyatnyky 91
Shivji, Issa 231
Sidi Bouzid 77
Sieci Prawdy 64
Sierra Leone 231
Sivas 191–2

slavery 45, *see also* abolition
Smallholders (Hungary) 211–12
Sochi Olympics 137
social media 12, 30, 40, 59, 75–6, 78, 91, 101–4, 106–7, 149–50, 152, 167, 171–2, 174, 261
social protests 11–12, 138–9, 141–3, 145–53, 170
  potential politicization of 149–51
Solidarity (Poland) 54, 208, 210–12, 214, 218
South Africa 229–30, 236
Soviet Bloc, collapse of 2–4, 14, 22, 27–9, 91–5, 205–6
  opposition within 54, 206
  political consequences of collapse 205–13, 215–17, 220–1, 243–6, 258–9
Soviet Union 4–7, 91, 206–8, 211, 214, 216, 250
Spain 57, 206, 209, 249
spontaneous popular mobilizations 10–12
Sreenivasan, Ambiga 122
Stephan, Maria 24–5
strikes 42, 93, 188–9, 210
Student Hunger Strike (Ukraine), *see* Revolution on the Granite
Suaram 124, 128
Sudan 41–2, 73, 82, 227–8, 230, 233, 236–40
  demonstrations in 228, 230, 238
  repression of opposition 228, 238
Sudan Professional Organization 238
Switzerland 28
Syria 34, 37–8, 40, 47–8, 73, 75, 183, 195, 215, 244, 257

Tahrir Square, demonstrations in 12, 39, 77–9
Tamarrod 79
Tanzania 80, 229
Teik, Khoo Boo 123, 126–7
term limits 137, 142, 163, 229–31
Thailand 44
theory of voluntary servitude 22, 25–7

Tiananmen Square protests 12, 47, 164–6
Tikhanovskaya, Svetlana 45
Tikhanovsky 45
Tito, Jozip Broz 29
Tocqueville, Alexis de 55
Together Party (Poland) 220
Tometi, Opal 45
Transitional Military Council (Sudan) 41–2
Trzaskowski, Rafał 219
Tsepkalo, Veronika 45
Tshisekedi, Felix 227
Tunisia 3, 12, 34–6, 38–41, 74–85, 233
Tunisian Confederation of Industry, Trade and Handicrafts (UTICA) 77
Tunisian Human Rights League 77
Tunisian Order of Lawyers 77
Turkey 14, 31, 54, 60, 163, 181–97, 217, 228
    coups within 181, 188, 190, 192–3, 196
    demonstrations in 9, 183, 188, 195–6
    Islamism in 182–5, 191–5, 197
    Kemalism in 181–5, 191, 193–5, 197
    masses as auxiliary power 182–3, 185, 191, 194–7
    mass violence in 182–4, 187, 189, 191–2, 195
    military role in politics 182–4, 188–93, 195–7
    nationalism in 182, 184–5, 189, 191
    pro-market stance in government 182
    repression of opposition in 13, 182, 190–2, 195–6
Turkish War of Independence 184
Trump, Donald 6, 16–17, 30, 31, 44, 244–5, 248, 251–2, 255–63
Twitter 102, 104, 256
Tyahnybok, Oleh 105

Uganda 140, 229
Ukraine 22, 89–107, 142–3, 148
    cross-sectional coalitions in 90–3, 95, 97–8, 100
    demonstrations in 11, 12
    radical right wing movements in 90, 95, 97, 100, 103–5
    Ukraine without Kuchma protests 90, 95–7
Ulbricht, Walter 40
Umbrella Movement (Hong Kong) 43, 173
United Kingdom 30–1, 115, 120, 137
United Malays National Organisation 118–21, 123–7
United Nations 33
United Peasant Party (Poland) 210
United Russia party 138, 142, 144
United States 30–1, 39, 54, 58, 74, 82, 143, 148, 173, 193, 228, 231, 233, 234, 246, 250, 255–63
    populism in 244–5, 251–2
Union Generale Tunisienne du Travail (UGTT) 75–7
Universiti Malaya 126
Updike, John 258

Vargas, Getulio 249–51
Velvet Revolution 3–4, 24
Venezuela 6, 31, 244, 249–50
Viatrovych, Volodymyr 103
Vietnam War 29
Volokolamsk 147

Wade, Abdoulaye 233
Wałęsa, Lech 211–12, 214
Wamba-dia-Wamba, Ernest 235
war on terror 4, 6, 260
Warsaw 220
WeChat 14, 167–8, 171–2
Weimar Republic 57
Welfare Party (Turkey) 191, 193
Wilders, Geert 248
Women, and Arab Spring 79–82
    as a check on violence in demonstrations 90, 100, 104
    and civil resistance 10, 22, 45–7, 220, 234

and civil society 120, 122–3
suffrage 45, 234
Workers' Defence Committee (KOR) 54
World Bank 230
World Cup 137–8

xenophobia 16, 34, 40, 62–3, 65, 197, 215, 217, 244, 251–2
Xi Jinping 13, 163–4, 166–72

Yanukovych, Victor 90, 98–100, 103
Yatseniuk, Arseniy 105
Yemen 34, 37–8, 40, 73, 75, 80
Y'en a Marre 233
Yevropeyska Ploshcha 103
Youngs, Richard 58
Young Turks 184
Yue Xin 169–70
Yugoslavia 29
Yugoslav Wars 29
Yushchenko, Viktor 98–100

Zainuddin, Daim 125–6
Zakaria, Fareed 31
Zelensky, Volodymyr 107
Zuma, Jacob 229

www.ingramcontent.com/pod-product-compliance
Lightning Source LLC
Chambersburg PA
CBHW060946230426
43665CB00015B/2076